The Ma
of A

Yvonne Aburrow

Illustrated by Dena Moore

Appendix Two Animal Pub Signs   483
Appendix Three Terminology   486
Bibliography and Further Reading   488
Index   497

Dedication

To Nick 'Longshanks' with all my love

Thanks also to my dad, who told me that animals have souls and introduced me to Tolkien and hence fairytales, runes and the world of magic.

For Nick "Longshanks"

Beloved, gaze in thine own heart,
The holy tree is growing there;
From joy the holy branches start,
And all the trembling flowers they bear.
The changing colours of its fruit
Have dowered the stars with merry light;
The surety of its hidden root
Has planted quiet in the night;
The shaking of its leafy head
Has given the waves their melody,
And made my lips amd music wed,
Murmuring a wizard song for thee.
There the Loves a circle go,
The flaming circle of our days,
Gyring, spiring to and fro
In those great ignorant leafy ways;
Remembering all that shaken hair
And how thew winged sandals dart,
Thine eyes grow full of tender care:
Beloved, gaze in thine own heart.

Introduction

I think I could turn and live with animals,
they're so placid and self-contained,
I stand and look at them long and long.
They do not sweat and whine about their condition,
They do not lie awake in the dark and weep for their sins,
They do not make me sick discussing their duty to God,
Not one is dissatisfied, not one is demented with the mania of owning things,
Not one kneels to another, nor to his kind that lived thousands of years ago,
Not one is respectable or unhappy over the whole earth.

(from *Song of Myself*, Walt Whitman, 1819-1892)

Animals represent instinctual wisdom, freedom, and the powers of Nature. They represent different spiritual qualities; each of us has an animal self whose wisdom we can draw on in times of need. This animal self is not an enemy to be conquered, but a potential ally - to live instinctually is to live in harmony with Nature. This is why Taoist philosophy often uses stories of animals to impart its wisdom. Similarly, folklore and mythology from all over the world is full of animal stories, and many (if not most) deities have animal totems associated with them. The animals, birds, trees, and places connected with each deity link all Nature in a web of symbols, showing that everything depends on everything else. The animal represents the power of the deity at work in the world, a visible manifestation of the numinous.

However, animal symbolism and mythology have not always been used for the enhancement of the psyche. Myths have also been used for ideological purposes. It is a mistake to regard myth as universal and timeless, the same archetype cropping up again and again in various different cultures and eras, but with inherently the same archetypal meaning. Not only does this view represent blatant cultural arrogance, it is also a gross oversimplification, and has been used to put forward the idea that myths are 'natural' and can therefore be used to justify either the status quo or some new

1

ideology. An apparently apolitical idea can be used to support two totally different political agendas. For example, William Blake's *Jerusalem* has been used to support the Tory idea that God is an Englishman - it is a very popular 'patriotic' hymn in public schools. It has also been used as an expression of the socialist ideal of creating an utopia - the biblical 'New Jerusalem' ('I shall not cease from mental fight, Nor shall my sword sleep in my hand, Till we have built Jerusalem, In England's green and pleasant land').

Myth is, on one level, an interpretation of historical events in an allegorical manner. Whether these events involve a political manoeuvre, a shift in consciousness, or a natural event, a myth will be evoked to explain and/or justify them. For example, an invading people bringing a new pantheon would marry off all their deities to the conquered people's deities (e.g. the Aesir inter-married with the Vanir in Norse mythology); or a new discovery such as fire, which must have provoked a shift in consciousness, as it gave humans apparent mastery over an element, was mythologised in the legend of Prometheus, or the legend of a bird or animal which fetched fire for humans; or earthquakes, which were explained as the Celestial Bull tossing the Earth on its horns.

Equally history, by selecting features of the past which are deemed significant, and ignoring other aspects, has mythical content. For example, history was taught in English schools as if England were the centre of the world, and as if kings and queens and battles defined their epochs. There was no attempt to examine the history of ideas, or to encourage people to exercise their critical and interpretative faculties. If we are to see history and mythology in a sensible light, it is necessary not to abandon our critical awareness. The interpretation of myth and symbol should be deeply personal. There is no absolute system of magical corres-pondences; each culture, each person, can develop their own symbol-systems. Each individual relationship to the landscape and spirit of place will be different in each locale. Just as a poet or a musician creatively interprets metaphor or music, so the magician should creatively embroider upon the tapestry of Wyrd. Magic is an Art, not a science. It is when we begin to take myth literally that the trouble starts; when we project mythical scenarios onto external situations instead of using them creatively within ourselves.

2

When reading a book on the subject of myth, then, it is important to be aware of the fluidity of the subject matter, and the cultural context of the symbol or myth being discussed. This is particularly relevant when thinking about a subject such as animal sacrifice. Clearly our ancestors did engage in this practice, which we are inclined to regard as barbaric. Vegetarians are of course entitled to this view; but meat-eaters might need to consider before condemning our ancestors' customs. As most forms of sacrifice involved the sharing of the animal's flesh as a communal meal afterwards, there is little difference between a sacrifice and the practice of eating roast beef on a Sunday (except that the sacrificial animal was probably reared and killed more humanely than the average modern cow). I am not suggesting the revival of sacrifice, merely that it is important to be aware of the cultural context of a custom in order to see it in a balanced perspective. Similarly, it is important not to remove the concept of the totem animal from its cultural context, and act as if it is the same in every culture - the differences are at least as significant as the similarities. (This will be discussed at length in the chapter on totem animals.)

In addition, there is no point in pretending that our ancestors lived in a politically correct and environmentally friendly manner. (For example, the Iron Age Celts, whom we love to think of as dreamy bards, mystical shamans, and honourable warriors, were an extremely warlike bunch of head-hunters. They had a slightly better attitude to women than some of their contemporaries, in that they were prepared to listen to a woman's opinion - unlike the ancient Greeks, who were by all accounts just about as misogynist as it was possible to be.) In this book, therefore, I have not tried to edit out the more gruesome bits of information about animals, and the strange things humans have done to them in the name of the sacred. It is counterproductive to inform the reader that the pig was sacred to Demeter without also mentioning that it was sacrificed to her, as the two facts are closely related. Our ancestors did not live in a pastoral idyll; on the other hand, nor were their lives necessarily "nasty, brutish, and short".

Our current cultural background is the accumulation of our ancestors' experience, constantly augmented by our own experience. Our ancestors are part of what we are, and we cannot deny their legacy - to do so would be to relegate it to the realm of the Shadow, where it could wreak havoc if left untended. (Look to the rock whence ye are hewn, and to the hole of the pit whence ye are digged.) If, however, we acknowledge both their strengths and their weaknesses, we may yet regain something that we have left by the wayside. For example, being much less "rational" than we are, their view of reality was much more fluid than our own; since they believed in magic, it was much easier for seemingly impossible things to occur, as they did not have to struggle against a consensus view that magic was impossible. Aleister Crowley once said that magic was much easier in the middle of the Mexican desert (where the consensus reality of the inhabitants allowed for the possibility) than in "civilised" countries (where consensus reality was much more rigid). The same idea was simply but aptly expressed by J M Barrie in *Peter Pan*, when Peter Pan says that Tinkerbell the fairy will cease to exist if children stop believing in her.

So how should we approach the magical lore of animals in our own day and age? Many people are drawn to the idea of totem animals, establishing a kinship with a particular animal, and learning from its characteristics (both actual and symbolic). This is obviously a much more fruitful avenue to explore than the exploitative one of sacrifice. However, it is important not to anthropomorphise animals. They are sentient beings, but they have a different consciousness from our own. When dealing with animals, therefore, one should never assume that they are exactly the same as a human; nor, conversely, treat them like an inanimate thing. Even scientists are now beginning to admit that animals have consciousness, as there are two forms of awareness, the unconscious proprioceptive senses, and the capacity to compare incoming visual data with stored memories. Animals demonstrably have this capability, and therefore it is likely that they have consciousness. The animal spirits which reach out to humans in the form of totem animals may be powerful guardians of the land, like the Aboriginal Ancestors of the Dreamtime; or they may be the animal aspects of the human psyche resurfacing from the pre-conscious mind. For example, it is possible to access the reptilian aspects of the mind (said to correspond to the limbic system in the

4

brain, which deals with sensory impressions, pleasure and pain) by meditating on the various qualities of reptiles and their mythical associations. Frogs and toads are generally associated with the sensual aspects of the earth, the underworld, and sexuality. Their amphibious qualities led them to be associated with the ability to exist on more than one level, so they also symbolise the incarnation of spirit in matter. The serpent is also associated with the earth and the underworld, representing the sinuous qualities of earth energies; it is associated with healing (Asklepios, Greek god of healing, had a snake entwined about his staff) and wisdom (Hermes and Mercury had as their attribute the caduceus, with two serpents entwined about it). The mammalian aspects of mind (generally regarded as corresponding to the thalamus and the hypothalamus) are associated with the emotions, a sense of community, and instinctual wisdom. The mammalian mind is more complex and multifarious, so that different mammals hold widely different symbolic meanings.

Another way of developing the animal aspects of the mind is to use the shamanistic technique of dressing as an animal, in order to acquire its characteristics. This practice survived into the dances of the medieval mummers (though its original meaning may have been forgotten), who often dressed as hares and other sacred animals.

Animals themselves frequently have an instinctual awareness of people's personalities. This awareness is perhaps similar to what we experience as a "gut feeling", a kind of pre-cognitive knowledge. We can learn to develop this awareness in ourselves by being aware of animals' responses to people.

In the past, animals were used as "cures" for various diseases. Some of these practices were extremely dodgy (e.g. fried mice as a cure for whooping cough). The therapeutic benefits of having animals around have been confirmed by research, however - it has been observed by psychologists that stroking a cat or a dog will lower a person's blood pressure and reduce stress.

The companionship of animals is an ancient pleasure. Since cats and dogs first moved in with humans, and various animals were

5

domesticated, humans have shared their lives with animals. The ancient Egyptians regarded the cat as sacred, so much so that the penalty for killing a cat was death.

Humans have also hunted animals for food and clothing. Many of the early rituals of humans were acts of sympathetic magic for success in the hunt. The spirits of the animals had to be propitiated, in order that they would not exact vengeance; the animals' remains had to be buried in a certain way, to ensure that their spirits could reach the underworld; and the guardian deity of the hunt would be invoked to provide plentiful game.

In modern Paganism, we tend to regard Nature and Nature spirits as wholly benevolent, in dialectical opposition to the supposedly orthodox Christian view that Nature is 'fallen' and sinful. However, the traditional view was more complex, and being older than Christianity, did not particularly take account of Christian orthodoxy (since most people did not have access to the Bible, a popular Christianity developed which was a hybrid of popular magic and Christian belief). In traditional thought, there is a creative tension between the view of humans as separate from nature and of humans as a part of nature. Western culture is beginning, with a growing ecological awareness, to recognise the value of the traditional world view. However, this world view does not necessarily regard nature spirits as entirely benevolent; they may be indifferent to humans or even hostile, though some are friendly and helpful. On the whole it is recognised that these beings are pursuing an entirely different agenda from our own, which is sometimes in accord with our desires, and sometimes not.

In Scottish folklore, for example, there is a whole class of water beings (usually occupying freshwater lakes) which may be malevolent, though some are helpful. The kelpie was a water spirit usually seen in the form of a young horse running along a river bank. When tired, it would strike the water three times with its tail, so heavily that each lash of its tail sounded like a crash of thunder; it would then disappear like a flash of fire into a deep pool. The kelpie also possessed a magic bridle, with which it enchanted people by looking at them through the eyelets of the bit. A magician could undo such enchantments by looking through the eyelet holes in the opposite direction; the kelpie's bridle could also be used in this manner to see elves, fairies, and other spirits. A kelpie's bridle was obtained by Seumas MacGregor, who lost his horse by Loch Slochd, and mistaking a passing kelpie for his horse, mounted it, only to find that it was trying to carry him off into the depths of the loch. So he called on the Trinity to save him, whereupon the kelpie threw him off, and he was left holding its bridle, which was passed down in the MacGregor family as a magical heirloom. There are also legends of water bulls and water cows. These spirits are not helpful, and may even be malevolent, but their magical qualities may be harnessed by humans for helpful purposes.

Both wild and domestic animals are rich in symbolic associations, which have developed over the centuries and cultures into an immense heritage of mythology and folklore. In our dealings with animals, it is well to be aware of their symbolic meaning as well as their characteristics, habitat, and position in the eco-system. Many of our attitudes to species affect our dealings with them. For example, when the wolf was regarded as a rapacious predator with no redeeming qualities (as in the Big Bad Wolf in the tale of *The Three Little Pigs*), it was hunted to extinction. Nowadays it is beginning to be seen as a symbol of freedom and the vanishing wilderness, representing the wisdom of instinct - partly because its social habits have been studied by naturalists. Because of this change in perception, there is talk of reintroducing the wolf to areas where it had become extinct, such as Scotland. The symbolism of an animal can change over time, and this will not only affect our dealings with it, but also reflect some change in the culture. The new attitude to the wolf has been constructed from various sources, but it probably represents a shift in tastes towards the truly wild, which is seen as the locus of freedom and individuality - symbolised by the "lone wolf" (although wolves are actually quite sociable animals). By observing such cultural shifts, we can discover a lot about the nature of consciousness and society. Symbolism and myth are never static. They are a constant internal process, fermenting in the vat of consciousness. As C G Jung put it:

"When one reflects on what consciousness really is, one is

7

profoundly impressed by the extreme wonder of the fact that an event which takes place outside in the cosmos simultaneously produces an internal image, that it takes place, so to speak, inside as well, which is to say: becomes conscious."

(Basel Seminar, 1934)

In his autobiography, Jung also put forward the idea that consciousness holds up a mirror to Nature; that perhaps this is the purpose of consciousness, so that Nature may be aware of herself. If this is so, humanity, as the maker and user of symbols (which are the building blocks of consciousness), has a tremendous responsibility, since we shall reap what we sow. When the symbols themselves are autonomous beings such as animals, there is a dual responsibility, since it is also desirable that the symbolic qualities of the animal reflect its actual nature (as we have seen with the example of the wolf).

Those who desire to work with the magical lore of animals need to be aware of these issues, and to treat animals with respect. We share this planet with them, and we are all part of the delicate balance of the environment. We ourselves are animals, though we have tried to divorce ourselves from Nature. We would do well, therefore, to look to the animals for inspiration in our search for ways of living in harmony with Nature.

Yvonne Aburrow

Chapter 1

Totems and Familiars

> "In the black furrow of a field
> I saw an old witch-hare this night;
> And she cocked a lissome ear,
> And she eyed the moon so bright,
> And she nibbled of the green;
> And I whispered 'Shsst! witch-hare,'
> Away like a ghostie o'er the field
> She fled, and left the moonlight there."
> (Walter de la Mare)

The word totem has been borrowed from one culture and applied indiscriminately to other cultures. Whilst the concept of kinship with animals is similar in many cultures, there are subtle differences between the various ways in which the concept is applied in everyday life, and the explanations given for it by its adherents. It is inappropriate to regard all these different concepts and social structures as totemism *per se*, as this is to underestimate the complexity of the cultures in which they arise. Similarly, the word 'shaman' has been applied inappropriately to practices which differ in significant ways from the one from which the word was borrowed, as Ronald Hutton has demonstrated in his book, *The Shamans of Siberia* (1993). I suspect that a similar process has occurred with the concept of totemism.

For example, in *The Golden Bough*, Frazer calls all totemic relationships "the external soul" in an animal. He has taken the concept of an external soul from Indo-European folk-tale, and applied it willy-nilly to other cultures, which would not necessarily regard the totemic relationship in the same way. Similarly, the group

9

totems of indigenous Americans have been taken as the basis for comparison with other cultures' relationships with animals.

So, what is the totemic relationship? In modern Paganism, the concept of a totem animal can be divided up into three distinct, though related, concepts:

a)   A species or an individual animal with which a person feels an affinity, either for its attributes or its symbolism;

b)   A kind of "spirit guide" in the form of an animal;

c)   The "animal self" of the person, i.e. an inner archetype.

These concepts come from a variety of sources. The animal as a spirit guide is partly derived from nineteenth century occultism, and partly derived from the popular idea of the witch's familiar spirit, which was believed to take the form of an animal, frequently a cat. The idea of the "animal self" is mostly derived from Jungian psychology. Jung interpreted mythology in the light of inner processes, and his theories are derived from his interpretation of the significance of myth and legend. The idea of an affinity with a species or individual animal is the closest to the practice of totemism in tribal societies, but it is not quite the same. In modern Paganism, totem animals are regarded as a personal totem. In tribal societies, the totem is often a communal one. It should be emphasised that the concept of totem animals in modern Paganism is just as valid as earlier forms of the concept. Traditions evolve constantly to adapt to changes in society; the fact that modern Pagans have developed a new way of looking at totem animals shows that Paganism is dynamic and not static. Also we no longer live in a tribal society in the formal sense of the word, although we may build up loose tribal affinities with like-minded people. The basis of this developing tradition, however, is personal experience with one's own totem animal. The relationship which is built up is one of mutual respect and affection, and provides a link with the spirit world and with planet Earth. It is based on respect for the environment and for our fellow beings, whether animal, bird, plant, or spirit.

Totem animals in tribal cultures

At first, anthropologists thought that mythology focussed on anomalous animals, but they then realised that what is considered anomalous depends on one's system of classification, which depends on one's culture. It was then suggested that similarity between animals and concepts formed the basis of myth and symbol. However, this too is culture-dependent, as metaphor does not depend on resemblance alone. The practice of referring to two objects metaphorically is what gives them their similarity in the mind of the individual. In order to be certain that we are interpreting another culture's metaphors correctly, we need to look for the underlying constructs of their world-view. It is not enough to explain their social structures using animal metaphors; this view is too simplistic. It is better to look at the medicinal and dietary theories of a society, and at how these are applied to relations with the animal world.

For example, among the Lele of Zaire, diviners are forbidden to eat the Nile monitor because of its spotted skin, which is associated with skin diseases such as smallpox. The Lele categorise humans according to whether they are equals, patrons, or clients, and their relations are governed by the principles of friendship or enmity among equals, and seniority and patronage among clients and patrons. Equal relationships have no territorial constraints, but patron-client relationships have a strong territorial element. Client-client relationships under the same patron require mutual honour and respect. The Lele apply this world-view to animals. If they want to understand how two different species share the same habitat, they apply their ideas of patron-client relationships. In order to understand the behaviour of carnivores, they apply their ideas of enmity. Animals which inhabit the territory of nature spirits are believed to be the clients of the spirits. If fish, lizards, water snakes, and wild boar inhabit the same stream, it appears that they have secured the protection of the water spirits and have become their clients; this means that the patron water spirit will avenge aggression against its clients, so it will not be safe to eat them if one is allied to a water-spirit. The Lele model assumes a commonality of intention and reaction between humans, animals, and spirits. If a human becomes the client of a certain spirit, they will not prey on their co-clients, just as they would not attack the co-clients of a human patron. To do so would be to incur the wrath of the patron. The taboos applied to diet are merely the surface manifestation of a complex theory about the nature of life and death, and to assume that these taboos represented being forbidden to eat a totem animal would be to miss the point entirely.

Among the Zapotecs of Central America, when a woman was about to give birth to a child, her relations gathered in the hut and drew various animals on the floor, then erased them. Whichever animal had not been erased when the child was born was its tona or second self.

In Mota, a Melanesian island, the "totem" animal or object was called a tamaniu. If a person with a *tamaniu* became ill, they would send someone to see if their *tamaniu* was similarly afflicted.

The Wotjobaluk tribe of South-Eastern Australia believed that the life of every man was connected with the bat (Ngunungunut), and the life of each woman with that of the nightjar (Yartatgurk), but they did not know which bat or nightjar was their own, so all bats and nightjars were protected and not killed. Occasionally fierce fighting broke out between the men and the women because a man had killed a nightjar, or a woman had killed a bat.

In Western Australia, the clan animal is called the *kobong*. In Central Australia, the totem clans are responsible for ensuring that their totem multiplies, so that the other members of the tribe may eat it. For example, the witchetty grub totem people perform a ceremony miming the emergence of the larva from the chrysalis.

The Bataks of Sumatra were divided into exogamous clans; each clan was known as a *marga*, and was forbidden to eat a particular animal. The reasons for this differed from one clan to another: it may be that they were descended from the animal, or that their souls passed into the animal when they died, or that the animal rescued their ancestors from some disaster. There was a clan associated with each of the following animals: tiger, ape, cat, crocodile, dog, dove, locust, white buffalo.

The Syrians of antiquity believed that if they ate fish, which they regarded as sacred, they would break out in ulcers, and their feet and stomach would swell up.

Among the Hopi, the men have *katsina* societies. These societies hold special dances throughout the time when the *katsina* spirits live among the people, which runs from the Soyala observance of the winter solstice to Niman, a few weeks after the summer solstice. The *katsina* societies are not the only religious grouping among the Hopi. The *katsina* group is not totemic, in that the spirits are not generally regarded as ancestors. Animal spirits may appear in animal or human form. The *katsina* may be a spirit of a plant, a geographical place, an insect, a force of nature, animals, or another people. Frogs are represented by Pakwabi, turtles by Yonyosona, bears by Honau, badgers by Honan (little brother of the bear), deer by So-wing, antelope by Chop, mountain sheep by Pang, cows by Wakas, chickens by Kowaku, roosters by Takawea, crows by Angwus, eagles by Kwahu, prairie falcons by Kisa, owls by Monswa. A *katsina* clan is called a *yom* (plural yomu). People and animals are part of the yom, which has a relationship with the *katsina*. Recently introduced species such as the cow and the chicken are not yet regarded as people, but they may be in the future. A similar case is the parrot, which was introduced to the Hopi nation by the Mexicans (before Europeans arrived in America); it is associated with the south, its feathers are used for religious items, and it has a yom associated with it. In some instances there is a *katsina* but no associated yom; in others, there is a *yom* but no *katsina*. For example, frogs and turtles have a *katsina* but no clan associated with them, whereas there is a coyote clan (Isau wuyomu) but no katsina. There is no taboo against a member of a *yom* eating the animal associated with it. There are some animals that no-one eats, either because they are too sacred and helpful (eagles, turtles, frogs), or because they are inedible (wolves). All animals with a position or role in the spirit world are treated with respect in the material world.

Anímal ancestors

Animal ancestors are frequently found in the mythology of tribal cultures. There are also legends of marriage between humans and animals, such as the bear ancestor of the Mongols. The seal appears in Celtic legend as an animal ancestor; there is an Irish legend of a wolf ancestor, and the bear appears frequently in Irish and Welsh names. The Merovingian dynasty was reputed to be descended from a fish. There are many animal groupings amongst Indigenous Americans and Australian Aborigines, in whose legend of Dreamtime the animal ancestors sang the land into being. In India, some families are believed to be descended from the Nagas, who are serpent beings. Some African peoples are believed to be descended from the leopard and the hyena; in Madagascar, there are tribes descended from cattle, sheep, and moths.

The totemic relationship is not necessarily between one group of humans and one animal species. Nor does it simply embrace the characteristics of the animal; it may include traditions, songs, places, and more than one species of animal. The Aboriginal peoples of Australia construct the world of ancestral beings from the attributes of animals. The ancestors can be analogies of events, processes, states and relationships. Among the Yolngu, their songs relate to specific clan animals, which are mythically associated with geographical places, which can be distinguished from neighbouring places by their different ecological characteristics. For example, the mangroves are associated with the tree *Exocarpus latifolia*, the little red flying fox, the black butcher bird, and the Ma:tjarra clan. The ancestors are called *wangarr* by the Yolngu.

In the island of Wetar (between New Guinea and Celebes), the people are believed to be descended from wild pigs, snakes, turtles, crocodiles, eels, and dogs. A person may not eat the animal from which they are descended; if they do so, they will become a leper and go mad. Amongst the Omaha nation (indigenous American), men descended from the elk believed that if they ate the flesh of the male elk they would break out in white spots and boils in various parts of their bodies. The belief that leprosy or some other skin disease will afflict you if you eat your totem animal is common to a number of totemic societies.

The pastoral peoples of Mongolia, particularly the Khoshut and Torgut of the Altai region, associate the tibia bone of the sheep (usually from the right hind leg) with a complex set of ideas about fertility, connections between the ancestors and the living, and patrilineal descent. Matrilineal descent is associated with the flesh of the sheep. At the birth of a child, the *dallag* ritual is performed, in which the child's personal bone is presented to the family altar. It is kept by the family until the child is aged seven, then it may be presented to the *ovoo* (the communal altar).

The local form of Buddhism incorporates tibia rituals. At a wedding, the groom breaks the bride's sheep tibia to signify that she is separated from her family and line of descent. The wedding guests compete for the groom's sheep tibia in a horseback contest. The groom's party retains the bone, and it is then carried to the new couple's yurt and thrown in through the smokehole to clear a path for the hearth-smoke.

This custom may be connected with the belief that the souls of children born to the couple will descend through the smokehole, which represents the cosmic axis. After the tibia has been thrown into the yurt, the couple grasp it between them and recite a prayer to the Sun (and sometimes the Moon), the parental protective spirits, and the tibia. At death, the tibia is displayed with the corpse in the yurt, and then buried with its owner. The tibia was also used for voluntary euthanasia, after the person had eaten a dish of sheep's tail (the tastiest part).

Bronze Age burials in Mongolia have also been found with the tibia of sheep and goats, so it is possible that the tradition dates back to that time. Although the atheism imposed by Soviet rule made considerable inroads into these traditions, there were still taboos observed around tibia, such as not throwing them out with refuse. Communal ceremonies such as New Year also make use of the tibia, but they mostly relate to family and individual ritual. The Yakut people use human tibia in a similar way.

Rites of passage

Among many tribal cultures, the children (usually the boys) are symbolically 'killed' and then resurrected as their totem animal. Among the Niska people (indigenous Americans), there are four clans: raven, wolf, eagle, and bear. When a man was initiated into a secret society known as the Olala, his friends would pretend to kill him. Then he would disappear for a whole year, and funeral rites were held for him. When he returned, he was carried by an artificial animal representing his totem.

The people of Nootka Sound (indigenous American) had the wolf as one of their major totems. There was a secret clan called the Tlokoala, into which novices were initiated by being seized by men wearing wolf-masks and wolf-skins who carried them off into the woods. When they were brought back they had to feign death, and were then revived by the village wizard.

Transmigration of souls

The Zuni people of New Mexico believe that their ancestors' souls pass into turtles. Turtles were killed annually at the festival of Kak'ok'shi (the Good Dance) as messengers to the realm of the dead. Among the Gilyaks of Siberia, it was believed that if a hunter was killed by a bear, his soul would pass into the bear. Some tribal peoples will not eat certain animals in the belief that after death, their ancestors' souls pass into those animals.

The external soul

The Yakut people of Siberia believed that shamans kept their soul (or one of their souls) incarnate in an animal for safe-keeping. A Yakut shaman was called an *oyuna*. One oyuna is reported to have said, "Nobody can find my external soul. It lies hidden far away in the stony mountains of Edzhigansk." Once a year these external souls appeared in the shape of animals near human habitation, at the time when the last snows melted and the earth turned black. They roamed all over the place, but only the oyuna could see them. The strong ones were noisy and roaring; the weak ones were quiet and furtive. They frequently fought amongst themselves, and an *oyuna* whose external soul had been beaten would fall ill or even die. The weakest *oyunas* were reputed to have their souls in dogs, which gnawed at their hearts and tore their bodies. The most powerful *oyunas* were those with stallions, elks, black bears, eagles, or boars for their external souls. The Samoyed people of the Turukhinsk region, among whom a shaman was known as a *tadibey*, believed that every *tadibey* had a familiar spirit in the shape of a boar, which was led about by a magic belt. When the boar died, the *tadibey* died. Many Siberian tales were told of shamans who sent their spirits to fight each other before they encountered each other in person.

In West Africa, wizards became blood brothers with an animal by an initiation ritual. Their lives became so closely linked that the death of one would cause the death of the other. Because of this, the relationship was always established with a ferocious animal such as a leopard, black serpent, crocodile, hippopotamus, wild boar, or vulture. The wizard acquired magical powers and invulnerability from the relationship, because he had deposited his soul outside his body.

The people of Calabar, at the mouth of the Niger, believed that everyone has four souls, one of which dwells in a forest animal such as a leopard, a fish, or a tortoise.

In a tale told by the Ba-Ronga of South Africa, the lives of a whole family were connected with a cat. The daughter of the family was married to a man from another village, and begged her family to let her take the cat with her. She kept it concealed, but one day it escaped, and began to taunt some children. They told the woman's husband, who found the cat making free with his weapons. He was very angry, and killed the cat. The wife promptly dropped dead in the field where she was working. Before she died, she asked her husband to take the cat back to her home village. When they saw the dead cat her relatives perished one by one, until the entire family was no more.

In a European folk tale, Punchkin, the hero, kept his life in a parrot, and when it was killed, he died. In an Indian folk tale, a lady called Bidasari kept her soul in a golden fish.

In a Magyar folk tale, an old witch kept a wild boar in a silken meadow; if it were killed, a hare would be found inside it, and inside the hare, a pigeon, and inside the pigeon, a small box, and inside the box, one black and one shining beetle. The shining beetle held her life, and the black one held her power. If both of these were killed, she would die. In Irish legend, the life of the hero Diarmuid was bound up with that of a boar, which when defeated, caused the death of its pursuer.

The "familiar spirit"

The name familiar is derived from the Roman belief that each family had protective spirits, usually ancestors. Popular beliefs about witchcraft included the idea of familiar spirits, but these were usually regarded as tame demons which took the form of an animal. However, the two concepts are evidently linked, as many cultures (including the Anglo-Saxons and the Celts) regarded the families of their monarchs as descended from, or in some way linked to, animals. So there is a connection between ancestor-spirits and animals. Beliefs about witches' familiars included the idea that they could shape-shift into the animal concerned, as the witch song which Isobel Goudie gave at her trial in 1662 shows:

> *"I sall gae intil a haire,*
> *Wi' sorrow and sych and meikle care;*
> *And I sall gae in the Devillis name,*
> *Ay quhill I com hom againe."*

An Edinburgh witch cast a spell on a local laird because he shot her familiar. Her son told what had happened:

> *"He shot her urchin - a hedgehog that folk ca'd her familiar. It slept in a cozy neuk o' her bed at nicht, but I thocht it weel awa', for it was a sair rival to me, and aye got a share o' my sowans and kail."*

Agnes Sampson, the Wise Wife of Keith, had a dog called Elva. Alexander Hamilton, a Lothian witch, had a crow, a cat, and a dog. A Shetland witch had a crow as a familiar. Scottish witches generally tended to have divining familiars, which they used to foretell the future.

In his research on dreams, Jung found that during an illness, people often dream of a visit by a helpful animal, or by animal-headed people. These often symbolise the healing process, and may be the reason why so many cultures have animal-headed deities. Helpful animals also appear in folk tales. The excellent book *The Wise Wound* by Penelope Shuttle and Peter Redgrove (1978) recounts an episode in the life of a friend of theirs, who began to began to hallucinate red ants on doorposts whilst menstruating. She came to the conclusion that the ants represented the instinctual processes occurring during her period. As this idea developed, she began to dream of little rat-like animals entering the house, and monkeys with auburn fur swinging through the trees. As she continued to communicate with animals, her instinctual life was enriched. This is a very similar experience to the acquisition of an animal familiar. Women's shamanistic practices are often organised around the menstrual cycle. The menstrual cycle is closely associated with the Moon, and many lunar animals are linked with witches in folklore (the hare, the toad, the magpie, etc.)

Shape-shifting into animals is also found in other cultures.

Shape-shifting

The indigenous people of Guatemala, whose life was connected with that of an animal, were believed to have been able to shape-shift into their totem animal. In Europe, witches were believed to be able to shape-shift into their 'familiar'. This was usually a hare, cat, fox, or magpie. It is possible that folk beliefs about werewolves were derived from a tradition of shape-shifters.

The indigenous peoples of Guatemala and Honduras had a tradition of the *nagual* or *naual*. This was generally an animal, which stood in relation to a person in such a way that their entire well-being depended on that animal. According to a sixteenth-century Spanish account, they could shape-shift into their nagual animal, and if they were shot at and wounded in their animal form, they would be similarly wounded in their human form. The most common *nagual* animals were deer (bucks and does), lions, tigers, dogs, and eagles. Legend has it that in the first battles with the Spanish on the plains of Quetzaltenango, the chiefs' *naguals* fought in the form of serpents. The highest chief's *nagual* was a great bird with green plumage, which the Spanish general Pedro de Alvarado killed with his lance. As the bird expired, so did the chief.

In the Northern Tradition, there are many legends of various warrior clans associated with animals: the Berserkers, Svinfylking warriors, and lfhenar. The Berserkers were believed to be shapeshifters; the power of shapeshifting was called *hamrammr*. This may have involved acting on the perceptions of observers, or some kind of out-of-the-body experience. For example, one famous Berserker, Bothvar Bjarki, who fought in the army of King Hrolf of Denmark, was said to have gone into battle in the form of a bear, whilst his human form lay in a trance in his quarters. The name of the Norse hero, Beowulf, means 'bee-wolf', which may be a kenning (metaphor) for a bear. The Ûfhednar wore wolf-skins over shirts of mail, and fought singly in battle. There were also Ûfhednar or wolf-shirts, who are thought to have gone into battle without mail, like the Berserkers. The animal warriors were reputed to have superhuman strength; a Saxon champion called Ordulf is reputed to have kicked in oaken gates at one blow.

In medieval England, outlaws were often referred to as wolf's heads. The Svinfylking warriors wore helmets with decorated with metalwork depicting boars; in the Skaldskaparmál, King Athal's helmet is called Hildigölt, 'battle-boar'. They fought in a formation called the Svinfylking or Boar's Throng. This was a triangular formation designed to smash the enemy's shield wall. Two warriors at the front formed the rani or snout. The Northern Tradition name for the constellation of the Pleiades is the Boar's Throng. The animal warriors also used the sound of their chosen animal to intimidate the enemy. It is thought that this technique temporarily lowered the blood-pressure of opponents, in order to catch them off guard. It appears that the Celts used similar techniques in battle. A Celtic Welsh princess of Radnor is said to have waged war against her enemies in the form of a wolf. In the 13th century, Irish warriors were believed to shapeshift into wolves. In Malory's *Morte d'Arthur*, one of Uther Pendragon's knights is called Ulfius; he later becomes King Arthur's chamberlain.

The process of becoming more attuned to one's animal nature is closely related to shape-shifting. In yoga and the martial arts, the postures and stances are inspired by animals. This enables the practitioner to become naturally graceful, accurate, and harmonious in their movements.

Heraldry and Totemism

It has often been speculated that heraldic animals associated with particular families are the 'totem animal' of those families. There are instances in folklore which would lend support to this view. For example, the lions kept in the Tower of London were said to fall ill when the monarch did, and to die when he or she died. Addison, in the *Free-Holder* (1 June 1716), relates that:

> "*Our first visit was to the Lions. My Friend [a Tory] enquired very much after their Health, and whether none of them had fallen sick upon ... the Flight of the Pretender? ... He had learned from his Cradle, that the Lions in the Tower were the best Judges of the Title of our British Kings, and always sympathized with our Sovereigns.*"

Needless to say, the lion is the heraldic symbol of the British sovereign.

The Anglo-Saxon kings, however, had several power animals. According to W A Chaney in *The Cult of Kingship in Anglo-Saxon England*, cult animals were:

> "*the touchstones of a dynamic relationship uniting the monarch to the divine sphere from which his mana flowed into him. The vitality of the gods and of the whole world of awe with which the ruler served as mediator for his folk was made palpable in the cult objects and hence in him.*"

The cult animals of the Anglo-Saxon kings were the boar, the dragon, and the stag.

The names of several Saxon kings were connected with animals. Various kings of Mercia had wolf names: Wulfhere (656-675), Cenwulf (794-819), Beornwulf (821-823), Bertulf (838-852), and Ceolwulf (874-877), the last king of Mercia, who lost the kingdom to Danish invaders. Some of the kings of Northumbria also had wolf names: Heodwulf (572-573), Freodwulf (573-580), Ceolwulf (729-737), Oswulf (757-759), and Erdulf (794-796 and 808-809). There was also a king of East Anglia called Aldulf, who reigned from 664 to 713. Two kings of Mercia had bear names: Beornred, who was king in 755, and Beornwulf, who was king from 821 to 823.

The Picts may represent an intermediate development between totemism and heraldry (the "missing link", so to speak). Around the seventh century of the current era, they began to carve symbols on standing stones. Anthony Jackson, in "Pictish animal symbols" (chapter in *Signifying Animals*, ed. R G Willis), speculates that symbols paired together represent marriages between lineages (the Picts were a matrilineal people), and may also have mystical significance. There is a clear geographical division between types of design carved on the stones: north of the Moray Firth, they were mostly geometrical designs; south of the Moray Firth, down as far as Fife, they were mostly animal designs. The Picts seem to have had a dualistic view of the world, and to have divided it into four regions (land, sky, forest, and water). Animals could also be divided into four categories (inedible/edible and mythical/ordinary).

According to Jackson, the species depicted in the carvings could be divided among these categories. The forest was represented by the wolf and the boar; the open land by the serpent and the stag; the sky by the sea eagle and the goose; and the water by the sea horse and the salmon. There were two different types of water. The first was that which was bounded only by the sky, i.e. rain (represented by the salmon and a carving which looks like an elephant) and lochs and the sea (represented by a deer's head or a stag). The second was that which was bounded by the land, i.e. rivers (represented by the sea horse or a beast's head) and springs (represented by the serpent and Z-rod or the serpent). The animals depicted may also have been related to the fourfold division of the year. However, we can only speculate on the classification and meaning of these carvings.

In Scotland, the Baird family was reputed to have been first granted land by King William the Lion for saving his life from a wild boar. The crest of the Baird family is "a boar's head erased, or". The war cry of the Camerons was "*Chlanna nan con thigibh a so's gheibh sibh feoil*" (Sons of the hounds come here and get flesh). Many other clans have animal, bird, tree, and plant crests and badges. The fortunes of the Hays of Errol were bound up with an oak tree: "While the mistletoe bats on Errol's aik / The Hays shall flourish, and their good grey hawk / Shall nocht flinch before the blast." Tradition has it that the Clan Skene originated in the eleventh century when a younger son of Robertson of Struan saved the king's life by killing a wolf with his *sgian* (knife), and was rewarded with the lands of Skene in Aberdeenshire.

Many English families also have animal crests, supporters, and blazons in their coats of arms. The Cavendish family have stags as supporters, stags' heads on their shield, and a serpent as a crest, and many other families have stags, lions, and various other animals in their coats of arms. The lion is the most frequently depicted animal in heraldry, being the king of the animals, and a solar animal.

Other solar animals depicted in heraldry are the horse, the leopard, the wolf, and the bull. Lunar animals depicted in heraldry are the bear, the unicorn, the dog (usually the talbot or the greyhound), and the boar. The stag is often found, and occasionally the fox (though usually only the head is shown).

Heralds had often never seen some of the more exotic animals they incorporated into their designs, hence the heraldic antelope and the heraldic tiger do not look much like their wild counterparts. The Bengal tiger, found in modern heraldry, and so called to distinguish it from the medieval depiction, is more realistic. The heraldic panther breathes fire and is often spattered with roundels. The legend of the panther repelling dragons with its sweet breath made it popular in European heraldry. The lynx is usually blazoned coward, that is, shown with its tail between its legs. The cat, wild cat, or cat-a-mountain is found mostly in Scottish and Irish heraldry. The squirrel is occasionally found. The seahorse is depicted with a fish's tail, webbed forefeet, and a horse's head; it occasionally has a fin-like mane. Goats, rams, sheep, lambs (especially in ecclesiastical heraldry), and fleeces are also found.

There is also the elephant and castle - an elephant with a howdah on its back. Otters, rabbits, hares, and badgers are occasionally shown. Stoats and weasels do not appear very often, though the Italian Sforza family had an ermine as its emblem. The hedgehog is referred to in heraldry as the hurcheon, urchin, herrison, or herizon. Mythical animals also put in an appearance: the cameleopard (a giraffe), the dragon, griffin (both the female winged griffin, and the male, not winged), opinicus, wyvern, cockatrice, centaur, and sphinx. The centaur carrying a bow and arrow was called the sagittarius. The mermaid was sometimes depicted, and more rarely, the merman or triton. The melusine (a two-tailed mermaid) appears occasionally, but is more common in German heraldry. The winged horse, or pegasus, is sometimes depicted. Another mythical beast is the enfield, a wolf with the head of a fox and the forelegs and talons of an eagle.

There is little doubt of the mythical origins of heraldry. The heralds were steeped in the lore of the medieval bestiaries, some of whose legends were derived from the ancient philosophers. The double-headed eagle of the Holy Roman Empire derives ultimately from Hittite art; the lion and unicorn as supporters of the shield may be derived from the Sumerian Moon-tree motif, in which the lion was the waxing Moon, the tree the full moon, and the unicorn was the waning Moon.

Summary

Types of totem:

- The animal as ancestor;
- The animal as representative of a clan;
- An external soul placed with an animal for safekeeping;

- The animal as friend or relation (if the animal dies, so will the human, but meanwhile the human obtains magical powers);
- The animal as an embodiment of a deity;
- The animal as an attribute of a human or deity;
- The animal as a guide to the spirit realms.

Further reading

Familiars - Animal Powers of Britain, Anna Franklin, Capall Bann Publishing

Sacred Animals, Gordon MacLellan, Capall Bann Publishing

Talking to the Earth, Gordon MacLellan, Capall Bann Publishing

Chapter 2

Transformations: Animals in Folk Tale

"The archetype of spirit in the shape of a man, hobgoblin, or animal always appears in a situation where insight, understanding, good advice, determination, planning, etc., are needed, but cannot be mustered on one's own resources."

C G Jung, *"Four Archetypes"*

There are three main animal motifs in folk tales: the animal groom, the animal helper, and the dangerous animal. The language of animals is also very important in folk tales, and represents instinctual wisdom. In the West, we tend to undervalue so-called fairy tales, thinking of them as merely stories for children. Children know better. We would do better to refer to them as folk tales, which better represents the idea that they are repositories of folk wisdom, and often provide psychological insights on a symbolic level, as C G Jung, Bruno Bettelheim (in *The Uses of Enchantment*), and the novelists Isabel Allende, A S Byatt, Robertson Davies, and many others have shown. This has always been known in India, where people of disturbed mind are given folk tales to meditate on. The cunning thing about folk tales is that they do not need to be analysed and understood by the linear-logical left brain; they appeal to the mythopæic consciousness of the right brain. Animal symbolism is particularly useful in this context, as animals often represent instinct, sexuality, and other cthonic qualities. Savage animals represent the shadow aspects of ourselves that we have not yet brought into consciousness; for example the wolf in *Little Red Riding Hood* represents sexuality.

Folktales are very definitely "of the people". They show that the humble and the poor can triumph by using their wits, even against a seemingly insuperable adversary. Jawaharlal Handoo, in "Cultural attitudes to birds and animals in folklore" (chapter in *Signifying Animals*, ed. R G Willis), has shown that animals in folk tales behave differently to animals in the "real world". In the "real world" we expect the larger animals to overpower the smaller. In folktale, the small and weak use their cunning or wisdom to outwit the big and strong; the humble hero, by use of observation and by making alliances with animal helpers, succeeds where the proud warrior has failed. In folk tale, the cunning always have the last laugh over the powerful. In India, animal tales, particularly the *Panchatantra*, are said to have been collected for the education of children and young princes.

The animal helper usually represents the hero's or heroine's instincts. The youngest brother, Jack, or the youngest princess, who is always the hero of the folk tale, is represented as a simple soul. The rest of the world views the youngest sibling as a bit of an idiot, since they do not appear to possess the qualities necessary for worldly success. However, their simplicity is that of the Fool in the Tarot; they instinctively follow Christ's injunction "Be ye wise as serpents and innocent as doves". Frequently the hero or heroine is mistreated because of this simplicity; in many tales it is because he or she is an orphan. Often it is the wicked stepmother who mistreats the orphan, in which case the dead mother is transformed into the animal helper. In many versions of *Cinderella* (Aschenpüttel), Cinderella's real mother is transformed into a helpful animal. In the Chinese version, she becomes a fish, which the wicked stepmother kills and eats; but a helpful old man tells the heroine where the bones are buried.

In many European and Eastern versions, the mother becomes a calf, a cow, or a goat. In *Rashin Coatie* (a Scottish version known as early as 1540), the mother gives Rashin Coatie a little red calf just before she dies, and this calf gives Rashin Coatie everything she asks for. The stepmother finds out and has the calf butchered, but it tells Rashin Coatie to bury its bones under a grey stone. At Yuletide, everyone puts on their best clothes to go to church, but Rashin Coatie is not allowed to go because she has no decent clothes. She goes to the grey stone and asks the calf to provide her with clothes, and when she gets to church, she meets the prince, drops a slipper, and the rest of the story proceeds in a similar fashion to the story of Cinderella.

In an Egyptian story, a stepmother and step-siblings mistreat two children, who beg the family cow to be kind to them as their mother was kind to them. The cow gives them good food, but the stepmother finds out and has the cow butchered. The children burn the cow's bones and put the ashes in a pot, from which a tree grows and bears fruit for them. In the Brothers Grimm version of the story, Aschenpüttel, the heroine is helped by birds. One day the father goes to the big city, and asks Aschenpüttel and the two step-sisters what they would like him to bring back. The stepsisters ask for 'beautiful clothes' and 'pearls and gems'; Aschenpüttel asks for the first twig that pushes against her father's hat on his way home. He gives her this, and she plants it on her mother's grave, watering it with her tears, so that it grows into a tree. A beautiful white bird alights in the tree and grants her wishes, including her desire to go to the ball, for which it provides a beautiful dress. When the Prince comes to the house with the slipper, and the stepsisters cut bits off their feet to fit into it, it is the birds who alert him to the fact that they are the wrong brides; and it is the birds who peck out the sisters' eyes at the end. It should be pointed out that the slipper is actually a fur slipper, not a glass one, and is clearly a metaphor for the vagina.

According to Jung's interpretation of folk tales, the animal helper represents the archetype of the Friend, which corresponds to Tifereth on the Tree of Life, the Christ archetype, and Khidr (the Green One) in Islam. According to Bettelheim's interpretation, the dead mother in the Cinderella tales represents the uncritical mother that the child encounters in infancy, whilst the wicked stepmother represents the later perception that the mother is a separate entity with her own agenda, which is experienced as a kind of betrayal (hence the "terrible toddler" phase at around two years old, when children realise that mother does not exist solely for their benefit). The transformation of the dead mother into an animal or tree implies that the child must internalise the nourishing aspect of the mother, so that the real mother can maintain her individuality. Of course, the views of Jung and Bettelheim are not inconsistent; they merely show two different aspects of the folk tale. Mythology is shaped by biology, but the process is reciprocal: the way we feel about our bodies is shaped by mythology. A crude deterministic interpretation of mythology does not do justice to the complexity of different cultures, which are also shaped by environment and history.

The animal groom represents the initial encounter with sexuality. There are various stories in which the heroine marries an animal, but discovers that he is actually a human under an enchantment. The most famous of these is *Beauty and the Beast*, closely followed by *The Frog Prince*, but some of the less famous are actually more interesting, such as *The Black Bull of Norroway* and *The Enchanted Pig*. In these tales, the transformation of the groom from animal to human form depends on the actions of the bride. In *The Enchanted Pig*, the heroine tries to restore the pig to human form by magic, but because her intervention is premature, he has to go away from her, and she has to seek him. In *The Black Bull of Norroway*, the bull tells the heroine to sit quite still while he fights with the Devil; if she does not remain motionless, he will not be able to find her when he returns. On perceiving that he has won the fight, however, she moves, so that he cannot see her or hear her however much she calls to him. Again, they are only reunited through strenuous effort on her part.

The animal groom is frequently restored to human form in the marital bed (e.g. in *Hans, my Hedgehog*). The implication is that the virgin bride perceives her new husband and his sexuality as some kind of animal to be tamed. It is her devotion and love which restores him to human form, particularly in the story of *Beauty and the Beast*. In *Snow White and Rose Red* (no relation to *Snow White and the Seven Dwarves*), the groom is a bear. In a Nordic folktale, *The Werewolf*, a princess's lover is changed into a werewolf. An old man tells her that to release him from the spell, she must put a white lily that she has always treasured into a cauldron of tar. When the werewolf comes, she must pour the tar over his head; this will release her lover from the spell. The lily is a symbol of virginity; the cauldron is a vessel of transformation; and the werewolf represents her fear of sexuality. In an African version of the story, a girl has to lick a crocodile's face to restore him to human form. According to G K Chesterton, the lesson of *Beauty and the Beast* is that "a thing must be loved before it is lovable".

The animal bride is often a bird, such as the girl who has been turned into a swan in the story of *The Drummer*. In *Cherry, or the Frog-Bride*, three princes set out into the world to seek their fortune, and come to a town where there lives a beautiful girl named Cherry, so called because that is all she will eat. Her mother goes to the garden of the nearby nunnery to get her cherries; when the abbess finds out, she is very angry. One day the three princes arrive in the town, and see Cherry combing her long hair at a window. She is so beautiful that they begin to fight over her. Hearing the noise, the abbess comes to the gate. Being of a contemplative frame of mind, she wishes that Cherry would turn into a frog, so that the uproar might cease. The source of their contention removed, the brothers become friends again. Later they return to their kingdom. Their father is dying, and wishes to decide which son shall inherit the kingdom. He sends the three brothers out to find a piece of linen so fine that it will pass through his gold ring. All three set out; the two older brothers set out upon pleasant ways, passing through many towns, where they buy the finest linen they can find. The youngest brother sets out upon a desolate way over uninhabited moor and marsh, where there are no towns. At length he sits down by a bridge, and a frog emerges from the river to ask what ails him. He tells her that he is seeking a piece of fine linen; she gives him a small rag. He thanks her, and pockets the rag. On his way home he feels it growing heavier in his pocket. When he arrives home, he meets the two older brothers laden with linen; but none of it will pass through the king's ring. They jeer at him for returning empty-handed, but he produces the cloth given him by the frog from his pocket, and it is the finest linen anyone has ever seen, and passes easily through the ring. The next task set by the king is to find a dog so small that he fits in a nutshell. The two elder brothers go and buy the tiniest dogs they can find; the youngest goes back to the frog, who gives him a hazelnut and bids him crack it open very carefully on his return home. On the brothers' return, the king has a large walnut, but none of their dogs will fit in it.

The youngest brother produces his hazelnut; when it is cracked open, there emerges a tiny white dog onto the king's hand, much to the delight of the court. The final task is to find the most beautiful woman ever seen; this time the youngest brother goes away with heavy heart, thinking the frog will be unable to help him, but he goes to her anyway. She tells him to start walking home, but not to laugh at anything he might see on the way. On the way back he sees a frog go past in a coach, but does not laugh because he is so preoccupied. As he rounds the next bend, the coach presents quite a different aspect - instead of the frog, there is the beautiful Cherry. They return to his father's kingdom in style, and Cherry is the most beautiful woman anyone has ever seen. The youngest son inherits the kingdom, and Cherry is his queen. The frog is a frequent metaphor for female sexuality, being both amphibious and cthonic.

The animal helper often represents the hero's instinctual wisdom. It is similar to a "totem" or power animal. In folk tales, animals are frequently anthropomorphised, representing human qualities and values. Folk tales are also animistic, attributing life to everything, in the same way as a child does. The belief expressed in folk tales is that if we do not understand animals, it is because we are insufficiently attuned to them; hence the hero, who is usually more instinctual than his clever elder brothers, often has or acquires the gift of understanding the speech of animals.

In the story of *The Queen Bee*, the obligatory three brothers set out on a quest. On the first night, they encounter a bees' nest, which the two older brothers want to ransack for honey. But the youngest brother prevents them. The next day, they encounter an ants' nest, which the two older brothers want to disturb, to see the ants running about in confusion. Again, the youngest prevents them. That evening, they see some ducks on a pond, which the two older brothers want to kill and eat. But the youngest stops them. Further on, they come to a castle, where an old king says they can marry his youngest daughter if they can complete three tasks; if they fail, they will be turned to stone. The castle courtyard is full of statues which were once men. Undaunted, the two elder brothers attempt the tasks, but fail and are turned to stone. Then the youngest brother begins the tasks. The first is to find the key of the princess's bedchamber at the bottom of the lake; his friends the ducks come and dive to the bottom of the lake, and retrieve it for him. The next task is to gather up a thousand pearls scattered in a wood; his friends the ants gather them for him. The final task is to guess which is the king's youngest daughter. His three daughters are lying asleep in a room in the castle, and they look exactly alike, but one of them has eaten some sugar, one has eaten some treacle, and the youngest has eaten some honey. The queen bee of the hive he saved from being ransacked alights on the lips of the youngest daughter, so that he knows which she is. Having completed all the tasks successfully, he marries the youngest daughter and inherits the kingdom. His two older brothers are released from their enchantment, and marry the other two daughters.

A similar story is told in Siberia, called *Mergen and his Friends*, by the Nanai people. The hunter Mergen is hunting in the woods when he finds a deer caught in a swamp. He frees it. Later, on another hunting trip, he comes across an ant trapped by a fallen branch; he frees the ant also. Next he finds a sturgeon stranded on a sandbank in the river; he heaves it into the water. Further on in his journey, he enters a clearing where the tents of a strange clan are pitched. He is greeted by an old man, who welcomes him to his tent. Then he hears behind him the tinkling of bronze earrings: it is the old man's beautiful daughter. The old man asks him what he thinks of her, and Mergen replies that he would readily take her for his wife.

The old man tells him that a hundred men have already tried, and they are all now his servants. He sets Mergen three tasks, each of which he must complete by nightfall. The first is to wear out a pair of iron boots. Mergen calls the deer to his aid, and the deer puts on the boots and vanishes at high speed over the mountains. When it returns at nightfall, there is nothing left of the boots but a shred of an iron ring at the top. Next day, the hunter's task was to gather up a sack of millet spread over the camp. This time, Mergen calls the ant to his aid, and the ant brings the whole ant tribe to help. Soon all the millet is gathered up.

The next day, the task is to retrieve a gold ring that the old man's father dropped into the river. So Mergen calls upon the sturgeon, which retrieves the ring for him. On his return to the camp, the old man offers himself and his servants to serve Mergen, but Mergen declares that henceforth there will be no servants, and they will all live peacefully together. Mergen also marries the beautiful daughter. In the story of *The Two Brothers*, the twin heroes meet a hare, a fox, a wolf, a bear, and a lion. They spare the lives of all these animals, and in return each animal gives them two of its offspring. When the brothers separate, they each take one of each species with them, which are their faithful companions, and help them to escape from great dangers. The qualities of the different animals represent various human qualities: courage, cunning, etc. The animal helper may also represent sexual initiation and the inner resources of the sub-conscious.

In *The Three Feathers*, a king cannot decide which of his three sons shall inherit the kingdom. He gives each son a feather (following a feather was an ancient German method of divination to decide which way to go), and says that the one who brings back the finest carpet will inherit the kingdom. The oldest and middle brothers' feathers are blown east and west. The youngest brother's feather comes to rest a few yards from the castle. The others laugh at him, and he feels a bit foolish, but sits down and waits. Then he sees a trapdoor nearby. This leads down into a cave, where there is a huge toad surrounded by smaller toads. They give him the finest carpet he has ever seen, and he returns to the castle and wins the contest, because the two oldest brothers have not tried, and have brought back some rag they got from a shepherd. The two older brothers demand another test, so the king sends them out to find the finest gold ring. The two older brothers knock the nails out of a carriage ring, still not expecting the youngest to come up with anything better. The youngest visits the toads again, and is given a beautiful gold ring, again winning the contest. The two oldest demand a third test, so the king sends them to find the most beautiful woman. The two eldest return with peasant girls; the youngest visits the toads and selects a toad from amongst them, who turns into a beautiful maiden. This time the two older brothers demand that the three girls must jump through a hoop,

33

thinking that their sturdy peasant girls will easily win. But the peasant girls break their legs, whilst the dainty maiden sails through gracefully. This time the victory is uncontestable, and the king awards the kingdom to the youngest son. The toads represent cthonic wisdom; the two elder brothers remain on the surface, but the youngest goes down within himself (literally beneath the earth of his own kingdom) to find the inner resources of sexuality and wisdom.

The wild beast is an externalised representation of our inner fears and conflicts. The hunter who protects the hero or heroine from the wild beast is often seen as a strong avuncular figure, in direct contrast to the inneffectual father figure who has been eclipsed by the wicked stepmother. The savage beast represents the fear of the unknown; it is perhaps, on a spiritual level, the guardian of the threshold. Such a figure appears in the Spanish/Portuguese story of *The White Parrot*, where a boy is sent to fetch silver water from the well, but an old man warns him that the well is guarded by a lion who 'sleeps with his eyes open and watches with his eyes shut'. The wolf who eats Red Riding Hood's grandmother is also a threshold guardian; he is the Eater of Souls, the transforming power of Death.

Being eaten is a frequent metaphor of initiation; what is eaten is transformed into a new substance. However, we also become what we eat, as is demonstrated in the story of *Brother and Sister* (another Brothers Grimm tale). A boy and a girl leave home because of the cruelty of their wicked stepmother. They come across a spring, and the little boy is thirsty, but the girl hears the spring murmuring, 'Whoever drinks of me will become a tiger', so she prevails upon her brother not to drink. The next spring they find whispers that whoever drinks from it will become a wolf; again the girl prevents her brother from drinking.

At the next spring she hears it say that its water will transform the drinker into a fawn, but she cannot this time prevent her thirsty brother from drinking. He is turned into a fawn, so she places her golden girdle about his neck and weaves a leash of rushes. He represents sexuality and innocence; she represents the psyche, that controls and contains desire. His transformation happens because he has no control, and he must regain control in order to regain his human form.

Wild animals are often associated with transformations. According to Jung, the appearance of animals in a folk tale indicates that "the contents and functions in question are still in the extrahuman sphere, i.e. on a plane beyond human conscious-ness". Frequently these animals appear in conjunction with a witch or the wicked stepmother, who represents the matrix of the unconscious from which monsters (repressed elements of the psyche) occasionally emerge to affright us. Talking animals represent the wisdom of the psyche, mediators between the conscious and unconscious mind. Horses appear frequently in this role; the function of knowing and intuition is represented by a riding animal, because the rider represents the ego in control of the unconscious (the ridden animal).

The language of animals is another important motif in folk tale. In the story of *The Three Languages*, an old count has a son who will not learn anything. He sends him away to a famous master; when he comes back after a year, the father is furious to discover that he has learnt 'what dogs bark'. So he sends him away again; this time he returns, having learnt 'what the birds speak'. Once more the father sends him away, and this time he learns 'what the frogs croak'. All three of these languages come in useful to him on his later adventures; eventually he ends up being Pope, with the help of the doves. The dogs represent control over aggression; the frogs represent sexuality and instinct; and the doves represent spirituality.

Chapter 3

The Folklore of Animals

Folklore, superstition, weather lore, and folktale all abound with references to animals. To town dwellers it seems a rarity to see a wild animal, but to country dwellers who did not use a variety of machines to till the earth, and had a much more symbiotic relationship with nature than we do today, wild animals would have been a part of their everyday experience, and knowing how to read omens from them would have been an essential part of country lore. If we want to recapture the sense of unity with Nature, folklore is a means to rediscovering the sense that everything is connected to everything else.

There are many superstitions relating to animals, particularly with regard to activities such as fishing. The fishermen of the east coast of Scotland had a number of taboos on mentioning certain animals whilst mending nets, setting lines, or going aboard their boats. If they saw certain animals, they would not put to sea. Amongst Yorkshire fishermen (1898), it was not a good omen if a four-legged animal crossed your path, especially when going down to the fishing-boat.

Conversely, on certain salmon rivers of Scotland, the first salmon grilse catch of the season was celebrated with considerable merrymaking. Herrings were said to dislike quarrels (Ross and Cromarty, 1853). When setting out on a journey, it was lucky to meet a horse or a horse and rider, especially for a bride (Scotland, 1881), but unlucky to meet a cat (Reginald Scot, 1584; Banff, Scotland, 1886), especially for fishermen. It was also unlucky for fishermen to meet a rabbit (1822).

Quarrymen on Portland Bill, Dorset (1953) would not go to work if they saw a rabbit cross their path. In the village of Portland, people would not say 'rabbit'; it was referred to as a 'Wilfred' or 'one of them furry things'. If someone wished you ill-luck, however, they would say "Rabbits to you". Even in the 1960s, the local paper was edited to ensure that the word rabbit did not appear. It was very unlucky to go to sea with a dead rabbit or hare on board the boat (perhaps this originated with an idea about not offending against the creatures of the Moon, who rules the tides). In Yorkshire, Cornwall, and Buckie in Banffshire, hare and rabbit were taboo words among fishermen. In some places, however, hares' and rabbits' feet were worn for luck, to prevent witchcraft, to allay cramp (16th c.), to alleviate gout (Pliny), to relieve colic (Pepys, 1664-5), and to ameliorate rheumatism (Northamptonshire, 1850s, and Northumbria, 1899).

In the seventh century, St. Eligius, Bishop of Noyon in Flanders, warned his congregation to avoid the following heathen practices: regarding sneezing as an omen; paying heed to birdsong (using it as an augury); leaving home on specific days, such as the first day of the new moon, or on the day of an eclipse; observing the month of May, and the festivals of moths and mice; the lighting of torches along the roadside; the passing of cattle through holes in the earth or holes in trees; the wearing of amber by women, either round their necks or in their 'zones' with invocations of Minerva; holding fountains sacred, or venerating trees (he also ordered that sacred trees should be cut down); the leaving of little representations of feet at crossroads.

Some of these customs are familiar to modern Pagans: using birdsong as an augury; regarding specific days as sacred; observing the month of May; the blessing of cattle; the wearing of amber; and the veneration of trees, wells, and crossroads. Less comprehensible however are the festivals of moths and mice (totem animals of the clan? some sort of propitiatory rite to stop them eating your clothes and your grain store?) and regarding sneezing as an omen. Presumably the feet at the crossroads were a charm for safe travel, but I wonder to which deity the Flemish held crossroads sacred? It may have been the local equivalent of Hecate, since the use of the name Minerva in the proscription against wearing amber is probably a Latin 'translation' of a local deity. I presume that the wearing of amber in your 'zones' means decorating your sexual organs with it in some way, and therefore relates to some sort of fertility magic. This glimpse of Flemish Paganism provides us with evidence that the customs we still practice are of ancient origin.

In many areas, it was believed to be lucky to step in animal excrement, especially that of dogs, horses, and cows; it is still regarded as lucky if a bird craps on you. There was a country saying "Muck is luck". Perhaps the fertility afforded by manure is the reason for this superstition; alternatively, perhaps it was a way of turning the apparent misfortune of stepping in muck into a happy occurrence.

There were various magical procedures involving animals. In the Cambridgeshire Fens, an eelskin garter was used as a preventative and a cure for rheumatism. Snake-skin headbands were used elsewhere as a cure for headaches. In the Norse tradition of shapeshifting, called hamrammr, a girdle of untanned wolf-skin, wolf hair, or wolf-leather was used to shapeshift into a wolf. A South American people, the U'wa (Tunebo) of Colombia, have a ceremony called Reowa, the purification chant. Fish and frogs are ceremonially eaten. The chant and the ceremony banish all harm from the universe, especially poisonous snakes and confused weather. The ceremony is performed for proper foetal development and safe birth. It is done in the temperate zone; the effects are transferred to the lowlands by the master chanter during the ceremony. (The distinction between highland and lowland areas is an important one in U'wa cosmology.)

Local traditions of animal worship, crop magic, and weather magic were widespread until well into the eighteenth century. St George, the renowned dragon-slayer, was celebrated in many local festivals. St George represents the airy powers of light, whilst the dragon represents the cthonic powers of darkness and primordial chaos. Many fairs and saint's day processions had figures of dragons, including Snap the Dragon, a figure formerly paraded through Norwich. These were related to the hobby horse, another seasonal figure (see Horse). The myth of the hero slaying the dragon dates back to Tiamat and Marduk. Tiamat was the goddess of the primordial waters, and was slain by the solar hero, Marduk, after a protracted battle in which Tiamat enlisted the aid of the Eleven Mighty Helpers. They were the Viper; Lakhmu the Shining Snake; the Great Lion; the Ravening Dog; the Scorpion Man; the Storm Winds; the Fish Man; and the Goat Fish. (They were the prototypes of the Zodiac.) They were armed with the Thunderbolt, an invincible weapon, and led by Kingu, god of the powers of darkness.

In Scotland, various animals were regarded as magical, and festivals and rituals reflected this. The serpent, the salmon, and the bull were particularly potent symbols. The serpent was the symbol of wisdom, perhaps a form of earth spirit. In the Isles, a serpent rite associated with the Day of Bride at Candlemas survived for a long time. In Ireland, there are no snakes; there, the symbol of wisdom is the salmon, particularly the salmon of the Pool of Connla, that eat the nuts that fall from the sacred hazel trees. These nuts were said to contain the knowledge of poetry and art, and their red colouring was said to give rise to the red spots on the underside of the salmon. The first person to taste the juice of the salmon as it was being cooked was said to become wise and be able to foresee the future.

In Scotland, where both snakes and salmon are widespread, both animals symbolise wisdom. There are drawings of both salmon and serpents on Pictish stand-ing stones. There are also bulls depicted on these stones. The custom of sacrificing bulls was widespread amongst the Celts, and even survived into the Christian era, when bulls were sacrificed to certain saints, e.g. to St Maol Ruadh in Ross-shire, and to St Cuthbert at Kirkcudbright. There was also a folk tale that St Martin was cut up and eaten in the form of an ox. The hide of bulls was also used in a ritual manner; there was a form of divin-ation, called taghairm, in which the seer lay under a waterfall in a bull's hide; in the Highlands and Hebrides, the leader of the Hogmanay guisers wore the head and hide of a bull.

The symbols of the Four Evangelists were well known in medieval times; the font at Minstead Church in Hampshire has one on each side (though the church leaflet will have you believe that they are animals associated with the life of Christ). The four animals were the Eagle, the Lion, the Man (sometimes an angel), and the Bull (sometimes an Ox). They also represented the Four Elements and the quintessence. The Man is associated with the gospel of Matthew, and represents the human nature of Christ (the incarnation). The Lion is associated with the gospel of Mark, and represents the royal nature of Christ. The Ox or Bull represents the sacrificial nature of Christ, and is associated with the gospel of Luke. The Eagle represents the divine nature of Christ and his ascension to heaven, and is associated with the gospel of John. The four cherubim guarding the throne of God and the four corners of Paradise are sometimes represented as a tetramorphic figure of a man, lion, ox and eagle. They also represent the Four Elements, and wield the sword of discrimination, the flaming sword that drove Adam and Eve from Paradise.

The same four animals appear in the forms of the cherubim guarding the gates of the palace of Ashurnasirpal II, who ruled from 883-859 BCE at Nimrud. These cherubim have the head of a man, the body of a bull, the wings of an eagle, and a lion's feet. In the Taurean Age (circa 2000 BCE), these were the animals of the solstices and equinoxes. (Aquarius, the Man, would have been at the Winter Solstice; Taurus, the Bull, would have been at the Vernal Equinox; Leo, the Lion, would have been at the Summer Solstice; and Scorpio, which is an eagle in its exalted form, would have been at the Autumnal Equinox.)

Animals are frequently associated with the Moon. According to folklore, plants will not grow and animals will not bear their young without the fertilising power of the Moon. There are various Moon deities, both male and female, who are held to control fertility. It was believed that the rays of the waxing Moon made seeds germinate. It has now been demonstrated that the phases of the Moon do actually affect growth. All nocturnal animals are associated with the Moon (e.g. cats, foxes). Animals which appear and disappear, such as bears that hibernate and reappear with their newborn cubs in Spring, are also lunar. The dog is lunar, perhaps because dogs howl at the Moon. Hecate was the three-headed hound of the Moon. Artemis, another Moon goddess, was associated with bears and dogs. The young girls of Athens danced in honour of Artemis Brauronia, the bear goddess. The Celtic Moon goddess was also associated with bears, particularly at Berne in Switzerland.

Animals of the waters are associated with the Moon, particularly amphibious animals such as the frog and the toad. The spiral is sacred to the Moon, hence also the snail. Cybele was a lioness, seated on a lion throne; her chariot was also drawn by lions, or in some versions, by goats, another lunar animal. Atargatis, the Queen of Heaven, was depicted riding a lion, her head surrounded by moonbeams. The ravening aspect of the Mother Goddess is often represented as a lion or a panther. The maternal aspect is depicted by the cow. Isis and Hathor were cow-goddesses. The cow's horns are associated with the crescent or horned Moon. The Moon Goddess is often depicted with horns or a horned headdress, in Greek, Egyptian, and Babylonian art. The Apis Bull was the incarnate soul of Osiris, who was the pilot of the lunar barque, the Boat of Millions of Years. The new Moon is the Bull Child, the Calf of his Mother. In her human form, the Moon Goddess is often accompanied by a cow, a goat, or a bull. Pasiphae, the Minoan Moon Queen, whose name means "She Who Shines for All" was the mother of the Minotaur, the bull child. One interpretation of this myth could be that Pasiphae was a Moon Goddess assimilated into another legend, where the idea that she is the mother of a hybrid becomes abhorrent because it is no longer understood as a symbol of the waning Moon giving birth to the new Moon.

The Moon is particularly associated with the hare in folklore, because of the way in which the craters of the Moon sometimes look like a running hare, particularly when the Moon rises at dusk. The lunar hare and the lunar toad are often three-legged to represent the three phases of the Moon, or past, present, and future. The rabbit is also a lunar creature. Another important aspect of Moon symbolism is the Moon Tree, which is often guarded by animals. In Assyrian and Phoenician depictions of the Moon Tree, it is guarded by lions, unicorns, goats, or winged beasts. In some myths, these attack and kill the Moon God. In other stories, they are there to guard the treasures of the tree from the hero who comes to steal them.

The Sun also has a number of animal associations. Horses, usually white or golden, draw the Sun god's chariot. The spider is solar, because it sits at the centre of its webs with rays in all directions. The lion, the ram, and the horse are all solar creatures. The winged or plumed serpent and the dragon are also associated with the Sun.

Many hunting cultures have customs and taboos surrounding the disposal of bones. They must be treated with respect and carefully buried, otherwise the spirit of the animal would be displeased, and the species as a whole would withdraw from the hunters. The Canadian Indians gathered and preserved the bones of the beavers they had hunted, and threw them in the river. Deer and elk were treated with similar respect by Indigenous Americans. In some places, this was to ensure that the animal's spirit could go to the other world, eventually to be reborn. This was the case among the Minitaree and Dakota peoples.

The Plains peoples arranged the skulls of buffaloes in a circle, and their other bones in a symmetrical pile, to await their resurrection. Among the Kwakiutl people of North America, it was believed that the souls of the salmon they had killed returned to the salmon country, so they threw its bones and offal into the sea. The Ottawa and Huron peoples did not burn fish bones; if they did the soul would be lost. There were various other taboos surrounding hunting. Among the Indigenous Americans of Nootka Sound, the Malagasy whalers, the fishermen of the Uap people in the Caroline Islands, and the turtle hunters of Mabuaig Island, it was taboo to have sexual intercourse before setting out, and fasting and ritual washing had to be performed. Among the Nootka, if fish did not appear, the shaman would make an image of a swimming fish and put it in the water in the direction from which the fish generally appeared, and prayed for fish to come. Among the Tlingit, a festival was held in honour of the first fish caught in the season, in which they were addressed as chiefs.

The Karok people of California held a dance for the salmon which swam up the Klamath River in Spring. A man goes into the mountains and fasts for ten days; no-one is allowed to eat any salmon until he returns to eat the first fish caught. In Peru, people adored the spirits of the fish on which they depended, because they said that the first fish that was made in the upper world was the ancestor of all other fish of that species, and would send its children to feed the people. In some areas, they revered sardines, in another, skate; also dogfish, golden fish, crawfish, or crabs. The Inuit of the Bering Straits would refrain from any work with iron implements for four days after a whale had been killed. Among the Lapp people, a man who had killed a bear was considered unclean for three days afterwards. The Baganda people fear the ghosts of slain buffalos. The head is eaten in open country, and must not be brought to a garden of plantains or a village. After the head has been eaten, the skull is placed in a small hut, beer is offered to it, and the ghost is beseeched to stay in the hut and not harm the hunters. The Toda, a pastoral people of southern India, live on the milk of their buffaloes. They never eat meat from the cow buffalo, and generally refrain from eating the bull, except for once a year, when a male calf is taken to the woods, killed with a club made from the Toda sacred tree (the Millingtonia), roasted on a sacred fire kindled by rubbing sticks together, then eaten by the men. Among many peoples, such as the Dyaks of Borneo, there was a taboo against killing crocodiles unless they had killed a human (in which case it was a matter of a blood feud), otherwise the vengeful spirit would follow the killer, and the other crocodiles would wreak vengeance on him.

Homeopathic magic is a very important aspect of identifying with animal spirits. Animals are often seen to possess qualities which humans would like to share, such as courage, swiftness, or strength. Homeopathic or imitative magic seeks to impart these qualities to humans by various means. A charm made from the fur, teeth, claws, or a symbolic representation of the animal, is held to endow the wearer with its attributes (e.g. the hornlessness of the ox, which makes it difficult to catch; the tenacity of the ferret; the agility of the frog; the strength of the bear). In Morocco, ants were given to lethargic people to eat to make them more energetic, and lion's flesh was given to cowards to make them braver, but people would not eat the hearts of chickens, because it would make them cowardly. In one of the ancient books of Hinduism, it is stipulated that when a sacrifice is offered for victory, the earth from which the altar is constructed should be taken from a place where a boar has wallowed, because the boar will have imparted its strength to that earth.

Many animals were associated with rain, particularly snakes and frogs. In Northern Australia, the Anula people killed snakes to make rain (presumably as emissaries to the spirit world). The explanation given was that the dollar bird, which is associated with rain, had a snake as a mate, which would spit up into the sky and make clouds and rainbows, so that the rain fell. In Java, a male and female cat were bathed and then let go to make it rain. In Sumatra, the women went to the river, waded in, and splashed each other. Then they threw a black cat in and made it swim about for a while, eventually letting it escape to the bank. In seasons of drought, the Garo people of Assam offered a black goat on the summit of a very high mountain. The Wambugwe of South Africa sacrificed a black sheep and a black calf, placed them on the roof of the communal hut, and scattered their entrails in all directions. The Wagogo people sacrificed black fowl, sheep, and cattle at the graves of ancestors. The Matabele sorcerers made rain-charms from the blood and gall of a black ox.

In Lithuania, the worshippers of Perkunas, the thunder god, offered a black heifer, a black he-goat, and a black cockerel to persuade the god to make it rain. They would be offered in the depths of the oak woods; a bonfire would be kindled and the people from the surrounding countryside would assemble at it, then prayers for rain would be made to the god whilst a bowl of beer was carried three times roud the fire and poured on the flames. Most of these customs involve a black animal, perhaps by association with black storm-clouds. The people of Timor sacrificed a black pig to the Earth goddess for rain, and a white or red pig to the Sun god for sunshine. It is always useful to have a method of stopping the rain once you have started it. In Egypt, sacred kings and sacred animals were threatened with death if they did not make it rain.

Many animals are specifically associated with a particular seasonal festival, often because a particular deity was celebrated at that time of year.

44

At New Year or at Yule, medieval mummers wore animal masks, possibly continuing an indigenous Pagan tradition. Animal masks included representations of stags and hares. At Hogmanay, in the Highlands of Scotland, it used to be customary for a man dressed in a cow's hide to run three times deosil (sunwise) round each house in the village. He was accompanied by young men with staves with rawhide tied to them. While he ran round the house, they would beat a hide and the walls of the house with their staves. After this they went into the house, and one of them would stand on the threshold and give a blessing, "May God bless the house and all that belongs to it, cattle, stones, and timber! In plenty of meat, of bed and body clothes, and health of men may it ever abound!" Then each of the young men singed the piece of rawhide on his staff in the fire, and touched the singed hide to the nose of every occupant of the house, including domestic animals. This was to protect them from disease, misfortune, and sorcery for the rest of the year. The ceremony was called the calluinn because of the noise made by beating the hide. The custom was observed in the Hebrides until the latter half of the eighteenth century, and may even have survived into the nineteenth century.

Bechuana warriors wore the skin of a frog on their cloaks, because frogs are slippery and hard to catch. Frogs and toads are thought to control rain because they live in water. Among the people of the Orinoco River, the frog or the toad was the lord of the waters. They did not kill frogs, but would keep them under a pot and beat them when there was a drought.

Chapter 4

The Lord of the Animals

The Horned God, the ancient deity of hunter-gatherer peoples, is often represented as the Lord of the Animals. It is an archetype found in many cultures.

In India, various deities have been identified with the Lord of the Animals; in the case of some animal species, there is a specific deity for that species. The Lord of the Elephants is Palakapya (or, in Vedic writings, Matangalua). It is related that the elephants were laying waste the jungle, pulling down trees, so King Hairyfoot of Anga sent emissaries to entreat with them. Amongst the elephants was Palakapya, who shone with divine light. He stays with the elephants all the time, protecting them. There is possibly also a Lord of Horses, called Salihotra. However, Indra is also referred to as Asvapati, Lord of the Horses.

There may be a Lady of the Animals as well. A possible candidate for the role is Padumavati, one of the Mrgas, who are associated with Rudra. Alternatively, it may be that Aranyani, Lady of the Wood, is also Lady of the Animals. Aranyani has a number of parallels with the Tamil wood goddesses, Katamarcelvi, Katteri, Katukilal, etc. The deities of Tamil Nadu are Dravidian in origin, and therefore pre-Vedic. There is also a goddess of the Chenchu (a caste near Hyderabad) called Garelamaisama, who has a special power over the wild animals of the forest, and can grant success (or cause failure) in the hunt. The Chenchus say that in ancient times only male animals were hunted. If female animals were hunted, it would make Garelamaisama very angry. In pre-Vedic times, the Lord of the Animals was Pasupati or Prajapati. A seal found at Mohenjodaro (dating from 3000 to 2000 BCE) has a depiction of an enthroned man sitting in the lotus position, with a huge pair of bison horns on his head. In the middle of the horns is something resembling a bunch of feathers (or possibly a flame, as is often found on depictions of stags in the West). This deity also has three faces, and is depicted as ithyphallic (semi-erect). He has heavy gold chains around his neck, and there are arm-rings on his arms. He is surrounded by four animals: a rhinoceros, a bison, a tiger, and an elephant. The first three are facing the god, whilst the elephant turns its back. It appears that this is a representation of the Lord of the Animals, indeed of wild animals, since there are no domestic animals depicted. In the *Rig Veda*, however, Pasupati is not mentioned anywhere, and Rudra is not described as the Lord of the Animals, but as a dangerous power who kills for pleasure. In pre-Vedic writings, Rudra is clearly identified with Pasupati.

"bhavasarvav-idam brumo rudram pasupatis-ca yah"

(Now we will speak of Bhava and Sarva, and to Rudra, who is Pasupati...)

And in another passage:

"You carry a yellow-gold bow, that hits thousands and kills hundreds, O Archer. Rudra's arrow goes forth, the divine shot..."

In the twelfth century text *'Vita Merlini'*, Merlin becomes the Lord of the Animals; dressed in antlers, he summons an enormous herd of stags and she-goats as a wedding gift for Guendoloena, who is amazed at his affinity with the animals. The name Gwendolen means 'white circle', and in this story Guendoloena appears to be a type of flower maiden. (In modern Welsh, *gwyn* or *gwen* means white or blessed, and *dolen* means a ring, link, loop, or bow.) It is appropriate that the Lady of the Flowers should be the consort of the Lord of the Animals. She represents the growth and burgeoning of nature; he represents the powers of hunting, culling, and death, which must occur so that the powers of fertility can progress without stagnation. Cernunnos is often identified with the Lord of the Animals, since he (or some other antlered god) is depicted on the Gundestrup cauldron with a stag and other animals, and holding a ram-headed serpent in one hand and a torc in the other.

In the *Mabinogion*, in the story of *The Lady of the Fountain*, the Lord of the Animals is described as "a black man of great stature on top of the mound. He is not smaller in size than two men of this world. He has but one foot, and one eye in the middle of his forehead. And he has a club of iron, and it is certain that there are not two men in this world who would not find their burden in that club. And he is not a comely man, but on the contrary he is exceedingly ill-favoured; and he is the woodward of that wood. And thou wilt see a thousand wild animals grazing all around him."

In European folktales, the Lord of the Animals makes an occasional appearance as an old man. In a Russian folktale, this old man appears as the King of the Forest, who is described thus: "all wrinkled he was and a green beard hung down to his knees. 'Who are you?' asked the peasant. 'I am Och, King of the Forest', said the little man." The King of the Forest lives underground in a green hut with his green wife and green children, in 'that other world under the earth'.

A South American people, the U'wa (Tunebo) of Colombia, have a deity called Ruáhama, the Master or Leader of Animals. At the making of the world, he cleared the thorny plants and bushes, while Thírbita (original Earth Sun) warmed the lake water. Then Ruáhama sowed the essential elements of life around the lakes. Ruáhama and Thrbita are shamanic deities. They are associated with Yagshowa, a tree turkey who can shape-shift, amongst other magical activities. The magic referred to is kwika, which signifies the reversal of order, changing of appearance and sexual practices. The first animals to emerge were the deer, hare, and peccary, but Thírbita promptly ate them (thus fulfilling their fate), leaving nothing but the bones. According to U'wa belief, animals change according to altitude, and things become what they eat. The faster animals, such as hare and deer, live in the highlands, whilst slower ones, such as monkeys, live in the lowlands. (See also Fox, Opossum, and Fish in the Animal Index.)

48

Chapter 5

Animal Sacrifice

The mythology of animals is intimately connected with their role as sacrifices and scapegoats. In the modern world, the idea of sacrifice is abhorrent to us, especially when more and more people are becoming vegetarians. However, we should not condemn the practices of ancient cultures without considering why they carried out sacrifices. Many animals were sacred to a particular deity because they were sacrificed to that deity. For example, at the rites of Eleusis, pigs were washed in the sea, then sacrificed to Demeter. In the ancient world, deities were propitiated with offerings because it was believed that giving them the best of everything would induce them to look favourably on the activities of humanity. In a worldview which regarded everything as having a soul, including Nature, sacrifice would not have been carried out lightly (at least in theory); rather it was the curtailment of an individual destiny for the good of the community. There is some evidence that some human sacrifices went willingly to their deaths in the belief that they were going to save their community from calamity.

There were various different kinds of animal sacrifice, depending on the relationship of the animal to the deity. If the deity was embodied by the animal (as Osiris was embodied by the sacred Apis Bull), the animal was killed when it reached a certain age, as an old and infirm animal could not be allowed to embody the god (in much the same way as the sacral king was killed when his luck ran out or he became too old). In this case, the animal was eaten as a sacral meal by the participants in the rite, who were then partaking of the body of the god. Sometimes the sacrifice had a fertility connotation, in that the failure of the crops was held to mean that the king or the animal was no longer bringing luck to

49

the people. Another kind of animal sacrifice was when the animal was sacred to the deity, and was therefore offered as a propitiatory sacrifice, to persuade the deity to accede to the prayer accompanying the sacrifice. Sometimes an animal would be sacrificed before starting a journey or an enterprise, in order to persuade the deity to look favourably on the endeavour. The animal was usually eaten in these rituals as well; a portion was reserved for the gods and burnt on the altar. However, it seems that the sacral meal, where the participants partook of the body of the god, was the origin of this custom. Another form of sacrifice was haruspicy, when an animal was sacrificed, and omens were taken from its entrails.

Sacrifices were also performed to make the crops grow. The Romans sacrificed red-haired puppies in spring to ward off the malign influence of the Dog Star, and to make the crops ripen and grow ruddy.

An example of a sacrificial rite can be found in Homer's "*Odyssey*" (Book III):

> "... *The ship drew into Pylos, the stately citadel of Neleus. There upon the foreshore were gathered the inhabitants, doing sacrifice to the Earth-shaker, Poseidon, the dark-tressed God. Nine congregations they made, each five hundred strong: and every congregation had offered nine victims, jet-black bulls free from any fleck of colour, to the God: in whose honour the leg-bones were now burning with fire while the assembly ate of the entrails and organs.*"

There follows a description of the prayers offered to the god and the feasting afterwards upon the flesh of the sacrificed bulls.

Sacrifice seems abhorrent to the Western mind because we have ceased to regard the meat we eat as the flesh of a dead animal. Meat comes in packets from the supermarket, and it is easy to forget that it had to be killed for us to eat it. The logical result of making the connection between the meat that we eat and the animal from which it came is either to become a vegetarian, or to ensure that the animal is treated humanely whilst alive, and killed in a humane way. Hunter-gatherer cultures treat their prey with great respect, because they have not ceased to make the connection between the live animal and the dead meat. The reindeer-hunting tribes of Siberia bury the bones of the reindeer they have killed, so that the animal can return to the spirit world and be reborn. If the sacrificed animal was eaten by the participants in the ritual, then it is little different from any other form of meat-eating. If one eats meat, it is rather hypocritical to condemn our ancestors for sacrificing animals. At least they treated the remains of the animal with some respect (especially when it was regarded as the embodiment of a deity) in the hope that it could thereby return to the spirit world and be reborn. Presumably the animal also had a reasonable quality of life before being killed, unlike today's factory-farmed animals. If one is a vegetarian, then of course killing animals is abhorrent in any circumstances, and this argument is irrelevant.

It is generally considered undesirable to revive such practices as animal sacrifice. There are plenty of other methods of making offerings to the gods: fruit, bread, wine, etc. can all be offered. Alternatively, one can pledge to perform a specific task, such as clearing a sacred site of rubbish. If it is desired to partake of the nature of the god by eating a consecrated meal, then any food can be consecrated to the deity. Of course, customs such as eating a goose at Michaelmas, or a pig or boar at Yule, were originally sacral meals: the goose was sacred to Odin; the boar was sacred to Thor. Meat-eaters may wish to continue the custom of eating pork at Yuletide and goose at Michaelmas (the Autumn Equinox was Odin's festival, so goose was eaten then); if so, it is worthwhile to try and obtain a free-range animal for the occasion, and ensure that it has been killed humanely.

Different cultures had different forms of animal sacrifice. In order to understand this practice it is necessary to look at the different customs of various cultures in more detail.

The Sacral Meal and the Animal Embodiment of the Deity

It is probable that taboos against eating certain animals originated in their being reserved for the sacral meal, which usually occurred annually, particularly where the rite related to the death and resurrection of a dying god, such as Attis or Adonis.

In Deuteronomy 14 (in the Old Testament of the Bible), the animals listed as clean and permitted to be eaten are: "the ox, the sheep, the goat, the deer, the gazelle, the roe deer, the wild goat, the ibex, the antelope and the mountain sheep" (all ruminants with cleft hooves). Unclean animals were the camel, the rabbit, the coney, and the pig (which either did not have a cleft hoof or did not chew the cud). Water creatures which were permitted were any with fins and scales; anything else was unclean. Insects were also unclean. Birds were permitted, except for "the eagle, the vulture, the black vulture, the red kite, the black kite, any kind of falcon, any kind of raven, the horned owl, the screech owl, the gull, any kind of hawk, the little owl, the osprey, the cormorant, the stork, any kind of heron, the hoopoe and the bat." It was also prohibited to seethe a young goat in its mother's milk.

The most well-known item on the above list is the prohibition against eating pork. The pig was sacred to Adonis and Attis, and it is this which has given rise to the theory that the pig was originally eaten as a sacral meal once a year on the festival of the god, and abstained from for the rest of the year. In later times, when the connection between the god and the animal was no longer obvious, it was thought that the animal was unclean. This theory is borne out by the rumour that certain Israelites gathered secretly in gardens to eat the flesh of pigs and mice; presumably this was a relic of an earlier sacral meal. On the other hand, the rumour may have been entirely unfounded, being merely an attempt to discredit the Jews. If it was the relic of a sacral meal, then perhaps a cult of Adonis existed among the Israelites.

The worshippers of Attis abstained from pork, regarding it as taboo. The legend that Attis was killed by a boar implies that the boar or pig was the sacred animal of the god. It is possible that the cry of "Hyes Attis! Hyes Attis!" which was uttered by Attis' worshippers meant "the pig Attis", as the Greek for pig is 'hys'. Adonis (a name which simply means 'Lord', and was probably a title rather than a name) also had the pig or boar as his sacred animal. There are various legends recounting the tale of Attis; he is not killed by a boar in every version. In a Greek version, the jealous Hephaestus killed him while he was hunting wild boars on Mount Lebanon. (Aphrodite had fallen in love with Adonis; Hephaestus, the smith god, was her husband.) Another story was that it was his birth that was linked with the boar - a boar cleft with his tusk the bark of the tree from which Adonis was born.

The Thebans and other Egyptians who worshipped the Theban god Amon regarded rams as sacred, and would not sacrifice them. But at the annual festival of Amon they killed a ram, skinned it, and dressed the image of Amon in the skin. Then they mourned over the ram and buried it with full ceremony in a consecrated tomb. The explanation given was that Zeus (who later acquired Ammon as an epithet, as in Jupiter-Ammon) had once appeared to Hercules dressed in the fleece of a ram and wearing its head. The ram was, however, the ancient theriomorphic deity of Thebes, just as Upuaut was the wolf-god of Lycopolis. It would appear that the ram was killed as an embodiment of Amon (hence the dressing of the god's statue in the animal's skin) rather than as a sacrifice to him.

At Memphis, there was the Apis Bull, worshipped as the incarnation of Osiris. There were actually two bulls at Memphis, one called Apis (Hapi in Egyptian) and the other called Mnevis, Menvis, or Merwer. They may originally have been entirely distinct deities, and only later merged with Osiris. They were also associated with the cult of Ra. Most of the other sacred animal cults were purely local, but the worship of Apis spread to the rest of Egypt. However, "although the bull Apis was worshipped as a god with much pomp and profound reverence, he was not suffered to live beyond a certain length of time which was prescribed by the sacred books, and on the expiry of which he was drowned in a sacred spring." (J.G. Frazer, in "*The Golden Bough*".) According to Plutarch, the bull's reign lasted twenty-five years; but inscriptions on the tomb of two of the bulls dating from the twenty-second dynasty relate that they lived for more than twenty-six years.

An unusual case of an animal being sacrificed as a re-enactment of the death of a deity is that of the goat and Artemis. In Arcadia, Artemis was known as the Hanged One, and an effigy of her seems to have been annually hanged in her sacred grove at Condylea. A remnant of a similar rite may be traced at Ephesus, where there was a legend of a woman who hanged herself, and was then clothed by the compassionate Artemis in her own divine raiment and called by the name of Hecate. At Melite in Phthia, the tale was told of a girl named Aspalis who hanged herself. After her death, her body could not be found, but an image of her was discovered standing beside the image of Artemis (she is evidently an aspect of Artemis herself), and the people gave it the title of Hecaerge ('Far-shooter'), one of the epithets of Artemis. Every year the virgins sacrificed a young goat to the image by hanging it, because Aspalis hanged herself. Hanging was a means of sacrifice whereby the person or animal sacrificed was sent to the underworld. Sacrifices to Odin were hanged.

The worshippers of Dionysos consumed a live goat in an ecstatic frenzy, tearing the unfortunate animal in pieces with their bare hands, presumably in the belief that they were devouring the god himself. According to legend, Dionysos had been changed into a kid by Zeus to protect him from the wrath of the jealous Hera. Again, when the gods fled to Egypt to escape from Typhon, Dionysos was transformed into a goat. One of his names was "the Kid". In Athens and Hermion, he was given the title "the one of the black goatskin", and a legend told that he had manifested wearing a black goatskin. He was also the god of the vine, and in the wine-growing district of Phlius there was a bronze image of him which the husbandmen plated with gold leaf to protect their vines from blight.

The horse was probably the sacred animal of Virbius, the first of the Kings of the Wood in Aricia. Horses were not permitted to enter the sanctuary of Virbius, because they were responsible for his death as Hippolytus. According to legend, the young Greek hero Hippolytus, who was chaste and fair, learned the skills of hunting from Chiron the Centaur. Hippolytus spent all his time in the forest chasing wild animals with Artemis, the virgin huntress. The divine company he kept made him immune to the charms of ordinary women. Aphrodite, goddess of love, was angered by his indifference, and inspired his stepmother Phaedra to fall in love with him. But he refused her advances, so she accused him falsely to his father, Theseus, who believed her, and prayed to his father Poseidon to avenge this slight upon her honour. Hippolytus was driving a chariot on the shore of the Saronic Gulf when Poseidon sent a great and fearsome bull forth from the sea. The horses of Hippolytus' chariot bolted, and he was trampled under their hooves. Artemis was grief-stricken, and persuaded Asclepius, god of healing, to bring him back to life. Zeus was angry with Asclepius for restoring a mortal to life, and sent the physician god to Hades. But Artemis concealed Hippolytus in a cloud and carried him to Nemi. There she entrusted him to the nymph Egeria, and he ruled there as king under the name of Virbius, and was worshipped as a god. He had a son, also named Virbius, who rode in a chariot drawn by fiery horses to fight with the Latins against Aeneas and the Trojans. It is possible that a horse was sacrificed annually in his grove, probably as an embodiment of him as a deity of vegetation.

A horse was sacrificed after the chariot races on 15th October on the Field of Mars in Rome. The right-hand horse of the victorious team was stabbed with a spear, then its head was cut off and decorated with a string of loaves. The head was then competed for by two teams from different districts. The tail was cut off and carried to the king's house, allowing the blood to drip on the threshold. The blood was kept by the Vestal Virgins and mixed with the blood of unborn calves sacrificed six days previously. This was then given to the shepherds to burn near their flocks in order to fumigate them. It is possible that the horse was the embodiment of the corn-spirit (which would explain the loaves); its tail, like the tails of other corn-animals in Europe, was the most fertilising part.

At one time the goat was the sacred animal or embodiment of Athena, who is portrayed dressed in a goatskin (the aegis). The goat was not generally sacrificed to her, nor allowed to enter her sanctuary in Athens, the Acropolis. This was said to be because the goat injured the sacred tree of Athena, the olive. However, Varro relates that once a year, the goat was driven onto the Acropolis, and there sacrificed. An animal that is only killed once a year is often the embodiment of the deity. Presumably the goat was Athena, and (as with the statue of Amon) her statue was probably dressed in its skin as a new aegis.

The pig was sacred to Demeter, and may originally have been the goddess herself. Pigs and cakes of dough were sacrificed to Demeter and Persephone at the festival of Thesmophoria, which was celebrated by women alone in October. They were thrown into deep ravines where there were snakes, which ate the remains of the pigs. The previous year's decayed flesh (that which remained uneaten by the snakes) was fetched from the bottom of the chasm by women, and sown with the seed corn to ensure a good crop. Later legend explained that this custom originated when Hades abducted Persephone. As Hades opened the earth to return to the underworld, a swineherd called Eubulus was herding his pigs nearby, and they fell down the chasm into the underworld. Probably Persephone's sacred animal was the pig.

The problem with taking myth too literally is graphically illustrated by the practice of the people of Rhodes, who annually sacrificed a chariot and four horses to the sun god, flinging them into the sea for his use. Believing that the sun god rode across the sky in a chariot, they thought he would need a new chariot and team every year, as the old ones would be worn out. Another example of this is the lamb annually sacrificed by the Argives to Hades. Dionysos was supposed to have gone into the underworld by way of the Alcyonian lake to rescue his mother Semele from the underworld, so they threw a lamb into the lake.

The story of the Golden Fleece is also a tale of sacrifice. Notice how the female character, Helle, is conveniently drowned. Athamas, a king of Thessaly, married Nephele, and she bore him a son, Phrixus, and a daughter, Helle. But then Athamas married Ino, and had by her two sons, Learchus and Melicertes. Ino was jealous of Phrixus and Helle, and plotted their death. She persuaded the women to roast the seed-corn before it was planted. The next year, there were no crops, which resulted in a famine. So the King sent a messenger to Delphi to consult the oracle as to what the cause of this might be. But Queen Ino bribed the messenger to say that the famine would not come to an end unless Phrixus and Helle were sacrificed to Zeus. Accordingly, Athamas sent for the children, who were with the sheep. But a ram with a golden fleece spoke to them and alerted them to the danger. They climbed on the ram's back and fled. He carried them over land and sea. As they flew over the sea, Helle slipped from the ram's back and was drowned. Phrixus arrived in Colchis and married the King's daughter. Afterwards he sacrificed the ram to Zeus and gave the fleece to the King, who nailed it to an oak tree guarded by a dragon who never slept. The tree grew in the sacred grove of Ares. Zeus took the ram and made it into the constellation of Aries, the Ram (Krios in Greek). Here we appear to have another example of the embodiment of a god being slain and its skin given to the god, this time in the form of an oak, the tree sacred to Zeus.

Similar customs were observed with animal deities in other parts of the world. It is often believed that the animal killed goes to intercede with the gods on behalf of the tribe. The Issapu tribe in Fernando Po killed the sacred serpent and hung its skin on a tree. Every child in the tribe had to touch the serpent's tail (possibly to bring the children under the deity's protection, or to make them identify with the tribe by touching the sacred animal). The Psylli, a snake clan of Africa in ancient times, used to put their newborn children amongst snakes, believing that the snakes would not harm them if they were true-born members of the tribe.

Among the Lapps, sacrificed animals were believed to go to Jabme-Aimo, the subterranean realm of the dead. They set aside the bones, eyes, ears, heart, male sexual parts, and some of the meat from each leg, and laid them in a coffin. The god to whom the animal was sacrificed was believed to give it new life in the underworld. The Lapps also buried the bones of bears which they had eaten.

The Todas, a pastoral tribe of Southern India, relied for their main food-source on the milk of their buffaloes. They held buffaloes sacred and treated them very kindly, even adoring them. They never ate the meat of the cow buffalo, and only ate the meat of the male once a year, when they killed a very young male calf, which was taken into the depths of the forest and killed with a club made of the wood of the Millingtonia tree (the Todas' sacred tree). They then made a sacred fire by rubbing two sticks together, and the calf was roasted on the embers of the fire, which had consisted of various trees. Only the men of the tribe partook of the meat.

The Kalmuck people, in the Caucasus, consecrated a white ram, called "the ram of the spirit" or "the ram of heaven". It was never shorn or sold, but when it grew old and its owner wished to dedicate a new one, the old one was killed and eaten at a feast to which the neighbours were invited. It was killed on an auspicious day, generally in autumn, by a sorcerer. Its meat was eaten, and some of the fat and the skeleton was burned on a turf altar, and the head, skin, and feet were hung up.

Oracular sacrifice

Another form of sacrifice was the oracular sacrifice. Among the Kuruvikkarans (a caste of beggars and bird-catchers in Southern India), the goddess Kali was believed to descend on her priest, and he gave oracles after drinking the blood which streamed from the slit throat of a goat. In the temple of Apollo Diradiotes at Argos, they sacrificed a lamb once a month by night, and a woman subject to a rule of chastity tasted its blood, and then prophesied or divined, inspired by the god. Similarly, the priestess of Earth at Aegira in Achaia drank the fresh blood of a bull before going down into the cave to prophesy. In Rome and Etruria, the entrails of sacrificed animals were read for omens; this was the practice of haruspicy (probably meaning 'entrail gazing'), which originated in Etruria, and most of its prominent practitioners were Etruscan. The College of Haruspices at Rome consisted of sixty members, who would interpret the liver of a sacrifice for a fee. The liver was considered to depict the universe in microcosm, and various areas of it were designated as belonging to specific deities. Presumably, if the liver of a particular sacrifice differed from the norm, it was interpreted accordingly.

In Celtic Iron Age Britain, the act of eating meat sometimes had ritual overtones. There was the rite of Himbas Forosnai, which involved chewing the meat of a red pig, a dog, or a cat, then singing an incantation over it and offering it to the gods, for the purposes of divination. In *Togail Bruidne Da Derga'* there is an account of a man eating a huge quantity of beef and then entering into a sacred sleep in which he would discover in a dream the identity of the future king. One of the functions of the vates was to interpret sacrifices, divining the future from their death-throes.

Intercessionary sacrifice

An ox was sacrificed in Greece around the end of June, to intercede for an end to drought and food shortages. All those present at the sacrifice blamed each other for the "murder of the ox" (*bouphonia*). The ox to be sacrificed was chosen by driving the animals round an altar with corn strewn on it. The ox that ate the corn was the one to be sacrificed (this could be interpreted as the god claiming the animal as his own). All the participants ate of the meat, and its stuffed body was yoked to a plough. The ox probably represented the corn-spirit. At Great Bassam in Guinea, oxen were killed at the harvest.

The Aino of Japan and Sakhalin killed a sacred bear to take their prayers to the bear-god. When they killed a bear whilst hunting, a ritual of propitiation was carried out, and bear-skulls were displayed in a place of honour in their houses. Many of the Aino who live in the mountains are called *kimun kamui sanikiri* (descendants of the bear), and they regard the bear as a minor deity. The Gilyaks (a Tungus people of Eastern Siberia) also held a bear-slaying ritual in January. It was similar to the Aino rite - both tribes killed the bear with arrows - and the Gilyaks believed that the bear went to the Lord of the Mountain to intercede on their behalf. Before being killed, the bear was led into each house in the village, to share its divinity among the people.

The Celts also sacrificed animals (and occasionally humans). Ritual deposits seem to have consisted mostly of domestic animals which had not been butchered for human consumption (which undermines the theory of the sacrifice as a sacral meal). In England and Wales, the skulls of cattle, horses, and dogs, and the bodies of horses and dogs have been found beneath Iron Age houses, and in the ditches or beneath the ramparts of forts. Presumably these ritually interred animals were 'foundation sacrifices'.

We know from the stories of Merlin that King Vortigern was told by his advisers that a human sacrifice was required for the foundations of his castle to stop it falling down, and that Merlin was going to be the sacrifice, but he managed to escape this fate by discovering that the castle was being undermined by the conflict of two dragons in a pool beneath the hill. Animal remains were also deposited in votive pits (found mostly in southern England), and can only be distinguished from domestic detritus by the way in which they are deposited (arranged in layers, not butchered, and sometimes only a part of the animal is deposited). Foundation rites were also performed when a well was sunk or a boundary ditch dug, and similar termination rites were deemed necessary when it was filled in again. Votive deposits of animal remains have been found in wells and boundary ditches, though their purpose is unclear, and it is not known to what deity, if any, they were offered. In the period of Roman occupation the presence of inscriptions and of temples dedicated to specific deities makes the task of identification easier. Most of the bones of sacrificial animals at the temple of Mercury at Uley in Gloucestershire were those of goats; there were also some cockerels sacrificed. Animal skulls were also placed in human graves, both in Roman Britain and in the early English kingdoms. Whole or cremated horses and dogs were sometimes interred in Anglo-Saxon burials.

Animals as Scapegoats

Animals were also used as scapegoats; symbolically loaded with the sins or illnesses of the community, they were sent out into the wilderness, or killed to expiate the sins of the people.

In Formosa, a lamb, goat, or camel was used to take on disease or evil or the sins of the community, then driven out into the desert. In Morocco wealthy Arabs used to keep a wild boar in the stables, so that djinni and evil spirits would enter the boar and leave the horses alone. Similarly, in the New Testament, Jesus cast a whole legion of evil spirits out of a man and into a herd of swine, which then rushed headlong into a lake. Afterwards, the people of that region (the Gadarenes) "pleaded with him to leave their region". (Matthew 8:28-34)

The Badagas of the Neilgherry Hills in Southern India laid the sins of a deceased person on a buffalo calf. This calf was then left to wander, and was never made to work again. In Central India, when an epidemic struck a village, they put dye or paint on an animal (a chicken, a goat, or a pig, depending on the seriousness of the crisis) and drove it out into the wilderness. The Bhars, Mallans, and Kurmis of India used a black female goat or buffalo when cholera struck them.

Among the Dinka people of the White Nile, a sacred cow was laden with the sins of the people when war, famine or other disasters threatened, and it was driven to the other side of the river. Some cultures carried out these rites annually. An example is the sacrifice of a goat and a monkey by the Garo people of Assam, or the stoning of a dog by the Bhotiyas of Jahur (in the western Himalayas), or the sacrifice of a red red horse or buffalo by the Bataks of Sumatra.

Another sacred animal (other than the pig) in the rites of Attis was the bull. One of the initiatory rituals was to crown the devotee with gold and wreath him with fillets. He would then descend into a pit. The mouth of the pit was covered over with a wooden grating. A bull decked with garlands and gold leaf was then driven onto the grating and killed with a consecrated spear. Its blood then poured over the eager worshipper below, who emerged bloody from head to foot, and was greeted with adoration by the other devotees as a person reborn to eternal life, with his sins washed away by the blood of the bull. This rite was carried out at Spring Equinox, when Attis was reborn. In Rome, it was probably done at the temple of Cybele on the Vatican Hill. Excavations in the catacombs of St. Peter's basilica uncovered a shrine of Cybele.

In France in the Middle Ages, cats were burned in the bonfires at Easter, Shrove Tuesday, or the first Sunday in Lent, occasionally at Midsummer (St. John's Day). The cat was believed to be a form taken by witches, and an animal of the devil. This singularly unpleasant custom was instigated in the belief that burning a cat was the same as burning the witch who had shape-shifted into a cat. J.G. Frazer suggests that it may have been a remnant of a Celtic sacrificial rite, because the cats were burnt in wicker baskets. Foxes and snakes were also burnt in the midsummer fires in the belief that they were witches in animal shape.

In South Africa, disease, suffering and sin was transferred to a goat by dripping a few drops of the patient's blood on the goat's head; the animal was then turned out on the veldt. The goat was also used to take cholera away in Central India.

Even as late as the nineteenth century, in times of cattle sickness, farmers in Cornwall, Wales, and some parts of Scotland would slaughter one member of the herd to protect the rest from sickness. It was believed that the voluntary offering of a victim would ward off the sickness, in accordance with a law of nature. These were not offerings to a deity; rather the slaughter was intended as a magical act. Animals were also buried under buildings or interred in the walls, a custom which prevailed until the early nineteenth century; this was believed to bring good fortune to the structure. It was even justified on the grounds that it improved the acoustics of the building. Again, this was a magical act rather than a votive offering.

In the context of Christian beliefs, sacrifice was clearly rendered unnecessary by the intercession of Christ on behalf of sinful humanity. However, in certain more remote areas, sacrifices to saints were made. Oxen were killed in St. Benyo's honour at Clynnog Fawr in Gwynedd, and at Wester Ross in honour of St. Maelrubha, but the Gwynedd custom was suppressed in 1589, and that at Wester Ross in 1678, by reforming churchmen.

Conclusion

Whilst sacrifice seems abhorrent to the modern mind, it evidently fulfilled a socially cohesive function in ancient societies: it united people in a common purpose; they shared a sacral meal (probably the only time some of them obtained any protein); and in times of emergency (famine, war, epidemics), it helped them to believe that the deities were on their side.

It is difficult to ascertain whether animals were sacrificed as an embodiment of the deity, or as an offering to the deity. J. G. Frazer attempted to prove that most deities were originally conceived of as animals, then went through a phase of being represented as part-animal, part-human, and were then represented as fully human, but retained the animal as an attribute or emblem. According to this view, the logical development of this process is for the deity to become more and more abstract, until a monotheistic religion arises as a result. Still later in the process, there is a rational attempt to explain the universe, and the logical outcome is either atheism or humanism. However, closer scrutiny of the mythological material (e.g. that of the Celts) has demonstrated that it was not necessarily always the case that an anthropomorphic deity developed out of a theriomorphic one. The relationship between a deity and the animals associated with him or her was more subtle, and often more complicated than this; sometimes a human hero or god was turned into an animal; sometimes the animal form was contemporary with the human form.

Whatever the purpose of sacrifice, it was a central feature of ancient religion. Among the Celts, according to Caesar, the Druids would 'excommunicate' rebellious elements by excluding them from sacrifices:

> *"When a private person or a tribe disobeys their ruling, they ban them from attending at sacrifices. This is their harshest penalty. Men placed under this ban are treated as impious wretches; all avoid them, fleeing their company and conversation, lest their contact bring misfortune upon them."*

In any case, being confronted with the concept of sacrifice forces us to think about our relationship to animals. The modern view of animals is a distorted one, in that we are divorced from nature. The ancients lived much closer to nature in the sense that they depended on it for survival; they were not necessarily animal lovers, nor environmentally friendly in the modern sense. They were almost completely at the mercy of the elements, and knew very little about fertilisers or crop rotation. Under these circumstances it is hardly surprising that they looked for divine assistance simply to survive, and were prepared to use any means at their disposal to secure the favour of the gods. In the modern world, on the other hand, we regard animals either as pets, in which case we anthropomorphise them, or as food, in which case we try and forget that they are animals at all. We forget that animals are wild creatures with a different form of consciousness; we also forget that humans are also a species of animal, and a predatory one at that. Personally, I feel that if one is going to eat meat, one should be capable of killing the animal (preferably humanely), and of acknowledging that the piece of meat on the table is a piece of animal. The logical outcome of recognising this would be to give the animal a reasonable quality of life, and to kill it humanely. It is the refusal to face up to the moral implications of meat-eating that allows factory-farming to continue. At least with sacrifice, the animal in question was left alone for most of the year (if its meat was taboo except for the occasion of the sacral meal), even pampered in some cases, and only killed once a year on the festival of the deity, if Frazer's interpretation is to be believed. This is not to advocate the revival of sacrifice, merely to put it into perspective.

Chapter 6

Animals in Mythology

Animals are seen in many cultures as divine messengers, intermediaries between this world and the next. Sometimes they are attributes and companions of deities, sometimes a deity will manifest as an animal. In some cultures certain animals are seen as being particularly divinely favoured. In Zoroastrianism, for example, the dog and the otter are regarded as clean animals. The dog is believed to accompany the dead to the spirit world.

In the *Mabinogion*, animals are often the means by which deities make themselves known to humans. For example, Pwyll, Lord of Arberth, is hunting a stag when he meets Arawn, King of Annwn (the underworld). Pwyll's dogs are set on a stag, but then another pack of hounds appears; these are Arawn's hounds, shining white with red ears. Pwyll claims the quarry for his own, so Arawn and Pwyll meet in anger. But Arawn needs a human hero to fight for him against Hafgan, a rival Otherworld king. There are also enchanted animals in the *Mabinogion*, such as Twrch Trwyth, a magical boar.

Before Culhwch can marry Olwen, he has to carry out a series of tasks for her father, the giant Ysbaddaden. These tasks culminate in the hunt for Twrch Trwyth, who is really a king who has been transformed into a boar. The task is to obtain the shears, comb, and razor from between Twrch Trwyth's ears. Culhwch obtains the help of Arthur and Mabon (the divine hunter) in his quest. First, however, they have to find Mabon. The Stag of Rhedynfre (one of the Oldest Animals) helps to find him. The Stag is a magical animal and can communicate with one of Arthur's men, Gwrhyr the Interpreter of Tongues. The idea of someone who can understand the speech of animals is a frequent one in myth and folktale, and often signifies a person in tune with their instinctual nature. The folk tale of *The Three Languages* (retold by the Brothers Grimm) tells of a boy who goes out into the world to obtain an education, and learns the language of animals, much to his father's chagrin. However, the acquisition of the language of frogs, dogs, and birds stands him in good stead on his travels.

Because of the urge to show a "natural" progression from animism to polytheism to monotheism to atheism, many interpreters of culture have tried to show that the idea of deity evolves from zoomorphic figures into anthropomorphic ones. This theory is not, however, supported by the Celtic evidence. The Celtic Horned God is frequently depicted with a ram-headed serpent, which is accorded such prominence that it may be a deity in its own right. The great bull of early Irish legend, Donn of Culánge, was originally a man but then metamorphosed into a bull. The souls of people were also held to transmigrate into animal forms.

In the *Mabinogion*, there are various references to older Celtic legends, lost fragments of mythology which perhaps derive from the oral tradition which preceded the written text. One of these is the myth of the Oldest Animals, which are the Ouzel of Cilgwri, the Stag of Rhedynfre, the Owl of Cwm Cawlwyd, the Eagle of Gwernabwy, and the Salmon of Llyn Llyw. These magical animals are very old indeed, and none of them had heard anything of the imprisonment of Mabon son of Modron except the Salmon of Llyn Llyw, who was the oldest.

In Hinduism, Vishnu is believed to have appeared on earth in various animal and human incarnations. The first was Matsya, the fish; the second was Kurma, the tortoise; the third, Varaha the boar; the fourth, Narasinha the lion-headed man; the fifth, Vamana the dwarf; the sixth, Parushurama or Rama; the seventh, Ramachandra; the eighth, Krishna; the ninth, Buddha; and the tenth, who is yet to come, is called Kalki, a giant with a horse's head, who will appear in a new and better world. Matsya, the fish avatar, is associated with ancient traditions of a flood. The tale goes that one day the wise Manu was having a wash, and found a tiny little fish in the palm of his hand. The fish begged him to allow it to live, so he put it in a jar.

66

The next day it had grown too big for the jar, so he carried it to a lake. After a while it was too big for the lake, so he threw it into the sea. Then the fish warned Manu of an impending deluge, and sent him a large ship, with orders to put two of every living thing aboard, along with the seeds of every plant. Manu did this, and had only just completed the task when the ocean overwhelmed the earth, and the only thing that could be seen was Vishnu in the form of a huge one-horned fish with golden scales. Manu moored his ship to the fish's horn with the great snake Vasuki. In this way, people, animals, and plants were saved from destruction. The next avatar was Varahavatara, the wild boar. After the earth was submerged by the deluge, it was captured by demons, but Varaha ran across the heavens and dived into the waters, retrieving the earth from the deeps by using his sense of smell. He killed the demon who was keeping the earth, and brought it back to the surface on the end of his tusks. Sculptors tend to represent Varaha as a giant with the head of a wild boar, holding the earth goddess in his arms. After the wild boar came Kurma, the turtle, who is connected with the legend of the churning of the sea of milk. Once Indra was cursed by a great rishi called Durvasas, so that Indra and the three worlds lost their vigour. In order to rectify the situation, Vishnu instructed Indra to take the snake Vasuki for a rope and Mount Mandara as a stick, make a pact with the demons and churn the great sea of milk. So the demons took one end of the snake and the gods took the other, and turned the mountain in the sea of milk. This caused the mountain to bore into the earth, so Vishnu supported the mountain in the form of a turtle. The next avatar of Vishnu was Krishna, the divine youth, subject of the *Bhagavad Gita*, the *Govinda Gita*, and other Hindu scriptures. The next avatar was Rama, the hero of the Ramayana, the great epic in which he and Hanuman rescue Sita from the demon king Ravana. The next avatar will be Kalki, the giant with the horse's head, who will close the iron age and destroy the wicked. When his work is complete he will be reabsorbed into Vishnu and a new cycle will begin.

It is interesting that the legend of the deluge described above makes mention of saving the animals from the waters. In this it is similar to the legend of Noah's Ark. The original source of the biblical version of the legend appears to have been a Sumerian story of the hero Utnapishtim, who built an ark in similar circumstances. The name Noah may be related to a Babylonian Moon-goddess called Nuah. There is also a Welsh deluge myth, where the goddess Dwyvach and the god Dwyvan build Nefyed Nav Nevion, an ark in which they and various animals escape from the flood caused by the serpent Addanc. The ark itself is a Moon and sea symbol, usually portrayed as crescent-shaped. It represents the feminine principle, the bearer of life, the womb, regeneration, preservation, the ship of destiny, and a vehicle for transmitting the life principle. The ark on the waters symbolises the Earth in the deeps of space. The rainbow is the corresponding symbol of life for the waters of the heavens, so the ark together with the rainbow represents universal rebirth.

In ancient Greece and Rome, many deities had specific animals associated with them. The serpent was sacred to Aesculapius. The wolf, the gryphon, and the cow were sacred to Apollo. The dragon and the panther were sacred to Bacchus. The stag was sacred to Diana, whilst Artemis was associated with the bear. The deer was sacred to Hercules. Juno was associated with the peacock and the lamb. The eagle and the bull were sacred to Jupiter and Zeus. The dog was sacred to the Lares. The horse, the vulture, and the woodpecker were sacred to Mars. The cock was associated with Mercury, and the owl with Minerva. The bull was sacred to Neptune, and the horse to Poseidon. The halcyon (kingfisher) was sacred to Tethys, and the dove, the swan, and the sparrow to Venus. The lion was associated with Vulcan. Each of these had a myth associated with it (see individual animal entries). Various deities also had chariots, which were drawn by an appropriate animal. The chariot of Admetus was drawn by lions and wild boars. Apollo had white horses for his chariot of the Sun. Ceres' and Medusa's chariots were drawn by winged dragons; Cybele's chariot by lions; Diana's by stags or unicorns; Dionysos'/ Bacchus' by panthers or goats; Eros'/Cupid's by leopards or goats; Hephaestus'/Vulcan's by dogs; Jupiter Dolichenus' by bulls; Pluto's by black horses; and Poseidon's/Neptune's by white horses or Tritons.

The Zodiac has many legends associated with it. One of these explains the origin of Sagittarius. The centaur Chiron, who taught

Achilles and other heroes the arts of music, medicine, and hunting, was placed by Zeus among the stars after he gave up his immortal status because of his wound. The constellation of Aries was said to be the ram that gave the Golden Fleece, and carried Phrixus and Helle (also placed in the sky by Zeus).

In ancient Egypt, various animals were associated with the four directions, and were guardians of the four canopic jars used in embalming. They were the four sons of Horus, and were also associated with the goddesses:

North, Earth
(Nephthys)
Lungs
Hapi (dog or ape headed)

West, Air
(Selkhet)
Intestines
Qebesenuf (falcon-headed)
He Who Cools His Brother

East, Fire
(Neith)
Stomach
Duamutef (jackal-headed)
He Who Praises His Mother

South, Water
(Isis)
Liver
Imsety/Imset/Mestha/Mesti
(human-headed)

Various other deities were theriomorphic: Osorapis (Ousir-Hapi), Apis (Hapi), and Mont (Menthu) all had the head of a bull. Osorapis was an amalgam of Osiris (Ousir) and Hapi; the Apis Bull was believed to be an incarnation of Osiris, and one of Isis' titles was the Cow of Memphis, whilst Horus was known as the Bull of his Mother. The goddess Bast was cat-headed; Nefertum, Sekhmet, and Tefnut were all lioness-headed. Hathor (Athyr), Isis (Aset), and Nut were all depicted with the head of a cow. Suchos (Sebek) was crocodile-headed. Hapi (one of the Four Sons of Horus) was ape- or dog-headed. Thoth (Tehuti) was depicted with the head of a baboon, because he was associated with the rising sun, and baboons appear to salute the rising sun. Set was sometimes shown as donkey-headed. Taueret, the hippopotamus goddess, was depicted as a pregnant female hippopotamus, standing on her hind legs, with pendulous human breasts, the hind legs of a lioness, and a crocodile's tail. In her avenging aspect she had the head of a lioness and carried a dagger. The red hippo was attributed to Set. The jackal was associated with Anubis (Anpu), the guide of the souls of the dead and the faithful companion of Isis. The wolf was the animal form of Upuaut and Khenti Amenti. Amon was depicted as a ram with curved horns, whilst Khnum and Hershef were depicted as rams with wavy horns. Khepri was shown with the head of a scarab; Selkhet with that of a scorpion; and Buto or Uadjet with that of a snake. The writer Porphyry explained that the Egyptians worshipped theriomorphic deities because animals represent 'the universal power which the gods have revealed in the various forms of living nature'.

Legends about animals also developed to try and explain why they are as they are. Classical writers perpetuated many strange theories about animals, such as the idea that bear cubs are born shapeless, and the mother bear licks them to give them form, hence the expression 'licked into shape'. Many of these ideas were carried over into the medieval bestiaries. These books were in great demand from the eleventh to the fourteenth century, and described the supposed habits and idiosyncracies of both real and mythical animals. Many were concerned to point a moral from these fables; others concentrated on imparting legend and lore. They were based on the *Physiologi* of late classical antiquity. The English bestiaries were mostly translations of European originals. Some of the most popular were the bestiaries of Philippe de Thaun, Guillaume le Clerc (*Le Bestiaire Divin*), and Richard de Fournival's satirical *Bestiaire d'Amour* (circa 1250).

Later, the classification of animals became more serious, but happily did not lose its mythical associations. The term fauna was first used by Linnaeus in 1746, in the title of his book, *Fauna Suecica*, a companion volume to his *Flora Suecica* (1745). Both are the names of Roman goddesses. Fauna was a rural goddess, the wife of Faunus, a good spirit of the field and forest, and a god of prophecy.

In Islam, there are certain individual animals which are believed to have been allowed to enter Paradise: Jonah's whale, Solomon's ant, the ram sacrificed by Abraham as a substitute for Isaac, the lapwing of Balkis, the camel of the prophet Saleh, the ox of Moses, the dog Kratim of the seven sleepers, Mohammed's steed Al Borak, and Noah's dove.

In China, animals are divided into five classes. The birds are represented by the feng huang, the Chinese phoenix; the furry creatures are represented by the ky lin, the Chinese unicorn; the naked creatures are represented by humanity; the scaly creatures are represented by the dragon; and the shelled creatures are represented by the tortoise. There are also Five Noxious Creatures: the snake, scorpion, lizard or gecko, and the toad. On the fifth day of the fifth month, ceremonies were held in the villages to get rid of them.

In Alchemy, animals are used to represent the various stages of the Great Work. Alchemy regarded all matter as animate, and hence depicted the stages of the alchemical process with living creatures. Toads, owls, and basilisks were associated with the darkness, witchcraft, the goddess Diana, and the Moon. The animals of alchemy are the dragon, a cthonic creature; winged serpents; the salamander; and the red and green lions. The creatures of the light were the phoenix, the eagle, the lion, and the ram. The ram was associated with the sign of Aries, the beginning of the Sun's course in the wheel of the year. In Giordano Bruno's book, *De Umbris Idearum* (On the shadows of ideas, Paris, 1582), the triumph of the creatures of the light over those of the darkness is described. In later 16th century texts, the grey wolf was used to symbolise antimony. Animals generally represent colours and processes in alchemy. The cthonic creatures (snakes, salamanders, and dragons) symbolised the obstacles on the path to enlightenment; they were fierce and venomous guardians of the threshold.

The mythology of animals describes a people's relationship to the environment, their understanding of the spiritual and material realms, the interrelationship between the two, and their responsbilities towards their environment. An excellent example of this is the Toba people of Formosa province in Argentina. The Toba draw a distinction between mythical animals and ordinary animals. Mythical animals are called *nanoiknagaik* (shapeshifters) - the name refers to the magnitude of their powers as well as their ability to change their morphology. The *nanoiknagaik* were active in the beginning of the world. The end of this time was brought about by a series of legendary catastrophes, after which they were no longer able to change shape at will. There are two categories of nature spirit: owners of species (Ioogot, Ita'a, or Iate'e), and spirits of natural phenomena such as wind and rain. The owners of species determine the success of hunters. If hunters throw away meat, that animal does not appear in the next hunt. The owners of species may also initiate shamans, bestowing their powers on them; they are also symbols of abundance, since they have many animals in their sphere of influence. There are also the helpful spirits (*Itagaiagawa*). There are several different classifications of animals: the form of a human (*shiagawa*); and the form of an animal (shigiak). There are several subcategories of *shigiak*: wild animals of regular size (*shigiak*); flying animals (*gojo*); snakes (*araganaq*); water animals (*njaq*); and domestic animals (*hil-lo*).

Chapter 7
Celestial animals

Zodiac Animals

Aries
The Ram is brave and fierce, and is renowned for putting its head down to charge anything it sees. The rushing ram represents the first burst of growth in Spring, the renewal of solar energy. The sigil of Aries is said to represent a ram's horns, or a human eyebrows and nose. The sign is ruled by Mars and the element of Fire. In Greek myth, the ram with the golden fleece, which carried Phrixus and Helle on its back, was eventually sacrificed to Zeus, who set it in the heavens as the constellation of Aries.

Taurus
The Bull represents the earth in the sense of fertility and sensuality; it is the Spring at its peak, the full expression of the powers of Nature. It depicts the qualities of generosity and kindness, but also jealousy and possessiveness, occasionally pomposity. The sigil represents a bull with horns, or the Full Moon surmounted by a crescent. The Full Moon signifies the celestial mother, growth, and fertility, whilst the upturned crescent depicts the gathering of material possessions. The sign is ruled by Venus and the element of Earth.

Gemini
The sign of Gemini is that of the heavenly twins, Castor and Pollux, the Dioscuri, who are depicted with half an egg on their heads. This is because they were born from the egg fertilised by

the union of Zeus and Leda, along with Helen and Clytemnestra. Pollux and Helen were the children of Zeus, whilst Castor and Clytemnestra were the children of Tyndareus, Leda's husband. Zeus appeared to Leda in the form of a swan. It is thought that Leda was originally a deity of the night. The sign is ruled by Mercury, and those born under it are said to be changeable, whimsical, and mercurial, though their sign symbolises the joining of two souls, one intuitive and the other rational. From this union creativity is produced, or the unity of mind and spirit. Like the other dual signs, the character of Gemini is often underestimated, their adaptability mistaken for fickleness. Like the other Air signs, it is often associated with intellectual prowess.

Cancer

The Crab represents a love of tradition, imagination and intuition. It depicts still waters. It is associated with Hera, who gave the Crab its place in the heavens. Close scrutiny of the constellation of Cancer will reveal the cluster of stars known as the Beehive, another creature associated with Hera. The sign of Cancer is said to be the gate through which the soul descends from heaven and enters the body; Porphyry called it 'the gate from the Milky Way to manifestation'. The sign is ruled by the Moon, and those born under it are said to be sensitive, affectionate, emotional and sociable. The sigil may represent the union of masculine and feminine, or perhaps the claws of a crab. When the Sun enters the sign of Cancer, it is the Summer Solstice. In Egyptian astrology, the sign of Cancer was a scarab.

Leo

The Lion represents the element of Fire in its controlled, fixed aspect, giving light and warmth. The animal is a symbol of life, strength, vigour, pride, clarity, dignity, authority and courage. It is the King of the Animals. The sigil represents the link between divine and human will. The season of the year associated with the sign of Leo is the heat at the height of summer and the crops ripening for the harvest. The sign is ruled by the Sun.

Virgo

The sign of the Virgin represents analysis and transformation. The season of the year with which it is associated is the harvest, when there is much activity on the land. The qualities associated with it are dependability and sincerity. The sigil represents female genitalia, or the head and part of the body of a serpent. The sign is ruled by Mercury and the element of Earth. The Virgin is sometimes depicted as a girl holding an ear of corn, and sometimes as a mermaid with a child in her arms.

Libra

The sign of the scales is ruled by Venus and the element of Air. The sigil represents the Sun sinking on the horizon, as the nights grow longer at this time of year. It also represents balance, beauty, order, and harmony; the equilibrium between our physical and spiritual natures. The upper line depicts the spiritual, and the lower depicts the physical realms. In paintings of the Zodiac, the scales of Libra are often depicted in the claws of the Scorpion.

Scorpio

The sign of Scorpio is associated with the scorpion and the eagle (see tetramorphs). The scorpion represents winter, which causes the animals to retreat into hibernation from its sting. Those born under the sign are said to be deeply emotional, self-disciplined, calm, intuitive, and steadfast. They are intense and sometimes withdrawn. The scorpion symbolises the ability to sting others, either through revealing their weaknesses, or by inspiration. The eagle stands for the ability to achieve spiritual transformation. The sigil represents a serpent or the male genitalia.

Sagittarius

The Centaur or the Archer represents a more expansive aspect of Fire, more spiritual than Leo. It is the transition between Autumn and Winter. The centaur, which is immortal, represents the combination of the rational soul of humanity with animal instinct. The sigil depicts the combination of the foundation of civilisation

with the arrow of inspiration. The archer is a symbol of questing
and spirituality. The sign of Sagittarius is ruled by Jupiter.

Capricorn
The goat-fish was originally the Babylonian deity Ea-Oannes, the
symbol of wisdom. It is the essence of Earth, representing stability
and structure. Those born under the sign are said to be cautious,
practical and orderly, but also mystical. They are stubborn,
determined, and loyal. The planet Saturn, which rules the sign, is
said to be a calming influence. The sigil represents the dual
nature of the goat-fish, being of both land and sea. The sign is also
associated with the crocodile, the dolphin, and the sea-serpent. At
this season of the year, the Earth is in the depths of Winter, but
life begins to prepare for Spring. When the Sun enters Capricorn,
it is the Winter Solstice, and the sign is said to be the gate of the
gods. From this time onwards, the days grow longer. Capricorn is
associated in Greek myth with the god Pan, who changed himself
into a goat in order to escape from Typhon, and was made into the
sign of Capricorn by Zeus.

Aquarius
The Water Bearer carries the water of knowledge, and embodies
compassionate, visionary, and hopeful qualities. The sigil can
represent the serpents of wisdom (intuition and rationality) or the
waves on the water of consciousness. The season of the year when
the Sun enters Aquarius is when the first signs of Spring appear;
it represents spiritual awakening. The sign is ruled by Saturn and
Uranus, and the element of Air. The waters carried by Aquarius
can also represent the waters of creation and destruction.

Pisces
The Fishes represent the ability to move in the unconscious, which
is often equated with the sea. Those born under this sign are said
to be emotional, sensitive, vague, unworldly, and adaptable. The
sigil represents two fishes linked by a cord. A more abstract
explanation is that one arc is the finite consciousness of humanity

and the other is the infinite consciousness of the Universe. The line between them is the Earth, where the spiritual and material realms coincide. The season of the year associated with Pisces is when the rains of late Winter and early Spring prepare the earth for the first burst of growth in Spring.

The Zodiacal belt was known as the girdle of Ishtar among the ancient Arabs, and the signs were called the Houses of the Moon (their calendar was lunar). Ishtar was said to ride across the sky in a chariot drawn by lions or goats. The Arab zodiac is represented by a fruit tree with twelve branches and the stars as fruits. The Islamic zodiac has six northern signs, which are regarded as wet, and six southern signs, which are regarded as dry. Aries, Leo, and Sagittarius are associated with the East, Fire, and the qualities of heat and dryness. Taurus, Virgo, and Capricorn are associated with the South, Earth, and the qualities of cold and dryness. Gemini, Libra, and Aquarius are associated with the West, Air, and the qualities of heat and moisture. Cancer, Scorpio, and Pisces, are associated with the North, Water, and the qualities of cold and moisture. The Egyptian Denderah has the symbols of the northern constellations at its centre, surrounded by the signs of the Zodiac. The Hindu zodiac is called the Rasi Chakra, the Wheel of the Signs, and is depicted with the chariot of the Sun at the centre, surrounded by the planetary deities: Rahu and Ketu, the dragon's head and tail (the planet Jupiter); the Buddha as the planet Mercury; Chandra, the Moon god; and Mars, Saturn, and Venus. The Zodiac is also known as the Serpent of the Heavens. In a relief carving from Modena, the body of Mithra is encircled by a snake and surrounded by the twelve signs of the Zodiac. The name Zodiac is derived from the Greek *zodiakos*, pertaining to animals, from *zoon*, an animal. Plato called the Zodiac signs the 'gates of heaven'.

In ancient Mesopotamian astrology, various constellations were regarded as important. In a Babylonian prayer dating from about 1800 BCE, the constellations are called upon as 'the great gods of the night' to provide a propitious sign, including the Fire-star, heroic Irra, the Bow-star, the Yoke-star, Sitadarru, Mushussu-star, the Wagon, the Goat-star, the Goatfish-star, and the Serpent-star. In another inscription from around 1000 BCE, the eighteen constellations around the ecliptic (the apparent path of the Sun) are listed. Aries was called 'the hired man'; the Pleiades were called simply 'the stars'; Taurus was called 'the bull of heaven'; Orion was called 'the true shepherd of Anu'; Perseus was called 'the old man'; Auriga, 'the hooked staff'; Gemini, 'the great twins'; Cancer, 'the crab'; Leo, 'the lion'; Virgo, 'the barley-stalk'; Libra, 'the balance'; Scorpio, 'the scorpion'; Sagittarius was called Pabilsag (a god); Capricorn, 'the goat-fish'; Aquarius, 'the giant'; Pisces, 'the tails'; south-west Pisces, 'the swallow'; and north-east Pisces was called Anunitum (a goddess). The Babylonian astrologers were concerned with the path of the Moon through the ecliptic. Some of these constellations are only just touched by the path of the Moon, and are not found in the modern Zodiac, but many of the signs are the same, though modern astrology is concerned with the apparent path of the Sun through the ecliptic, and the positions of the planets.*

The Chinese Zodiac
(The Twelve Terrestrial Branches)
The signs of the years are the Rat, Ox, Tiger, Hare, Dragon, Snake, Horse, Goat, Monkey, Cock, Dog, and Boar. There are six wild and six domestic animals, six yin and six yang. The Chinese year is divided into twelve sections, and the day is divided into twelve two-hour periods. Each of these is associated with a zodiacal animal. In ancient China, time was measured by the cycle of twelve two-hour periods, and each period was imbued with the qualities of the animal (beginning with the Rat at midnight).

* A. Kitson (ed.), "*History and Astrology: Clio and Urania confer*", Mandala/Unwin, 1989. Chapter 1, "A Sketch of the Development of Mesopotamian Astrology and Horoscopes", by C. B. F. Walker.

Animal	Chinese name	Time of day	Years
Rat	*da shu* or *lao shu*	24:00 to 02:00	1936, 1948, 1960, 1972, 1984, 1996
Ox	niu	02:00 to 04:00	1937, 1949, 1961, 1973, 1985, 1997
Tiger	*hu*	04:00 to 06:00	1938, 1950, 1962, 1974, 1986, 1998
Hare	*tu-z*	06:00 to 08:00	1939, 1951, 1963, 1975, 1987, 1999
Dragon	*lung*	08:00 to 10:00	1940, 1952, 1964, 1976, 1988, 2000
Snake	*she*	10:00 to 12:00	1941, 1953, 1965, 1977, 1989, 2001
Horse	*ma*	12:00 to 14:00	1942, 1954, 1966, 1978, 1990, 2002
Goat		14:00 to 16:00	1943, 1955, 1967, 1979, 1991, 2003
Monkey	*hou*	16:00 to 18:00	1944, 1956, 1968, 1980, 1992, 2004
Cock	*gong-ji*	18:00 to 20:00	1945, 1957, 1969, 1981, 1993, 2005
Dog	*gou*	20:00 to 22:00	1946, 1958, 1970, 1982, 1994, 2006
Boar or Pig	*zhu*	22:00 to 24:00	1947, 1959, 1971, 1983, 1995, 2007

Rat

The rat is the first animal of the Chinese zodiac. According to Chinese folktale, the ox was at the head of the queue to be zodiacal animals. However, no-one noticed that the rat had climbed on the back of the ox, and jumped down to get to the head of the queue. The rat is associated with money; a rat heard scrabbling at night is said to be counting its money.

Ox

The word niu is a generic term for oxen, cows, bulls, etc. It signifies a beast of burden, the creature that draws the plough and helps with the harvest. Therefore many Chinese people do not eat beef, believing it ungrateful to such a helpful animal. The ox symbolises the Spring, as work on the land began at that season. It is also associated with water and rivers. An old story tells how two black and two blue oxen came out of the river at Lo-yang, and fought with each other. At one time, if the dykes seemed to be about to give way, stone or bronze figures of oxen were thrown into the river.

Tiger

The tiger is the king of the wild animals and a yang creature. A white tiger symbolised Autumn and the West, which is associated with the yin principle. The tiger was greatly feared, and in some places its name was taboo, so that it was referred to as *da chong* (big insect or king of the mountains). At one time sacrifices were made to it because it ate the wild pigs which laid waste the village fields. Several gods are depicted riding on a tiger. A boy on a tiger symbolises filial piety, because there was a legend where a boy rode a tiger to divert it from his father. A tiger carved on a door-post protects against demons, and small children are given tiger caps to protect them.

Hare

The hare lives in the Moon. It has a pestle and mortar with which it pounds cinnamon twigs, and is a symbol of longevity. A picture showing six boys round a man with a hare's head standing on a table refers to the lunar festival held on the fifteenth day of the eighth month, and expresses the wish that the children of the recipient will have a peaceful life and ascend the social scale.

Dragon

The dragon is a symbol of luck in China. There are four kinds of dragon: *tian-long*, symbolising the regenerative powers of the heavens; *shen-long*, or spirit dragons, which cause the rain to fall (often by playing with a ball or a pearl among the clouds); di-long, or earth dragons, which rule springs and watercourses; and fu-*cang-long*, or treasure-guarding dragons. There were also four *long-wang* or dragon-kings ruling the four seas of the earth. The blue dragon is the creature of the East.

Snake

The snake is one of the five noxious creatures, and is regarded as clever but also wicked. River gods were often portrayed as snakes; the god of the Yellow River was a small golden-coloured snake with a square head and red dots under its eyes. Theatrical shows were performed to keep this god in a good mood. Some snake gods demanded the sacrifice of a young girl on a certain day every year, until a hero came dressed in women's clothing to kill the snake. Snakes are also associated with sensuality and the penis, and are believed to be attracted to the smell of women's underwear. A snake with a triangular head is a female symbol. Snakes symbolise transition and change, because they can slough their skins.

Horse

The horse is a yang creature when it is contrasted with the cow in later Chinese mythology, but in the Yi-jing it is yin, in contrast with the dragon as yang. In Buddhist texts, a white horse symbolises purity and loyalty. The expression "getting off the horse" refers to a shaman who asks the gods to visit. Among prostitutes, "riding the horse" meant menstruating. "The horse shakes its hoof" is a position in sexual intercourse.

Goat

The goat is the eighth animal of the Chinese zodiac. It is a yang animal and symbolises peace and goodness.

Monkey

The monkey-god in China is called Sun Wu-kong. He accompanied the Buddhist pilgrim Xuan-Cang to India, rescuing him from many perilous situations. The downside was his fondness for practical jokes and his volatile temper. He was one of the chief characters in the Song Dynasty novel *The Journey to the West* by Wu Ch'ê ng-ên (also known as Monkey, which was a television series in the late seventies and early eighties). In South China, the monkey god was revered as Qi-tian da-sheng (the great saint equal to heaven) and many temples were built to him. The monkey is often shown holding a peach, as in the novel Feng-shen Yan-yi (The metamorphoses of the gods). According to legend, the peach was stolen from the garden of Xi-wang-mu (the great fairy goddess of the West, who lives in the Kunlun Mountains).

Cock

The cock is not eaten in China. A red cock wards off evil, and protects the house from fire. A white cock on a coffin wards off demons. There is said to be a cock in the Sun, although in some traditions it is a three-legged raven. The cock represents masculine vigour, benevolence (because he calls the hens to eat the food he finds), reliability (as a timekeeper), achievement, and fame.

Dog

In Northern China, paper dogs are given to the dead to drive away evil spirits, and are thrown into the river on the fifth day of the fifth month so that they will bite the evil spirits. The dog is associated with the West, and therefore could only be eaten in Autumn and Winter, not in Summer. If a dog runs towards you, it is a sign that you will become rich. The dog is the companion of the god Er-lang, who rids the world of evil spirits. In South China, there are many stories of faithful dogs, such as the dog whose master was lying in a field when the crop caught fire. He could not wake him, so he carried water from the river and prevented the man from being burnt, but unfortunately died of exhaustion.

There are legends of men with dogs' heads, also stories of the Yao people, who are descended from the union of a dog and a princess. The emperor was having trouble with his enemies, so he said that whoever brought him the head of the rebel leader could marry his daughter. A dog brought the head, and so the princess had to marry him. The Yao people still wore dog caps and abstained from eating dog as late as 1934.

Boar

The pig symbolises virility. The Chinese pig can be black or white. The black pig was associated with Water, the North, and a salty taste. White is the colour of Autumn and old age.

Norse animal constellations

Norse name	Explanation	Classical or modern name
The Boar's Throng	From the Svinfylking battle formation	The Pleiades, the Seven Stars
The Battle of the Gods	Includes the goats of Thor's chariot, and Heidrun, Odin's goat whose milk was mead given to the warriors of Valhalla	The constellation of Auriga and the star Capella α Aurigae)
The Greater Wolf's Jaws	These stars form a semi-circle around which is Tir's sword. The Fenris Wolf will break free at Ragnarok and fight Tir	Includes Andromeda, the Pole Star, part of the Milky Way, and forms a semi-circle of stars through Pegasus to Cygnus

| The Lesser Wolf's Jaws | Also the jaws of Fenris, threatening the sun's path; it faces the constellation of the Battle of the Gods | Hyades and Aldebaran, which lie directly on the ecliptic |

When the Fenris Wolf was fettered, the god Tir put his hand in the wolf's mouth as a pledge of good faith. When the fetters closed on the wolf's limbs, his jaws closed on the god's hand. Afterwards the wolf's jaws were wedged open with a sword, and two streams of saliva run out of his mouth until the end of the world These are Wan and Wil, the two streams of the Milky Way (which was known to the Anglo-Saxons as Ermine Street). Tir's sword arm stretches from the Pole Star into the Greater Wolf's Jaws.

Conclusion

Celestial animals are very important in mythology and cosmology because they connect the earth to the heavens, the macrocosm to the microcosm. Many cultures have myths of animals being placed in the heavens as constellations, or being associated with the qualities of a certain time of year.

Amphibia

Frog

Latin name *Rana temporaria* **Polarity** Feminine

Family *Ranidae* **Element** Water

Sub-order *Anura* **Order** *Salientia*

Planet Moon

Etymology Old English *frogga*, pet name from *forsc, frosc, frox*, from Old High German *frosc*, Old Norse *frosk*, from Germanic *froskaz* (compare modern German *Frosch*)

Deities Aphrodite, Venus, the Nymphs, Hekat, Isis

Varieties

There are approximately 1700 species of frogs and toads. Families include tree frogs (*Hylidae*), which are represented in Europe by the bright green Common Tree Frog (*Hyla arborea*); and true frogs (*Ranidae*), which include the Edible Frog (*Rana esculenta*), the Marsh Frog (*Rana ridibunda*), the Field Frog (*Rana arvalis*), the Dalmatian Frog (*Rana dalmatina*) and the Common Frog (*Rana temporaria*), all of which are found in Europe.

Folklore

The nickname of frogs applied to the French originally only meant the people of Paris, because the heraldic device of Paris was three frogs or toads. At the court of Versailles in 1791, it was fashionable to ask, *"Qu'en disent les grenouilles?"* (What do the frogs [people of Paris] say?). Paris was originally built on a swamp called Lutetia, a name meaning 'mud-land'. The nickname was used by the English to mean the French in general because of their habit of eating the hind legs of frogs.

In folk tales, frogs represent sexuality and desire. In the story of *The Three Languages*, the hero learns the language of frogs, which symbolises his coming to terms with his sexuality. In the original version of *The Sleeping Beauty*, the king and queen desired a child so much that every day they wished for one. One day, when the queen was sitting in the bath, a frog came to her and said, "Your wish will be fulfilled; before a year is over, you will bring a daughter into the world."

The frog symbolises sexual fulfilment and fertility. In the story of *The Frog Prince*, the frog lives in a well, which is another obvious symbol of sexuality. The frog also represents the sexual organs; a child perceives sex as something animal-like and a bit slimy, but the frog is transformed by kissing it, and the sexual act is transformed by the participation of a beloved other. A version of this tale is mentioned in the 13th century, called The Frog King. In *The Complaynt of Scotland* a similar story called *The Well of the World's End* is mentioned.

Frogs were used as a remedy in folk medicine. In Yorkshire (1898), frog soup was a cure for whooping cough. In Cheshire, whooping cough was transferred to frogs by breathing on them. In the 1850s, people swallowed live frogs as a cure for consumption. A child with thrush of the mouth had a live frog or toad placed in its mouth (this was a cure by transference). A Roman writer, Marcellus, recommended curing toothache by spitting into the frog's mouth and asking it to carry away the ache. This must be done whilst wearing boots and standing under open sky on bare earth.

Mythology

In Egypt, the green frog of the Nile symbolised the inundation, and the renewal of life that it brought. Frog amulets have been found in Egyptian tombs, probably representing resurrection. The frog is an attribute of Hekt (also known as Hequet, Heket, or Hekat), the protector of mothers and the newborn, as the frog represents embryonic life in the waters. Hekt was sometimes depicted as frog-headed, and was the mother of Haroeris, a variant of Horus. The frog is also a symbol of Isis. The Ogdoad of Hermopolis were the first eight living beings created by Thoth (Tehuti). The males were frogs and the females were serpents, brought into being by the sound of Tehuti's voice.

In Graeco-Roman mythology, the frog is associated with the swamps of the underworld. In Ovid's *Metamorphoses*, the Lycian peasants were changed into frogs for trying to prevent Leto (the mother of Diana and Apollo) from drinking from a fountain in Delos with her children in her arms to slake her thirst. A fountain at Versailles depicts the metamorphosis of the Lycians into frogs, to illustrate the divine and royal power over the waters (Louis XIV, the Sun King, identified himself with Apollo). According to Plato, the frog is a bringer of rain and is associated with the nymphs. It is a symbol of Aphrodite and Venus, representing fertility, licentiousness, and harmony between lovers.

To the Celts, the frog represented the Lord of Earth and the powers of the healing waters.

In China, the frog represents the lunar Yin principle. A frog in a well depicts a person of limited understanding. In Taiwan, it is taboo for young girls to mention the green frog because it is supposed to resemble a girl's body. In some provinces there was at one time a frog cult, which made it taboo to eat frogs. The frog was often referred to as *tian-ji*, the celestial cock, because it was believed that frog spawn fell with the dew from heaven. An ancient Chinese text says that one of the two souls of a human being resembles a frog. The term frog-mouth refers to the glans of the penis.

In Burmese and Indo-Chinese mythology, the first man and woman resembled tadpoles. The first woman was called Yatai (or Ya-Hsek-Khi) and the first man was called Yatawn.

In Huron (indigenous American) mythology, the hero Ioskeha created humanity after defeating the Great Frog who had swallowed the waters of the earth. The Great Frog is the power of the waters, a bringer of rain, and represents initiation by water. In magic, it is regarded as a cleansing power; it is also a totem animal.

Among the Hopi, the frog is never teased, molested, or eaten, because the frog *katsina*, Pakwabi, is a helpful spirit, associated with water and rain.

Symbolism

The frog's moist skin represents the renewal of life and the abundance of the waters, in contrast to the dryness of death. The amphibious nature of the frog, and its development from a tadpole, represents the move from primitive consciousness to full awareness. In Hinduism, the Great Frog which supports the universe is the *prima materia*, dark and undifferentiated, the primordial waters and the matrix of creation. In Egypt, the frog represented prolific new life and fertility, abundance, longevity, strength, and the reproductive powers of nature.

Christianity's view of the frog is ambivalent: as an amphibian, it represents new life and resurrection; but it also represents greed, heresy, and sin.

Poetry

The Frog Prince
I am a frog
I live under a spell
I live at the bottom
Of a green well

And here I must wait
Until a maiden places me
On her royal pillow
And kisses me
In her father's palace.
The story is familiar
Everybody knows it well

But do other people feel as nervous
As I do? The stories do not tell,

Ask if they will be happier
When the changes come
As already they are fairly happy
In a frog's doom?

I have been a frog now
For a hundred years
And in all this time
I have not shed many tears,

I am happy, I like the life,
Can swim for many a mile
(When I have hopped to the river)
And am for ever agile.

And the quietness,
Yes, I like to be quiet
I am habituated
To a quiet life,

But always when I think these thoughts
As I sit in my well
Another thought comes to me and says:
It is part of the spell

To be happy
To work up contentment
To make much of being a frog
To fear disenchantment

Says, it will be heavenly
To be set free,
Cries, Heavenly the girl who disenchants
And the royal times, heavenly,
And I think it will be.
Come then, royal girl and royal times,
Come quickly,

I can be happy until you come
But I cannot be heavenly,
Only disenchanted people
Can be heavenly.

Stevie Smith

Toaò

Latin name *Bufo bufo*

Family *Bufonidae*

Folk name ha-ma (Chinese)

Polarity Yin

Element Earth

Planet Moon

Etymology from Old English *tadige, tadde, tada*, of unknown origin

Deities Hecate, Sabazios

Varieties

The True Toads (*Bufonidae*) include the Common Toad (*Bufo bufo*), found in central and northern Europe and parts of Asia. In America the commonest species is *Bufo americanus*. The Natterjack (*Bufo calamita*) lives in northern and western Europe, but is sometimes found in central Europe. The Green Toad (*Bufo viridis*) is distributed through western and central Europe as far as Mongolia. The Giant Toad (*Bufo marinus*) is found in Central and South America; the males make a loud barking noise. There are approxiamtely 1,700 known species of frogs and toads. Among the Pelobatidae, the Spadefoot Toad (*Pelobates fuscus*) is found in north-eastern central Europe and throughout central Asia. The Discoglossidae include the Red-bellied Toad (*Bombina bombina*), found in central and eastern Europe; the Yellow-bellied Toad

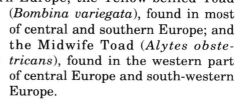

(*Bombina variegata*), found in most of central and southern Europe; and the Midwife Toad (*Alytes obstetricans*), found in the western part of central Europe and south-western Europe.

Folklore

The toad is often associated with witchcraft. It represents the wisdom that sees the sacred in everything. It was once believed to have a jewel in its head, which was called the Borax, and was believed to be antidote to poison. According to Pliny and Aelian, the toad could spit poison.

In China, a ten thousand year old toad (called a 'flesh-mushroom') should be caught on the fifth day of the fifth month, then dried and eaten as a cure for boils. It was also believed that if you scratched the earth with a toad's leg, a spring would gush forth. Eating a toad was believed to make you invulnerable.

Mythology

In China, the toad symbolises the lunar, yin principle. It represents the unattainable (because it is said to swallow the Moon when there is an eclipse), longevity (because it lives to a great age), wealth, and the creation of wealth. The three-legged toad lives in the Moon, and its three legs symbolise the three phases of the Moon. Another tradition has it that the toad in the Moon is Chang-e, the wife who stole the elixir of immortality from her husband and fled to the Moon, where she was turned into a toad. In Taoism, the toad is an attribute of the immortals Hon Hsien-Hing and Liu Hai. In southern China, the Tanka (a minority boat-dwelling people) hold a ceremony in honour of a newly-wed couple on the fifteenth day of the eighth month, which is a Full Moon. They put a cinnamon tree with a hare and a toad under it at the door of the bridal chamber. The bridal bed has curtains around it and candles burning beside it. The sacred space thus created is called the Toad Palace. An old woman acts the part of Xi-wang-mu, the Queen Mother of the West, stepping on to a platform near the front of the boat with lucky objects on it (ground-nuts, gourd seeds, cinnamon cakes, tea, and wine). When all the family are gathered, the newly-weds appear in their wedding clothes and stand in the moonlight. They go into the bridal chamber, the Moon Palace, but pause at the Gate of the Moon-hall (the sacred space) whilst Xi-wang-mu utters words of wisdom. She then leaves, the couple embrace each other and kiss, and are led to the Toad Palace (the nuptial bed).

This was originally a lunar festival celebrated all over China.

In Japan, the toad Sennin Gama is a wizard, and one of the Taoist Immortals.

In indigenous American mythology, the toad is the Dark Manitou, the lunar waters, and the powers of darkness and evil which were overcome by the Great Manitou.

In Mexico, the toad symbolises the earth, and the toad and toadstool represent the sacred mushroom bestowing enlightenment.

In Celtic myth, the toad often takes the place of the serpent as the power of destruction. This belief was carried over into Christianity, and toads were associated with witches, both as familiars and as an ingredient in the witch's brew.

In Greek myth, the toad was associated with Sabazios (a late syncretistic deity), and was depicted on the Votive Hand of Sabazios. In Zoroastrianism, the toad represented Ahriman, and hence evil, envy, greed, and avarice, but it was also a fertility symbol.

In Witchcraft, the toad is good luck, and represents witches (see *The Call of the Horned Piper* by Nigel Aldcroft Jackson).

Symbolism

The toad is associated with the Moon and the waters. Because it appears and disappears, it is a symbol of resurrection and of the waxing and waning of the Moon. It is also a symbol of evil, loathsomeness, and death. In Alchemy, the toad represents the darker side of nature, but also the fertility of the earth. Avicenna (Ibn Sina) said, "Join the toad of the earth to the flying eagle and you will see in our art the Magisterium." In Oceanic symbolism, the toad represents death. In European folk tales, the toad and the frog symbolise sexuality. In the story of *The Three Feathers*, the toads help the youngest son. The toads live in a cave underground, and they give the youngest son a beautiful bride.

Poetry

"When busy at my books I was upon a certain Night,
This vision here expressed appear'd unto my dimmed sight:
A Toad full ruddy I saw, did drink the juice of Grapes so fast,
Till over-charg'd with the broth, his Bowels all to-brast..."

In this poem by George Ripley, the toad passes through the colours of the Great Work. The toad dies by imbibing its own poisonous venom, becoming "like coal for colour black". This alludes to the Nigredo (the blackening, the first stage of the Great Work). After this comes the stage of putrefaction, when the alchemist heats the rotting carcass, and perceives the colours of the cauda pavonis, the Peacock's Tail. The alchemist creates an elixir from the toad's venom. This elixir is the poisonous mercury, which, properly treated, becomes the elixir of life and the mystical medicine of metals.

Literature
In Kenneth Graeme's *The Wind in the Willows*, the Toad is a fickle creature who has many fads and enthusiasms, most of which have disastrous consequences. He is also pompous and incredibly vain.

Arthropods

Scorpion

Latin name *Buthus eupeus*

Family *Scorpionidae*

Class *Arachnoidea*

Planet Mars

Polarity Masculine

Element Water

Constellation Scorpio

Etymology Middle English, from Old French, from Latin *scorpionis*

Deities Ishtar, Nina, Sabazios, Selkhet, Set

Folklore

The scorpion is said to carry with it an oil which is an antidote to its stings. Oil was extracted from the scorpion's body and given to the person who had been stung; it was also used to break up kidney stones.

It was also believed that if the scorpion was surrounded by fire, it would sting itself to death.

Mythology

In Sumer, scorpions or scorpion-men were the guardians of the Gateway of the Sun, the Mountains of the East, and the Twin Gates. They appear as such in the *Epic of Gilgamesh*. Scorpions were also associated with Nina, and the Phrygian

Sabazios, and they were the cult animals of Ishtar in her dark underworld aspect.

In ancient Egypt, the scorpion was an attribute of Set, who took the form of a scorpion to sting Horus. But Isis prayed to Ra, who sent Thoth (Tehuti) to cure Horus. It was also attributed to Selkhet as the protector of the dead and a divinity of the underworld. She was also a fertility goddess, a patroness of marriage, and protected one of the four sources of the Nile. She was portrayed as a scorpion with the head of a woman, or a woman crowned with a scorpion. Seven scorpions accompanied Isis (Aset) in her search for Osiris (Ousir). One of them stung a boy after his mother had shut the door in their face because she was afraid of the scorpions, but Isis restored the boy to life.

In Mithraism, the *dadophoroi* are a Bull holding a torch upwards, representing the rising Sun and life; and a Scorpion holding a torch downwards, representing the setting Sun and death.

Scorpio is the eighth sign of the Zodiac, and the Sun enters it around 24 October. In Greek mythology, Orion boasted that he could kill any animal the earth could produce. A scorpion was sent to punish his hubris, and it stung him to death. Zeus later raised the scorpion to heaven. (Of course, the mythological origins of the identification of that constellation with the scorpion are much older than this myth, as the Mesopotamian culture of around 1,000 BCE was already calling it *Mul Gír-Tab*, the Scorpion, and the name may date back even earlier to the Old Babylonian period).

Symbolism

Generally the scorpion represents death, destruction, darkness, and disaster. In Christianity, it represents evil, torment, treachery, and Judas Iscariot. In Hebrew symbolism, it signifies venom and death. In the Torah (1 Kings 12:11), the scorpion represents a scourge ("My father scourged you with whips; I will scourge you with scorpions").

Spider

Latin name various; see below

Families *Araneidae* (true spiders); *Tetragnathidae*; *Agelenidae*; *Lycosidae* (wolf spiders); *Pisauridae*; *Eresidae*; *Thomisidae* (crab spiders); *Salticidae* (jumping spiders).

Deities Holda, the Norns, Neith, Athene, Arachne, the Moerae, Persephone, Harmonia, Old Spider, Young Spider, Ishtar, Atargatis, Anansi

Folk name *Spinner* (German), *zhi-zhu, xi-mu* (Chinese)

Folklore

The rhyme about Little Miss Muffet is based on a real person; apparently she was the daughter of an arachnologist called the Rev Dr Thomas Mouffet.

In 1936, a policeman was cheered when he held up traffic on Lambeth Bridge to let a spider cross the road.

In Japan, Spider Women snare travellers. The Goblin Spider shape-shifts into various forms to cause people harm. An enormous spider called Tsuchi-Gumo caused a lot of trouble, until it was trapped in a cave and suffocated with smoke, since it could not be killed with steel.

In China, the spider is a good omen. A spider descending from its web symbolises good luck descending from heaven. In Central China, the spider is called *xi-mu*, the one returning to his mother, and portends a son returning from far away, or the visit of a guest.

It was formerly believed that fever could be cured by wearing a spider in a nutshell around the neck. A cure for jaundice was to swallow a live house spider smothered in butter; in Ireland this was a remedy for ague. If a spider ran onto your clothes it was good luck or a sign that you would get some money. Tiny spiders are often called money spiders for this reason. It was also believed that spiders only spin their webs on dark days.

Robert the Bruce was said to have been inspired by the tenacity of a spider in his resistance to the English. He was in hiding on the island of Rathlin, when he noticed a spider trying to fix its web to the ceiling. It tried six times, only succeeding on the seventh attempt. The Bruce had also failed six times, but decided that the seventh would be different. He left the island in 1307, and began the campaign which culminated in the Battle of Bannockburn.

Islamic legend tells that when Mohammed fled Mecca with the Koreishites pursuing him, he hid in a cave. An acacia tree sprang up outside the cave, a woodpigeon nested in it, and a spider spun its web between the tree and the cave. When the Koreishites saw this they thought that no-one could have been in the cave recently, so they did not bother to search the cave, and went on.

Mythology

The spider represents the Great Mother in her terrible aspect as the weaver of destiny. Lunar goddesses are weavers of fate and spinners of the thread of life.

The Cosmic Spider is the Creatrix who spins the thread of life from her own substance, attaches humans to herself by the umbilical cord, and weaves them into the pattern of fate. The spider at the centre of the web represents the cosmic centre, the Sun surrounded by its rays, the Moon as the wheel of birth and death, weaving the web of time.

To indigenous Americans, the spider is the wind and the thunder, and protects from harm. Some peoples regard the spider as a creatrix, who wove the dream of the phenomenal world, then the web of fate, then the first writing. Then she created plants and animals and named them; then she created humans.

The spider can also be a trickster figure in some cultures. The Sia people have a god called Sus'sistinnako, who created humanity by singing and accompanying himself on a harp made from a spider's web. Old Spider was a member of the Animal Council which helped the people to recover the light.

The Ashanti people of Ghana have a culture hero called Anansi, who provided the materials with which Nyame (the sky, storm and creator god) made the first humans. He married Nyame's daughter Akonole and they had a son called Kwakute. Ghanaian male children born on Wednesdays are called Kwakute. Anansi acted as an intermediary between humans and Nyame. He is renowned for his wisdom. The stories of Anansi, who is also a trickster, were taken to the Caribbean by Africans. They are often associated with traditional songs. In the Caribbean his son is called Tacoma, his wife is called Crookie, and he also has a daughter (whose name is not mentioned). Pamela Colman-Smith, the artist who drew the Rider-Waite Tarot deck, published an illustrated version of the Anansi stories in 1899 in New York. The Anansi tradition is strong in Jamaica, where Colman-Smith was brought up. The stories are often used to explain anomalies and apparently fantastical things in nature. Anansi got the forest god to agree that all animal stories should be called Anansi Stories by completing an impossible task. He then persuaded the god to give him eight legs instead of the usual six possessed by the other insects by performing another three impossible feats. However, the other animals thought he looked ridiculous, so he had to go off and hide, and this is why spiders always hide in dark corners. There is an Anansi web site on the Internet, where traditional stories can be found.

In Norse and Germanic mythology, the Norns and the goddess Holda are the spinners and weavers of destiny, the Web of Wyrd. In ancient Egypt, the spider was attributed to Neith as the weaver of the world.

In Greek mythology, it is an attribute of Athene as the weaver of the world, and of Persephone, Harmonia, and the Moerae (the Fates) as spinners of destiny. Arachne, the spider goddess, was a Lydian girl skilled in weaving who dared to challenge Athene to a contest. When the contest was held, Arachne's weaving was perfect, but depicted some of the gods' disreputable deeds, including Zeus abducting Europa. Athene flew into a temper and turned Arachne into a spider, so that she would always have to spin thread from her own body. Arachne was possibly originally a spider goddess in her right, weaving fate and reality from her own substance, but subdued by patriarchal religion, of which Athene was very much a part (having been created without recourse to a woman).

In Hinduism and Buddhism, the spider is the weaver of the web of illusion or maya, but is also the creator because it weaves the thread from its own substance. In Oceanic mythology, Old Spider created the universe. On Nauru Island, Micronesia, they say that Old Spider created the Moon, the sea, the sky, the Earth, and the Sun from a clam-shell that she found with two snails in it. Her son, Young Spider, created fire. The North West monsoon can be represented as a spider, unreliable and temperamental, but also bestowing fertility. In Australian Aboriginal mythology, the Great Spider is a sky hero.

Symbolism
To the Celts, the spider's web was a symbol of the web that holds all life together.

To the Greeks and Egyptians, the web symbolised the weaving of the fates.

In Christianity, the web symbolised the snare of Satan, the miser sucking the life out of the poor.

To the Romans, the spider represented business acumen and good fortune.

Poetry

"If you want to live and thrive
Let the spider run alive."

Crustacea

Crab

Latin name various

Family *Crustaceae*

Suborder *Brachyura*

Planet Moon

Polarity Feminine

Element Water

Order *Decapoda*

Zodiac Sign Cancer

Etymology Old English *crabba*, cognate with Middle Dutch *krabbe*, Old Norse *krabbi*, related to Middle High German *krabben*, from Old Norse *krafla*, to scratch

Deities Nina

Varieties

Hermit Crabs (Order: *Anomura*, Family: *Paguridae*) are a transitional group between crayfish and crabs. The Common Hermit Crab (*Eupagurus bernhardus*) is found in the North Sea and the Atlantic, including the coasts of Britain. Velvet Crabs (*Portunus holsatus*) live on the coasts of the Atlantic. The Freshwater Crab (*Potamon potamii*) lives in various parts of Europe.

The Mitten Crab (*Eriocheir sinensis*) originated in China but was brought by ship at the beginning of the twentieth century to the mouths of the Weser and Elbe rivers.

There are various species of Spider Crab, including Inachus scorpio, from the Mediterranean. On British coasts there are Spider

Crabs (*Macropodia rostrata*), Common Shore Crabs (*Carcinus maenas*), and the Mitten Crab.

Mythology

In Inca mythology, the crab denoted the terrible aspect of the Great Mother, the waning Moon, and the devourer of the temporal world.

In Sumerian mythology, crabs, lobsters, scorpions and fish were associated with the goddess Nina, lady of the waters. Nina was a marine and lunar goddess who was later merged with Ishtar. She was the daughter of Ea, and her temple was at Nineveh (which was presumably named after her) where she gave oracles.

In ancient Egyptian mythology, Set dismembered Osiris, then threw the pieces in the Nile. Isis managed to gather all the pieces and magically reassemble Osiris, but unfortunately the Nile crab had eaten the phallus, so Osiris lacked a vital part.

In Graeco-Roman legend, Juno sent Cancer the Crab against Hercules when he fought the Lernean Hydra. Cancer bit Hercules' foot, but he killed it, so Juno took it up into heaven as a constellation.

Symbolism

The apparent retrograde motion of the Sun after the Summer Solstice resembles the sideways motion of the crab. The astrological sign of Cancer is associated with the Tarot card of the Chariot.

The crab generally symbolises dishonesty, unreliability, and money-changers.

In Buddhism, the crab represents the sleep of death, the period between death and rebirth (the Bardo), and regeneration between consecutive incarnations.

Lobster

Latin name *Homarus vulgaris*

Family *Homaridae*　　　**Element** Water

Order *Decapoda*　　　**Planet** Moon

Etymology Old English *lopustre*, corruption of Latin *locusta*, a crustacean

Varieties
The Lobster (*Homarus vulgaris*) is related to the American Lobster (*Homarus americanus*), the European Rock Lobster or Langouste (*Palinurus vulgaris*), the River Crayfish (*Astacus fluviatalis*), the Mud Crayfish (*Astacus leptodactylus*) and the Stone Crayfish (*Astacus torrentium*).

Symbolism
Lobsters occasionally appear in designs for the Tarot card of the Moon. They are generally depicted emerging from the sea. According to Juliet Sharman-Burke, they symbolise inner fears forcing their way to the surface of consciousness. The sea represents the unconscious.

In Japan, the lobster symbolises congratulations, a happy event, and longevity. It is particularly associated with the New Year festivities.

Starfish

Latin name *Asteria rubens*

Family *Asteroidea*

Order *Echinodermata*

Deities Stella Maris

Polarity Feminine

Element Water

Planet Venus

Varieties

The Common Starfish (*Asteria rubens*) is abundant everywhere in the North Sea and the Atlantic. In the Pacific, the most common starfish is Valvaster striatus.

Mythology

In Europe, the starfish represents Stella Maris (star of the sea), divine love, and the inexorable power of love. In Christianity it is a symbol of the Holy Spirit, religion, charity, and the Virgin Mary as Stella Maris. The title Stella Maris was originally applied to Isis. Many of the Virgin Mary's titles and attributes were appropriated from Pagan goddesses (e.g. the attribute of the peacock and the title Queen of Heaven from Hera/Juno, the Moon from the various lunar goddesses, etc.).

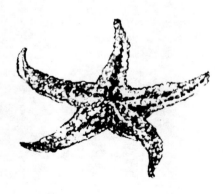

Sea Urchin

Latin name various

Family *Echinoideae*

Order *Echinodermata*

Polarity Yin

Element Water

Planet Moon

Etymology from hurcheon, a hedgehog

Varieties

Centrostephanus rodgersi (from the shores of South Australia) and *Strongylocentrotus franciscanus* (from the Californian coast) are sea-urchins and have rotational symmetry. Other species are only bilaterally symmetrical; these are known as Irregular Sea Urchins, the *Irregularia*. These include  *Meoma ventricosa* (found in the Bahamas) and *Encope grandis* (found near the Antilles).

Folklore

The sea urchin was so named because of its spines, which bore a passing resemblance to those of a hedgehog.

Mythology

In Celtic mythology, the sea urchin represented the serpent's egg, the seed of life, and latent force.

Físh

Class Pisces

Planet Moon

Polarity Masculine

Constellation Pisces

Etymology from Old English *fiscian*, cognate with Old Saxon *fiskon*; from Old High German *fiskon*, Old Norse *fiska*, Gothic *fiskon*, Germanic *fiskojan*

Deities Atargatis, Derketo, Nanshe, Ea-Oannes, Dagon, Hatmehyt, Ichthys, Isis, Venus, Christ, Khidr, Te Tuna

Folklore

The sea is a mysterious domain, indeed an essentially hostile one in which humans cannot survive for long except by artificial means. Hence the mythology of the sea is often ambivalent, regarding it as a hostile environment inhabited by creatures and beings either harmful or indifferent to humans, though some may be helpful.

In order to understand why this is so, it is necessary to look at the social, technological, and cultural context in which the mythology was formed. Even today, many (if not most) fishermen cannot swim. This point was graphically illustrated for me recently when I went snorkelling. I emerged from the water and said hello to a man cleaning a boat on the shore. He said that like many coastal folk, he could not swim, and did not actually like the water. I remarked that many fishermen cannot swim, and he said there would not be much point, when with all the heavy gear they wear (seaboots and so on) they would sink straight to the bottom.

His family had lived on the coast for at least the last three generations, as the boat he was cleaning had been found by his great uncle in 1924. Also, in the past, the technology available was much more limited. There were no wetsuits, snorkels or aqualungs; no radar or satellite navigational systems; no accurate maps or charts; even the compass was a relatively late introduction. However, there were methods of navigation; people used the stars to steer by at night, and by day there were landmarks, and various fishing grounds were delineated by landmarks and traditional nomenclature. When looking at attitudes to the sea, it is important to remember that ancient peoples were relatively powerless in relation to the sea. Therefore it was also seen as an unpredictable, sometimes hostile entity in the magical sense as well (not that the magical world view was separate from the general one, since magic was a part of the technology, not a separate activity, though there were magical specialists).

In Iceland, where Norse mythology survived the longest, indeed long enough to be written down by Snorri Sturluson and others, an ambivalent attitude to the sea remained embedded in the folklore of fishing. From the ninth century CE to the early twentieth century, metaphors of fish were prevalent in popular discourse. Modern Icelandic still contains a number of references to fish in its metaphorical usage. For example, if an idea or thing is of no value, it is said not to amount to many fish (uppa marga fiska); a person who keeps quiet is said to be 'silent as a fish' (pögull sem fiskur).

The sea was seen as a hostile force, beyond human control. On the other hand, fish were an important commodity in Iceland; they were the staple diet, and dried fish was for a long time the most important monetary standard. However, access to the fishing grounds, via the harbours, was restricted by the landowners, and the price of fish was kept artificially low to give precedence to agricultural products. Hence the technology of fishing never developed much beyond the open boat with individual fishermen using hand lines to catch fish, because there was no economic incentive to develop the technology. The mythology therefore retained the view that the sea was an otherworldly realm, innately hostile to humans. The view of the sea from an open boat (a relatively insecure position) differs radically from the view from a larger vessel, less likely to be inundated by the next wave.

In Icelandic folklore, the sea is populated with a variety of mythical creatures, as well as fish, seals, whales, and otters. Medieval manuscripts describe 'sea women' (saekona), protective beings that 'have the nature of fish while in the sea but look like humans while ashore'. They are sexually attractive, and sometimes have sailors' children. There are also mermaids (marg´ygur) with huge breasts, the hinder parts of a whale, and the head of a giant woman; they sing beautifully, but destroy ships and kill people. Another mythical sea dweller was the öfuguggi, a species of fish with reversed fins, which swims backwards, is poisonous and has red flesh because it eats the bodies of drowned sailors. Another malevolent fish was the hairy trout (lodsilungur), which was believed to have been created by giants as a punishment for human misdemeanour. These fish were also believed to inhabit certain lakes. There were also strange water beings that attempted to drag humans into the sea or destroy their boats: sea men (hafmenn), water horses (vatnanykrar), sea dogs (saehundar), and flying fish (flugfiskar), amongst others. It can be seen from all this that most of the beings believed to inhabit the sea were hostile to humans.

The ancient Celts had a similarly ambivalent attitude to the waters. Supernatural beings that emerged from the waters were often hostile. Fresh water lakes, springs, and rivers were generally regarded as benevolent (except, as we have seen, in the myth of the kelpie), whilst the sea was an unpredictable force. Fresh water was the source of life and fertility; the sea was a source of fish, but also the abode of strange supernatural fish and monsters.

In the medieval story of the Fisher King, the castle of the King stood in the middle of the Waste Land. The land was barren, the minds of men and the wombs of women were barren. The Fisher King lay wounded in his castle. But in this castle was the Grail, and a lance that dripped blood. In order to restore the land, the Questing Knight had to come to the castle and eat and drink with the Fisher King and his maidens. He then had to ask the right questions, which were "What do these wonders mean?", "Whom does the Grail serve?", and "Why does the Lance bleed?" If he failed to ask the questions, the castle would vanish from his sight and he would be back in the Waste Land with no sign of the castle. But if he asked the question, the King would be healed and the land restored to full and joyous life. The story is related to the legend of Osiris, whose wound was the loss of his phallus (the "wound in the thigh" is perhaps a circumlocutory way of saying this). The Grail and the Lance are the spear and the cauldron of Celtic Pagan mythology, but they are also the cup from the Last Supper and the lance that pierced Christ's side at the crucifixion. The barren land represents the psyche without consciousness. The importance of the questions is that the seeker must understand the symbolism of the mysteries, otherwise he remains uninitiated. The Grail Chapel is often situated by the sea in these tales; the sea represents the Great Mother and the realm of the unconscious.

In the folk tale of *The One Who Went Forth to Learn Fear*, the hero was challenged by his father to make something of himself, so he decided to learn to shudder, as that was something he didn't understand at all. He undertakes many frightening adventures, but still does not shudder. Eventually he gains the hand of a princess by disenchanting her father's castle, but he still has not felt fear. One day, the princess pours a bucket of gudgeons (little minnow-like fish) over him while he is in bed - and then he shudders. The fish represent sexuality, and the heroic deeds represent sublimated sexuality. The ability to shudder symbolises the ability to let go, to be free from the rigid control of the ego.

There are many superstitions surrounding fish and fishing. When fishing, it is unlucky if the first fish caught is a ling or a salmon. In Aberdeenshire and Banffshire, the scales from the herring must not be washed off the deck or the fishermen's boots, because the luck would go with them.

In some places, a trout was used as a cure for whooping cough. A trout was drowned in ale or cider. The patient had to drink this, then the trout was fried and given to them to eat. A live trout was placed on the stomach as a cure for worms.

Mythology

The fish represents the Mother Goddess and all lunar deities. Many of the mystery religions had a sacramental meal of fish with bread and wine (compare the story of the Loaves and Fishes in the Bible). Fish meals and sacrifices were part of the worship of many lunar, underworld, water, love, and fertility deities. An example of this was the Babylonian goddess Atargatis, whose son Ichthys was the Sacred Fish. The fish was also sacred to the goddesses Isis, Ishtar, Nina, and Venus, whose day was Friday, and in whose honour fish was eaten on that day. All this fish symbolism was carried over into Christianity and reinterpreted.

In Chaldaea, a fish in a bowl was the emblem of Nanshe, the goddess of springs and canals, interpreter of dreams. She was the daughter of Ea and the sister of Inanna.

In Sumer, the fish skin was used as ritual garb by the priests of Ea-Oannes, Lord of the Deeps, who was portrayed as a fish-goat or a fish-ram (the original of the constellation of Capricorn). The fish headdress of the priests of Ea-Oannes was later developed into the mitre of the Christian bishop (though some say it came from the hats of the priests of Dagon). The fish is an attribute of Ea and Tammuz as phallic and masculine, but it also represents the feminine principle, love, and fertility, and is associated with Ishtar. Adapa (the wise one), son of Ea, is depicted as a fisherman. The Phoenician deity Dagon was either a sea god or a corn god; his priests wore fish hats. The Babylonian god Oannes (half-man, half-fish) was concerned with wisdom. He was said to have been the father (by the goddess Atargatis) of Semiramis, a historical queen of Babylon. Atargatis was sometimes represented as a mermaid. In the daytime, Oannes walked among humans and gave them his knowledge of the arts and sciences; but by night, he returned to the waters of the Persian Gulf. There was also a fish goddess, Derketo, who was sometimes a divinity in her own right, but her name was also applied as an epithet to Atargatis, the Phrygian moon-goddess. Derketo was a great leviathan who caused a flood and lamented that her children became like the fishes of the sea; she was also the consort of Oannes.

In Phoenicia, Phrygia, and Syria, the fish was the sacral meal of the priests of Atargatis, who had sacred pools of fish dedicated to her. The fish was an attribute of deities of love and a symbol of good fortune.

In Assyrian art, the fish is portrayed with the axe. Possibly the fish represents deities of the Moon and the waters, whilst the axe represents Sun and sky deities. The fish and the axe are also depicted together in Crete.

In ancient Egypt, the fish represented the phallus of Osiris. When Isis found the body of Osiris, she had the child Diktys (whose name means "the Fish") in the boat with her. When she embraced the dead Osiris, she showed her full radiant glory, and Diktys fell overboard and was drowned. Fortunately Isis rescued him and restored him to life. The title Diktys was applied by both orthodox Christians and Gnostics to Christ. Two fish represented the creative principle, the abundance of the Nile, and fertility. The fish was also an emblem of Isis and Hathor. The barbel fish symbolised hatred and uncleanness, and was an attribute of Set as the irrational and passionate element of nature. In the North East Delta, the fish goddess Hatmehyt was worshipped, together with her consort Banebdjedet, the ram god. (Perhaps they were sidereal divinities representing the constellations of Aries and Pisces?)

In Greek myth, the fish was an attribute of Aphrodite as goddess of love and fertility, and associated with Poseidon as the power of the sea. In the worship of Adonis, people offered fish for the dead. Orpheus was known as the Fisher of Men. According to Hyginus (a Greek writer several centuries after Homer), Aphrodite was born from an egg which dropped from the sky, and she was brought ashore by fish.

In ancient Rome, the fish was a funerary symbol representing continuing existence in the afterlife; it was an attribute of Venus as love and fecundity. Priapus, the ithyphallic patron of orchards and gardens, was also the patron of fishing harbours on the coast of Asia Minor, and statues of him were erected there to ensure a good catch. On 17 June, the Romans held the Ludi Pescatori, a festival of fishermen and divers, in honour of Tiberinus, the god of the River Tiber.

In the Hebraic tradition, the fish is the pure meal of the Sabbath, and the food of the blessed in Paradise. Fish in the sea represent the faithful in the pure waters of the Torah. The old Jewish festival of Passover was in the month of Adar, the fish.

In Christianity, the fish represents Christ, as the Greek for fish is an acronym for Christ's titles (*ichthyos*: Iesous Christos Theou Huios Soter, which means Jesus Christ, Son of God, Saviour). The apostles were called 'fishers of men'. Three fishes signify the Trinity. Three fishes with one head represent the Triune principle of the Godhead. This symbol is found in Egyptian, Celtic, Indian, Mesopotamian, Burmese, Persian, and French iconography. Three intertwined fishes also represent the Trinity. In the Grail legend, the Fisher King lived in a castle at the heart of a waste land. His wounds kept him and the land in a wasted state. In order to heal him and the wounded land, it was necessary for the Grail Seeker to ask the right questions.

In Christian art, the sacramental fish, bread and wine represent the Last Supper. Christ's disciples were called fishers of men, and the early church referred to the faithful as *pisciculi*. The fish represented Christ in the Roman church, but not in the Greek Orthodox. The fish is also an attribute of St Peter. The fish also represents baptism, immortality, and resurrection (by association with the story of Jonah and the whale). A medieval hymn called Christ "the little Fish which the Virgin caught in the fountain" - so he is both fisher and fish, transcendent and immanent, human and divine.

The Icelandic world view appears to divide the world into two domains, the sea and the land. Some fish inhabited both realms (e.g. the salmon, which occurs in rivers and in the sea). In *Snorra Edda*, Loki changes into a salmon to escape the punishment of the gods, and has two choices: to head out to sea, or to go inland, up the river. The salmon is regarded as a creature of transformation, because it belongs to both the sea and the land.

In Scandinavia generally, the fish was an attribute of Frigga as goddess of love and fertility (but this may have been borrowed from classical myth). The dwarf Alberich or Andvari could shapeshift into a fish. He was the guardian of the treasures of the gods, including the Tarnkappe, the cloak of invisibility.

In Welsh legend, Gwion changed into a fish to escape the anger of Cerridwen (see also otter, dog, and hare). Nodens was a fisher god of the river, and was depicted with a fish hooked on a line at his temple at Lydney Park on the River Severn. It has been suggested (O'Rahilly, 1946) that both the fisherman and the fish are depictions of the god.

In Shropshire legend, Wild Edric was a Saxon ealdorman who resisted William the Conqueror, because he had been dispossessed of his lands by the conquest. He was said to have been condemned to wander, unable to die, because he did not give up the resistance soon enough, and he led the Wild Hunt across the Shropshire hills. Sightings of him occurred before the outbreak of wars, riding in the direction of enemy territory. He was associated with a fish in Bomere Pool near Shewsbury which wore his sword at its side and could not be caught with a net. It was said to have received the sword in trust when Edric disappeared; it was probably the guardian spirit of the pool.

In Oceanic legend, the lover of Hina, the Moon goddess, was Te Tuna, a giant fish who lived in the depths of the ocean. But one day Hina tired of his embraces and went to seek another lover. She lay in the foam on the shores of the world and waited for a lover. Then the hero Maui came to her, and they made love. When Te Tuna heard of it, he was jealous, and came to fight Maui. After a terrible battle, Te Tuna was killed, and his remains lay on the beach. Later, from the place where he lay, there grew the first coconut palm, which is the mainstay of Oceanic existence, so he is remembered as a benefactor and a valiant foe.

In Hinduism, Brahma and Vishnu sometimes appear in fish form. Vishnu's first incarnation was as a great horned fish called Matsya. He saved humanity from the flood and began the present cycle of existence by starting a new race of people. The fish is also the symbol of Varuna, the golden fish who embodies the power of the waters and redeemed the Manu from the flood. The *Artha´sastra* (Textbook on the Art of Winning), a classical Indian treatise on political life, expounds the Law of the Fish (*matsya-nyaya*), which expresses the moral order of the world by which kings and princes function: "The big ones eat the little ones and the little ones have to be numerous and fast". The *Artha´sastra* was written sometime between 321 bce and 297 bce, probably by Kautilya, the counsellor of Chandragupta I, the founder of the Maurya dynasty.

In Aztec mythology, Opochtli was the god of fishermen and bird-snarers.

In the 18th Sura of the Koran, in the story of Khidr and Moses, Moses sets out to seek Khidr, the green one of Islamic legend, who dwells at the place where two seas meet. They stop to cook a fish that they have caught, but Moses' servant splashes it with water from the sea, and it is miraculously revived and jumps back into the sea and swims away. It is only when they stop later on for breakfast that they realise what has happened and its significance, so that they have to turn back. This often happens on the spiritual path, where you have to go back and look again for something that you have missed. It is only when Moses and his servant turn back that they meet with Khidr. Khidr is sometimes described as living in rivers and riding on a fish, and he is sometimes known as Dhu-n-Nun, 'he who possesses the fish'. He is the inner being, the one who restores life, and green shoots spring up wherever he goes. The two seas symbolise the meeting place of life and death, the eternal and the temporal, the spatial and the unmanifest. They are similar to the Sumerian concept of Tiamat and Apsu, the salt water and the sweet water (see snake).

According to Jung, the fish represents Nun (the Hebrew letter and path on the Tree of Life), the father of the shadow, the carnal being (sexuality), who comes from the dark world of the Creator, the depths of the sea. The sea is a symbol of the primordial unconscious. Where the fish dived into the sea, it became solid ground, and Khidr appeared there seated on a throne of light. The fish may be a manifestation of Khidr. The immortal being comes from something humble and forgotten, which is a source of nourishment, representing the fertility of the unconscious mind, which maintain the consciousness by a continual influx of energy. This interface between the conscious and unconscious mind is represented by the meeting place of the two seas. Nun, the fish, is the path between Hod and Netzach, directly below Tifereth on the Tree of Life.

Fish deities and sea gods riding on fish or dolphins represent the ability to move at will in the waters, and infinite possibility.

Symbolism

Fish symbolise life moving in the depths. Deep water signifies the unconscious, so fish moving within it symbolise inspiration and creativity. The fish also represents the instinctual side of women

In Alchemy, fish represent the Arcanum, the arcane substance, the "round element", the germ of the "animate stone", the philosophers' stone.

Fish moving downwards depict the incarnation of spirit in matter; swimming upwards, they denote the separation of spirit from matter. Two fishes represent temporal and spiritual power.

Fish also represent disciples and devotees swimming in the waters of life. Fish and birds together symbolise earth and funerary mysteries, and symbolise the hope of resurrection.

In Hinduism, the fish symbolises wealth and fertility. Two fishes touching nose to tail portray the yoni (the vulva).

In Buddhism, the fish is sometimes drawn in the footprint of Buddha to symbolise detachment and freedom from desire. Buddha is sometimes called the Fisher of Men.

In China, the fish represents abundance (the word for fish sounds similar to the word for abundance), wealth, regeneration, harmony, and the people as subjects of the Emperor. A single fish depicts a loner, an orphan, a bachelor, or a widow. A pair of fish depicts the joys of marriage, union, and fertility. The fish is an attribute of Kwan-Yin, the goddess of compassion, and an emblem of the T'ang Dynasty.

In Japan, the fish is an attribute of Kwannon, who is the same deity as Kwan-Yin. Tatsuta-Hiko, the wind god, and Tatsuta-Hime, the wind goddess, are venerated by sailors and fishermen, and prayed to for good harvests.

In ancient Greece, the fish was a phallic symbol, and signified fecundity and the life-giving powers of water.

The fish is still a phallic symbol, representing fertility and procreation, and the renewal and sustenance of life. It is regarded as the origin and the preserver of life.

In Zodiacal symbolism, the fish represents the unconscious and the spiritual principle. In the constellation of Capricorn, the goat-fish, the fish denotes the power of the waters and the unconscious. In the constellation of Pisces, the two fish swimming in opposite directions (one upwards, the other downwards) represent the exchange of energies between spirit and matter, and the cord between them represents the golden cord linking the soul to the body.

Poetry

Out then he drew his shining blade,
    Thinking to stick her where she stood,
But she was vanished to a fish,
    And swam far off, a fair mermaid.

O mother, mother, braid my hair,
    My lusty lady, make my bed.
O brother, take my sword and spear,
    For I have seen the false mermaid.

(from *"Clerk Colvill"*)

The Song of Wandering Aengus
I went out to the hazel wood,
Because a fire was in my head,
And cut and peeled a hazel wand,
And hooked a berry to a thread;
And when white moths were on the wing,
And moth-like stars were flickering out,
I dropped the berry in a stream
And caught a little silver trout.

When I had laid it on the floor
I went to blow the fire a-flame,
But something rustled on the floor,
And someone called me by my name:
It had become a glimmering girl
With apple blossom in her hair
Who called me by my name and ran
And faded through the brightening air.
Though I am old with wandering
Through hollow lands and hilly lands,
I will find out where she has gone,
And kiss her lips and take her hands;
And walk among the dappled grass,
And pluck till time and times are done
The silver apples of the moon,
The golden apples of the sun.

(W B Yeats, 1865-1939)

Literature

One of the most lyrical books about fishing is *"The Silver Darlings"* by Neil M Gunn, which is about the beginning of herring fishing on the East Coast of Scotland after the Highland Clearances. It describes the experiences of Catrine and her son Finn after her husband was press-ganged on his first fishing trip, and Finn's growing up alongside the development of the herring fishing.

Carp

Latin name *Cyprinus carpio*

Family *Cyprinidae*

Order *Cypriniformes*

Folk name li

Etymology Middle English, from Old French *carpe*, from Provencal or from Late Latin *carpa*

Varieties
The Carp is related to the Crucian Carp (*Carassius carassius*), the Minnow, the Tench, the Roach, the Bream, the Eastern European Bream, the Silver Bream, the Orfe, the Chub, the Dace, the Asp, the Bleak, the Bitterling, the Nase, the Barbel, the Rudd, and the Gudgeon.

Symbolism
In China, the carp symbolises literary eminence, perseverance in the struggle against difficulties, and courage. The carp is said to 'leap the Dragon Gate' by persistence and become a dragon. A successful scholar in literary examinations is known as a carp that has leapt the Dragon Gate. Twin carp represent the union of lovers. The carp's beard is a symbol of supernatural powers. In the story of Monkey by Wu Ch'êng-ên, Monkey is captured by a river dragon that has escaped from Kuan-Yin's pond, where it was a carp.

In Japan, the carp signifies Samurai as courage, dignity, endurance, good fortune, and resignation to fate. It also symbolises love, as the word for carp sounds like the word for love.

Eel

Latin name *Anguilla anguilla* **Polarity** Yin

Family *Anguillidae* **Element** Water

Order *Apodes* **Rune** Ior

Etymology from Old English Êl, Old High German al, Old Norse ·ll, Germanic Êlaz

Deities Badb

Folklore

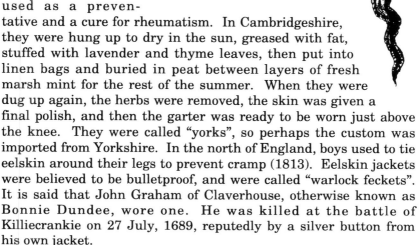

In Castleford, Yorkshire and in the Cambridgeshire Fens, eel-skin garters were used as a preventative and a cure for rheumatism. In Cambridgeshire, they were hung up to dry in the sun, greased with fat, stuffed with lavender and thyme leaves, then put into linen bags and buried in peat between layers of fresh marsh mint for the rest of the summer. When they were dug up again, the herbs were removed, the skin was given a final polish, and then the garter was ready to be worn just above the knee. They were called "yorks", so perhaps the custom was imported from Yorkshire. In the north of England, boys used to tie eelskin around their legs to prevent cramp (1813). Eelskin jackets were believed to be bulletproof, and were called "warlock feckets". It is said that John Graham of Claverhouse, otherwise known as Bonnie Dundee, wore one. He was killed at the battle of Killiecrankie on 27 July, 1689, reputedly by a silver button from his own jacket.

Mythology

In Celtic mythology, the raven goddess Morrígan appeared on a standing stone to warn the bull of Cuálnge of the danger he is in. She also appeared in bird form to Cú Chulainn, whose love she desired, but he denied her. Up to this point she had been protecting him, but she then turned against him and hindered him in single combat by distracting him, appearing first as an eel tangled around his feet, then a heifer, then a wolf. After this he no longer won every fight. Badbh is sometimes identified with the Morrìgan. The word *badbh* in Irish and Scottish Gaelic signifies a hag or unpleasant woman.

Cú Chulainn beheld at this time a young woman of noble figure coming towards him, wrapped in garments of many colours.

"Who are you?" he said.

"I am King Buan's daughter," she said, "and I have brought you my treasure and cattle. I love you because of the great tales I have heard."

"You come at a bad time. We no longer flourish here, but famish. I can't attend to a woman during a struggle like this."

"But I might be a help."

"It wasn't for a woman's backside that I took on this ordeal!"

"Then I'll hinder," she said. "When you are busiest in the fight I'll come against you. I'll get under your feet in the shape of an eel and trip you in the ford."

"That is easier to believe. You are no king's daughter. But I'll catch and crack your eel's ribs with my toes and you'll carry that mark for ever unless I lift it from you with a blessing."

"I'll come against you in the shape of a grey she-wolf, to stampede the beasts into the ford against you."

"Then I'll hurl a sling-stone at you and burst the eye in your head, and you'll carry that mark for ever unless I lift it from you with a blessing."

"I'll come before you in the shape of a hornless red-eared heifer and lead the cattle-herd to trample you in the waters, by ford and pool, and you won't know me."

"Then I'll hurl a stone at you," he said, "and shatter your leg, and you'll carry that mark for ever unless I lift it from you with a blessing."

Then she left him.

Then Cú Chulainn went to fight Loch at the ford, and she came from the dwellings of the Sidhe to destroy him, first appearing as the white, hornless, red-eared heifer with fifty cows linked together with a chain of silvered bronze. The cattle rushed through the waters of the ford and caused confusion, and Cú Chulainn cast at the Morrìgan and shattered one of her eyes. Then he resumed his fight with Loch, but then the Morrìgan appeared again as a black, slippery eel, coiling three times around Cú Chulainn's legs, until he lay on his back in the ford, whereupon Loch wounded him in the chest. The watching armies began to taunt Cú Chulainn for being bested by a fish. He became very angry and crushed the eel's head with his foot, destroying half its brains and breaking its ribs. Then the Morrìgan appeared in the form of a "rough grey-red bitch-wolf", bit him in the arm, and drove the cattle against him. Cú Chulainn cast a stone at her with his sling and took out her other eye. Loch wounded him again while he was distracted by the Morrìgan, and Cú Chulainn was so enraged by this that he killed him with the gae bolga, his magical spear. Later the Morrígan tricked him into healing her by appearing in the guise of an old woman with a cow, and giving him milk. As she gives him the milk from each teat, he blesses her and she is healed. She does this because only he can heal those whom he has wounded.

Symbolism
In China the eel is a symbol of carnal love. It is generally a phallic symbol, and represents the quality of slipperiness.

Poetry
Ior by‚ eafix;   and deah a brucep
fodres on foldan;   hafap faegerne eard,
wætre beworpen,   dær he on wynnum leofa‚.

The eel is a river-fish; and yet it enjoys
food in the fields;   it has a fair home,
surrounded by water,   where it dwells in delight.
(Anglo-Saxon Rune Poem)

Salmon

Latin name *Salmo salar*

Family *Salmonidae*

Order *Clupeiformes*

Polarity Masculine

Element Water

Planet

Etymology Middle English, from Anglo-French *samon, saumon,* Old French *saumon,* Latin *salmo, salmonis*

Deities Nodens, Finn, Latis, Murigen, Boann

Varieties
The Salmon is related to the Trout, the Huchen, the Alpine Charr, the Freshwater Houting, and the Grayling.

Mythology
The Celts regarded the salmon as a creature of wisdom, prophecy and inspiration, perhaps because of its instinctual ability to return to the river in which it was spawned. The Irish myth was that the Pool of Connla contained wise salmon, who fed on the nuts which fell from the nine hazel trees growing around the pool. In Celtic mythology, both salmon and trout were associated with sacred wells, symbolising divine knowledge and prescience. Heads are also associated with sacred wells. A Gallo-Roman altar depicts a fish (possibly a salmon) whispering into the ear of a human head. There is an Irish legend of a severed head speaking when a salmon is cooked and shared amongst the company, so there is evidently a connection between the two. The salmon was known as *eá fis*, the

salmon of wisdom. In the Welsh legend of Culhwch and Olwen, the salmon of Llyn Llyw (associated with the River Severn) is one of the oldest animals, and so it is consulted about how to complete the tasks set by the Giant Ysbaddaden. In Irish legend, Finn MacCumhal was apprenticed as a child to a magician called Linn Feic. They fished for the salmon in the Pool of Connla at the source of the Boyne. Finn gained his wisdom by sucking his thumb, which he burnt while cooking the salmon. Murigen was an Irish lake goddess who later became a salmon, possibly one of the salmon of the Pool of Connla.

In Britain, Latis was goddess of the pool or of beer, worshipped at Birdoswald on Hadrian's Wall. She fell in love with a salmon, and out of pity for her the other gods turned him into a handsome young warrior. Every winter he turns back into a salmon, and the winter rains are the tears that Latis weeps for him until he returns as a man in spring.

Among the Tsimshian and the Nootka (Indigenous Americans), twins were believed to be related to salmon. As a result, they were believed to be able to call up salmon, control the weather, and make wishes come true. Among the Kwakiutl, twins were not allowed near water in case they turned into salmon. They were not allowed to catch or eat salmon either.

Poetry

Cresses green culled beneath a stone,
And given to a woman in secret.
The shank of the deer in the head of the herring,
And in the slender tail of the speckled salmon.

(from "The Consecration of the Cloth", *Carmina Gadelica*)

Shark

Latin name various **Class** *Chondrichthyes*
Order *Selachiformes*

Etymology 16th century, origin unknown

Mythology

In Polynesian mythology the shark can represent sacred beings who appear in either human or shark form, or it can be the incarnation of important ancestors such as chiefs. It can also be the familiar of a sorcerer. In some areas, the shark is addressed as 'Grandfather'.

In Hawaii, there are shark gods, and ancestral spirits can manifest as sharks.

The shark is also sacred in parts of West Africa. If a shark is killed accidentally, propitiatory rituals must be performed. If a shark bone is cast into the sea, it becomes a shark serving the Ocean Spirit.

In ancient Greece, it was taboo to eat shark meat at the women's festival of the Haloa.

Insects

Ant

Latin name *Lasius niger*   **Element** Earth

Family *Formicidae*

Folk name *ma-yi* (Chinese); *emmet* (Devon)

Etymology ant and emmet from Old English Êmete, from West Germanic *amaitja* (a meaning off, mait meaning cut)

Varieties
Black or Garden Ant (*Lasius niger*); Red Wood Ant (*Formica rufa*)

Folklore
In Devon, the ant is known as the emmet; this is also the local slang for a tourist.

In the Brothers Grimm story of *The Queen Bee*, the youngest brother prevents his brothers from destroying a nest of ants just to watch the ants' terror. Later he is set the seemingly impossible task of gathering pearls scattered in the forest, but the ants come and gather them for him. A similar tale is told in Siberia called Mergen and his Friends, in which Mergen saves an ant which is trapped by a fallen branch, and later the ants help him gather up the seeds which the magician has scattered in order to test Mergen for marriage to his beautiful daughter.

The moral of the story is that if we co-operate with Nature, it will help us; also that if we work with our instincts, it will help us to achieve our conscious aims.

A similar story appears in the legend of Culhwch and Olwen in the *Mabinogion*, when Gwythyr son of Greidawl saved an anthill from the fire, and the ants brought the flax seed which Ysbaddaden had said must be obtained to make a veil for Olwen's wedding.

> *"And as Gwythyr son of Greidawl was one day journeying over a mountain, he heard a wailing and a grievous lamentation, and these were a horrid noise to hear. He sprang forward in that direction, and when he came there he drew his sword and smote off the anthill level with the ground, and so saved them from the fire. And they said to him, "Take thou God's blessing and ours, and that which no man can ever recover, we will come and recover it for thee." It was they thereafter who came with the nine hestors of flax seed which Ysbaddaden Chief Giant had named to Culhwch, in full measure, with none of it wanting save for a single flax seed. And the lame ant brought that in before night."*

The Apalai people (Indigenous Americans) made travellers sting them with ants to purify them of any disease that the traveller might be carrying. Some tribes in Guiana use the same means to 'purify' women after menstruation.

Mythology

In Graeco-Roman mythology, the ant was an attribute of Ceres and Demeter. In Greek myth, Aeacus was the son of Zeus and the nymph Aegina; he ruled the island named after his mother. The jealous Hera sent a plague against the island, so Aeacus appealed to Zeus for help. Zeus turned a colony of ants into humans to repopulate the island. They were the Myrmidons, who later fought under Aeacus' grandson Achilles in the Trojan War. In Hinduism, the ant represents the transitory nature of existence. This is illustrated by the story of *The Humbling of Indra*. Vishnu appeared in Indra's palace in the form of a beautiful boy. A procession of ants marched across the floor, and the boy Vishnu laughed, because each of the ants had been an Indra in a previous existence. Each, by virtue of selfless deeds, rose to the rank of a king of the gods, but then they became proud and self-satisfied, and returned through many births to the condition of an ant.

Symbolism

The ant is a symbol of right conduct, virtue, and patriotism in China; it also symbolises self-interest, and in the Shanghai area, the village wheeler-dealer is called an 'ant'. The folkname '*ma-yi*' means the righteous insect.

In general, the ant symbolises industriousness.

Literature

In T H White's *The Sword in the Stone*, Merlin turns the boy Arthur into various animals for a day at a time. He spends a day being an ant, and discovers that the anthill is a very conformist society. The nearest thing to an abstract concept is 'Done' or 'Not-Done' (i.e. permitted or not permitted). Possibly White meant this as an allegory of totalitarianism.

Bee

Latin name *Apis mellifica*   **Polarity** Feminine

Family *Apidae*   **Element** Ether/Spirit

Folk name *mi-feng* (Chinese), bumble-bee, dumble-dore (Dorset); *abeille* (French); *Biene* (German)

Constellation The Beehive (located in Cancer)

Etymology from Old English *beo*, Old High German *bia*, Old Norse b´y, Germanic *bion*

Deities
Hera, Demeter, Cybele, Pan, Priapus, Zeus, Diana, Dionysos, Artemis of the Ephesians, Melissa, Cupid, Vishnu, Shiva, Kama, Soma, Ra, Mellonia, Nantosuelta

Varieties

Blue Carpenter Bee (*Xylocopa violacea*), found in southern and central Europe; Leaf-cutter Bee (*Megachile centuncularis*), found in warm parts of Europe; Potter Bee (*Anthidium manicatum*), which lives in warm areas of Europe; Horned Bee (*Eucera longicornis*), found in southern and central Europe; Black Burrowing Bee (*Andrena carbonaria*), found in most of Europe; Hairy-legged Mining Bee (*Dasypoda hirtipes*), central Europe; Mourner Bee or Armed Melecta (*Melecta armata*), central Europe; Digger Bumble Bee (*Bombus terrestris*), central Europe; Rock Bumble Bee (Bombus lapidarius), black with red-tipped abdomen, central Europe, also found in Britain; Honeybee (*Apis mellifica*), found all over Europe and in Britain, possibly originated in India.

Folklore

The folklore of bees is extensive; bees were regarded as the repository of all knowledge and wisdom. A country proverb was "Ask the wild bee what the Druids knew", and it was customary to tell the bees everything that occurred in the family: births, marriages, and deaths. When buying bees, it was regarded as better not to give money in exchange for them, but some other commodity (Lupton, "*Thousand Notable Things*", 1720); either that, or gold had to be given for them (W. Ellis, "*Modern Husbandman*", 1750). The belief that one must barter for and not sell bees was also found in Devon (1813), Hampshire (1854), N.E. Scotland (1881), Essex (1881), Shropshire (1883), and Somerset (1923).

"If you wish your bees to thrive
Gold must be paid for every hive;
For when they're bought with other money
There will be neither swarm nor honey."

(E.V. Lucas, collected in Sussex)

According to Pliny (77 CE), bees do not like dirty people, thieves, or menstruating women. In Northamptonshire (1850), it was believed that bees would not thrive in a quarrelsome family. In Shropshire (1883), it was the belief that bees must not be carried across running water, or they would die; also, that bad language must not be used near bees, as it would disturb and annoy them. Bees do not like arguments either - in Oxfordshire (1854), it was said that if a man quarrelled with his wife, the bees would leave; in 1904, the belief was still current that if anyone argues over a swarm of bees, the swarm would benefit neither party. It was a particularly bad omen if the bees left the hive; in many parts of England and in Ireland, it was believed to portend the owner's death; in Somerset, it meant that your luck would leave you. If the bees swarmed on dead wood it was a sign of a death in the family.

Various customs had to be observed with regard to the bees on important occasions: when their owner died, the beehive had to be lifted a a few inches clear of the bee bench when the coffin left the house, or turned away from the road, otherwise they would die. It was also believed that they had to be moved to a new location after their owner's death, or they too would die. In 1961, the *Shrewsbury Chronicle* recorded that "Sam Rogers was devoted to his bees. And when he suddenly died ... his children ... walked round the 14 hives telling the bees - to stop them, as legend has it, flying away. But as a memorial service was being held in the Shropshire village church of Myddle, the bees left their hives and settled in a great swarm all over the flowers on Sam's grave." In Dulwich, London, in 1984, a woman whose neighbour's son came round to tell her that he was getting married asked if his father had told his bees. "Of course", came the reply.

In Yorkshire (1827), it was the custom to drape the hives in black crepe for a funeral, to tell the bees who had died, and to leave some of the funeral biscuit at the entrance to the hive. At weddings, the bees had to be given a piece of the cake, and informed of the names of the married couple. In 1986, in Killorglin, Co. Kerry, a young boy died and they forgot to tell the bees, which swarmed on the day of the funeral and were found next day on the grave a few miles away. In Suffolk (1868) it was believed that a bumble bee entering the house meant that a stranger would come; if it was a white-tailed bee, it would be a woman, and if it was red-tailed bee, it would be a man. In Somerset a bee entering the house was a portent that someone would never leave the house alive.

There is a tradition that the bee came from Paradise.

Mythology

To the Celts, the bee represented secret wisdom from the other world. In the Romano-Celtic synthesis, a staff surmounted by a bee was a symbol of Nantosuelta and Mellonia.

In Anglo-Saxon mythology, bees were associated with the Valkyries (*Waelcyrge*), whose name means slaughter-choosers. The honeycomb was called the bee-web, and bees were described as weaving it. Bee-stings were associated with spears and spindles. The *waelcyrge* were also called Sigewif (victory-women), and bees are addressed as sigewif in the Anglo-Saxon charm *Wid Ymbe*. All the Germanic peoples regarded mead (honey wine) and metheglin (triple-distilled mead) as the drink of the gods.

The association of bee-stings with spindles might explain the spindle in the Germanic story of *The Sleeping Beauty*. After all, spindles are not sharp, so it is rather improbable that Dornröschen could have pricked herself with one. The old woman in the tower with the spinning wheel is clearly one of the Fates or Norns (she was the thirteenth fairy who was not invited to the feast), and the humming of the spinning wheel resembles the buzzing of bees.

In Egyptian mythology, the tears of Ra, the sun god, became bees as they fell to the ground. Upper Egypt was represented by the reed, and Lower Egypt by the bee. When the two kingdoms were united in 3550 bce, it was said that the Reed had been joined to the Bee. The bird-fly, or Abait, was probably a bee; it was the guide of souls on their way to the fields of Aarru, the land of honey. The bee's ability to find its way directly to the hive symbolises the unerring ability of the soul to find Aarru, even when lost in the darkness of Amenti, the Land of the Dead in the West. The name of the astral soul, the *ba*, may be related to the bee, as *ba* was also a word for honey. The Egyptians used honey in embalming.

Among the Hittites, the bee was sacred to Hannahannas, the mother goddess. She sent a bee to find the fertility god Telepinus, whose absence had caused famine and drought. Others had failed, but the bee found him.

In Greek myth, Demeter was "The pure mother bee". Hera, the wife of Zeus, was associated with the bee and the constellation of Cancer. In the middle of Cancer (not visible with the naked eye, but possible to see with binoculars) is the constellation of the Skep or Beehive, hence the esoteric connection of Cancer with bees. The Great Mother was also known as the Queen Bee; she was represented by lions and bees in Greek art, and her priestesses were the Melissae (bees). The Pythian priestesses at Delphi were called the Delphic Bees. The celebrants at Eleusis were called Bees. Bees were regarded as the givers of song and eloquence (hence perhaps the expression "honeyed words"). The appearance of a bee portended the arrival of a stranger.

The bee was an attribute of Cybele, Artemis, and Pan, and as such was lunar and virginal. Pan and Priapus were protectors and keepers of bees. Cretan Zeus was born in a bee cave and looked after by the bees and fed by the goddess Melissa. Dionysos was also said to have been fed by bees. The bee was also an attribute of

Cupid, who was stung by a bee, and of Artemis of the Ephesians (not to be confused with the Greek Artemis). It was also associated with the goddess Rhea.

Aristaeus, whose name means "the very good", was the son of Apollo and the nymph Cyrene (or in another legend, the son of Uranus and Gaia). He was an important deity in Thessaly. He was brought up by the centaur Chiron, who taught him medicine and soothsaying, and he was the protector of the olive, the vine, flocks, and agriculture. He was said to have invented bee-keeping. The symbolism of honey is associated with that of the nectar of the gods and the sweetness of divine experience, which bestows immortality. Plato (circa 429-347 bce) was known as the Athenian Bee, owing to the tradition that a swarm of bees alighted on his mouth as he was lying in his cradle, endowing his words with the sweetness of honey.

Sophocles, Virgil, and Lucan were said to have been fed by bees, or had their lips touched with honey, as infants. Sappho and Pindar were also said to have had their mouths filled with honey by the bees. Xenophon (circa 430-354 bce) was also known as the Athenian Bee or the Bee of Athens.

In the *Gospel of the Witches* by Charles Leland, the goddess Diana persuaded Lucifer to love her after she had lain with him by singing a song that was like the buzzing of the bees, or a spinning wheel spinning life.

In Hinduism, a bee on a lotus is a symbol of Vishnu. Krishna is portrayed with a blue bee on his forehead; the blue bee also signifies the element of Ether. A bee surmounting a triangle is an emblem of Shiva Madheri (the suave one). Kama, the god of love, has a bow whose string is made of bees, which symbolise the sweet pain of love, and he is followed by a swarm of bees. Soma, the Moon god, was sometimes referred to as a bee. The bee is often depicted with the lion.

In South America, the U'wa (Tunebo) people of Colombia have a Bee Chant. This is performed by the men after collecting honey, to ensure the welfare of the bees. The chanting begins after dusk.

The men sit cross-legged on the floor in the eastern half of the house, facing east. The women remain at the back of the house where the mead and beer is kept, and do not chant. The men's chanting is led by a chanter while the other men follow. When the chant mentions the bees travelling, the men walk up and down between the east door and the middle of the house. At dawn, when the chant is finished, the men and women drink beer together, and may make love.

The South American stingless bee makes combs without geometrical patterns; instead, they are made up in horizontal layers or spheres. The Kubaruwa visualise the universe as being made up of similar spheres. The symbols of wealth among the Kubaruwa are the products of bees (honey and wax), fertility, exchange goods, and (more recently) money. Honey is pure, free of contamination, sickness, and mortality, and bestows strength and fertility. Wax is traditionally an item of exchange. The bees' most important attribute is their chewing. They are seen to chew pollen and wood, which they transform into wax. The female bees are said to chew the yellow earth of the plains, which they make into the yellow core of the nest (*kuna*). By chewing, the bees also produce *kanoba* (honey).

Amongst the U'wa, there are various meanings of the word for honey, *kanoba*. It can mean saliva; honey (produced by the chewing of the bees); beer (a fermented drink produced by the chewing of the women); the act of chewing to produce beer; maize chewed to bait traps for small rodents; the rain of certain seasons, which is thought to be produced by the chewings of the immortals. The U'wa compare themselves to bees; they live socially, construct houses (similar to hives), and have gatherings, ceremonies, and chants. The U'wa make ceremonial beer (also called kanoba) in pots (kumtas). Both men and women drink honey to maintain health and vitality.

The U'wa also have a Hives (Bee Order) Chant. This chant has a fourfold structure. In the first part, it is related that the forests of the middle world are dry. The deities of the upper and lower worlds, Rukwa and Kanwara, co-operate to produce *kanoba* by chewing and spitting into large pots. In the second and third parts, Rukwa tells his children the bees that they must go down to the middle world. Yagshowa and Ruáhama lead the bees' *kanoba* through the coloured spheres. The bees bathe and develop bodies in the "wealth-lakes" of yellow; then they fly over the red lake of Kanwara, where some of the bees bathe and are touched by Ruáhama. Then they develop bodies with blood, and are named Kanwara's sisters' daughters. The bees that came through the red lake undergo an initiation ceremony and are given coca, peppers, ginger, and tobacco to eat. (These plants are used medicinally by the U'wa, to cleanse and produce a trance state.) As payment for inhabiting the middle world, they are given crowns, seeds, clothing, yellow soil (gold), and musical instruments. The bees who entered the red lake became flies, wasps, and other stinging winged insects, and they eat animal excreta. They flew to the highlands and entered the door of a cave, from which they emerged as highland and lowland deer, hares, and peccaries. They are led by Ruáhama and have Kanwara's illnesses. In the fourth part of the chant, Yagshowa takes the bees' kanoba from the yellow lake and plants it in the middle world, where it grows into coca, peppers, and ginger. The bees settle and chew the pollen of palms, other trees, and squashes, which become wax. The male bees give their sisters yellow earth (*kuna*) and the pollen of a hallucinogenic vine (*shebara*) to chew so that they can breed.

The bees domesticated by the U'wa are stingless, and inhabit the temperate zones. Their larvae is the embryonic female seed. They frequent the shebara vine, which shamans use to perform kwika (magic, the reversal of order, shape-changing and sexual practices). The U'wa believe that bees are incestuous (incest is a form of kwika). The bees' production of honey and wax is also regarded as a form of magic, and since they chew hallucinogenic pollen, are believed to be able to access shamanic states. The U'wa view of bees is dominated by their symbolic purity. Incest is regarded as pure, in that no sexual liquids are exchanged. Honey is believed to be a pure substance, and the bees feed off sacred plants.

Symbolism

In general, the bee symbolises immortality, rebirth, purity, industry, order, and the soul. Bees were believed to be parthenogenetic, so they represented chastity and virginity. They were regarded as divine; honey was often offered to supreme deities. Bees can also represent the stars, and are regarded as messengers to the spirit world, and messengers of oak and thunder gods. They were often carved on tombs to portray the concept of immortality. The bee gathering the nectar of flowers represents the immortal soul gathering life experience on earth. The bee pollinating the flowers represents the soul linking the spirit to the body.

Honey was a symbol of immortality, initiation, and rebirth. It was believed to bestow fertility, virility, and vigour, and was used as an aphrodisiac. Because bees were believed to be parthenogenetic, honey was regarded as a pure food. In astrology, they were associated with the Moon, hence also with increase and growth. In China, honey represented false friendship. In Christianity, honey symbolised the earthly mission of Christ and the sweetness of the word of God. In Greece, honey represented eloquence, wisdom, and poetic genius. It was used in cthonic rites. In Hinduism, the honey of the lotus blossom of knowledge is the food of the Hamsa, the divine swans which dwell in the Great Mind. Honey is forbidden in Jainism because it is offered to fertility spirits and is an aphrodisiac. In the Minoan culture, honey was used in rituals as food for both the living and the dead. In Mithraism, it was offered to Mithra, and poured on the hands and tongue of initiates. In Sumer, it was regarded as the food of the gods.

In Egypt, the bee was regarded as the giver of life, so it signified birth, death, and resurrection. It was also a symbol of industry, chastity, harmonious living, and royalty, particularly the Pharaoh of Lower Egypt.

In Mithraism, the bee represented the soul, the vital principle springing from the bull slain by Mithras. Both bees and oxen, as sexless creatures, were regarded as androgynous. A bee with a caduceus represents Mercury, the shepherd of souls. The soul is represented by the bee.

To the Romans, swarms of bees were an omen of misfortune. The headless bee and the headless frog averted the evil eye. Virgil called the bee "the breath of life", and said that it ascends alive into heaven; hence it is an image of the immortal soul. Porphyry associated it with justice and sobriety. According to Seneca, it was a symbol of monarchy.

In Greece, the bee symbolised industry, prosperity, immortality (the souls of the dead could transmigrate into bees), and purity.

The bee was the emblem of the Merovingian dynasty of France. Golden bees were sewn onto Napoleon's coronation cloak in an attempt to borrow the Merovingians' symbolism.

In Christianity, the bee symbolises diligence, order, purity, virginity, chastity, courage, economy, prudence, sweetness, co-operation, religious eloquence, the monastic life, and Mary's virginity (with Christ as the honey she produced). The bee was believed never to sleep, so it signified christian zeal and vigilance. A bee in flight represents the soul entering the kingdom of heaven. The beehive represents the Church, with the bees as the faithful. The bee was also the emblem of St Bernard of Clairvaux and St Ambrose. It was said that a swarm of bees landed on Ambrose's mouth when he was in his cradle, bestowing eloquence upon him. In the *Apocrypha*, the bee was said to have been created by God or Jesus. Christ was called the ethereal bee.

In Africa and Australia, the bee is a tribal totem. Among the Kung Bushmen, they are believed to possess supernatural power. The honeyguide bird sings to guide the Bushmen to the nests of bees. The honeybadger has also learnt to follow the honeyguide. The Bushman or woman will extract the honeycombs and share them with the badger and the bird.

A legend from South China tells how a bee helped a young man to find the right bride from a whole row of beautiful girls.

In the Brothers Grimm story of *The Queen Bee*, the youngest brother saves a nest of bees from his older brothers, who want to break it open to get the honey. Later, he has to select the youngest princess from three identical sleeping princesses. The queen of the hive he saved from destruction alights on the lips of the youngest princess.

Amongst the Essenes, the priestly officials were known as 'king bees'.

In Islam, bees symbolise the faithful, intelligence, wisdom, and harmlessness. They are associated with souls, and there is a legend that Mohammed admits them to Paradise. According to Ibn al-Athir, bees "benefit fruit blossom, practice useful things, work in the daytime, do not eat food gathered by others, dislike dirt and bad smells, and obey their ruler; they dislike the darkness of indiscretion, the clouds of doubt, the storm of revolt, the smoke of the prohibited, the water of superfluity, [and] the fire of lust."

In China, the bee symbolises thrift and industry. It is known as *mi-feng*. In Chinese art it represents a young man in love, while the peony it sits on depicts the girl he loves. The expression 'to call the bee and bring the butterfly' means to have an extra-marital affair.

Poetry
"May your holy churn be filled with honey cheese." (Ancient Sumerian blessing)

Beetle

Latin name various

Families *Cicindelidae* (Tiger Beetles);
Carabidae (Ground Beetles); *Dytiscidae*
(Water Beetles); *Gyrinidae* (Whirligig
Beetles); *Hydrophilidae* (Water Scavenger
Beetles); *Staphylinidae* (Rover Beetles); *Silphidae* (Sexton and
Carrion Beetles); *Lucanidae* (Stag Beetles); *Scarabaeidae*
(Chafers); *Buprestidae* (Metallic or Flat-headed Woodborers);
Elateridae (Click Beetles); *Cantharidae* (Leather-winged beetles);
Cleridae (Chequered Beetles); *Anobiidae* (Death-watch Beetles);
Tenebrionidae (Darkling or Pineate Beetles); *Meloidae* (Blister or
Oil Beetles); *Curculonidae* (Snout Beetles or Weevils); *Scolytidae*
(Bark Beetles); *Cerambycidae* (Longicorn Beetles); *Chrysomelidae*
(Leaf Beetles); *Coccinellidae* (Ladybirds)

Order Coleoptera

Folk names Dharrig Dael, Death-watch Beetle, Sun Beetle

Etymology from Old English *bitula* (biter) from *bitan*, to bite.

Folklore

Green and gold beetles that come out in the sunshine were called
sun beetles in southern England (1879). It was believed that if you
stepped on one, it would make it rain. The same was also believed
of black beetles, as late as 1981. The Dharrig Dael, a black beetle,
was believed in southern Ireland to be the creature of the devil,
and to have betrayed Christ to the soldiers in the Garden of
Gethsemane.

The Death-watch Beetle (*Anobium pertinax*) was commonly held to
be an omen of death when it was heard ticking in the wall, due to
its resemblance to a clock ticking (1671, 1691, 1708, 1735, 1828,
1879, 1882, 1941).

138

Butterfly

Latin name various

Polarity Feminine

Families *Satyridae* (Meadow Browns); *Nymphalidae* (Fritillaries); *Lycaenidae* (Hairstreaks); *Papilionidae* (Swallowtails); *Pieridae* (Whites).

Element Air

Order Lepidoptera

Folk name God's fool

Planet Moon

Etymology from Old English *buttor-fleoge*

Deities Hina, Psyche, the Great Mother

Folklore

A fairly widespread folk belief has it that the soul can appear as a butterfly. There is an old folktale where a man lay asleep on a cliff top, and his soul left his body in the form of a butterfly. His friend watched it fly out of his mouth and flutter along until it found an old sheep's skull, where it fluttered for a while and eventually returned to the sleeping man. When he awoke he said that he had had an amazing dream where he was flying over a broad road with lots of flowers and then entered a white palace with many pillars and curved walls. His friend explained to him what he had seen.

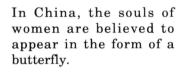

In China, the souls of women are believed to appear in the form of a butterfly.

Mythology

In Polynesian mythology, the Moon goddess Hina was a butterfly who flew through space, separating the worlds of land and sky.

The butterfly represented the Minoan Great Mother. A Mycenean coin from around 1500 bce has a butterfly on it. The shape of the butterfly echoes that of the labrys (the Minoan double-headed axe).

In Greek art, Psyche was depicted as a butterfly.

Symbolism

The butterfly symbolises immortality and the soul. As it changes from a caterpillar to a butterfly, it represents rebirth and resurrection, the transition from the material to the spiritual realm. The chrysalis represents metamorphosis, the transformation from apparent death and corruption into beauty.

To the Celts, the butterfly was a symbol of the soul and of fire.

In China, plum blossom and butterflies symbolise long life and immaculate beauty; chrysanthemums and butterflies signify beauty in old age. A butterfly sipping nectar from a flower represents a lover paying court to a woman. Sexual intercourse is referred to as 'the love-crazed butterfly and the wild bee'.

In Japan, the butterfly represents a vain woman, a geisha, or a fickle lover. A pair of butterflies denotes marital bliss. A white butterfly represents the spirit of a dead person.

To the Maoris, the butterfly symbolises the soul.

In Christianity, the butterfly denotes resurrection; it is sometimes depicted in the hand of Christ as a child.

In Greece, the butterfly represented immortality and the soul.

Caterpillar

The caterpillar is the larva of a butterfly or moth. In Shropshire folklore the caterpillar is called a Tom Tailor, and it is lucky if one crawls on you (Burne, 1883).

The word caterpillar is probably derived from an Anglo-French variation of Old French *chatepelose*, meaning hairy cat, with the addition of the obsolete word *piller*, a ravager.

Centipede

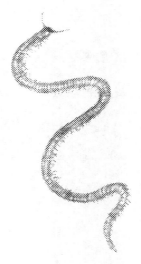

Latin name *Lithobius forficatus*

Class *Chilopoda*

Order *Lithobiomorpha*

Folk names *wu-gong, yan-yu*

Etymology from French *centipéde*, from
Latin *centum* (a hundred), *pedis* (foot)

In China, the centipede (*wu-gong*) is the arch-enemy of the snake.
Many folk tales relate how the hero was saved from a snake which
was about to attack him by a centipede. Big centipedes (*yan-yu*)
are poisonous, and hence regarded as one of the Five Noxious
Creatures.

Cícaða

Latin name *Cicadetta montana* (Mountain cicada)

Order *Homoptera* (Plant-bugs)

Sub-order *Cicadoidea*

Folk name guo-guo, shan (Chinese); cicala, cigala

Etymology from Latin *cicada*; Italian from Latin *cicala*; Italian *cigala*

Deity Apollo

Mythology
In a Chinese legend, the queen of Qi in eastern China turned into a cicada after she died, so the cicada was called "the girl of Qi".

Symbolism
The cicada represents the cyclical alternation of light and dark, day and night.

In China, it represents resurrection, immortality, eternal youth, happiness, and the absence of acquisitiveness and vice. Jade cicadas were placed in the mouth of a deceased person to ensure immortality; later, a fish was used instead. A cicada on a hat represented an honest and principled man.

In Greece, the cicada represented immortality, as it was believed to be bloodless and live on dew. It was sacred to Apollo. It was also

143

associated with Tithonus, whose wife Eos (the goddess of the dawn) loved him so much that she asked for immortality for him, but forgot to ask for eternal youth, so Tithonus grew older and feebler, and Eos shut him up in a chamber, until eventually the gods took pity on him and turned him into a cicada. This story illustrates the old saying "Be careful what you pray for, you might get it" very well. Magic has an uncanny habit of taking things absolutely literally.

CRicket

Families *Gryllidae* (Crickets); *Gryllotalpidae* (Mole Crickets)

Etymology Middle English, from Old French *criquet*, from the verb *criquer*, to creak.

VaRieties
Old World Field Cricket (*Gryllus campestris*); House Cricket (*Acheta domestica*); Common Mole Cricket (*Gryllotalpa gryllotalpa*).

FolkloRe
In the 17th century, it was believed that if the crickets forsook the chimney corner of a house where they had lived for many years, there would be a death in the house (1620); if a cricket chirped in a house where there were none before, someone would die (1650).

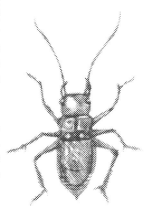

In East Anglia, it was believed to be an ill omen if crickets left a house they had been living in (1830). In Craven, Yorkshire (1910), it was lucky to hear a cricket whistling.

Throughout the 19th century, it was believed to be unlucky to kill a cricket, possibly because it was a breach of hospitality.

Symbolism
In the West, the cricket is a symbol of the domestic hearth. In China, it represents summer and courage.

Poetry

To Larr

No more shall I, since I am driven hence,
Devote to thee my graines of Frankincense:
No more shall I from mantle-trees hang downe,
To honour thee, my little parsley crown:
No more shall I (I feare me) to thee bring
My chives of Garlick for an offering:
No more shall I, from henceforth, heare a quire
Of merry crickets by my Country fire.
Go where I will, thou luckie Larr stay here,
Warme by a glit'ring chimnie all the yeare.

Robert Herrick, 1591-1674

Dragonfly

Latin name   various

Families   *Odonata* (Dragonflies); *Zygoptera* (Damsel Flies); *Anisoptera* (Giant Dragonflies)

Element Air

Etymology   dragon from Greek *drakon*, a serpent; fly from Old English *fleoge*

Symbolism
Because of its erratic flight, the dragonfly signifies instability. Like the butterfly, it represents immortality and regeneration.

In indigenous American symbolism, it denotes swiftness, activity, and the whirlwind.

In China, it represents summer, instability, and weakness.   In Japan it denotes irresponsibility and unreliability, but it is also a national emblem.

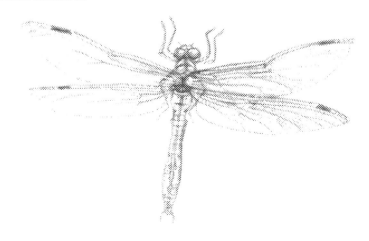

Firefly

Latin name *Lampyris noctiluca*

Family *Lampyridae*

These beautiful little beetles are seen on summer nights on heathland, the edge of woods, and in damp forest clearings. Both males and females give off light.

In Buddhism, the firefly signifies shallow knowledge incapable of creating enough light to dispel the darkness of ignorance.

Fly

Latin name various

Family *Ffimoxidae, Hippoboscidae*, etc.

Order *Diptera*

Deities Marmoo

Varieties

There are about 75,000 species of fly. The hoverflies are useful because their larvae eat aphids. Hoverflies resemble bees and wasps. They include the Currant Hover-fly (*Syrphus ribesii*), the Bee-fly (*Bombylius major*), and the Drone-fly (*Eristalis tenax*).

The Fruit-fly (*Drosophila funebris*) feeds on fermenting sour substances. Some species of Fruit-fly, such as *Drosophila melanogaster*, are used in the study of genetics because they form interesting mutations. The Small House-fly (*Hamalomyia canicularis*) is attracted to lights; the Common House-fly (*Musca domestica*) often contaminates food. The larvae of the Blow-fly (*Calliphora vomitoria*) live in refuse and can cause disease. The bite of the Horse-fly or Cleg (*Haematopota pluvialis*) can be very painful. St Mark's Fly (*Bibio marci*) appears early in Spring. The Green-bottle (*Lucilia silvarum*) lays its eggs in the nostrils of toads. The larvae cause the toad a very painful death. (Horse-ticks or Forest-flies) *Drosophilidae* (Fruit-flies), *Calliphoridae* (Blow-flies), *Muscidae* (True Flies), *Larvaevoridae* (Caterpillar-flies),

The Common Stable-fly (*Stomoxys calcitrans*) is common in cattle country, and transmits diseases such as anthrax and cholera. Other members of the Blow-fly family are the Bluebottle (*Calliphora vicina*), which lays its eggs in excrement, animal carcasses, cheese, and meat; the Gold Blow-fly (*Lucilia caesar*) which lays its eggs in rotting animal carcasses and human excreta; and the Common Flesh-fly (*Sarcophaga carnaria*). The

149

Caterpillar-fly (*Exorista larvarum*) lays its eggs in caterpillars, usually those of the burnet moth; the larvae eat the caterpillar.

Etymology from Old English *fleoge, flyge*, Old Saxon & Old High German *flioga*, from West Germanic *fleugo* or *fleugjo*, from Germanic *fleugan*, to fly

Deity Beelzebub/Baalzebul

Folklore
Witches were often believed to have flies as familiars. In County Durham, it was believed to be lucky to have a fly in the house between Christmas and New Year.

Mythology
In Syrian mythology, Beelzebub, the Lord of the Flies, was a personification of the destructive power of swarms of insects. In Phoenicia, Beelzebub was the agent of destruction and putrefaction. The name was originally Baalzebul, meaning "Baal the prince", but he later came to be known as lord of the flies or the dunghill. A Chaldaean goddess, Orore, was a creatrix portrayed with the head of an insect, a pregnant belly, and sometimes a giant eye.

The name Beelzebub later became associated with the Christian devil. The fly is usually associated with evil and corruption; devils were often portrayed as flies, and in Christianity, the fly denotes evil, pestilence, and sin. The fly was depicted in Christian art as disease, with the goldfinch as Christ. In Greek mythology, Bellerophon attempted to fly up to heaven on Pegasus, but Zeus sent a gadfly to sting the horse, and Bellerophon was thrown off.

The Aborigines of south-eastern Australia tell the story of Nungeena the Mother Spirit and Baiame the Father Spirit, who saved the world from the swarms of insects released by Marmoo the Spirit of Evil, which were devastating the land. Nungeena and Baiame created birds to eat the insects.

150

Grasshopper

Latin name *Tettigonia viridissima* (Katydid or Green Grasshopper)

Families *Tettigoniidae* (Green Grasshoppers); *Acrididae* (Field Grasshoppers)

Sub-order Saltatoria

Order *Orthoptera* (Straight-winged Insects)

Folk names Katydid

Etymology grass- from Old English *graes* from Germanic *grasam*; -hopper from the verb to hop, derived from Old English *hoppian*, Middle High German *hopfen*, Old Norse *hoppa*

Symbolism

In China, the grasshopper symbolises abundance, many sons, the virtues, and good luck.

In Europe, it represents irresponsibility, improvidence, and the pleasures of Summer.

In ancient Greece, a golden grasshopper signified nobility, a native aristocrat.
In Hebrew symbolism, it denotes a scourge.

Poetry

The Grasshopper
O thou that swing'st upon the waving hair
    Of some well-fillèd oaten beard,
Drunk every night with a delicious tear
    Dropt thee from heaven, where thou wert rear'd:

The joys of earth and air are thine entire,
    That with thy feet and wings dost hop and fly:
And when thy poppy works, thou dost retire
    To thy carved acorn-bed to lie.

Up with the day, the Sun thou welcom'st then,
    Sport'st in the gilt plaits of his beams,
And all these merry days mak'st merry men,
    Thyself, and melancholy streams.

Richard Lovelace

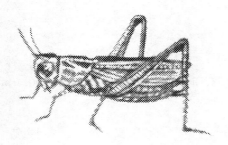

Ladybird

Latin name various (see below)

Family Coccinellidae

Folk name Mari Gorri, Lady Lanners, King Gollowa, Bishop Barnabee, Doctor Ellison, God Almighty's Cow, lady-cow

Planet Moon

Deity Mari

Polarity Feminine

Element Earth, Fire

Varieties

Seven-spot Ladybird (*Coccinella septempunctata*); Two-spot Ladybird (*Adalia bipunctata*); Eyed Ladybird (*Anatis ocellata*); Four-spot Ladybird (*Exochomus quadripustulatus*).

Folklore

In Scotland, the ladybird is called Lady Lanners, King Gollowa, Bishop Barnabee, and Doctor Ellison. In Shropshire it was called the lady-cow; in Herefordshire, the marygold. In Essex, it was unlucky to kill a ladybird; if you did, you had to bury it, stamp on the ground three times, and say the traditional rhyme:

"Ladybird, ladybird, fly away home
Your house is on fire and your children have flown."

In Somerset it was called God Almighty's Cow; it was very unlucky to kill one. In County Durham and Edinburgh it was regarded as lucky if a ladybird landed on you.

Mythology

In Catalonia, Mari was the supreme goddess of the Basques. She was sometimes an earth goddess, but mainly lunar. It is within her power to control rain and drought. She lives in the depths of the earth, but crosses the sky at night. Her husband or son is called Sugaar, the male serpent. She travels across the sky in a cart pulled by four horses, in the form of a burning sickle or crescent, riding on a broomstick in a ball of fire, or engulfed in flames. Her divinatory animal is the ladybird, known as Mari Gorri (Red Mari), and it is often asked to predict the weather. Mari's other totem animals are the horse, the heifer, and the crow or the raven.

Poetry

"Ladybird, ladybird, fly away home
Your house is on fire and your children have flown."
                    (traditional rhyme)

This lady-fly I take from off the grass,
Whose spotted back might scarlet red surpass.
Fly, Lady-Bird, North, South, or East or West,
Fly where the man is found that I love best.

He leaves my hand, see to the West he's flown,
To call my True-love from the faithless Town.
                    (Gay, *Shepherd's Week*, 1714)

Doctor, Doctor Ellison, where will I be married?
East, or west, or south, or north?
Take ye flight, and fly away.
                    (From the north of Scotland, 1818)

Lady Lady Lanners,
Lady Lady Lanners,
Tak up your clowk about your head,
An' flee away to Flanners.
Flee ower firth, and flee ower fell,

Flee ower pule and rinnan' well,
Flee ower muir, and flee ower mead,
Flee ower livan, flee ower dead,
Flee ower corn, an' flee ower lea,
Flee ower river, flee ower sea,
Flee ye east or flee ye west,
Flee till him that lo'es me best.

(From Clydesdale, 1818)

King, King Gollowa,
Up your wings and flie awa',
Over land and over sea,
Tell me where my love can be.
(From Kincardineshire, 1842)

Bishop, Bishop Barnabee,
Tell me when my wedding be:
If it be tomorrow day,
Take your wings and fly away!
Fly to the east, fly to the west,
Fly to them that I love best!
(origin unknown, 1850)

Lady-cow, lady-cow, fly away, flee!
Tell me which way my wedding's to be,
Up hill, or down hill, or towards the Brown Clee!
(Shropshire, 1883)

Marygold, marygold, flitter to fly,
Tell me where doth my lady-love lie?
(Herefordshire, 1912)

Lady-bird, lady-bird, fly away home,
Thy house is on fire, thy children all roam;
Except little Nan, who sits in her pan,
Weaving gold laces as fast as she can."
  (Jesmond, Northumbria; a lady-bird was set free with this rhyme)

155

Locust

In China, the great general Pa-Cha was invoked to ward off locusts; he was depicted as a man with the beak and feet of a bird and clawed hands, wearing a kilt.

Moth

In the seventh century, St. Eligius, Bishop of Noyon in Flanders, warned his congregation to avoid the heathen practice of celebrating the festivals of moths and mice.

The moth was associated with the goddess Psyche in Greece.

Mosquito

In China, the mosquito symbolised rebellion and wickedness.

Praying Mantis

Latin name *Mantis religiosa*

Order *Mantodea*

Etymology from Greek *manteia*, divination

Deities Cagn, Hyrax

Mythology
The Bushmen have a praying mantis deity called Kaggen or Cagn.
He is a Trickster figure. His wife is called Hyrax.

Symbolism
In China, the praying mantis is a
symbol of greed. In Greece, it
was associated with divination
(manteia). In Christianity, it
represents prayer and adoration.

Scarab

Latin name *Scarabeus sacer*

Polarity Masculine

Family *Scarabaeidae*

Planet Sun & Moon

Etymology
from Latin *scarabaeus*, from Greek *skarabeios*

Deities Khephra

Varieties
The species which was most revered in Egypt was *Scarabeus sacer*.
It is part of the Chafer family (*Scarabaeidae*).

Folklore
The ancient Egyptians believed that all scarabs were male, so they
represented virility, the power of self-generation, and masculine
fertility. They were also supposed to possess the secret of eternal
life (if they were of one sex only, they would be unable to reproduce), hence their use as amulets.

Mythology
Khephra or Khepera was the Egyptian scarab god, the creator of
the universe. He merged from Nu, the primeval waters. The
scarab was associated with creation because of the way it rolls
dung into a ball in which it lays its eggs. Khephra was one of the
Ogdoad of Hermopolis; he is sometimes identified with Ra.

The ancient Egyptians made brooches and amulets in the form of *Scarabeus sacer*. They were made of polished or glazed stone, metal, or glazed faience. By the time of the Thirteenth Dynasty, they were being used as seals, pendants, and signet rings.

Symbolism

In Africa and the Congo, the scarab is attributed to the Moon, and symbolises eternal renewal.

In ancient Egypt, the scarab represented the Sun, the path of the Sun, resurrection, immortality, the wisdom of the gods, and the intelligence which governs the cycles of nature.

Silkworm

Latin name *Bombyx mori*

Family *Saturniidae* (Giant Silkworm Moths)

Deities Hani-Yasu-No-Kami, Lady Horse-Head, Sien-Tsan

Etymology Silk from Old English *sioloc* or *seolec* (compare Old Norse silki) from Latin *sericum* from Greek Seres, an Oriental people; worm from Old English *wyrm*, from Old High German *wurm*, Old Norse *ormr* (serpent), Gothic *waurms*, Germanic *wurmiz*, *wurmaz*

Mythology

In Japanese mythology, the silkworm and the mulberry tree sprang from the goddess Hani-Yasu-No-Kami's head, whilst from her navel came the five cereals, hemp, millet, rice, corn, and pulses.

In China, Lady Horse-Head is the patroness of silkworm breeding; she is one of the concubines of the August Personage of Jade. Sien-Tsan is the goddess of silkworm culture. She was the wife of the early emperor-god Shen-Nung, who taught the people agriculture.

Varieties

The silkmoth (*Bombyx mori*) comes from East Asia. Silk is obtained from the cocoon after the pupa has been killed. Mulberry leaves are the only things the larvae will eat.

Tachinid fly

Latin name *Hystricia pollinosa "van der Wulp"*

Deity Dontso

Mythology

The tachnid fly is a regarded as a spiritual messenger and a bringer of news and guidance in Dineh (Navaho) mythology, because the fly has a habit of landing on people's shoulders or chest. It is called Dontso. In their sand paintings of the corn stalk which represents the stages of initiation, a flash of lightning strikes the centre of the stalk. At this point the two aspects of Dontso appear, which are called Big Fly and Little Wind.

Mammals

Antelope

Latin name various

Family *Bovidae*

Planet Moon

Zodiacal sign Capricorn

Element Earth

Etymology   Middle English from Old French *antelop* or from medieval Latin *ant(h)alopus* from late Greek *anthalops*

Deities Siva, Soma, Chandra, Pavana; the Great Mother; Astarte, Ea, Ea-Oannes, and Marduk.

Varieties

The eland, the oryx, the gazelle, and the gnu are all species of antelope. The chamois is a member of the Goat-antelopes, a subfamily of the Caprinae. The largest member of the antelope family is the Giant Eland (*Taurotragus derbianus*). There are two species of this eland, which are found in most parts of Africa. The Oryx genus includes the straight-horned antelopes (*Hippotraginae*), the South African Gemsbok (*Oryx gazella*), the White or Scimitar Oryx (*Oryx algazel*). Antelopes also include the Blackbuck (*Antilope cervicapra*), the Brindled Gnu (*Gorgon taurinus*), and the *Strepsicerotini* group, which is characterised by spirally twisted horns.

The Pronghorns (*Antilocapridae*) found in America are not true antelopes. They are unique in being the only hollow-horned ungulate to have branched horns and to shed them annually.

Mythology

The Bushmen (Kung and San) of Africa, believe that the dwelling place of their god is known only to the antelope, and that the god can manifest himself in the form of an antelope.

In Asia Minor and Europe, the antelope is associated with the Moon and the Great Mother.

In Egypt, the antelope was sacrificed to Set, but could also represent Osiris and Horus as the enemies of Set. The goddess Sati or Satet, whose name means 'to sow seed', and who personified the rain, was depicted with a vulture head-dress, and the white crown of Upper Egypt surmounted by antelope horns.

In Vedic mythology, the antelope is the emblem of Shiva, the Creator and Destroyer, the male generative principle in Hinduism. Soma (god of the water of life, the Moon, the sacred soma, and light; one of the eight divine attendants of Indra) and Chandra (probably a pre-Vedic Moon-god, possibly related to the Romani name for the Moon, O Chion *) have chariots drawn by antelopes; and Pavana, god of the winds, has an antelope as a steed.

In the Jain religion, there is a deity called Harinagamesi, the man with the antelope head, who is the general of the heavenly infantry.

In Sumerian myth, the antelope is a form of Marduk (the god of the spring sun, also known as Bel, and the champion of the gods, who killed Tiamat, the Great Dragon) and of Ea, the Babylonian creator-god. Ea-Oannes is 'the antelope of the subterranean ocean'

* Footnote: The Romani or Gypsies probably originated in the Sind valley in India, and began to migrate westwards about 1000 c.e.

163

(called the Apsu) and 'the antelope of creation'. Ea-Oannes is a combination of Ea, who divided the Apsu (the primordial waters) and Oannes, a deity who brought culture to humanity, and appeared in a form half-man, half-fish. This deity was the origin of the Zodiacal sign of Capricorn. The dragon aspect (its fierceness) is interchangeable with the bull, buffalo, or the cow. The antelope as a Moon animal is sacred to Astarte, the fertility goddess of the Semitic cultures, known as the lady of horses and chariots, depicted as lioness-headed; also associated with the planet Venus and the sea.

Among the Hopi, pronghorns are a source of food. Before the hunt, prayers are said and offerings are made to make the antelope willing to be caught. After being caught they are covered with a white blanket or manta, then they are smudged (smoke is blown over them), an act of blessing or a prayer offering of thanks. (Other large animals are treated with the same respect.) Members of the antelope clan are believed to be able to treat problems with urination. Rabbits, deer and prong horns are regarded as related species because of their tendency to speed, lope, and circle back. The rabbit is the smallest animal to be accorded the *manta* ceremony.

Symbolism
In Heraldry, the antelope is depicted as fierce, strong, and dangerous, with a tiger's head, a stag's body, a unicorn's tail, and tusks on its nose - a fearsome beast from the imagination of some medieval artist.

Ape

Latin name various

Family *Pongidae*

Etymology from Old English *apa*, Old High German *affo*, Old Norse *api*, from Germanic **apan-*

Deities Hanuman, Kenemet, Hapi, Nephthys

Varieties
The Great or Anthropoid Apes (*Pongidae*) include four genera of Apes. These are the Gibbons (*Hylobates*), the Orang-utan (*Pongo pygmaeus*), the Chimpanzee (*Pan troglodytes*), and the Gorilla (*Gorilla gorilla*).

Mythology
In ancient Egypt, the ape was a symbol of Kenemet, an early Egyptian mother goddess, who was later replaced by Mut, the Great Mother, creatrix, and Great Sorceress. One of the four sons of Horus the Younger was Hapi, the dog- or ape-headed guardian of the lungs, associated with Earth, the North, and the goddess Nephthys.

In the Cameroons, the Yaunde tribe have as their supreme deity Zamba, who created the Earth and came to live on it. He had four sons: N'kokon the wise, Otukut the idiot, Ngi the gorilla, and Wo the chimpanzee. Zamba taught the Yaunde people, and allocated their duties.

In Hinduism, the ape signifies benevolence and gentleness, and is an emblem of the monkey-god Hanuman, who played such a vital part in the epic of the Ramayana, by building a bridge across the sea to Ceylon so that Rama and his army could rescue Sita from the clutches of the demon-king Ravana. Hanuman was the general of a king of the monkeys. (See monkey)

Symbolism

In Christianity, the ape is a symbol of malice, cunning, lust, sin, unseemliness (!), levity, luxury, Satan, "perverters of the Word", and idolatry. An ape in chains symbolises the conquering of sin. An ape with an apple in its mouth symbolises the Fall. The Christian symbolism of animals frequently reflects a dualist world-view, with the animal or bird symbolising either something wholly good or something wholly evil; there is never a holistic approach.

Ass / Donkey

Latin name *Equus asinus*

Family *Equidae*

Order *Perissodactyla* (odd-toed ungulates)

Polarity Yin

Element Earth

Planet Moon

Deities Set, Dionysos, Typhon, Priapus, Cronos, Saturn, Epona, Ravana.

Etymology The word "donkey" has only been in use since the late eighteenth century; it was at that time pronounced to rhyme with monkey. The names donkey and ass are interchangeable. The derivation of the word ass is from Old English *assa*, from Old Celtic *as(s)in*, from Latin *asinus*. The word donkey is possibly derived from *Duncan*, or from *dun*, brown.

Varieties

An ass is a small, usually grey, long-eared animal of the horse genus. A mule is the offspring of a male donkey and a mare, and is a sterile hybrid. The offspring of a stallion and a female donkey is

called a hinny. Members of the Horse family (*Equidae*) include zebras, horses, kulan, onagers, wild asses and kiang (*Equus hemionus*). The domestic ass (*Equus asinus*) is probably descended from the Nubian Ass (*Equus asinus africanus*), and may have been domesticated earlier than the horse.

Folklore

The ass was a central feature in the Feast of Fools, usually held on St. Stephen's Day (26 December), St. John's Day (27 December), and Holy Innocents' Day (28 December). The Mass was burlesqued, and the usual responses were often replaced by braying. Obscene jests and dances and songs were also customary. The Feast of Fools was sometimes known as the Feast of Asses (*festum asinorum*). In some areas the Feast of Asses was a separate festival in its own right. It was very popular in the Middle Ages, and was not suppressed until the Reformation; in France it survived a lot longer. It was officially a festival commemorating the flight of Mary, Joseph, and the infant Jesus into Egypt, but it has some strangely Pagan overtones. In Beauvais, France, the ass procession went right into the church, and a girl stood by the altar with the ass. At the end of each part of the mass, the congregation would bray. Even the priest had to bray three times at the conclusion of the Mass. In some places, the ass was decked with a golden canopy carried by four distinguished canons of the church, and those who attended the service had to wear festive clothing. A special hymn was sung, the last verse of which was:

Amen, dicas, Asine	Say Amen, o Ass,
Jam satur de gramine.	Now you've had your fill of grass,
Amen, amen, itera,	Repeat Amen, Amen,
Aspernare vetera.	Ancient paths are left behind.

The god of the Jews had from ancient times been believed by outsiders to be an ass; it is possible that theriomorphic overtones crept into this festival. The ass is usually depicted as one of the animals in any Nativity scene, and Mary is often depicted riding on an ass, particularly in pictures of the flight of the holy family into Egypt. There is, however, no mention of this in the Bible, although the ass does appear bearing Christ on his triumphal entry into Jerusalem, treading on the palm leaves strewn by the inhabitants. Folklore has it that the cross-shaped marking on the donkey's back and shoulder was conferred on the animal by Christ for performing this service. The donkey's cross marking was also believed to have magical healing properties. Hairs taken from the cross marking were used as a charm. These hairs were also regarded (as late as 1853) as a cure for whooping cough, worn in a black silk bag hung round the neck. Presumably this worked by sympathetic magic, in that the donkey's bray resembles the cough of a sufferer. A similar remedy was used in Dorset in 1892 for bronchitis and whooping cough, but it had to be nine hairs from the cross marking of a white she-ass, also worn in a silk bag around the neck. In Kent (1885), hairs taken from the cross marking were sprinkled on a slice of bread and butter and given to a person with measles to eat. In Herefordshire (1912) teething children were given a necklace woven of the hairs from a donkey's cross.

Donkeys were also used for cures by transference, i.e. in the belief that the illness would be transferred to the animal. In Keswick, Cumbria (1823), the practice was to pass the child three times under the ass's stomach as a cure for whooping cough. In Hampstead (1827), it was three times over and three times under the donkey (also for whooping cough). In Hoxton (1845), the same method was used for rickets, with the added refinement that the mother of the child did the odd numbers, and the owner of the donkey did the even numbers. Three times over, three times under was also the method in Honiton in Devon (1862) for consumption, but it had to be done at a full Moon at a crossroads. Donkeys were also used as a cure for scarlet fever in Devon. The procedure in Cornwall (1865) was the most complicated. A three year old female donkey must be used. The child was passed naked over its back and under its belly nine times. Then three teaspoonfuls of milk were drawn from its teats, and three hairs from its belly and three hairs from its back were steeped in the milk for three hours, and the child drank this in three sips. The whole procedure was repeated on three consecutive mornings.

Note the importance of three and nine in this remedy (traditionally magical numbers in the Northern Tradition). In Glasgow (1887), two mothers stood on either side of the donkey, and the child had to face the ground while going underneath the donkey, and the sky while going above it. This process was carried out three times, then the mother took her child to the head of the donkey and gave it biscuits or bread to eat out of the child's lap. In some farming areas (Yorkshire, 1799; Durham, 1799; Worcestershire, 1900; and Wiltshire, 1973), it was believed that keeping a donkey with cows or horses would prevent them from dropping calves or foals prematurely.

Its association with Christ has not stopped the ass being regarded as the epitome of stupidity. The much-quoted phrase "The law is an ass" comes from Dickens' *Oliver Twist*. The donkey is probably regarded so unfavourably because it looks like a caricature of a horse. It is also associated with the jester and the Devil, however. The traditional Fool's hat had a pair of donkey's ears and a coxcomb, which symbolised both folly and obscenity. The donkey was associated with witches, who were believed to lust after its sexual potency. The donkey's bray was said to be the voice of the Devil.

The donkey has on occasion received respectful treatment on account of its association with Christ. A woman in Cambridge (1970) remembered that her grandfather had always taken his hat off to donkeys. It was also believed that if a pregnant woman met a donkey, the child would turn out pious and learned.

In China, the ass symbolises stupidity. A Chinese saying is "The year of the donkey and the month of the horse", meaning 'Never'.

Mythology

In ancient Greece, the ass was sacred to Dionysos, as a symbol of lust and licentiousness; and to Typhon as the brute beast. It was also sacred to Priapus (originally a fertility god from Asia Minor, and the protector of orchards and gardens) as the procreative principle, and to Cronos (Saturn), the god of time and restriction. Silenus (the tutor of Dionysos, and one of his retinue) was sometimes depicted riding an ass. Midas, having acquired the fatal ability to turn everything he touched into gold, and then prayed to Bacchus to take the baneful gift away from him, retired into the countryside and worshipped Pan. One day Pan challenged Apollo to a contest of musicianship; all the others who witnessed the contest preferred Apollo's lyre to Pan's pipes, but Midas preferred the music of Pan. In revenge, Apollo turned his ears into asses' ears. Embarrassed by this new turn of events, Midas tried to conceal his ears by wrapping them in a purple turban, but his barber saw them. He wanted to tell someone about what he had seen, so he went and dug a hole in the ground and whispered the secret in it. But reeds grew on the spot, and whispered in the wind "Midas has asses' ears". (See also satyr.)

For the Romans, the ass was sacred to Vesta, the goddess of fire and the hearth (both in a domestic and a ritual context). In *"The Golden Ass"* by Lucius Apuleius, the hero is transformed into an ass by magic, and has various trials and tribulations before he is restored to human form by the Goddess Isis. The story is a clear parallel of the initiatory traditions of the mystery cults (Apuleius was an initiate of the Mysteries of Isis), in that the hero becomes one with his animal nature before he can become truly human in the full sense of the word.

In Shakespeare's *A Midsummer Night's Dream*, Bottom the weaver is changed into an ass, and Titania, who has been condemned to fall in love with the first being she sees on awaking from sleep, falls in love with him. He is later restored to his former self having been thoroughly petted by Titania and her handmaidens.

Amongst the Celts, Epona (the horse goddess) was sometimes depicted riding an ass. In Europe, Mullo was the patron god of muleteers; he may originally have been a mule totem divinity (see mule).

In Egypt, the ass was a symbol of Set in his destructive aspect, of evil power lying dormant. Set was originally a sun-god of a pre-dynastic tribe which had a pig-like animal as its totem. He later became the ruler of Upper Egypt, but when the Osirian religion became prevalent, he became the chief adversary, who murdered

Osiris. His cult survived into the nineteenth dynasty; his followers, known as Typhonians, were said to have red hair. In the initiatory rites of Isis, the initiate was transformed into a red ass and then maltreated or abused, and underwent a ritual death. Set (Typhon) was the god of lust, so the initiate was tempted in every possible way; s/he had to "be" experience her/his instincts fully before being redeemed by the power of Isis. Within the secret sanctuary, the initiate became one with Osiris, dying and resurrecting. The next morning, the initiate was crowned with garlands of palm leaves and hailed as the reborn Osiris.

In Hebrew legend, there is the story of Balaam and the ass. The prophet Balaam was riding his ass, when the ass saw an angel with a drawn sword standing in road ahead, and turned aside into the field, whereupon Balaam beat her. Further on the angel appeared again, and the donkey pressed herself against the wall, crushing Balaam's foot, so he beat her again. Then the angel reappeared in a narrow place where the donkey could not turn aside, so she lay down in the road. Balaam became very angry, and beat the ass with his staff, so Yahweh gave her the ability to speak, and she asked why he was beating her when she was not in the habit of being recalcitrant. Then Balaam saw the angel, and realised that Yahweh was angry with him. In this story, the ass becomes the wise fool, humbling the pompous Balaam. It was traditional for kings, prophets, and judges to ride a white ass.

According to Islamic legend, the prophet Mohammed had a white mule called Fadda.

In the Hindu epic poem, the *Ramayana*, asses drew the chariot of Ravana, the demon king of the Rakshasas, when he abducted Sita, the bride of Rama.

Symbolism

To the Greeks the ass symbolised sloth and infatuation, lust and licentiousness. In general it is a symbol of humility, patience, peace, and fertility, but also of stupidity, obstinacy, and lewdness. As a beast of burden it is a symbol of poverty. To the Hebrews, it symbolised stubbornness. In Christianity, it symbolises Christ's nativity, the flight into Egypt, and the triumphal entry into Jerusalem. It also appears in a story about transubstantiation as a symbol of humility and spirituality, where St Anthony of Padua rebuked those who scoffed at the idea of Christ's presence in the host by offering the host to a hungry donkey; instead of eating it, the donkey knelt before it. In Sassanian symbolism, the three-legged ass is a symbol of purity and a defence against evil. It is also lunar, as the three phases of the Moon.

In general usage, the word ass is used to refer to a fool, e.g. "making an ass of oneself". Hence also the *pons asinorum* (the asses' bridge), which is the fifth proposition in the first book of Euclid's geometry, and which has proved for some to be an impassable barrier to further learning.

Don Quixote's side-kick, Sancho Panza, rides an ass called Dapple, which he rides like a patriarch. Dapple is humourously contrasted with Don Quixote's rather sad horse, Rocinante.

Another literary donkey is of course Eeyore in *Winnie-the-Pooh*, who is a melancholy beast given to introspection and living in sad boggy places. He is convinced that no-one likes him or is interested in him. However, on his birthday, Pooh and Piglet remember that it is his birthday just in time, and Pooh gives him a Useful Pot to put things in, while Piglet gives him a red balloon (which unfortunately bursts on the way) which just fits into the Useful Pot.

Aurochs

Latin name *Bos primigenus*

Family *Bovidae*

Planet Mars

Folk name Wild ox

Deity Thor; Bel, Enlil

Polarity Masculine

Element Fire

Rune Uruz / Ur

Etymology from Old High German *urohso*; *ur* (urus) + *ohso* (ox)

Varieties

The Aurochs was a fierce wild ox which is now extinct, but which once roamed Europe and Asia (see Cattle for related species).

Folklore

In ancient times, the rite of passage for Germanic tribes was for a young man to go out and kill an aurochs, bringing back its horns as proof that he had done so. The horns were greatly valued as drinking horns.

Mythology

In Assyrian and Sumerian mythology, the aurochs was the sacred animal of Bel or Enlil, ruler of heaven, earth, and fate. Enlil was the Sumerian god addressed as the 'Great Mountain' and 'Lord of the Storm'; he was also known as Rimn (Rimmon), 'wild ox'. Bel was a sky or sun god, and became an aspect of Marduk.

Symbolism

The aurochs (and the rune Ur) symbolises primeval force and energy, strength and will. It represents the spurt of growth and renewal at the beginning of Spring. It is also a symbol of Fire; just as the rune Feoh represents the primeval cow, Audhumla, licking the first man from the ice, so the rune Ur and the wild ox symbolise the first fire, which melted the ice and produced Middle-earth (Midgard).

Poetry

Ur byþ anmod anmod oferhyrned,
felafrecne deor feohte mid hornum
mære morstapa; þæt is modig wuht.

(The Aurochs is fearless and huge of horn,
 a ferocious beast, it fights with horns,
 a famous moorstalker, that is a mettlesome wight.)

Anglo-Saxon Rune Poem

Baboon

Latin name *Papio spp.*   **Polarity** Masculine

Planet Sun

Etymology Middle English, from Old French *babuin*, or medieval Latin *babewynus*

Deities Thoth, Hapi, Babi, Khons

Varieties
The Yellow Baboon (*Papio cynocephalus lestes*) comes from central Africa. The Chacma Baboon (*Papio porcarius*) lives in the dry upland areas of South Africa.

Mythology
In Egypt, the baboon was sacred to Thoth (Tehuti). Thoth was sometimes depicted as a baboon, because baboons chatter at dawn, greeting the rising sun.

Thoth was one of earliest Egyptian gods, and was represented as an ibis-headed man or a dog-headed ape. He was the inventor of numbers, arithmetic, geometry, astronomy, and other sciences. He knew the magic formulae for the dead to pass through the underworld.

He was also a moon god. Another Egyptian baboon deity was Babi, a fierce and dangerous god representing virility and the warrior aspect of the Pharaoh. Babi's phallus is the bolt of the door of heaven, and the mast of the ferryboat that travels through the Underworld. There were spells to protect people from him, but he could also be invoked against snakes and stormy waters. He lived on human entrails.

The baboon was also sacred to Hapi, one of the Four Sons of Horus, depicted as ape-headed or dog-headed, and the guardian of one of the Four Canopic Jars (the one containing the viscera). Another deity to whom the baboon was sacred was Khons, whose name meant the Wanderer, and who was originally a Theban moon god. Later, in the Age of Pyramids, Khons was held to be the son of Amun-Ra and Mut, and was called upon in times of war.

Symbolism
The Egyptians called the baboon 'Hailer of the Dawn'. Depicted with uplifted hands, it symbolised wisdom saluting the rising sun.

Badger

Latin name *Meles meles*

Family *Mustelidae*

Planet Moon

Polarity Masculine

Element Earth

Folk name Brock, *huan* (Chinese), *tanuki* (Japanese)

Etymology 16th c., perhaps from *badge*, because of its white forehead mark

Varieties

The European Badger (*Meles meles*) is the largest member of the *Mustelidae* family found in Europe.

Other members of this family include weasels, stoats, pine martens, ferrets, and otters (sub-family *Lutrinae*).

Folklore

In the Kalahari the honeyguide bird sings to guide the Bushmen to the nests of bees. The honeybadger has also learnt to follow the honeyguide. The Bushman or woman will extract the honeycombs and share them with the badger and the bird.

The other name for the badger, brock, is related to the adjective brockit or brocked, meaning variegated, particularly black and white. It comes from a Celtic word via Old English *brocc*. In Gaelic, the word is *broc*.

According to Japanese folklore, the badger turns himself into a fat-bellied abbot or mendicant monk, "out of his mind with excitement, beating on his stomach" (Shikitei Samba).

Symbolism

The Chinese word for badger, *huan*, is a homonym of the word meaning 'to enjoy oneself, to be glad'. Hence it is shown with the magpie as a symbol of happiness, the magpie being joy from heaven, the badger being joy on earth. The badger is a lunar, yin animal symbolising supernatural powers, playfulness and mischief. In Japan, the badger represents supernatural powers, and is said to produce will-of-the-wisps and to act as a *fata morgana*.

In Europe, the badger is regarded as a symbol of clumsiness, and the steed of Avarice.

Mythology

Among the Hopi, the badger is regarded as the little brother of the bear. The *katsina* (spirit) of the badger is called Honan, and the *katsina* of the bear is called Honau. The badger is believed to have curative powers derived from its intimate association with roots and plants. The badger can cure snakebite, arthritis, and rheumatism. People of the badger clan can also cure these ailments. The Hopi who belong to the badger clan regard Badger as an ancestor and the badgers as their relatives, but they do not necessarily believe that they are directly descended from the badger, who is also represented in *katsina* form.

Literature

In *The Wind in the Willows* by Kenneth Grahame, Badger is a dependable, sensible character, very wise and gruff, but likeable. He is also brave and fierce, hospitable and kindly.

Bandicoot

Latin name *Bandicota indica*

Family *Peramelidae* (20 species)

Deity Karora

Etymology from Telugu *pandikokku*, pig-rat

Varieties

The bandicoot is a ratlike marsupial mammal of a family found in Australia, Tasmania, and New Guinea. Bandicoots are mainly carnivorous, eating insects, worms, and grubs. They are about the size of rabbits, and are shy and retiring creatures, building nests from grass and leaves amongst dense vegetation.

Mythology

In Australia, Karora is the creator god of the bandicoot totem tribe. Karora himself is a bandicoot. He dreamt in the primeval darkness, and caused the Sun to appear; he then created bandicoots, and then the first man.

Bat

Latin name various

Order *Chiroptera*

Polarity Feminine

Planet Moon

Sub-orders *Megachiroptera* (fruit-bats), *Microchiroptera* (insectivorous bats)

Deities Persephone,

Folk name Fledermaus, Bawkie-bird Camazotz,

Etymology 16th c. alternative of ME *bakke*, *Fu Hsing* from a Scandinavian word.

Varieties

Rhinolophidae: Greater Horseshoe Bat (*Rhinolophus ferrumequinum*), Lesser Horseshoe Bat (*R. hipposideros*). *Vespertilionidae*: Whiskered Bat (*Myotis mystacinus*), Natterer's Bat (*M. nattereri*), Bechstein's Bat (*M. bechsteini*), Mouse-eared Bat (*M. myotis*), Daubenton's Bat (*M. daubentoni*), Serotine Bat (*Eptesicus serotinus*), Leisler's Bat (*Nyctalus leisleri*), Noctule Bat (*N. noctula*), Common Pipistrelle (*Pipistrellus pipistrellus*), Nathusis Pipistrelle (*P. nathusis*), Barbastelle Bat (*Barbastella barbastellus*), Long-eared Bat (*Plecotus auritus*), Grey Long-eared Bat (*P. austriacus*). All these bats are found in Britain, and are *Microchiroptera* (insectivorous bats). There are 831 known species of *Microchiroptera*, and 150 known species of *Megachiroptera* (fruit bats). Bats are mammals, not birds, but being winged, were regarded as birds by many cultures.

Folklore
The indigenous Americans regard the bat as a bringer of rain. In a Chinese folk-tale, the bat did not go to the phoenix's (Feng-huang) birthday party because it claimed to be a quadruped; later on it did not go to the unicorn's (Ky-lin) birthday party, claiming to be a bird. Both the unicorn and the phoenix had to admire its cunning. In Scotland, the bat is called the bawkie-bird, and is connected with witchcraft. In England, a bat in the house was said to be an omen of death, especially if it knocked over a candle. It was also deemed unlucky to see a bat during the day. According to *The Gospell of Distaues* (1507), bats flying round a house is an omen that it will burn down. A bat in your room or flying against your window was held to be an omen of misfortune (Somerset, 1923). In Shropshire, it was regarded as very unlucky to kill a bat or to bring one into the house.

Mythology
The bat is an attribute of Persephone as Queen of the Underworld; it is a symbol of Fu Hsing, the Chinese god of happiness; and among the Quiche tribe of Guatemala the bat is a god, Camazotz (the equivalent of the Mayan deity Zotzilaha Chimalman). In the mythos of the Kulin and Wotjobaluk tribes of S. E. Australia, Balayang the Bat discovers the two ancestors of women, Kunnawara (Black Swan) and Kururuk (Native Companion) in the river mud and takes them to the creator god Bunjil, who gives them life, and says, "Man is not complete without you, nor will you be complete without him." The bat is also the totem animal of the men of the Wotjobaluk tribe.

Symbolism

In Africa, the bat is ambivalent, symbolising perspicacity as well as darkness and obscurity. To the alchemists, it represented the androgyne, as being of dual nature (both bird and mouse). In Buddhism, it signifies a darkened understanding. In Chinese symbolism, the bat is yin because it is nocturnal. The word for bat, *fu*, is a homophone of the word for happiness, implying good luck, wealth, longevity, and peace. Two bats indicate good wishes and are an emblem of Shou-hsing, god of longevity. Five bats symbolise the Five Blessings (health, wealth, long life, peace, happiness). A white bat symbolises longevity, referring to a story of a 1000-year-old bat hanging head downwards from a bough. A red bat symbolises good fortune (red being the Chinese lucky colour).

In Christianity the bat is 'the bird of the Devil', an incarnation of the prince of darkness (Satan is depicted with bat's wings). As a supposed hybrid of bird and rat, it is a symbol of duplicity and hypocrisy; as haunting ruins and lonely places, it symbolises melancholy. In European folklore the bat represents black magic, witchcraft, cunning, wisdom, and revenge. To the Hebrews, the bat denoted impurity and idolatry. In Japanese symbolism, it is unhappy restlessness, a chaotic state.

Poetry

> *"Bat, bat,*
> *Come under my hat."* (Nursery rhyme)

> *"Come into the garden, Maud,*
> *For the black bat, Night, has flown"*
>   (from *Maud*, by Alfred, Lord Tennyson)

> *"By day the bat is cousin to the mouse,*
> *He likes the attic of an ageing house -*
> *But something is amiss or out of place*
> *When mice with wings can wear a human face."*
>   (from *The bat*, by Theodore Roethke)

183

Bear

Latin name *Ursus arctos*   **Polarity** Feminine

Family *Ursidae*   **Element** Earth

Folk Name Bruin   **Planet** Moon

Deities Artemis, Callisto, Artio, Andarta

Etymology from Old English *bera*, Old High German *bero,* West Germanic *bero*

Varieties

The Brown bear (*Ursus arctos*) is the only species of bear which survives in Europe. The Himalayan Black Bear (*Selenarctos thibetanus*) is found in south and central Asia. The Sloth Bear (*Melursus ursinus*) lives in India and Sri Lanka. The smallest bear is the Malayan or Sun Bear (*Helarctos malayanus*), which is only 4'6" long. The largest bear is the Baribal or American Black Bear (*Ursus americanus*); the second largest is the Polar Bear (*Thalarctos maritimus*). The last wild bear in England was killed a thousand years ago; even in North America, there are only seven hundred grizzly bears left. In the 1970s, the numbers of brown bear were increasing in Poland and Czechoslovakia.

Folklore

There is considerable evidence that the tradition of the Berserkers represented the remnants of a bear-cult. The word berserk (which is used nowadays to mean flying into a rage) is derived from the Old Norse, and means 'bear-sark' (bear shirt). The berserkers possibly wore bear-skin shirts in order to draw on the strength of the bear. Similarly, there was a technique practised by Norse warriors, called 'bear's warmth', where warriors sat naked in the snow and generated their own warmth. (A similar technique is still practised by Tibetan monks.) The berserker warriors were also reputed to be shapeshifters. The technique of shapeshifting was known as *hamrammr*; sometimes it involved manipulating the perceptions of observers to make them believe they were seeing a bear; at other times it involved an out-of-body experience for the practitioner. For example, Bothvar Bjarki (a famous berserker) fought in the army of King Hrolf of Denmark in the form of a bear; meanwhile his human body lay as if sleeping in his quarters. The name Beowulf (bee-wolf) may well be a kenning for 'bear', as bears like honey. Two kings of Mercia had bear elements in their names: Beornred (755 CE) and Beornwulf (821-3 CE).

In the Middle Ages, it was thought that bear cubs were born without form, and licked by their mothers until they were bear-shaped (hence the expression 'licked into shape').

Among the indigenous peoples of South America, the hearth stone is called the bear, signifying underworld and cthonic powers and the point of communication with them.

The name 'Bruin' for a bear was the name of the bear in *Reynard the Fox* (the Low German beast epic), from the Dutch *bruin*, meaning 'brown'.

In medieval mummers' plays, the bear pursues little boys dressed as lambs, who are rescued by the Shepherd Hero.

The Shushwap and Thompson peoples of the north-eastern seaboard of the Americas believed that twins were related to grizzly bears. Twins had supernatural powers throughout their lives. One of these was an ability to control the weather (see also salmon).

The 'Teddy Bear' symbolises reassurance, warmth, innocence, love, dependability, and calm wisdom. Each teddy bear has a personality for the child, but the Teddy is an archetypal image. The name came from Theodore Roosevelt (US President 1901-5), who was out hunting and not having much luck, so his hosts offered him the chance to shoot a tame bear, but he refused to shoot a tame and helpless animal. The most famous teddy bear of all is Winnie-the-Pooh, whose adventures are recounted by A A Milne (and reinterpreted as a Taoist symbol by Benjamin Hoff in *The Tao of Pooh*, where P'u means 'the uncarved block' and hence innocent wisdom).

The bear even appears in urban myth. In the story of the fake Russian bear hunt, a Russian businessman tries to attract American trade by holding a bear hunt. He buys an ageing circus bear. The Americans chase the bear through the woods, and finally catch up with it in a roadside clearing. They are just about to shoot it, when a peasant rides past on a bicycle and falls off it in surprise. The bear, remembering its circus training, jumps on the bicycle and rides off as fast it can.

In fairy tales, the bear frequently appears as a bridegroom. In *Snow White and Rose Red*, the two heroines befriend the bear and help the dwarf in spite of his nastiness. Eventually the bear kills the dwarf and regains his human form as a prince. Snow White marries the prince, and Rose Red marries his brother. The reason there are so many tales where the bridegroom is an animal is that, until love comes on the scene, sex is perceived as something animal-like; hence a man is perceived as an animal until perception is transformed by love. In a Norwegian fairy tale, *East of the Sun and West of the Moon*, the bride perceives that her husband is not a white bear, as a he appears by day, but a handsome prince. Because she has seen him in human form before the appointed time, however, he has to leave her. He would have regained his human form in a year's time, but now she must wander east of the Sun and west of the Moon to find him. The tale is a metaphor for the situation whereby sex looks different by day than at night in bed; hence the husband is a bear during the day and a man at night. However, the fear of sex is something implanted by society - it is the mother who suggests that the woman should look at her husband by the light of a candle, in case he is a troll.

The origins of *Goldilocks and the Three Bears* are not very ancient; it is not a genuine folk tale, as it was not collected in its present form from the oral tradition. The story first appeared from the Scottish oral tradition as a cautionary tale in which three bears are intruded upon by a vixen. The bears eat the fox. In 1894, another version of the tale from the oral tradition became widely known, in which the intruder helped herself to milk, sat in the chairs and rested in the beds of the bears, which lived in a castle in the woods. The bears tried to throw the intruder into the fire, drown her, or drop her from the church steeple. In a version by Robert Southey (1837), the intruder is an old woman, but she escapes. In 1849, Joseph Cundall published a version of the tale where the intruder was called Silver Hair, which was the origin of the name Goldilocks (which first appeared in 1904). In *Mother Goose's Fairy Tales* (1878), the three bears became Father, Mother, and Baby Bear. The story then became much more popular, as it reflected the situation of a stranger intruding on family life, rather than merely a cautionary tale. I have a postcard with a picture of Mother and Father Bear looking on while Baby Bear, looking at his empty porridge bowl, says "How in God's name can a small bear get the nourishment he needs if people steal the sodding food from under your very nose?"

Mythology

Cults of the bear have existed since earliest times. Neanderthal bear shrines have been found with bear skulls and bones interred ritually with human bones. There is one of these in the Alps. The book *The Clan of the Cave Bear* by Jean M Auel gives an interesting conjectural picture of Neanderthal life and customs. The bear is also one of the oldest sacrificial animals. Hunter-gatherer peoples revered the bear as a symbol of strength (and a source of food). In areas where farming was the means of sustenance, the bear ceased to be revered, as it was a symbol of the wilderness, which had to be kept at bay.

The bear was an attribute of Artio, a Celtic Moon goddess attended by bears, and probably the goddess of Berne in Switzerland (Berne means 'bears'); she may have been the consort of Esus (god of the Essuvi and god of agriculture, also depicted cutting down a tree). Artio was depicted sitting by a tree in front of a huge bear, with a basket of fruit beside her, possibly signifying that she was also a goddess of plenty. The bear was a lunar animal amongst the Celts. It is also associated with Arthur, whose name means 'bear'. A Celtic depiction of Minerva from Lavington in Wiltshire depicts her with a bear's head for a head-dress and her foot on an owl. At Risingham in Norfolk, the divine bear Matunus was invoked (the name may be related to Mathonwy in the *Mabinogion*). A small cameo of a bear, which may have been imported, was found at South Shields. A bear also appears with the depiction of the horned god on the Meigle stone from Perthshire. Another Celtic bear goddess was Andarta, probably meaning 'powerful bear'. Many Celtic names were derived from the word for bear (*matus* in Gaulish, *math* in Welsh).

In ancient Greece, the bear was sacred to Artemis (goddess of the Moon and of hunting), and an attribute of Atalanta and Euphemia. Girls participating in the rites of Artemis of Brauronia were called she-bears and wore yellow robes; they performed a bear dance as part of the rite. Adonis was killed by a bear, an aspect of Aphrodite. Artemis turned Callisto into a bear; this was probably a late myth. Callisto was originally a Greek goddess of the Moon, to whom the she-bear was sacred amongst the Arcadians. The region of Arcadia is named after her son, Arcas, whose father was Zeus. In another version of the myth, it was Hera who turned Callisto into a bear out of jealousy. Zeus then set Callisto and Arcas in the sky as constellations (she as Ursa Major, and he as Ursa Minor).

The name Callisto means 'beautiful'. She was seen as the axis on which everything turns, because of her association with the constellation of Ursa Major. She was also called Helice (that which turns); the willow-tree was also sacred to her. At her festival, two little girls dressed as bears attacked the boys taking part. Yet another version of the myth connecting her to Ursa Major was that she was an Arcadian nymph turned into a bear by Zeus. Her son Arcas was hunting in the forest, and would have killed her but for the intervention of Zeus, who turned him into a bear and placed them both in the heavens as constellations.

In Hindu myth, Jambavati, the wife of Krishna, is one of the family of Jambavan, King of the Bears.

In Norse and Teutonic myth, the bear is sacred to Thor. The she-bear Atla (grandmother) represents the feminine principle; the he-bear Atli represents the masculine principle. The name Atli is sometimes given to Thor. The Berserkers were also associated with bears. In mythology, they were the sons of Berserk, the grandson of Alfhilde and the eight-handed Starkadder. The bear is also sacred to the lunar goddesses of the waters in Scandinavian myth.

In Shamanism, the bear was a messenger of the forest spirits. Most Siberian cultures regard the bear as a mythological ancestor, as do the Aino of Japan. It is also the Animal Master, imparting wisdom to the shaman. The Ostyaks regard the bear as a messenger from the spirit world. When they hunt the bear, they honour it with a special feast and bury the bones in the forest. Among indigenous North Americans, the bear was called Grandfather Bear, and regarded as a close relative or an ancestor. It was the patron of wisdom; thought to be sleepy and not paying attention, but actually listening intently. In Chinese legend, the Great Yu, the hero who diverted the great flood which his father had been unable to stop, was a bear.

The bear is associated with the constellations Ursa Major and Ursa Minor. Ursa Major is particularly associated with Artemis and Callisto.

Symbolism
The bear is a symbol of resurrection, because it emerges from hibernation with a new-born cub in the Spring. It also symbolises new life, initiation, and rites of passage. In myths of heroes, the bear is a symbol of the Sun; in inundation myths, it is a symbol of the Moon.

In Alchemy, the bear represents the Nigredo or the prima materia. The Nigredo is the first stage of the Great Work, when the dross is burnt away, and the alchemist dies to the outer world.

Amongst indigenous Americans, the bear is a symbol of supernatural power, strength, courage, and the whirlwind.

To the Chinese, the bear represents strength and bravery. Also, the bear symbolises a man, whilst the snake stands for a woman. To dream of a bear signifies that you will have a son.

In Christianity, the bear symbolises the Devil, cruelty, greed, and carnal appetites. Because it was thought that bear cubs were born without form (see Folklore above), the bear also represented the transforming power of Christianity over the heathen. It is an emblem of St Blandina, St Gall, St Florentinus, and St Maximus. David's fight with the bear symbolises Christ's conflict with the Devil.

In Japan, the bear symbolises benevolence, strength, and wisdom. It is a culture hero and a divine messenger among the Aino.

The bear is also an emblem of the kingdoms of Persia and Russia.

In Heraldry, the bear and ragged staff was the crest of the Nevilles, and later became the device of the Earls of Warwick. The first earl (according to legend) was Arthgal of the Round Table, who adopted the bear as his emblem after having strangled one in combat. Morvid, the second earl, was said to have slain a giant with a club made from a young tree stripped of its branches, and so added the ragged staff. Later, the device was made famous by Warwick the Kingmaker, and became an inn sign. It may be, however, that originally the bear was a power or totem animal of the family, and that the ragged staff (one of Odin's attributes) was acquired through association with Odin).

Beaver

Latin name *Castor fiber*

Order *Rodentia*

Etymology Old High German *bibar*, Old Norse *björr*, from Germanic *bebruz*, from Indo-European *bhebhr's*, from the root *bhru*, brown.

Varieties
Both the European Beaver and the Canadian Beaver are forms of *Castor fiber*. The European form has paler fur.

Symbolism
The beaver is a symbol of industriousness, as in the expression "working like a beaver". In Christianity it symbolises chastity and asceticism (it was believed to castrate itself if pursued); also vigilance and peacefulness.

Literature
Beavers appear in *The Lion, the Witch, and the Wardrobe* by C S Lewis, where they help Lucy (the heroine) and Peter and Susan.

European Bison

Latin name *Bison bonasus*   **Family** *Bovidae*

Folk name Wisent

Etymology Middle English from Latin, from Germanic *wisand*

Varieties

The European Bison is not the same as either the American buffalo (*Bison bison*) or the wild aurochs (*Bos primigenus*); it is a species in its own right.

Folklore

It was said that three men could sit between the bison's two horns.

Symbolism

The bison of the Polish royal forest of Bialowieza symbolised the heroic tenacity of the Polish people and land. As a quarry for the hunt, it was important to the Polish cult of knighthood, which saw itself as descended from the ancient Sarmatian nobility. The bison was a large, ferocious, and strong animal, and was perceived as a relic of a tribal, prehistoric past. As long as the bison survived, so would Poland's military prowess.

Poetry

There is an ode to the Lithuanian Bison by the Polish poet Mikolaj Hussowski (published in 1523) *Carmen de Statura, Feritate ac Venatione Bisontis* - one thousand and seventy lines of Latin verse describing the bison, its habitat, and its heroic qualities. Hussowski was a hunter as well as a poet, the son of a Master of the Hunt of the royal forest of Bialowieza, a huge area of forest in northern Poland which symbolised the freedom of the Polish people.

Boar

Latin name *Sus scrofa*   **Polarity** Masculine

Family *Suidae*   **Element** Water

Planet Sun and Moon

Deities Brighid, Derga, Adonis, Ares, Mars, Demeter, Atalanta

Etymology from Old English *bar*, Old Saxon berswin, Old High German *ber*, from West Germanic *baira*

Varieties

The wild boar is the ancestor of domestic pigs; it is widespread in Europe, Asia, and North Africa.

Folklore

When hunting boar, it was necessary to use a spear with a cross-piece, because the boar would rush up the spear and gore the hunter if there was nothing to stop it.

In the Northern Tradition, there was a band of warriors who had the boar as their totem; they were called the Svinfylking (the Boar's Throng, also the Norse name for the Pleiades). Their battle-formation was a triangular wedge, with two champions at the front forming the rani (snout).

In a Celtic folk tale, a bishop called Caenchomrac was given a young wild pig. The clerics began to roast the pig, but a tall man emerges from the bottom of the loch and tells them that the pig they are roasting is a transformed youth, turned into a pig for rebelliousness. He and others lived in a monastery underwater. They give him the body for burial. After that the bishop goes to visit the underwater monastery several times.

In Thüringen, when the wind blows through the corn, people used to say "The Boar is rushing through the corn." In Sweden and Denmark, it was the custom at Yule to bake a loaf in the form of a boar, which is called the Boar. It was usually made from the corn of the last sheaf of the harvest. It stood on the table throughout Yule, and was kept until spring, when part of it was given to the ploughmen and oxen to eat, and part of it was mixed with the seed-corn. In ancient times, a real boar was sacrificed at Yule. In Sweden, an old woman with a blackened face would pretend to sacrifice a man dressed in a boar-skin.

Among the Estonians of the island of Oesel, the last sheaf of the harvest was called the Rye Boar, and the man who cut it was hailed with a shout of "You have the Rye Boar on your back!" In reply, he would sing a song, in which a prayer for plenty was included. In some parts of Oesel, a long cake with either end turned up would be baked and called the Christmas Boar. It stood on the table until the morning of New Year's Day, when it was given to the cattle. In other parts of the island, the custom was for the housewife to fatten a small pig in secret, which was then killed on Christmas Eve, roasted in the oven, and stood on the table for several days.

In other parts of Estonia, the Christmas Boar was baked from the first rye cut at harvest. It was made in a cone-shape, with a cross impressed on it with a pig bone or a key. Alternatively, three dents were made in it with a buckle or a piece of charcoal. Throughout the festive season it stood on the table with a light beside it. Before sunrise on New Year's Day or on Twelfth Night, some of the cake was crumbled with salt and given to the cattle. When the cattle were driven out to pasture in the Spring, the rest was put in the herdsman's bag to be divided

194

among the cattle to keep them from sorcery and harm. In some places, the Christmas Boar was shared between farm servants and cattle at the time of the barley sowing, to ensure a good crop.

Mythology

In ancient Greece and Rome, the boar was sacred to Ares / Mars, the god of war. As the beast which killed Adonis and Attis, it was also a symbol of Winter, and the slaying of the Boar of Calydon heralded the coming of Spring. The legend was that Oeneus, King of Calydon in Anatolia, neglected the sacrifices to Artemis, so the goddess sent a ferocious boar to ravage his lands. A band of heroic hunters gathered to kill it; Atalanta wounded it, and Meleager killed it. The boar is also an attribute of Demeter and Atalanta. Heracles captured the wild boar of Erymanthus. Hecate was sometimes depicted with three heads, one of a boar, one of a dog, and one of a horse. In Mycenae, the warriors wore boar's-tusk helmets.

In Hinduism, the boar Varahi was the third incarnation of Vishnu or Prajapati. In the form of a boar, he saved the world from the waters of chaos by diving to the bottom of the sea, whence the earth had been dragged by Hiranyaksha. Varahi also taught humans agriculture. The boar also represents Vajravarahi, the goddess of dawn and the Queen of Heaven, who as the sow, is the source of fertility and life. In pre-Vedic times, the storm-god Rudra was the boar of the sky. There is also the earth goddess Varahini, the wife of Vishnu in his boar incarnation, and herself an incarnation of Lakshmi; she is depicted with an infant on her knees. She corresponds to Sukarapreyashi ('Beloved of the Boar'), also said to be the wife of Varahi (Vishnu's boar avatar); she is depicted as a seated woman, with Vishnu in his boar form by her side.

In Iranian mythology, the shining boar is connected with the sun in the Zendavesta.

In Sumero-Semitic mythology, Tammuz was slain by a winged boar; but the boar could also be a messenger of the gods. Tammuz was the brother and lover of Belili, and later became the consort of

Ishtar (the Assyro-Babylonian goddess of love and fertility). He was known in Syria as Dumuzi, the ritual husband of the harvest goddess. In Autumn the Tammuz festival was held to commemorate his death and celebrate his resurrection, brought back from the Underworld by Ishtar. The boar that slew him could also have been an aspect of Ishtar, however, as the Terrible Mother who must slay the harvest god in order to renew the land.

In Teutonic and Scandinavian cultures, the boar symbolised fertility, the harvest, and the power of the storm. It was sacred to Odin (Woden) and Frey and Freyja, who ride boars. Frey has a golden boar called Gullinbursti (Golden Bristles), whose bristles are the rays of the Sun. In another legend Frey's boar was called Slidrugtanni (Fearful Tusk) and he rode on it to Balder's funeral (according to the late tenth century text *Husdrapa* by Ulf Uggason). Freyja had a boar called Hildisvin (Battle Pig); one of her by-names was Syr (Sow). Warriors wore boar masks and helmets to put themselves under the protection of Frey and Freyja. Amongst the Aestii (a tribe of the Baltic region), Tacitus relates,

"they worship the Mother of the Gods. They wear, as emblem of this cult, the masks of boars. These act as an armour and defence against all things, making the worshippers of the goddess safe even in the midst of enemies."

(Germania, 45)

A helmet with a boar on it was found at Benty Grange (near Monyash in Derbyshire). Protective boars on helmets are mentioned several times in Beowulf; among the gifts of King Hrothgar to Beowulf was a standard in the form of a boar's head. Amongst the Sutton Hoo treasure, there were ten representations of boars, including a clasp with a design of interlaced boars with tusks and crested backs, their bodies and haunches made of plate garnets; and an iron helmet on which each bronze eyebrow terminates above the cheek-guard in a small stylised gilt bronze boar's head. In the *Skaldskaparm·ál* (a Norse saga), King Athal's helmet, taken from King Ali, is called Hildigölt (battle boar). The boar-helmet is mentioned five times in the lay of *Beowulf*. The boar was a power animal for Anglo-Saxon kings, and the Anglo-Saxons also carried boar-banners. In *Elene* (an Anglo-Saxon text), the Emperor Constantine sleeps under his boar-banner. Clearly the writer assumed that the boar-banner was an essential attribute for a king. The royal and magical associations of the boar may therefore have continued into Christian times.

The Merovingian kings (the pre-Carolingian royal dynasty of France) were reputed to have bristles on their spines, like boars.

The constellation of the Pleiades (also known as the Seven Stars) was called the Boar's Throng in Norse cosmology, due to its resemblance to the battle formation of the Svinfylking warriors, which was used to break through the enemy's shield wall.

In the saga of King Heidrek the White, a boar was sacrificed to Frey at Yule to persuade the god to grant a good year. It was the *sonargoltr*, the 'atonement boar'. King Heidrek and his followers took their most solemn oaths on this animal by placing their hands on its head and bristles. According to the *Grimnismal* and *Gylfaginning*, the Einherjar (the warriors of Valhalla) feast on the boar Saehrimnir, which is constantly replenished no matter how much is eaten. The ceremony of bringing in a boar's head at the Yuletide festivities survived a long time both in England and Scandinavia. In some myths, Frey appears to have been a sacrificed vegetation god, like Tammuz or Adonis; Brian Branston (in *The Lost Gods of England*) argues that the myth of the vegetation god was brought from the Mediterranean, probably via the Dacians. Frey's name at Uppsala was Fricco, meaning darling (probably from the Indo-European root word *pri*j, beloved); the name Frey means Lord. Adonis also means Lord, and Adonis/Tammuz was also addressed as 'the beloved'; moreover, the boar is sacred to both deities. However, the cult of Nerthus was associated with the boar among Germanic tribes, and the cult of Frey was derived from that of Nerthus, so it is likely that this was the source of the boar imagery in Frey's cult. It is certain, however, that the boar was associated with fertility and plenty, and hence with the king, whose duty it was to maintain fertility and plenty. The Old Norse word for a boar, öfurr (Old English *eofer*) survived only in poetic language as a word for a chief.

The boar was a sacred animal amongst the Celts, a symbol of the supernatural, prophecy, magic, war, the protection of warriors, and hospitality. It was connected with gods, magic powers, and trees, also the wheel, ravens, and the cult of the human head. It was sacrificed to Derga. The boar's head was a symbol of health and preservation from danger, the power of the life force, the vitality contained in the head. It also symbolised good luck and plenty in the coming year. The boar and bear together were a symbol of spiritual and temporal rule. Some Druids called themselves Boars, probably solitary Druids who had withdrawn into the forest. The sacrificial fire was called the Boar of the Woods. The boar was one of the three sacred animals of the goddess Brighid, goddess of poetry, fire, and healing (the other two sacred animals being the ox and the ram). In a relief found at Bordeaux, a boar is depicted with a horned god of the waters and his consort. Boars are sometimes depicted with three horns, which indicates that they are supernatural. A boar and a serpent are also depicted with Vitiris (probably meaning the Mighty One or the Wise One), a north British deity occurring in the area of Hadrian's Wall. There is also a relief from the Carlisle region depicting a genius loci with a boar. Boars also occur frequently in Irish mythology. In the Welsh epic, the *Mabinogion*, King Math turned Gilvaethwy and Gwydion first into a stag and a hind, then into a boar and a sow, then into a wolf and a she-wolf, for raping his foot-holder Goewin.

The boar was an extremely widespread cult animal amongst the Celts. On the Gundestrup cauldron, warriors are depicted with boar-crests on their helmets; a similar engraving was found in Gaul. Also on the Gundestrup cauldron there appears a figure of a deity holding aloft two male figures carrying boars. The boar was

Reconstruction of bronze carnyx with boar's head terminal.
(After A. Ross)

also associated with Celtic ritual feasting. From early times, grave goods included pig bones and whole joints of pork. The boar is also depicted on Celtic and Gaulish coinage and battle standards, and a stylised boar's head was used as a terminal for the carnyx (the Celtic trumpet). The boar appears on pre-Roman Celtic coinage, and altars from the Roman period are carved with reliefs of boars. The name of the deity at Langres was Moccus (pig), who was equated with Mercury. Votive stone statuettes of boars were offered at the temple in the Forêt d'Halatte in France. Small bronze boars have been found at Hounslow in Middlesex (they were probably helmet crests originally); also at Lexden in Essex, Wattisfield in Suffolk, and East Cheap in London. An elegant stylised outline of a boar was found on the Witham shield.

In Celtic literature, the boar was an important ingredient in the ritual of the otherworld feast. In Irish tales, pork was the proper meat for the feasts of kings and gods alike. The flesh of a red pig was chewed for the divinatory rite of *Himbas Forosnai*. Many early tales tell of the hunting of an invincible magical boar, often a metamorphosed prince, such as Twrch Trwyth in the *Mabinogion* and Oc Triath in the Irish tales.

The hunting of the otherworld boar seems to have been one of the most popular Celtic cult legends. As pork was regarded as the food of the gods, so the boar hunt came to be the noblest pursuit. Presumably it was the ferocity of the animal which the Celts found so inspiring. In Irish legend, the life of the hero Diarmuid was bound up with that of a boar, which when defeated, caused the death of its pursuer. Magical swine figure significantly in Welsh legend: the sow Henwen gave birth to a grain of wheat and a bee in Gwent; a grain of barley and a bee at Llonion in Pembroke; a wolf-cub and an eagle at the Hill of Cyferthwch in Eryri (Snowdonia); and a kitten at the Black Stone in Llanfair in Arfon. Coll son of Collfrewy, who guarded her, threw the kitten into the Menai; afterwards it became Palug's Cat, fostered by the sons of Palug in Mon (Anglesey).

The swineherd was also a powerful figure in Welsh legend: the Three Powerful Swineherds of the Island of Britain were Pryderi son of Pwyll, Lord of Annwfn (because no-one could deceive or force him); Drystan son of Tallwch (whose pigs no-one could take by force); and Coll son of Collfrewy, guardian of the sow Henwen. The name Henwen means 'the Old White One'. Note that some of her gifts are beneficial, others harmful (such as Palug's Cat, which wreaked destruction upon the land), as is the often the case with otherworldly gifts. Even the introduction of pigs into Britain is said to be by supernatural means.

In the *Mabinogion*, Gwydion goes to King Math, and tells him that strange creatures have arrived in the south called *hobeu* (pigs). Arawn king of Annwn (the otherworld) gave them to Pwyll as a gift; they now belong to his son Pryderi. Gwydion goes to obtain the pigs from Pryderi, but he is told that they cannot be given away until they have bred to double their present number. He then offers to exchange for them twelve magnificent stallions, twelve greyhounds, and twelve golden shields (which he has made by magic, and which will only last for one day). One of the punishments inflicted by Math on Gwydion and his brother for the rape of Goewin was to be transformed into a boar and a sow, in which form they produced a piglet. Math changed him to human form and gave him the name Hwchdwn.

The story of Culhwch and Olwen has as its central theme the hunting of the boar Twrch Trwyth, who is a king transformed into a swine. Olwen's father, the giant Ysbaddaden, will only give her in marriage to Culhwch if he performs one of several seemingly impossible quests (all interlinked) culminating in retrieving the comb and shears from between the ears of Twrch Trwyth; only with these can Ysbaddaden's hair be dressed. Twrch Trwyth has seven followers, all magical boars. One of these is called Grugyn Silver-Bristle, who speaks with Gwrhyr Interpreter of Tongues. One of the lesser tasks is to obtain the tusk of Ysgithyrwyn the Chief Boar for Ysbaddaden to shave himself with. The name Culhwch means 'pig-run', so Culhwch may originally have been the personification of a pig. Legend has it that his mother was frightened by some pigs, and gave birth to Culhwch amongst the pigs, then abandoned him. He was found by the swineherd, who named him after the circumstances of his birth. In Irish legend, the life of the hero Diarmuid was bound up with that of the magic boar of Gulban. When he killed it, it caused his own death. He was trapped into this by Fionn MacCumhal. The tale related that Grainne, daughter of the King of Ireland, was betrothed to Fionn, but fell in love with Diarmuid O'Duibhne and ran away with him. Fionn pursued the lovers for seven years, and finally pretended to make peace with them, but then trapped Diarmuid into being killed by the boar. Many dolmens in Ireland are known as Diarmuid and Grainne's Bed, because they were said to have sheltered beneath them. One such is the Poulnabrone dolmen in the Burren, which is a particularly spectacular dolmen wedged into the limestone pavement on a hilltop. After Diarmuid's death, he was taken to Brugh na Boinne by Angus mac Og, who 'breathed aerial life' into him.

In the Fenian tales of Ireland, the boar of Formael, a 'black, shapely, dusky swine' without ears, testicles, or a tail, and with horrible long bristles, killed fifty men, fifty hounds, and the hero Failbhe Finnmaisech all in one day. In the story of Magh Mucrime, six magically transformed pigs wreak destruction upon the land; they are the swine of Derbrenn. Aengus mac Og commits them to the care of Buichet of Leinster, but then Buichet's wife longs to eat one of the pigs, and they are hunted. Aengus mac Og cannot save them until they have 'shaken the tree of Tarbga and eaten the salmon of Inver Umaill'. They fail to do this, and five of them are taken and their heads brought to a burial mound. Interestingly, in South Uist, there is a mound dating to around the beginning of the Christian era in which several pig jaws were found buried. Possibly there is a mythological connection here. Certainly pigs are associated with the underworld, and often the hunt for a supernatural pig leads the heroes of the old tales into otherworldly realms.

In the story *Belach Conglais*, Glas son of Donn Desa meets one of the red swine of Derbrenn in the midst of the plain of Tara; he and his hounds and the pig are all killed. In another tale, Manannan's hounds give chase to an enormous pig, which springs into a lake where all the dogs are drowned; the pig swims off to an island in the lake. Thereafter the lake is called Loch Con (loch of the dogs) and the island Mucc-Inis (Pig Island). Another group of magical pigs was the Muc Slangha in the Fenian tales; one of them was said to have nine tusks in each jaw. It is eventually killed by

Caoilte, and provides a feast for many warriors for a long time; those who partake of its flesh are preserved from ill and made joyous and happy. Many magical pigs could be cooked and eaten, and then reappear alive the next day. The Dagda had such a pig; the tale relates:

> *"Wonderful, then, is that land. Three trees with fruit are there always and a pig perpetually alive, and a roasted swine and a vessel with marvellous liquor, and never do they all decrease."*

In the story of the slaying of Cian by the sons of Tuirill Biccreo, the sons are given the task of obtaining the hide of the Pig of Duis, which could heal wounds and sickness and was as thick as four ox-hides; they also had to obtain the six pigs of Essach, which could be eaten and then return to life the next day, provided their bones were not broken in the eating.

In another Fenian tale, Finn brings to bay an enormous boar, which utters a hideous shriek. This summons a huge man, who threatens the Fenians if they kill his pig. He then picks up the pig and carries it on his shoulder. This casts a spell over the warriors so that they have to follow him to his underworld dwelling. When they arrive, he strikes the boar, turning it into a splendid young man, who is his son. The purpose of leading the warriors to his domain was to persuade Finn to marry his daughter, which he does.

The lord of the underworld was frequently depicted carrying a roasted pig over his shoulder, still squealing, for the otherworld feast. In the tale *Togail Bruidne Da Derga* (The destruction of Da Derga's hostel), the hero Conaire meets a man with one arm, one eye, and one leg, holding an iron fork and carrying a roasted pig, still squealing. This figure is reminiscent of the lord of the forest archetype.

When feasting, the hero's portion (*cauradmir*) was always a piece of pork.

Symbolism

The boar is both solar and lunar. As a solar animal, it represents the masculine principle. The white boar, however, is lunar, and represents the feminine principle and the element of Water. The boar also represents intrepidity, lust, and gluttony.

In Japan, the white boar is the Moon, and symbolises courage, conquest, and all the qualities of the warrior.

In China, the boar represented the wealth of the forests; a white boar was a symbol of the Moon.

In Siberia, the boar was a symbol of courage, conquest, steadfastness, and the qualities of the warrior.

In ancient Egypt, the boar was an attribute of Set in his destructive aspect, when he swallowed the eye of the God of the Day.

In Christianity, the boar connotes brutality, fierce anger, evil, and the sins of the flesh; also cruel princes and rulers.

In Hebrew symbolism, the boar is the enemy of Israel, destroying the vine.

In Heraldry, the boar is one of the four heraldic animals of venery (hunting).

Poetry

"The swine all golden, the boar iron-hard" (*swyn eal gylden, eofer iren-heard*)

(from *Beowulf*, the description of the funeral pyre of Hnaef the Scylding)

Buffalo

Latin name various   **Deity** Yama

Family *Bovidae*

Etymology probably from Portuguese *bufalo*, from Late Latin *bufalus*, from Greek *boubalos*, an antelope or wild ox.

Varieties

The Indian Water Buffalo or Carabao (*Bubalus bubalis*) occurs in India, and has been successfully introduced to Asia, Asia Minor, parts of Africa, and south-eastern Europe. The Pygmy Buffalo (*Anoa depressicornis*) is found in India, Burma, and Indonesia. There is also a South African buffalo (*Syncerus caffer*). The North American Bison or Buffalo (*Bison bison*) was systematically destroyed by white settlers in an effort to wipe out the food source of the indigenous peoples. It is making a comeback, and there are about 30,000 of them. This is still a depressingly low number compared to the numbers before the extermination.

Mythology

Yama, the god of the dead in Vedic and Buddhist mythology, is sometimes depicted riding a water buffalo, as buffalo-headed, or in the form of a buffalo. In Chinese mythology, Yama is the King of the Seventh Hell. In Vedic myth, he has a twin sister called Yami.

Symbolism

In indigenous American cultures the buffalo or bison is a symbol of strength, endurance, the whirlwind, and supernatural power. The reverent attitude of the indigenous Americans to the buffalo was in harmony with their environment: they only killed as many buffalo as they needed to eat, and performed rituals for the buffalo's spirit. The White Buffalo Cow brought the sacred pipe to the Lakota people for their rites.

Indian water buffalo

Camel

Latin name various

Family *Camelidae*

Etymology Old English, from Latin, from Greek *kamelos*, from Semitic

Varieties

The *Camelidae* are a member of the Even-toed Ungulates (*Artiodactylae*), within the suborder *Tylopoda*, which includes Llamas. The Bactrian Camel (*Camelus bactrianus*) was used in Central Asia until modern times as a beast of burden, particularly for carrying salt. Sven Hedin used a camel to cross the Gobi Desert in the 1920s.

Folklore

There are ninety-nine names of God known to humanity. In Arabic folklore, it is said that the camel knows the hundredth name.

Mythology

In Iranian mythology, the camel is associated with the dragon-serpent.

In Islamic legend, Mohammed's favourite camel was Al Kaswa. The mosque at Koba covers the place where Al Kaswa knelt when Mohammed fled from Mecca (then known as Jahilia). Mohammed considered that the camel kneeling was a sign from Allah, and hid at Koba for four days. The swiftest of Mohammed's camels was Al Adha, fabled to have completed the whole journey from Jerusalem to Mecca in four bounds, thereby meriting a place in heaven.

Symbolism

The camel is the meaning of the Hebrew letter Gimel, which symbolises self-reliance and the completion of a triad, and links Kether and Binah on the Tree of Life.

In Christianity, the camel symbolises temperance, dignity, royalty, obedience, and stamina. It is associated with the three Magi or Kings, and also with John the Baptist, who clothed himself in camel hair. The camel also symbolises humility and docility, as it kneels to receive its burden.

The camel was depicted on Roman coins as the personification of Arabia.

The Chinese regard the camel as a lazy beast, but also as an animal of great endurance. The art of the Tang dynasty (618-906 ce) abounds with images of the camel. One of the best known paintings, by Wu Dao-zi (c. 750 ce) shows the dying Buddha Sakyamuni under the sala trees, with the camel, water buffalo, elephant, tiger, and other animals grieving around him.

Cat

Latin name *Felis catus Linnaeus* **Polarity** Feminine

Family *Felidae* **Element** Earth

Planet Moon

Folk names Puss, Pither, Pyewacket Mao (Chinese)

Deities Freyja, Bast,

Etymology Old and Middle English *catte, catt*; Old High German *kazza*, Old Norse kˆttr, Anglo-French and Old Northern French *cat*, from late Latin *cattus, catta*.

Varieties

The cat was named Felis catus by Linnaeus in 1758. There are twenty-six species of wild cat belonging to the genus Felis. Among these are the Scottish wild cat (*Felis sylvestris*); the African wild cat (*Felis sylvestris libyca*); the Asian wild cat (Felis sylvestris ornata); Pallas's cat (*Felis manul*), found from Iran to Western China in mountainous country and steppe; the golden cat (Felis temminckii), a cat found in forests from Southern China to Sumatra; the leopard cat (*Felis bengalensis)*, found from eastern Siberia through to Baluchistan and South-east Asia; and the sand cat (*Felis margarita*). The closest relatives of the domestic cat appear to be the various species of *Felis sylvestris*. Most species of the genus Felis have nineteen pairs of chromosomes. The big cats are also part of the Felidae family: there are three species of Lynx, six species of large cats (*Panthera*), and the cheetah (*Acinonyx*).

Folklore

The cat is an animal to which it is almost impossible not to respond in some way. Few people are indifferent to cats. They have an air of the magical about them. Perhaps it is the way they gaze out into the night and seem to respond to things that we cannot see, giving the impression that they can see spirits. (It is hardly surprising that they were associated with witches.) Perhaps it is their dignified air, the impression they give that they are doing you a favour by condescending to sleep in your armchair and eat your food. Either way, cats have been the focus of many superstitions, and the subject of much anthropomorphising by pet "owners". One cannot own a cat, it just lives in one's house. It is interesting to note that legally, cats are still classified as wild animals.

In popular superstition, the black cat is an omen of evil and death. Only in modern times has the black cat been regarded as a lucky animal. The white cat is often regarded as a supernatural animal, and therefore treated with suspicion by country people. Cats in general are regarded as the familiars of witches, and witches are believed to shapeshift into cats. "A Cat hath nine lives, that is to say, a witch may take on her a cats body nine times." (W Baldwin, 1570). Cats and dogs were also employed in rain-making ceremonies, which may be the origin of the expression "It's raining cats and dogs".

The cat was supposed to have great influence on the weather; sailors used to say "The cat has a gale of wind in her tail", when they saw an unusually frisky cat. In mid-19th century Scarborough, sailors' wives would keep a black cat to ensure their husbands' safety at sea. It was also believed that if a cat sat with its tail towards the fire, there would be a change in the weather; if it lay with its forehead on the ground, it would rain (London, 1959); and if it frisked about and chased its tail, there would be a storm (hence the expression, "She's got the wind in her tail"). Shutting a cat in a cupboard would also cause stormy weather (1831, 1883, 1895).

There are many recorded instances (from 1507 to

1984) of the belief that a cat washing itself is a portent of rain, especially if it washes behind its ears. It was also believed that a cat washing itself portended a visit from a stranger (1755, 1922, 1955) - perhaps because the cat had to make itself look smart for the visitor! In the early 20th century, some football teams would take a black cat onto the field with them for luck. In the twenties in Somerset, a black cat was regarded as lucky for its owner, but nevertheless a creature of the devil.

Seaside postcards often used to include a black cat in the picture, and an old lady in Yorkshire was recorded in 1983 as saying she always kept the postcards with a black cat in them. It is believed to be lucky to touch a black cat (1953, 1961). Meeting a black cat, or one crossing your path, was generally regarded as unlucky (1620, 1797, 1882, 1885, 1890, 1898, 1909, 1922, 1952, 1962) and only more recently regarded as lucky (1971, 1983). In Shetland, it is lucky if a black cat runs in front of a fisherman, but unlucky if it crosses his path (1882). In Somerset (1922), it was believed that it was lucky if the black cat came towards you, but unlucky if it walked away from you; it was also very unlucky to kill or drown a cat, especially for farmers, as it brought bad luck to the cattle.

It is unlucky to buy a cat, but lucky if it is given to you, especially if it is black. Being visited by a black cat is good luck, and it is bad luck to chase it away. Another superstition is that if a kitten and a baby are born on the same day, only one of them will thrive.

Stones with natural or artificial depressions, used to make offerings in rituals for raising the wind, are sometimes called cat troughs, in the belief that they were used to make offerings to sacred cats. The cat is sacred to Freyja, so it would not be an unreasonable conclusion.

Spectral cats (e.g. Exmoor Cats, the Surrey Puma) occur frequently in folklore and legend.

The cat is also associated with harvest customs. Near Kiel, the children were warned not to go into the fields because the Cat would be sitting there. In the highlands of Eisenach, children were told that the Corn-Cat would come and fetch them, or that it was in the corn. In parts of Silesia, when the last corn was cut, they said that the Cat was caught, and the man who gave the last stroke at the threshing was called the Cat. Near Lyons, the last sheaf and the harvest-home were both called the Cat. In Vesoul, they said as they cut the last corn that they had the Cat by the tail. At Briançon in Dauphiné, a cat was decked in ribbons, flowers, and ears of corn at the beginning of the reaping. If one of the reapers was cut, it was made to lick the wound. At the end of the reaping, a dance was held in its honour, and then its finery was removed by the girls. At Gr.neberg in Silesia, the reaper who cut the last corn was called the Käter (Tom-cat). He was swathed in green withes and rye stalks and given a long plaited tail. He was sometimes accompanied by a Katze (Quean-cat), which was a man similarly dressed. They would run after everyone they saw and beat them with a long stick. Near Amiens in France, the expression for finishing the harvest was killing the Cat; when the last corn was cut, they killed a cat in the farmyard. In some parts of France a live cat was placed under the last sheaf to be threshed, and killed with the flails. It was then roasted and eaten on the next Sunday.

In China, the cat is a yin animal because of its nocturnal habits. It represents the powers of evil, and the ability to shape-shift and enchant people. Seeing a strange cat is an omen of unfavourable change; seeing a black cat is an omen of misfortune or illness. If a strange cat has her kittens in your house, it is an omen of poverty, because the cat is said to know that there will be plenty of rats in the house. Cat flesh is not eaten in Northern China, but people do eat cats in Southern China. In the northern province of Gansu, the cat was a sacred animal. Because of its very good eyesight, the cat is said to be able to see spirits in the dark. In the province of Zhejiang, white cats were not kept, as they were said to get onto the roof at night and steal the moonbeams, and were also liable to turn into mischievous spirits. It was also seen as a bad idea to bury dead cats, in case they turned into demons; for this reason they were hung up on trees instead. This is still the custom in Taiwan, where one may occasionally see a tree with dead cats in its branches. It was also believed that if a cat jumped over a coffin, the corpse would become one of the undead. Cats were regarded as having demonic powers. A girl who flirts a lot is called a 'black cat'.

The proverbial metaphor for insincerity is 'the cat weeping over the mouse'. In Buddhism, the cat and the snake were the only two animals who were said not to have wept at the death of the Buddha, and were therefore under a curse.

During the Middle Ages in Europe, cats were treated very cruelly, as it was believed that they were the familiars of witches. They were often burnt in bonfires during Lent.

The earliest English legend to tell of a cat being heroic was the story of Dick Whittington and his cat. Richard Whittington was born in Gloucestershire in around 1360, and became Lord Mayor of London in 1397, and again in 1406 and 1419. The first reference to him and his cat is in the play Eastward Hoe (1605); there is also a ballad, *A Song of Sir Richard Whittington* by Richard Johnson (1612), a biography, *The Famous and Remarkable History of Sir Richard Whittington* by T.H. (c. 1670), and an early 18th C. chapbook tale, *The Adventures of Sir Richard Whittington*. The story tells that Dick Whittington was a poor boy who went to London to seek his fortune, and became a turnspit in the house of Hugh Fitzwarren. He bought a cat to keep down the rats and mice in his attic, and then Fitzwarren asked everyone in his household to invest something in his next venture, a voyage to North Africa. As Whittington had only his cat, the cat was sent on the voyage. The Moorish king whose court the captain visited was so taken with the cat (who killed all the rats and mice in his court) that he gave much gold for her. Thus Dick Whittington became rich, and married Alice Fitzwarren, who had always been kind to him. He became a merchant, and subsequently Lord Mayor of London. It appears that an older folktale of a turnspit and his cat (similar tales are told in the Persian, Danish, and Italian traditions) has become attached to the historical figure of Richard Whittington.

The expression 'to bell the cat' comes from the prologue to William Langland's *Vision of Piers Plowman* (c. 1362), in which a rat suggests fixing a collar with a bell around the neck of a cat which has been chasing the rats and mice. However, none of the rats or mice are brave enough to venture near the cat. One of the mice says that even if they succeed in getting rid of this cat, another cat or its kitten will replace the first one. This was an allegory of the contemporary political situation; Edward III was the cat, his grandson Richard was the kitten, and the rats and mice were the people. The fable became so well known that Lord Gray alluded to it in a speech to the conspirators against James III of Scotland. Archibald, Earl of Angus, responded by saying, "I am he who will bell the cat"; he subsequently became known as Archibald Bell-the-Cat.

The saying that a cat has nine lives seems to be derived from the notion that a witch could only assume the form of her cat nine times. This belief is referred to in *Beware the Cat* (1560) by Baldwin: "it was permitted for a witch to take her cattes body nine times." It is perhaps also significant that nine is the most sacred number in the Northern Tradition, being associated with Odin. It is also three times three, the number of the Triple Goddess tripled.

The tale of *Puss-in-Boots* was originally told in Straparola's *Nights* (1530). In the story, the cat procures Constantine a fine castle and the heiress to the kingdom. The tale was translated from Italian into French in 1585, and appeared in Perrault's *Les Contes de ma Mere l'Oye* (Tales of Mother Goose) in 1697. This was translated into English.

Mythology
The Celts kept domestic cats. One such was excavated at Danebury Ring in Hampshire. In Celtic mythology, the cat represents cthonic powers, and sometimes featured on Gallo-Roman funerary monuments. Monster cats (such as Palug's Cat) appear in Celtic saga, and are fought by heroes. The Cor Anmann (the earliest written version of which appeared in the twelfth century) mentions Cairbre Cinn-cait (Cairbre Cat-head):

> *"Thus was Cairbre the cruel who seized Ireland south and north, two cat's ears on his fair head, a cat's fur through his ears."*

In the story of *Morann MacMain's Collar*, Cairbre is referred to as the cat-headed King of Ireland. He was the father of Morann, and every son that was born to him had a blemish, so he killed them.

In Welsh myth, Cath Paluc (Palug's Cat) was the offspring of the magical sow Henwen. It is referred to in two of the *Trioedd Ynys Prydein* (The Triads of the Island of Britain). It slew nine-score warriors and ate them; it was eventually slain by Fair Cei.

It is possible that there were Celtic cat deities; presumably the ferocity of the wild cat would have recommended it to the warlike Celtic aristocracy. There was a tribe called the Chatti, reputed to have a cat as their totem.

In Egypt, the cat was a sacred animal, associated with the Moon. It was sacred to Set as the darkness, and as watchfulness. As a lunar animal, it was sacred to Isis and Bast. It also represents pregnant women, as it was thought that the Moon made the seed grow in the womb, and the cat was associated with the waxing and waning of the Moon. Bast or Bastet was the goddess of Bubastis in the Delta from circa 2300 BCE onwards. When Bubastis was the capital of Egypt in 950 BCE, Bast became a national deity. She was originally lion-headed, representing the beneficent powers of the Sun, by contrast with Sekhmet, who was the destructive power of the Sun. According to one tradition, Bast accompanied Ra across the sky in his Boat of a Million Years (the Sun), and at night she fought with the serpent Apep, which tried to kill Ra. She was said to be Ra's daughter, sister, or wife; in one story she bore the lion-headed god Maahes. She was a kindly goddess of joy, dancing, and music. Barge processions and orgiastic ceremonies were held in her honour. She protected humanity against evil spirits and contagious diseases. Both she and Sekhmet were the wives of Ptah at Memphis, and their son Nefertum (god of the setting Sun and the lotus blossom) is the third deity in the Memphis Triad. Bast was depicted as a cat-headed woman, with a sistrum and a basket. She was also depicted as a cat. In either form, she often had kittens at her feet. At Speos Artemidos (the Caves of Artemis), east of Beni Hasan, Bast was known as Pakhit, depicted with the head of a cat or a lioness. Another Egyptian cat-goddess (predating Bast and Sekhmet) was Mafdet, a cat or lynx goddess. The Egyptians domesticated the cat very early on; they were useful as destroyers of snakes. They were sacred animals, much loved by the Egyptians, and dead cats were often mummified. A Roman visitor to Bubastis who killed a cat was lynched by the people of the city.

In Graeco-Roman mythology, a cat lies at the feet of the goddess of Liberty. The cat is also an attribute of the lunar Diana. In *Aradia: Gospel of the Witches* (written down at some time during the nineteenth century), Lucifer, the light, had a fairy cat which he dearly loved, and which slept on his bed at night. Diana, desiring to lie with Lucifer, prevailed on the cat to change forms with her, and so lay with him, assuming her own form in the darkness; thus she became the mother of Aradia. Diana also assumed the form of a cat in classical mythology, to infuriate the giants.

In Scandinavian mythology, the cat is an attribute of Freyja, the Lady. She is a Moon goddess (though she may originally have been a Sun goddess), and she rides in a chariot drawn by two cats. In a twelfth century wall-painting in Schleswig cathedral, Freyja is depicted riding a striped cat (possibly a Siberian tiger). In another wall-painting there, Frigg is depicted riding a distaff. Possibly these mythological associations are the origin of the association of witches, broomsticks, and cats.

Alternatively, the association of witches and cats may have arisen from a classical legend of Galenthias, a lady who was turned into a cat and became a priestess of Hecate.

In Bangladesh, there is a goddess called Shashti, protector of children and patroness of childhood, who rides a cat. In Hinduism she is known as Shosti, the goddess of birth. Shosti also rides a cat, as a symbol of prolific fertility.

In indigenous American mythology, Wild Cat is a hunter god, the younger brother of Coyote.

The Wild Cat is also the totem of an Australian Aborigine tribe.

Among the Araucanian people of Chile, Ngurvilu, the god of water, rivers, and lakes, assumes the form a wild cat with a claw at the end of his tail. He is usually responsible for boating and swimming accidents.

Symbolism

By virtue of its variable eyes, the cat symbolises the waxing and waning of the Moon, and the annual cycle of the Sun. As a creature of the night, the cat represents the splendour of the velvet night, the stealth of the hunter, the desire of the lover, and the liberty bestowed by the darkness. The cat is also associated with domesticity, as a frequenter of the hearth; and with cruelty, because of the way it hunts.

To the indigenous Americans, the wild cat is a symbol of stealth.

In Japan, the cat is a symbol of peaceful repose and the powers of transformation.

In Christianity, the cat is associated with Satan and the powers of darkness. It represents lust and laziness. Cats were regarded as the familiars of witches, and both were thought to be in league with the devil.

Poetry

"I and Pangur Ban, my cat,
'Tis a like task we are at:
Hunting mice is his delight,
Hunting words I sit all night.

Better far than praise of men
'Tis to sit with books and pen:
Pangur bears me no ill-will,
He too plies his simple skill."

(probably written by a 9th C. Irish scholar; translated from the Gaelic by Robin Flower)

Isobel Goudie's Witch Song (17th c.)

I sall gae intil a hare
Wi' sorrow and sych and meikle care
And I sall gae in the Devillis name
Ay quhill I com hom againe.

Haire, haire, God send thee care
I am in ane hairis likeness just now
Bot I sall be in a womanis likeness evin now.

I sall gae intil a catt
Wi' sorrow and sych and a blak shat
And I sall gae in the Devillis name
Ay quhill I com hom againe.

Catt, catt, God send thee care
I am in ane cattis likeness just now
Bot I sall be in a womanis likeness evin now.

I shall gae intil a craw
Wi' sorrow and sych and a blak thraw
And I sall gae in the Devillis name
Ay quhill I com hom againe.

Craw, craw, God send thee care
I am in ane craws likeness just now
Bot I sall be in a womanis likeness evin now.

Cattle

Latin name *Bos spp.*

Family *Bovidae* (hollow-horned ungulates)

Polarity Masculine or feminine

Element Earth

Planet Moon

Deities Lahar, Pales, Volus, Volusu, Walgino, Metzik

Etymology Middle English, Anglo-French and Old Northern French, *catel*, from Old French *chatel*, from Latin *capitalis*, *caput* (head). Related to *chattel*.

Varieties
Domestic oxen were developed from the Wild Ox, Aurochs or Urus (*Bos taurus primigenius*) which was indigenous to Europe and became extinct in historical times. Celtic cattle were smaller, lighter, and slenderer than either Roman or modern cattle. Celtic cattle belonged to a shorthorn type, Bos longifrons, which is now extinct. In India, various forms of Zebu have been developed from the wild cattle (*Bos indicus*). A form of the Zebu is found on the African savannahs; it is the Anhole or Watussi Ox, which has horns that can grow to a length of five feet. The Yak (*Bos grunniens*) is found wild in Tibet, but domestic varieties have been bred in Tibet and Northern China. The Banting or Tsine (*Bibos sondaicus*) is found in eastern India, Burma, and Indonesia.

Folklore
Somewhere in Australia is the mythical cattle-station called The Speewah, where everything is bigger and better than anywhere else in the world. A number of legends are associated with it, which are tall tales in the tradition of Baron Munchausen or the mythical Yiddish city of Chelm.

If a lamb, a foal, or a calf died, the carcass was hung in a rowan or thorn tree to protect the rest of the flock or herd. When cows calved, the afterbirth was hung on a white thorn bush to prevent milk fever and other ailments (Norfolk, 1935). If a cow miscarried of its calf, the dead calf had to be buried in a gateway, or all the other cows would lose their calves (Suffolk, 1785, 1905).

The Circassians regarded the pear tree as the protector of cattle. They would cut down a pear-tree in the forest, take it home and adore it as a divinity. Nearly every home had a pear tree. It was brought into the house on the day of the autumn festival with music and ceremony, then adorned with candles. A cheese was fastened to its top. After the festivities, it was bidden goodbye, and taken out into the courtyard for the rest of the year.

In many places, cattle were associated with bonfires. In the Poitou region of France, shepherdesses and children lit bonfires on the Eve of St John (Midsummer Eve) and passed nuts and sprigs of mullein across the fire. The mullein was to protect the cattle from sickness and sorcery, and the nuts were to cure toothache. In Hesse, the ashes of the midsummer bonfire were mixed with the cattle's drinking water to make them thrive and prevent them getting plague. They were also sometimes driven through the embers of the fire.

In north-east Scotland they lit bone-fires on the second of May (using the Julian calendar) to prevent witches stealing the milk and putting spells on the cattle. A bonfire which included rowan and woodbine was particularly efficacious. In Upper Bavaria, cattle were driven through the midsummer fires to cure sick animals and prevent healthy ones from falling ill. In Bohemia, girls threw wreaths across the midsummer bonfire to their sweethearts. The wreaths were given to sick and calving cattle, burnt on the hearth to prevent thunderstorms, or used to fumigate the byre and the house. In Prussia and Lithuania, the fires were believed to ward off cattle disease, witchcraft, thunder and hail. The cattle were driven over the ashes the next morning. In Estonia, midsummer fires were believed to prevent witches from harming the cattle. A needfire could be kindled at any time to ward off sickness from the cattle. This was done all over Europe for cows, pigs, and horses. In some places, a needfire was kindled every year, often at Beltane. In Poland, the needfire was kindled every year on St Roche's Day, and the cattle were driven through it three times to protect them from murrain.

Mythology

In Africa, the Hottentot god Heitsi-Eibib is said to have been born either of a cow, or of a virgin who ate a magical herb. He is willing to help humans, and can assume the shape of any animal. He did not create animals, but he gave them form and characteristics. He is a dying and resurrecting god; cairns are erected for him in mountain passes. When people walk past them, they place a stone on the pile for luck, and say, 'Give us more cattle'.

It was probably the Druids who drove the cattle between the needfires at Beltane to protect them from disease and make them fertile. The Irish epic, *Tain Bo Cuálnge* (Cattle-Raid of Cooley) tells of the desire of Queen Medhbh of Connacht to acquire as splendid a bull as that owned by her consort Ailill. Ailill's bull had originally been hers, but it had decided that it did not want to be owned by a woman, so it took itself off to Ailill's herd. She set her heart on getting the Brown Bull of Cuálnge in Ulster. The Brown Bull was thick-breasted, narrow-flanked, with a magnificent mane and glaring eyes. Cattle were a status-symbol to the Celts, and hence the most valuable item of property. Queen Medhbh and King Ailill also had enormous flocks of sheep. It all started when Medhbh and Ailill were comparing their assets one night as they lay in bed, and they found that all their assets were of the same value, except for Ailill's magnificent bull. So Medhbh sent emissaries to the owner of the Brown Bull, who lived in Ulster. They were to borrow the bull in exchange for many gifts so that it could sire equally magnificent cattle on Medhbh's cows. The envoy went well and the emissaries were about to leave with the bull, when one of them remarked how easy it had been to negotiate the loan of the bull, and his companion said that if it had not been easy, they would have taken the bull by force. Unfortunately the owner of the bull heard this remark, and changed his mind. The emissaries returned to Medhbh empty-handed, but instead of punishing them, she decided to take an army into Ulster and take the bull by force. This army was harried constantly by CúChulainn, whose superhuman prowess took considerable toll on their numbers. They eventually succeeded in getting the bull out of Ulster, but not before Cú Chulainn had killed many of their number, and was nearly killed himself in a single combat with his best friend, who was in Medhbh's army.

In Greek myth, Hermes stole Apollo's cattle. The story is told in Ovid's *Metamorphoses*; it is also excellently recreated in The Trackers of Oxyrhynchus by the poet Tony Harrison. While Apollo was wandering in Elis and the fields of Messenia after killing his lover Coronis out of jealousy, his cattle strayed into the fields of Pylos. There Hermes saw them, and drove them off, hiding them in the woods. He roasted and ate some of them, and made a lyre from their skeletons and gut. When Apollo discovered that his cattle had been stolen, he went in pursuit of the thief. Eventually the two gods were reconciled when Hermes gave Apollo the lyre.

In Roman mythology, Pales, a deity so ancient that it is now unclear whether it is a goddess or a god, or even a divine couple. Most writers seem to incline to the view that it is a goddess. Pales was the deity of flocks, pastures and cattle, and the protector of shepherds. As a god, Pales was associated with Faunus; as a goddess, with Vesta. The Palatine Hill was also named after Pales. The festival of Pales was the Palilia, celebrated on 21 April. At the festival, houses were decorated with greenery, sheepfolds were festooned with boughs, and people made a large bonfire of beanstraw and laurel. An offering of dried blood and sacrificial ashes was thrown onto the fire, and an offering of cakes and milk was made to Pales. Prayers were said, then all present sprinkled their hands with holy water from a laurel branch, and jumped three times through the flames. This festival evolved from a purely pastoral occasion into a national and urban celebration, said to be the day on which the building of Rome was begun.

In Sumerian and Chaldaean mythology, Lahar was the cattle-god; Enlil created Lahar at the same time as Ashnan, goddess of grain and cultivated fields.

In Poland, the god who protected cattle was called Walgino. In other Slavonic cultures, the cattle god was Volos or Volusu; originally a god of animals, and occasionally of war, he became a god of the peasants, the protector of cattle and shepherds.

In Estonia, there was a male wood-spirit called Metsik who was the patron of cattle.

In Hinduism, Shiva is a herdsman, and Krishna is associated with the gopis, the girls who tended the cows. One night he appeared individually to each of a thousand gopis, and made love to them all.

Bull

Polarity Masculine   **Element** Earth

Planet Sun

Deities Mithras, Attis, Dionysos, Adad, Asshur, Ramman, Marduk, Enlil, Teshub, Ea, Baal, Dumuzi, Jupiter, Zeus

Etymology Middle English, from Old Norse *boli*, cognate with Middle Low German and Middle Dutch *bulle*

History

One of the most famous bearers of the name of Bull was Sitting Bull (c. 1834 - 1890), a chief of the Teton (Sioux or Lakota nation) indigenous Americans, who resisted the U.S. government policy of reservations for his people. He defeated Custer in 1876 at the Battle of Little Bighorn, which was fought for the sacred hills of the Lakota, the Paha Sapa or Black Hills. He was killed whilst resisting arrest during the Sioux rebellion of 1890.

Folklore

At Koenitz in West Prussia, when the wind ruffled the corn, people said "The Steer is running in the corn". In parts of East Prussia, where the corn was growing particularly thickly and strongly, people said "The Bull is lying in the corn". In Graudenz, West Prussia, if a harvester over-stretched or lamed himself, people said that the Bull had pushed him. In Lorraine, when this happened, it was said that the man 'had the Bull'. Near Chambery, a sickle wound was called 'the wound of the Ox'. In Bunzlau, Silesia, the last sheaf of the harvest was made into the shape of an ox, stuffed with tow and wrapped in corn ears. It was called the Old Man. In some parts of Bohemia, the last sheaf of the harvest was made into a man-shape and called the Buffalo-Bull. In Rosenheim, Bavaria, people set up a straw bull on the land of a farmer who was late getting his harvest in. It was made of stubble on a wood frame, with flowers and leaves, and was adorned with doggerel verses ridiculing the man who was late with his harvest. At Pessnitz, near Dresden, the man who threshed the last corn was called the Bull. He had to make a straw man and set it up in front of the window of a neighbour who had not finished threshing. At Auxerre, when the last corn was bring threshed, they would call out twelve times, "We are killing the Bull".

Until the Reformation, a ceremony called the Oblation of the White Bull was carried out every year by the people of Bury St. Edmunds. The bull set aside for the ceremony was not to be used for ordinary farm work or bull baiting, but allowed to roam in the fields in peace and plenty until it was needed. When a married woman desired a child, the bull was adorned with garlands and ribbons and led through the streets to the main gate of the monastery. The woman walked beside it, stroking its sides and dewlaps. Once at the monastery, the bull was left outside, and the woman went to make vows at the shrine of St. Edmund, and to kiss the flagstones there.

There is an English folktale called *The Black Bull of Norroway*, in which three daughters set off to find their way in the world. The first two daughters go down to the cottage of a wise woman, and when they look out of the back door, a handsome coach comes for them. The youngest daughter sets off likewise, and sees a black bull which comes from the North. She mounts on its back, and the bull carries her off. On three succesive nights they come to a castle where one of the bull's brothers lives; each of his three brothers gives her an apple, a pear, and a plum, which she is not to break open until she is in great need. Then the bull carries her to a valley, and tells her to sit on a rock. He has to go further on and fight the Devil, during which time she must keep absolutely still; if she moves, he will not be able to find her when he comes back. If the bull wins the fight, everything will turn blue; if the Devil wins, everything will turn red. The girl keeps quite still until she sees everything turning blue, at which she is so happy that she crosses her legs in contentment. Unfortunately this means that when the bull comes back he cannot see her, however much she calls to him. He wanders off, and the girl sees a glass mountain. If only she could get to the top of the mountain she would be able to find her way home. She finds a cottage nearby where an old man lives, who says he will make her a pair of iron shoes with which she can reach the top of the mountain, but she has to work for him for seven years.

At the end of seven years, he gives her the shoes, and she climbs to the top of the mountain. From there, she can see her home valley, and she goes back to the wise woman's cottage. There she finds the wise woman trying to wash some bloodstained shirts. She asks the meaning of this, and the woman says that the shirts belong to a knight, who says he will marry the girl who can wash them. Both she and her daughter have tried, but to no avail. So the girl washes the shirts, and the bloodstains are washed away. The knight is asleep, however, so when he awakes, the woman pretends that it was her daughter who washed the shirts clean. The girl looks at the sleeping knight and recognises him as the black bull, now released from his enchantment. Perceiving that she is now in great need, she breaks open the magical apple given to her by the first brother, and finds jewels, which she gives to the wise woman's daughter in exchange for postponing her wedding to the knight by one day. But the wise woman learns of this and puts a sleeping potion in the knight's wine. So the girl's attempts to wake the knight and tell him what has happened are unsuccessful.

The same thing happens the next day; the girl breaks open the magical pear, and gives the jewels to the daughter in exchange for another postponement. Again the woman puts a sleeping potion in the knight's drink, but this time his companion hears the girl's attempts to wake him. The next night, the girl breaks open the magical plum, and again persuades the daughter to postpone the wedding by giving her the jewels. This time, however, the knight says that his wine needs sweetening, and whilst the wise woman goes out to get him some honey, he tips it away and substitutes fresh water. When the girl comes to him in the night, he is awake, and they tell each other their stories. The next morning, the knight and his companion kill the wise woman and her daughter. The knight and the girl are married, and they go back up the mountain to visit the girl's mother.

Mythology

Bulls were sacrificed in the worship of Attis and Mithra and at ancient New Year festivals. Bull sacrifice was called the Taurobolium. In the worship of Attis, a bull adorned with flowers and garlands and gold leaf on its forehead was driven onto a grating and killed with a consecrated spear. The worshipper waited underneath and was drenched with the blood of the bull. This washed away his sins, and he was reborn to eternal life. The rite was performed at the Spring Equinox. In Rome, it was done at the shrine of Cybele, on what is now the Vatican Hill in the basilica of St Peter. All Sumerian and Semitic cults included some bull legends. The celestial bull ploughed the great furrow of the sky. In the *Epic of Gilgamesh*, Ishtar conjured the Bull of Heaven to go in pursuit of Gilgamesh, to avenge herself for his indifference to her advances. The Bull of Heaven caused a seven-year drought, but Gilgamesh and Enkidu finally succeeded in killing him. For this deed, one of them had to die. The lot fell on Enkidu; thereafter Gilgamesh was alone in his adventures. Enkidu was himself half-man, half-bull; he grew up in the desert with the wild animals:

> "With gazelles he ate the grass,
>   With the cattle he quenched his thirst,
>   With the flocks his heart rejoiced to drink."

Many deities were called the bull of heaven, including Ramman, Asshur, and Adad, who were depicted riding on bulls. Asshur was the head of the Assyrian pantheon, a god of war and fertility; he was originally the Moon and war god of a city which was named after him. Gudibir, the bull of light, is an aspect of Marduk. Sin, the Moon god, sometimes takes the form of a bull. The roaring and stamping of the bull represents Dumuzi, the Phoenician god whose voice was the thunder, and the Canaanite god Baal or Bel. The Sumerian Sun god, called Enki or Enlil, was known as the savage bull of the sky and earth. The Hittite sun god, Teshub, also takes the form of a bull. Ea, in his aspect of lord of magic, appears as a bull, and was often depicted in Sumerian art holding door posts. Baal or Bel, the Syrian and Phoenician god of pastoral and agricultural fertility, also had the bull as his symbol. In Akkadia, the 'directing bull' began the Zodiacal year. All over the Semitic world, guardian spirits were depicted as winged bulls.

In ancient Egypt, the bull Apis was sometimes regarded as an incarnation of Osiris, and sometimes as an an incarnation of Ptah, or 'the second life and servant of Ptah'. The Apis Bull was said to be conceived when the generative rays of the Moon shone upon a cow in heat. The Apis Bull was very popular throughout Egypt. It was worshipped at Memphis, and called there 'the renewal of Ptah's life'. According to legend, Ptah manifested as a celestial fire (the Moon's rays were often associated with fire) and impregnated a virgin heifer, and was reborn from her in the form of a black bull. The Apis Bull could be identified by his mystical markings: a white triangle on the forehead, the figure of a vulture with outstretched wings on his back, a crescent moon on his right flank, a scarab on his tongue, and double hairs in his tail. Children born on the day that the new bull was discovered were often called 'Apis-is-found'. The bull was fed on delicacies in the temple, and let loose in the courtyard every day. There his devotees and curious travellers could catch a glimpse of the magnificent beast. His movements were interpreted as portents for the future. The reason he was venerated was apparently because oxen helped to plough the fields and sow the corn. He was normally allowed to die of old age, but if he lived beyond a certain age he was drowned in a fountain, according to Ammianus Marcellinus. When he died, his devotees would shave their heads. The bodies of the successive Apis Bulls were mummified in huge underground chambers at Saqqara. They were rediscovered in 1851. The temple, which was called the Serapeum, was situated above the burial chambers, and there the rites of the funeral cult of the dead bull were performed. When an old bull died, the priests would search for a new one; when he was found, the whole of Egypt would rejoice. The other sacred bulls in Egypt were Merwer (Mneuis or Menvis), the light-coloured bull at Heliopolis, sacred to Ra Atum; Bukhe (Buchis), the bull sacred to Menthu at Hermonthis, who was said to change colour every hour of the day; and Aa Nefer (Onuphis), which means 'the very good', was the bull in whom the soul of Osiris was said to be incarnated.

Also in Egypt, one of Isis' titles was 'the Cow of Memphis', and Horus was known as 'the Bull of his Mother', and regarded as Osiris himself reborn. Later, the Pharaohs were known by this title; the early Pharaohs had called themselves 'bulls'. Sarapis, the god of the sacred bull, was the Greek version of Osiris, and became Isis' consort in the Greek version of the Egyptian pantheon. The name Sarapis is derived from Asar-Hap or Usar-Hapi.

The bull was also worshipped in the form of Menvis and Merwer (the incarnation of Ra). The bull was sacred to the solar Ra, who daily impregnated the sky goddess Nut in the form of the Bull of Heaven. Neb or Geb, the Earth God, was also the bull of the Sky Goddess. The bull's thigh was the North Pole and the phallic leg of Set, denoting fertility and strength. A Theban war-god of c. 2000 BCE onwards, Mont (also called Montu or Menthu), was portrayed as bull-headed or falcon-headed.

To the Romans, the bull was an attribute of Jupiter as the sky god, and of Venus and Europa as Moon goddesses. Europa, goddess of the dawn, is carried across the sky by the bull of the sun. Bulls were sacrificed to Mars. The citadel of Carthage, which the Romans laid waste, was called Bursa (a hide). When Dido went to Africa and founded Carthage, she bought as much land as could be encompassed by a bull's hide. The agreement having been made, she cut the bull's hide into thongs, and used them to measure out enough space for a citadel. Similarly, when the Russians invaded Siberia, it is said that the Yakut people granted them as much land as they could encompass with a cow's hide, but the Russians cut the cow's hide into strips and obtained enough land for the port of Yakutsk. These stories are perhaps a folk memory of a ritual for claiming and blessing new territory.

In both Roman and Greek myth, Jupiter Dolichenus and Dionysos Zagreus were associated with bulls.

In ancient Greece, the bull was the attribute of Zeus as the sky god; Zeus assumed the form of a bull in order to carry off Europa (daughter of Phoenix or Agenor, King of Phoenicia and Telephassa); Europa was gathering flowers with her friends by the sea when she caught sight of the bull, by which she was enchanted; she hung a wreath of flowers on its horns and playfully climbed on its back, whereupon it charged off across the sea, coming to a stop at Gortyna in Crete, where Zeus raped Europa under a plane tree. Zeus also took the form of a bull when he fathered Persephone with Demeter. The bull was also an attribute of Dionysos, who was horned and sometimes bull-headed when representing the masculine principle. In his bull form, Dionysos was called Zagreus; in this aspect he was torn to pieces by the Titans. In Crete, a live bull was torn to pieces and eaten by the devotees of Dionysos, in a re-enactment of his death. Dionysos was often represented as a bull, or with the features of a bull. One statue shows him dressed in a bull's hide. He is sometimes portrayed as a child with the head of a calf, or wearing a calf's head. The bull was also sacred to Poseidon, whose wine-bearers at Ephesus were known as 'bulls'. Aphrodite (as the lunar humid principle) also had the bull as her attribute. In Ovid's *Metamorphoses*, Achelous, a river-god, turned first into a serpent, then into a bull, whilst wrestling with Herakles. The Centaurs are associated with bulls in that the name 'centaur' means 'one who rounds up bulls' (a cowboy). Centaurs were originally portrayed as hairy giants, and were only later depicted as half-man, half-horse.

In Minoan art, the Great God was represented as a bull. Bulls were sacrificed to the Earth and the god of earthquakes. In some societies, the cosmic bull was thought to cause earthquakes by tossing the Earth on its horns. The noise of the quake was its roaring. In Crete, the bull seems to have symbolised the reproductive principle of Nature. In Greek myth, Pasiphae, daughter of Helios, was the wife of King Minos of Crete. Poseidon made her fall in love with the white bull of Minos, and as a result of her union with the bull, she gave birth to the Minotaur (whom her daughter Ariadne helped Theseus to overcome). It is probable that Pasiphae and Ariadne were originally Moon goddesses, with the bull as their cult animal. The association of their cult with the labyrinth where the Minotaur dwelt gives credence to this view, since the spiral is often associated with the Great Mother. There was also a Cretan bull goddess called Tauropolos, the Lady of the Bull. The bull was a celestial divinity, bearing the epithet 'Asterius' (starry), and may have been widely worshipped in the Aegean. The epithet recurs in the name of Asterion, king of Crete, who married Europa after she was carried off by Zeus in the form of a bull. Afterwards Asterion was assimilated to Zeus. The Cretan form of Zeus was unusual, due to his mixture of animal and human features. In the Aegean, as in many Asiatic cultures, the bull was the symbol of strength and creative energy, and thus became the symbol of the Great God, an important figure in Cretan legend.

In Buddhism, the bull is an attribute of Yama, the king of the dead, who is sometimes depicted as bull-headed or buffalo-headed.

In Hinduism, Shiva, guardian of the west, rides the bull Nandi. Nandi is the son of Kasyapa and Surabhi, the marvellous cow who was produced from the Churning of the Ocean of Milk. Nandi is Shiva's chamberlain, steed, and principal attendant; he produces the music for his Tandava dance as Shiva Nataraja (Lord of the Dance); and he is the guardian of all quadrupeds. A statue of him often stands before temples of Shiva, such as the magnificent one at Mysore, India. He is generally depicted as being a milky-white colour. The bull is also an attribute of Agni (the god of fire and lightning), the 'Mighty Bull', who rules the earth. Agni is the son of Dyaus the sky-god and Prithivi the earth-goddess, herself a cow. He is said to have three bodies and three births: born of water, he was a calf who grew annually to a bull; born of a fire drill, he was a glutton with a fiery tongue; and born in the highest heaven, he was an eagle. He is also said to be born from wood or in the embryo of plants. Indra in his fertile aspect takes the form of a bull. The bull is also the vital breath of Aditi, the all-embracing. The power of Soma is often compared to that of the bull. Rudra, the storm god, is called a bull in the Vedas and has a cow goddess as his consort.

In Southern Arabia, the Moon god was called Almaqah, with the bull as his cult animal.

In Iranian mythology (pre-Islamic), the bull is the soul of the world. Its generative powers are connected with the Moon and the rain clouds, producing fertility. A bull called Gosh and the god Gayomart were the first created beings, but they were slain by Ahriman. From Gosh's soul came all later creation, and Ahriman's posthumous twin children, Mashia and Mashiane (born from his semen buried in the Earth for forty years), became the father and mother of humanity. The myth embodies the concept that all creation springs from ritual sacrifice.

In Mithraism, the bull was the solar god. The sacrifice of the bull was the central ritual of Mithraism, representing victory over man's animal nature, and the gift of life through death. Mithras was the god of light and moral purity, later a Sun god and god of victory in battle. The killing of the bull was a fertility rite; the shed blood of the bull made vegetation flourish; it was also used in baptismal rites.

In China, the bull is one of the animals of the Twelve Terrestrial Branches (the Chinese Zodiac).

In Celtic mythology, bull-gods represent divine power and strength. Both Celtic and pre-Celtic cults attributed great power and importance to the bull. To the Druids, the bull symbolised the Sun, while the cow symbolised the Earth; according to Pliny, they sacrificed white bulls to the sun after cutting the mistletoe at the winter solstice. An early British bull-god was called Tarvos, possibly the same deity as Tarvos Trigaranus, whose altar was discovered at Notre Dame de Paris, carved with a picture of The Bull With Three Cranes (Tarvos Triganarus) standing by a willow tree. These cranes are actually egrets, which perch on the backs of cattle and clean them of lice, and nest in willow trees. Tarvos Trigaranus was also associated with the Gaulish god Esus.

Bulls' heads are often depicted with birds; an example was found in Denmark and at Ribchester in Lancashire, England. Bulls were also associated with the raven, a bird with underworld and solar connotations in Celtic mythology. At Maiden Castle in Dorset, archaeologists found a three-horned bull with three goddesses on its back, possibly of Belgic origin. Three-horned representations of animals seem to be depicting supernatural animals.

The Celts also frequently depicted bulls with knobbed horns (possibly a phallic symbol). Real bulls were fitted with balls on the ends of their horns to stop them injuring people; one would have thought this would lessen the power of the image, so the precise reason for the statuettes of bulls with knobbed horns remains a mystery. On a stela from Reims, the bull is depicted with the stag-god. The horned god is sometimes depicted with bull's horns, sometimes with stag's antlers. A relief carving of a bull-horned god from Unterhambach in Germany shows him carrying a purse and accompanied by serpents. He was apparently the local equivalent of Mercury. In the *Tain Bo Cuálnge* (The Cattle Raid of Cooley), the Bull of Cuálnge was capable of human understanding and reason.

In the early Welsh triads, there were three bull spectres of the Island of Britain (the spectre of Gwidawl, the spectre of Llyr Marini, and the spectre of Gyrthmwl Wledig); three bull protectors of the Island of Britain (Cynfawr Host-Protector, son of Cynwyd Cynwydion, Gwenddolau son of Ceidiaw, and Urien son of

Cynfarch); and three bull chieftains of the Island of Britain (Elinwy son of Cadegr, Cynhafal son of Argad, and Afaon son of Taliesin).

In Welsh verse, the term *tarw*, meaning a bull, was used as a poetic description of a warrior (as were *aergi*, battle hound; and llew, lion). This usage may have derived from the earlier tradition in which the tribal gods of the Northern Britons were sometimes seen as bull-horned warriors.

In Scandinavia, the bull was an attribute of Thor as the thunder god, and sacred to Freyja as goddess of fertility.

Symbolism

The bull usually symbolises the masculine principle in Nature, the generative force of the Sun. It is sacred to all sky gods, and denotes fecundity, male procreation, royalty, and kingship. Many ancient kings had a horned crown or head-dress (Celtic, Egyptian, and Assyrian). The king was considered to be an incarnation of the Moon god; Egyptian kings all had Osiris (Ousir) as one of their names, just as British monarchs have all had Arthur as one of their names (Arthur is associated with the bear, also a lunar animal). This was partly for political reasons, to legitimise their rule by claiming descent from a god or a divine king, but it was also for spiritual continuity.

The bull is also the Earth and the humid power of nature; in this case it pertains to the Moon, and is ridden by Moon goddesses such as Europa and Astarte. The bull ridden by a goddess signifies the taming of the masculine and animal nature. The bull of light ridden by a god indicates that the god is a warrior deity connected with the sky, the Sun, and storms.

The roaring of the bull and the stamping of its feet symbolises thunder, rain, and fertility. Storm and solar gods are depicted as bulls from earliest times onwards. The bull-man is usually a guardian figure who protects a central place, a gateway, or treasure. It wards off evil. The bull's head signifies sacrifice and death. The slaying of the bull at New Year symbolises the death of

Winter and the rebirth of the creative life-force. The slain bull of Minoan, Cretan, and Sumerial religion was a lunar animal, the 'lord of the rhythm of the womb'. He was an embodiment of the lunar king; the waxing and waning of the Moon was linked with the ritual killing of the king. The Moon was the other husband of the woman; he died each month, to be reborn as her physical child. The menstrual cycle was thus given cosmological significance.

In the Zodiac, Taurus the bull is a solar symbol of the creative resurgence of life in the Spring.

In Buddhism, the bull symbolises the moral self, the ego.

In Hinduism, the bull is a symbol of strength, speed, fertility, and reproduction in Nature.

In Mithraism, the bull and lion together symbolise death.

In Christianity, the bull symbolises brute force. It is an emblem of St. Eustace and St. Thecla.

In Hebrew symbolism, the bull is the might of Yahweh, and Yahweh is called the 'Bull of Israel'.

Calf

Etymology   from Old English *cælf*, Old Saxon *calf*, Old High German *kalb*, West Germanic *kalbha*

Folklore
If cow dung was smeared on the calf's mouth before it suckled its mother, it prevented faeries and witches stealing the milk, according to Robert Kirk's *The Secret Commonwealth of Elves, Fauns, and Fairies*, Aberfoyle, Perthshire, 1691. A similar custom was observed in Killearn, near Stirling, in 1795, when cow dung was forced into the calf's mouth immediately after birth so that the witches and faeries could not do it harm.

In parts of France, the first calf born in Spring was adorned with flowers and ears of corn at the harvest and led three times round the farmyard in a procession which included all the reapers with their tools. It was then chased by the reapers. Whoever killed it was the King of the Calf.

In Austria, the Muhkälbchen, a mythical calf, is seen amongst the sprouting corn in Spring, and pushes the children. When the wind ruffled the corn, people would say "The Calf is going about."

Mythology

In Vedic mythology, the calf is the mind of Aditi, the All-Embracing, who was originally the Mother of the Gods, from whom everything came. She was the personification of the creative powers of Nature. She was also symbolised by the Tree of Life and the Zodiac; she was the mother of the Adityas, the gods of the months, and may also have been a Sun goddess in this context.

The golden calf worshipped in the book of Exodus (Chapter 32) may have been a representation of Hathor, the Egyptian cow goddess, who was the patroness of the Sinai mining area.

In ancient Semitic mythology, the bull-child, the son of the Moon Mother, is the hero who comes to Earth to bring salvation for humanity. He stands between Earth and Heaven, since he is both a mortal man and the immortal son of the Moon Mother, both human and divine in nature.

Mythologically, Christ was such a divine son; the Virgin Mary is often depicted with the Moon.

Cow

Polarity Feminine   **Element** Water

Planet Moon   **Rune** Feoh / Fehu

Deities Hathor, Isis, Io, Audhumla, Hera, Prithivi, Surabhi, Nirriti

Etymology Old English *cu*, Old Saxon *ko*, Old High German *cuo*, Old Norse *k'yr*, from Germanic *k(o)us*

Folklore

In Shropshire, there is a valley called Mitchell Fold, where the Dun Cow was said to have been kept, according to a twelfth century legend (probably a local version of an even older tale). The Dun Cow's milk was inexhaustible, but one day an old woman wanted to fill her sieve as well as her pail. The cow became so enraged that she broke loose and wandered to Dunsmore Heath, becoming wild and savage. She was eventually killed by Guy of Warwick.

In fairy tales, the cow symbolises the mother figure, as the giver of milk. When the good cow Milky White stops giving milk in *Jack and the Beanstalk*, it is a symbol of expulsion from the infantile paradise in which Jack has hitherto lived. No longer will his every need be satisfied at a moment's notice; he must work to fulfil his desires. In *Jack and his Bargains* (a less well known Jack tale), Jack barters three of his father's seven cows for a stick that will beat his enemies senseless, a bee that sings, and a fiddle that plays marvellous tunes. These possessions enable him to gain the hand in marriage of a princess, by making her laugh.

In Schwaben, Germany, the last sheaf of the harvest was called the Cow. The man who cut the last ears of corn 'had the Cow', and was himself called the Cow, Barley-Cow, or Oats-Cow. He was given plenty of drink and a posy of flowers at the harvest-home, but no-one liked to be the Cow, because it involved a lot of teasing. The Cow was sometimes represented by the figure of a woman made from cornflowers and ears of corn, which was carried to the farmhouse by the man who cut the last handful of corn. The neighbours laughed at him and the children ran after him, until he gave the Cow to the farmer. In Switzerland the man who cut the last ears of corn was called the Corn-Cow, Corn-Steer, Oats-Cow, or Wheat-Cow, and was the butt of jokes. At Wurmlingen in Thuringia, the man who gave the last stroke at threshing was called the Cow. He was dressed in straw and two sticks were mounted on his head to represent horns. Then two lads led him on a rope to the well to drink, and on the way he had to low like a cow. At Obermedlingen in Schwaben, the man who gave the last stroke at the threshing 'got the Cow', which meant that a straw figure dressed in a petticoat, hood and stockings was tied to his back, his face was blackened, he was tied to a wheelbarrow with straw ropes and paraded round the village. In Switzerland also, importance was attached to the man who threshed the last corn. In Schaffhausen canton he was called the Cow; in Zurich canton, the Thresher-Cow; and in Thurgau canton, the Corn-Bull. At Arad, in Hungary, the man who gave the last stroke at the threshing was dressed in straw and a cow's hide with horns.

The breath of cows was believed to cure consumption (TB). If a cow wandered into the garden from the field, it portended a death in the family (1850, 1895, 1923). In Sweden, people gathered mistletoe on St John's Eve (Midsummer Eve) and hung it on the cows' cribs to keep trolls away.

Mythology

In Celtic legend, the cow is cthonic, and is depicted as red with white ears. She often appears in Celtic myth as the provider of perpetual nourishment, like the magic cows of Manannan, which were always in milk. However, if such a gift was abused, then it was speedily withdrawn. There is one tale (similar to the tale of the Dun Cow above) of a magic cow which visited many farms, until one day a woman tried to milk it dry; thereafter the cow was never seen again. This is a timely warning that using up the Earth's resources is an abuse of hospitality, and an irreversible process; once they are gone, they are gone forever.

In Scandinavian mythology, Audhumla, 'the Nourisher', the primal cow, emerged from the ice, and licked it with her warm tongue to produce the first man. She also nourished the giant Ymir with four streams of milk.

In China, the cow is the principle of yin and the Earth, with the horse representing yang and the Heavens. In Sumeria, Ninhursag, 'She Who Gives Life to the Dead', was originally a cow goddess; her temple had a sacred herd of cows. In Zulu mythology, humanity was belched up by a cow.

In Egypt, the great mother goddess, Hathor, was the primordial cow. She was the sky-goddess, often depicted as a cow with stars on her body, or as a woman with a cow's head. In other depictions she had a human face shaped liked a sistrum and cow's ears, or a crown with a solar disk between two horns. She ruled the month of Athyr (17 September to 16 October), the third month of the Inundation season. According to Plutarch, Set killed Osiris on 17th Athyr, and the Egyptians mourned him annually for five days thereafter; these days corresponded to the time at the Winter Solstice when the image of Isis was brought forth from the temple. Upper and Lower Egypt was represented by a double-headed cow.

The goddess Nut is also the celestial cow; her legs are the four quarters of the Earth; the stars of the firmament are on her underbelly. She is said to give birth to Ra, the sun god, every morning. Isis was also depicted as a cow, though she appears to have acquired this aspect by partially assimilating Hathor. Isis, Hathor, and Nut may all be depicted as cows or with horns, or crowned with the crescent Moon. In ancient times, Hathor was the sky, Osiris was the Moon, and Isis was Nature. Then Osiris became the Sun god, so Isis and Hathor both became the Moon goddess, and Isis eventually acquired Hathor's head-dress of the cow-horns surrounding a solar disc (her original head-dress was an ideogram of a throne, the hieroglyph of her name, Aset).

The absorption of Hathor by Isis is explained in the legend of Osiris' return from the underworld. He came back from the dead and appeared to his son Horus, to prepare him to avenge Osiris' murder. Horus fought with Set, and after a long struggle, eventually won. He brought the defeated Set before Isis. However, Isis being Nature, and therefore all-merciful, refused to kill him, and released him. Horus was angry at this, and tore off his mother's crown (in some versions, he beheaded her). When Thoth heard about it, he made Isis a new crown (or gave her a cow's head in place of her original one). In this way Isis was killed or maimed, losing her crown of light, and was restored to new life by Thoth, becoming Hathor, the Horned Crescent. One of the reasons why the Moon is identified with the cow is that the horns of the crescent Moon resemble a cow's horns. Isis was known as the Cow of Memphis; Horus was known as the Bull of His Mother. At the Winter Solstice, a statue of Isis in the form of a golden cow, covered in a black robe, was carried seven times around the shrine of Osiris, to represent Isis' wanderings around Egypt in her search for the dismembered parts of Osiris. This was done at night, and people fastened oil-lamps to the outside of their houses. At Sais in Lower Egypt, the image was made of wood and had a golden sun between its horns.

Another cow goddess is Shentayet, the goddess of weaving, who wove the mummy-wrappings of Osiris. There is also Sopdet (known to the Greeks as Sothis), the goddess of the Arrow-head Star (Sirius) which rises in Egypt on 19 July, heralding the return of the constellation of Orion, which in Egypt was Osiris himself. Sopdet was depicted either as a woman or as a cow seated in a boat, with three stars on her back and Sirius between her horns. A pre-dynastic Egyptian cow goddess was Mehueret, also a celestial cow, a Great Mother, and the goddess of the beginning. She was depicted as a woman with a cow's head, large breasts, and a sceptre with a lotus flower entwined around it. She was the mother of Ra, and was called 'Lady of Heaven and Mistress of Earth'. The terrestrial counterpart of the great cow of the heavenly ocean was Methyer, 'The Great Cow in the Water'. She is possibly an aspect of Mehueret. Neith was sometimes depicted as a cow, giving birth to Ra every morning; usually, however, her emblem was the crossed arrows of a pre-dynastic clan. She symbolised the female mysteries.

In Greece, the cow was a form of Hera (Zeus often manifested in the form of a bull), and of Io, who was a priestess of Hera at Argos who was desired by Zeus, and either turned into a heifer by Hera out of jealousy, or by Zeus to hide her from Hera. She was originally a pre-Greek Moon goddess to whom cows and barley were sacred. In Ovid's *Metamorphoses*, she is identified with Isis.

The heifer is one of the attributes of Mari, the Basque lunar and fire goddess (see also Ladybird).

In Hinduism, the cow is the sacred animal, a symbol of fertility, plenty, and the Earth. It is a commandment in the Rig Veda that the cow shall not be killed; it has been revered since Indo-Iranian times as the source of life and nourishment. Nandini, the wish-fulfilling cow, gives freely of her milk, and bestows an elixir of life upon her worshippers. She is the cow of plenty, the sister of Nandi, the milk-white steed of Shiva; they are both calves of Surabhi, the cow of plenty. Nandini is said to belong to Vasishtha (a Supreme Being and Vedic scholar). Aditi, the All-Embracing, the original source of life, is depicted as a cow. Prithivi, an early Hindu fertility and Earth goddess, is also depicted as a cow. She is the wife of Dyaus, the sky god, and the mother of Indra, the storm god. Her symbol is a square, her sacred colour is orange-red or yellow, and she represents solid matter. The cthonic cow is the consort of the bull of heaven. The four castes are represented as the four legs of the sacred cow. Nirriti, the goddess of ill-luck and disease, has as her sacred animal a barren black cow. By contrast, Surabhi is the cow of plenty. She was produced at the Churning of the Ocean of Milk. Her name means 'Pleasant, Friendly', and she is known as 'the marvellous cow, the mother and nurse of all living things'. Another cow goddess is Rohini, invoked to cure jaundice; she is associated with the constellations of Hyades and Scorpio, and also the stars Antares and Aldebaran (in the constellation of Taurus). There is also Prisni, the Earth and cow goddess; her name means 'the many-coloured earth'. She is the wife of Rudra, the storm god, and the mother of the eleven Maruts who became the companions of Indra, also a storm god. The Hindu goddess of sound, of the mystic speech through which occult wisdom is passed on, and of the power of speech, is envisaged as a melodious cow, personifying the nourishing aspect of Nature. She is called Vach; her name means 'Speech'. In one of the rituals associated with her, initiates pass through the womb of the statue of a heifer. The same ritual is used for purification after travel.

In Christianity, the Virgin Mary acquired the characteristics, attributes, and epithets of many goddesses. From Isis she acquired the titles 'Star of the Sea', 'She Who Initiates', 'Throne of the King', 'Mistress of the World', and 'the Heifer who has brought forth the spotless Calf'.

Symbolism

The cow is a symbol of the Great Mother, and of all Moon goddesses in their nourishing aspect. It is also a symbol of the productive powers of the Earth, representing plenty, procreation, and motherhood. The cow's horns symbolise the crescent Moon. The cow is both a celestial and cthonic animal, an emblem of both Earth and Moon goddesses.

Milk was a sacred substance in ancient times. The milk of the Mother Goddess provided nourishment for the gods. As milk and honey were given to newborns, they were also given to initiates to symbolise rebirth. Bedouins regard the sale of milk as an act of impiety. Milk is also used in funeral rites as the food of Paradise. The libation to the Muses consisted of milk, water, and honey.

Milk and water mixed symbolised the union of spirit and matter (milk was spirit, water was matter); they also symbolised weakness. In Buddhism, the Buddha Dharma is nourished by milk. In Christianity, milk is a symbol of the Logos; it is the heavenly milk of the mystic bride, the Church. The newly baptised were given milk and honey, as they were the foods of the newborn. Milk also symbolises the simple teachings imparted to the neophyte, before initiation entitles him or her to the wine of the sacrament. In the Greek mysteries of Orpheus, the initiate entered the womb of the Earth Mother; he or she was then reborn, and given milk from her breasts. Milk is also sacred to the Zoroastrians as a product of the cow. Milk and honey are the foods of Paradise; in Hindu mythology, there is a tree in Paradise which gives milk. The cow and the bee are linked with the tree of the Great Mother in many spiritual traditions.

Poetry

> "Weave a circle round him thrice,
> And close your eyes with holy dread,
> For he on honey-dew hath fed,
> And drunk the milk of Paradise."

(from *Kubla Khan*, by S T Coleridge)

Bless, O God, my little cow,
>   *Bless, O God, my desire;*
Bless Thou my partnership
>   *And the milking of my hand, O God.*

Bless, O God, each teat,
>   *Bless, O God, each finger;*
Bless Thou each drop
>   *That goes into my pitcher, O God!*

Ho, my heifer!
The night the Herdsman was out

No shackle went on a cow,
Lowing ceased not from the mouth of calf
Wailing the Herdsman of the flock,
        Wailing the Herdsman of the flock.

        Ho my heifer! ho my heifer!
        Ho my heifer! my heifer beloved!
        My heartling heart, kind, fond,
        For the sake of the High King take to thy calf.

The night the Herdsman was missing,
In the Temple He was found.
The King of the moon to come hither!
The King of the sun down from heaven!
        King of the sun down from heaven!

(from the Carmina Gadelica)

Ox

Polarity Yin   **Element** Earth

Planet Moon

Deities Hu Gadarn, Brighid, Nu-Wang, Bacchus

Varieties

In 1994, a hitherto unknown species of mammal, the pseudoryx or Vu Quang ox, was discovered in the forests of Vietnam.

Folklore

In the *Gospel of the Witches*, Diana uses an ox-bladder in her creative magic (see Mouse).

At Pouilly, near Dijon in France, it was the custom, when the last ears of corn were about to be cut, to lead an ox garlanded with ribbons, flowers, and ears of corn into the field, followed by all the reapers, dancing. A man disguised as the devil then cut the last ears of corn and slaughtered the ox. Part of the ox was eaten at the harvest supper, and the rest was pickled and kept till the first day of sowing in Spring.

Mythology

In Taoism and Buddhism, the ox represents the ego. In Taoism it is the untamed animal nature, which is dangerous when uncontrolled, but powerful and useful when subdued. This symbolism is reflected in the Ten Ox-herding Pictures of Taoism and Ch'an Buddhism (the Chinese forerunner of Zen Buddhism). In these pictures, the ox is at first depicted as wholly black, then gradually becomes white and finally disappears altogether. It is accompanied by a sage whose animal nature it represents; when it finally disappears, it signifies that the sage has transcended nature. After Lao Tzu had spread the teachings of Taoism and given the *Tao Te Ching* (Book of the First Principle and its Virtue) to his disciple, Yin Hsi, he is said to have mounted a green ox and disappeared into the West, never to be seen again. In Chinese festivities, the ox represents Spring, agriculture and fertility (instead of the more usual bull). The ox is the second animal in the Chinese zodiac (the Twelve Terrestrial Branches). In Chinese Buddhism, the white ox represents contemplative wisdom. The ox also features in the tale of the Heavenly Spinster.

In Celtic mythology, the ox is a symbol of Hu Gadarn, an early culture hero, who had a team of oxen which dragged the monster Addanc from the lake of Llyon-Llion, the Lake of Waves. Addanc was a dwarf or marine monster who dwelt by or in the lake and caused a flood. The ox is also an attribute of the goddess Brighid:

> *"Brigit the poetess, daughter of the Dagda, she had Fe and Menn, the two royal oxen... she had Triath, King of the Boars... she had Cirb, king of the wethers"* (rams)

In Greece, the ox was one of the main sacrificial animals. According to Varro, it was a capital offence in ancient Attica and the Peloponnese to kill one, except in sacrifice. Even when the animal was sacrificed, a scapegoat had to be found to carry the blame for the killing. This was either a person, or the knife which had been used was thrown away.

At Pompeii, there is a painting of Bacchus and Ariadne in a triumphal car drawn by oxen. Ariadne was abandoned on the island of Naxos, where she was discovered by Bacchus. A Christian catacomb painting shows Jacob and his sons travelling to Egypt in carts drawn by oxen. The Hebrew Torah forbids oxen and asses being yoked together (Deuteronomy 22:10).

In China, there was a god of oxen, Nu-Wang, and the golden-haired buffalo protected against epidemics among oxen. This buffalo was the spirit of the star T'ien-wen, and his image was placed on stables for protection.

Symbolism

The symbolism of the ox is interchangeable with that of the bull, in which case it is solar and represents fertility, but as the castrated ox it loses its connotations of fecundity and becomes a lunar symbol. To the Greeks and Romans, the ox was a symbol of agriculture and sacrifice. In Christianity, the ox represents patience, strength, the yoke of Christ, and Christ as the true sacrifice. It is an emblem of St Luke, who emphasised the sacrificial aspect of Christ in his gospel. In Nativity scenes, the ox is frequently depicted with the ass, to represent the idea that Christ became incarnate for both the Gentiles and the Jews. The ox is also an emblem of Saints Blandina, Julietta, Leonard, Medard, and Sylvester.

The saying "The black ox hath trod on your foot" or "The black ox hath trampled on you" means that misfortune has befallen you, or that you are henpecked. This may be associated with the Roman custom of sacrificing a black ox to Pluto, lord of the underworld, whilst a white one was sacrificed to Jupiter.

> *"Venus waxeth old; and then she was a pretie wench, when Juno was a young wife; now crowes foot is on her eye, and the blacke ox hath trod on her foot."*
>
> (from *Sapho and Phao*, IV, ii, by John Lyly)

Coyote

Latin name *Canis latrans*   **Planet**   Moon

Family *Canidae*

Etymology Mexican Spanish from Aztec *coyotl*

Deities Quetzalcoatl, Chinigchinich, Olle

Varieties

The Coyote is related to dogs, wolves, dingoes, foxes, fennecs, and jackals.

Folklore

Coyote is the indigenous American trickster figure. He is a transformer, a hero-saviour, who leads the people out of danger.

Mythology

In indigenous American mythology, Coyote is a lunar animal, a bringer of floods, the spirit of night, the Trickster of the tribes of the western mountains. The figure of Coyote is common to many of the indigenous American nations: the Achomawi, the Aschochimi, the Maidu, the Navaho or Dineh, the Sia, the Tuleyone, the Yana, and the Yokut. He is usually said to be cunning, resourceful, mischievous, and malicious. In the Tuleyone creation myth, he is Olle, the saviour of the world. (Usually he is the agent of destruction, but in this myth, it is Sahte who is the destroyer.) Sahte, an evil spirit, tried to destroy the world with a fire, but Coyote put it out with a flood, which submerged everything except one mountain peak, where the survivors gathered. In another version, it was the falcon Wekwek who stole fire from Heaven and set the Earth on fire, so that Olle had to put it out by sending rain.

In the Yana creation myth, Coyote accompanied a man in need of fire to a mountain which emitted sparks to steal some fire. On the way back, however, Coyote dropped the fire, and everything in the world was destroyed by fire. Many of Coyote's tricks represent the natural phenomena which are beneficial to humans.

In the Maidu creation myth, Coyote and Kodoyanpe survived the flood, then created humans from wooden images.

The Acagchemem people of California had a god called Chinigchinich, who was portrayed as a coyote.

In Aztec mythology, the double coyote is the cthonic form of Quetzalcoatl.

Deer, Stag

Latin name *Cervus spp.*

Family *Cervidae*

Order *Artiodactyla*

Suborder *Ruminantia*

Folk name Hart

Polarity Feminine (hind)
Masculine (stag)

Element Earth

Planet Moon (hind) Sun (stag)

Deities Apollo, Artemis, Athene, Diana, Flidass, Isis, Vaya, Fukurokuju

Etymology from Old English *deor* (animal or deer) Old Saxon *dior*, Old High German *tior*, Old Norse *d´yr*, Gothic *dius*, from Germanic *deuzam*, from Indo-European *dheusúm*, creature that breathes. (Compare modern German *Tier*, an animal.)

Varieties

Common Fallow Deer (*Dama dama*), originally from the Mediterranean region and Asia Minor, were brought to Europe in the tenth and eleventh centuries and bred for hunting, but later escaped from game preserves and lived wild in the forests. Red Deer (*Cervus elaphus*), with various subspecies throughout Europe, Asia, North Africa, and North America, inhabits both mountains and plains. Roe Deer (*Capreolus capreolus*) are distributed over most of Europe and parts of Asia. The Sika Deer (*Cervus nippon*) was introduced to Britain from Japan and northern China. It could be mistaken for a fallow deer but for its antlers. Another recent introduction to Britain is the Barking Deer or Muntjac (*Muntiacus muntjac*), a very small species. Other species of deer are the Wapiti or American Elk (*Cervus canadensis*); the Altai Wapiti or the Maral (*Cervus elaphus sibiricus*) which lives in Asia; Père David's Deer (*Elaphurus davidianus*) from China; the Axis Deer (*Axis axis*) which lives in

India and Sri Lanka; the White-tailed Deer (*Odocoileus virginianus*), found in the western half of North America; the European Elk (*Alces alces*), known in America as the Moose, which is the largest member of the deer family; and the Caribou or Reindeer (*Rangifer*), the most northerly of the deer family, which is unique in that both stags and hinds carry antlers.

Folklore

Medieval mummers were depicted wearing various animal masks, including a stag's head. This was clearly derived from a Pagan New Year custom, as the Council of Auxerre (578 CE) forbade dressing up as a stag or a calf on the Kalends of January.

The Well of St. Mary at Pilleth in Lancashire is "reputed to be haunted by a stag-headed former tenant" (Kightly, *The Customs and Ceremonies of Britain,* p. 231). Perhaps this apparition represents a local memory of a Pagan stag-god, who may have been Herne or a local variant of him. The water of the well is reputed to cure sore eyes and skin complaints.

In Devon, the custom of the Skimmington Ride took the form of dressing the victim (a man or woman who had been unfaithful to or ill-treated their spouse) as a stag, and pursuing them with mounted huntsmen and lads dressed as dogs.

The Berkshire coat of arms depicts an oak and a stag. Michael Drayton's poem of the battle of Agincourt, written in 1627, refers to this:

> *"Barkshire a Stag, under an Oake that stood*
> *Oxford a White Bull wading in a flood."*

According to Pliny and Aristotle, if a deer is wounded by an arrow, it will seek out the herb dittany (*Dictamnus albus*), which causes the arrow to be ejected from the body. This belief may have been derived from the slightly arrow-shaped leaves of the dittany plant.

In the Siberian folktale *Mergen and his Friends*, the hero saved a deer which was stuck in a swamp; he had been about to shoot it with his bow and arrow when it spoke to him with a human voice and asked him to pull it out of the swamp. When he did so, it told him to call upon it if he needed help. Later he met a magician with a beautiful daughter, who said that he could marry his daughter if he could accomplish three impossible tasks, the first of which was to wear out a pair of iron boots in one night. So Mergen called on the deer, which came to him, pulled the boots onto its hind legs, and rushed off into the hills, leaving a trail of stars and comets behind. In the morning it returned with only the tattered tops of the boots.

Mythology

Drawings of stags have been found in prehistoric graves, so it appears that they were associated with the dead from the very earliest times. Gods of the wind and the Wild Hunt were also associated with both stags and the dead. In Shakespeare's *The Merry Wives of Windsor*, it is said that Herne the Hunter 'blasts the tree', and the stag Eikthyrni consumes the branches of Yggdrasil; Herne 'makes the milch kine yield blood', and Frey (god of fertility) was slain with the antlers of a deer. All these customs and legends probably derive ultimately from Mesolithic hunting magic, which possibly relied on the magician's ability to communicate with the realms of the dead, where the spirits of hunted animals went. Shamans are often depicted dressed as stags; the stag was a symbol of wisdom in Shamanism.

To the Hittites, the stag was the steed of protective male deities. The Hittite God of Animals stands on a stag.

At the Sumerian temple of Ninkhursag at Tell-el Obeid, near Ur, a large copper panel depicts Imdugud, the divine lion-headed eagle, with two stags. Imdugud was a personification of the benevolent rainstorm after drought. In Sumero-Semitic rituals, the fertility god was sometimes dressed as a stag for the sacrifice. The stag's head was an emblem of Reshep, a god of lightning also known in Syria and Egypt (where he was known as Reshpu). Both Ea and Marduk were sometimes depicted with antlers.

In Egypt, the deer was sacred to Isis at Phocis.

In Mithraism, the stag and the bull together represent the moment of death.

In Greece, the deer was sacred to Artemis, Athene, Aphrodite, and Diana as Moon goddesses, and to the Delphic Apollo. Diana is frequently depicted with a fawn. The fawn was also the emblem of the Bacchantes and the devotees of Orpheus, who wore a fawn skin and sandals made of fawn-skin. Artemis transformed Actaeon the hunter into a stag to punish him for seeing her bathing naked, whereupon he was torn to pieces by his own hounds. The translation by Golding of Ovid's *Metamorphoses* has Diana sprinkling Actaeon with water from the spring, and the first phase of his transformation was the sprouting of hart's horns on his head. In the sixteenth century, Actaeon was a slang name for a cuckold.

The stag was a cult animal of the Anglo-Saxon kings. An iron 'standard' found among the grave goods of Sutton Hoo has a bronze stag with widespread antlers at its top. Hrothgar's hall in *Beowulf* was called 'Heorot' (Hart-hall). It is possible that the god Frey was the Germanic equivalent of the Celtic horned god. In Gylfaginning, Frey killed the giant Beli with a stag's horn. Germanic tribes held processions with stags, which were forbidden by the Church.

In Norse myth, four stags (representing the four winds) nibble the shoots of Yggdrasil. They are called Dainn, Dvalinn, Duneyrr, and Durathrorr. The reindeer is sacred to the Scandinavian Great Mother Isa or Disa, meaning ancestress. Interestingly, one of Freyja's titles is Vanadis (ancestress of the Vanir, the elder pantheon of Norse gods); she could possibly be identified with Disa. Both the Anglo-Saxons and the continental Germanic peoples regarded the stag as a symbol of kingly power and political authority. Woden (from whom the Anglo-Saxon kings claimed descent) was led to the halls of the troll-queen Hulda by a deer. In at least two extant texts, Odin himself was referred to as an elk or a stag.

The Siberian hunters in the region of Lake Baikal give formal burial to the bones of the reindeer they have killed for food. They regard the deer as a psychopomp, guiding the souls of the dead to the other world.

The Inuit (Eskimo) earth god is Tekkeitsertok, their most powerful deity. All deer belong to him, and sacrifices are made to him before the hunting season.

In Japan, the deer is an attribute of Fukurokuju, the god of wisdom and longevity.

In Vedic mythology, the wind god Vaya rides a deer. In India, the antlered storm god Rudra leads the Maruts, a host of the dead, and is also Lord of the Animals. In another Hindu myth, Brahma once got so drunk that he pursued the twilight goddess Samdyha. Samdyha took the form of a hind; Brahma took the form of a stag. Shiva shot off the stag's head with an arrow. Brahma said afterwards that he had been right to intervene.

In Celtic mythology, deer are supernatural animals of the faery world; they are the cattle of the faeries and the messengers of the gods; they can also convey souls to the Otherworld. Deer skins and antlers were used as ritual garments, possibly because of a desire to borrow the deer's ability to travel between the worlds. Flidais, the goddess of hunting, has a chariot drawn by deer. She is the woodland goddess, the queen of animals; the Cattle of Flidais were named after her. She is also possessed of great sexual stamina; she is the wife of Adammair, or of Fergus; when Flidais was away it took seven ordinary women to satisfy him. Deer were also associated with wealth. Sadhbh or Sadv, an Irish deer goddess whose name means 'goodly habitation', was the wife of Fionn and the mother of Oisin. She was enticed from Fionn's house by a Druid before the birth of Oisin, who turned her into a deer. Fionn searched for her for many years, but never found her.

The boy Oisin (whose name means 'fawn') returned to his father and grew up to be an inspired poet. He was also the only man on record to stand up to St Patrick in an argument. He was also known as Ossian. In 1762, a Scottish poet, James McPherson published his popular series of poems (alleged to be a translation of Ossian's poems), which sparked off a Celtic revival and were read by Goethe. Fionn's true name was Demne, meaning 'small deer'; Oisin's son was called Osgar (he who loves the deer). Fionn, Oisin, and Osgar came from Leinster, and there is a part of Leinster called Osraige (people of the deer).

Another Irish deer goddess was Garbh Ogh, a giantess whose chariot was drawn by elks; she lived on venison, milk, and eagles' breasts, and hunted the mountain deer with a pack of seventy hounds who were all named after birds. Irish goddesses are often transformed into cailleachs, who could be encountered at their sacred wells or driving their herds of deer over their sacred hills. In the *Tain Bo Cuálnge*, Cú Chulainn subdues wild deer and wild swans, which he yokes to his chariot. The Irish god Donn mac Midir appears in the shape of a deer in three stories. The Morrigan can also shape-shift into a stag. Supernatural stags also appear in Irish texts: in the *Colloquy of the Ancients*, a three-antlered stag is mentioned.

The stag is an attribute of the North British Celtic hunting god Cocidius, who was equated with Silvanus, god of the hunt and guardian of forests and fields; it is also a form of the Horned God, and an attribute of Vosegus, the patron deity of the Vosges region of France. The stag is occasionally depicted with three antlers in Celtic art; this signifies that it is a supernatural animal, possibly related to the cult of the horned fertility god. A three-antlered stag is mentioned in the Colloquy of the Ancients (an Irish text, 'Agallamh na Senorach') as 'the grey one of three antlers' (*liath na dtri mbenn*); it was eventually killed by Caoilte. Three was a sacred number in Celtic tradition. Also in the *Agallamh*, the warrior Salbhuide dies in pursuit of a magical deer.

Celtic stag gods are also depicted with purses full of gold and cornucopiae, signifying wealth and plenty. A relief from Luxembourg shows money pouring from a stag's mouth. Reliefs showing the stag god have been found at Cirencester, Avon, and Meigle, Perthshire. A relief of Mercury from York shows him with a stag; Mercury was sometimes equated with the Horned God. A relief from Castlecary in Stirlingshire shows stags fighting in a wood; a hunter stands on one side holding a bow. An altar to Cocidius found at Risingham shows him hunting stags in a wood. He is also depicted in other reliefs, carvings, and intaglia as hunting or accompanied by stags. Horned goddesses were rare but not unknown in Britain; there is a bronze statuette portraying an antler-bearing goddess. The stag also appears as an attribute of the Horned God on the Gundestrup Cauldron from Denmark. A god with vestigial horns is shown holding aloft by its hind legs a stag in each hand. In Celtic mythology, deer frequently entice heroes into the otherworld; there are many legends where the hunting of a deer leads the protagonists into unexpected magical situations.

In Welsh legend, King Math of Gwynedd could only rule when his feet were placed in a virgin's lap (unless he was at war). The virgin was his daughter Goewin, whose marriage would mean his death (this may signify that the king ruled by virtue of being married to the queen - hence if Goewin married, her consort would be king in Math's stead). Arianrhod's brothers Gwydion and Gilfaethwy lived at Math's court, and Gilfaethwy desperately wanted Goewin. So Gwydion and Gilfaethwy started a war which meant that Math had to be away from court, and raped Goewin while he was away. When Math discovered what had happened, he turned the brothers first into a stag and a hind, then into a boar and a sow, then into a wolf and a she-wolf. In each form they returned to court after a year with offspring of that species, each of which turned into a boy. The boy who had been a fawn was called Hyddwn; the boy who had been a piglet was called Hwchdwn; and the boy who had been a wolf cub was called Bleiddwn. The tale is related in the *Mabinogion*.

In another Welsh legend, Amathaon (the plough god and magician) stole a dog and a roebuck from Arawn, Lord of the Underworld. This theft caused the Battle of the Trees (Cad Goddeu) between Gwydion and Arawn.

In the twelfth century text *Vita Merlini*, Merlin becomes the Lord of the Animals; dressed in antlers, he summons an enormous herd of stags and she-goats as a wedding gift for Guendoloena, who is amazed at his affinity with the animals. The name Gwendolen means 'white circle', and in this story Guendoloena appears to be a type of flower maiden. (In modern Welsh, 'gwyn' or 'gwen' means white or blessed, and 'dolen' means a ring, link, loop, or bow.) It is appropriate that the Lady of the Flowers should be the consort of the Lord of the Animals. She represents the growth and burgeoning of nature; he represents the powers of hunting, culling, and death, which must occur so that the powers of fertility can progress without stagnation. Cernunnos is often identified with the Lord of the Animals, since he (or some other antlered god) is depicted on the Gundestrup cauldron with a stag and other animals, and holding a ram-headed serpent in one hand and a torc in the other.

In indigenous American mythology the deer symbolises swiftness, and is famed for being fleet of foot.

In Aztec mythology, Mixcoatl the god of hunting is accompanied by a two-headed deer. In South America a deer can be the incarnation of a sorcerer or of a dead ancestor. In Inca mythology, Urcaguay is the god who guards underground treasures; he is depicted as a snake with a deer's head and a tail adorned with gold chains.

In Christianity, the hart is a symbol of piety, religious aspiration and fervour, the Christian thirsting after knowledge, God, solitude, and purity of life, 'as the hart panteth after the water brook' (Psalm 42). The hart trampling on the serpent represents Christ triumphing over evil.

The hart was also the quarry of the Wild Hunt in Christian legend. Originally associated with Odin in Germanic legend and Herne in Anglo-Saxon myth, the Wild Hunt became the entourage of Satan in some medieval stories. The connection was inferred from a reference in Psalms to Satan as a hunter who lays snares to catch the souls of the unwary. *"Quoniam ipse liberavit me de laqueo venantium, et a verbo aspero."* (For He has freed me from the snare of the hunter, and from harsh words. - Psalm 91.3).

254

This image is developed further in various texts. Hugh of St. Victor wrote that "*Cerva est casta et munda anima. Sagittae sunt desideria mala. Venatores sunt daemones.*" (The hart is the chaste and pure soul. The arrows are evil longings. The hunters are devils.)

So the Pagan myth of the Wild Hunt as the divine Hunter and his crew purifying by selection and sacrifice was distorted into the Christian devil hunting down souls. This distortion was brought about by the fear of death induced by belief in hell as a place of torment. Whereas the Pagan view is that souls descend into the Underworld to be renewed, and sees the Lord of the Forest as the guide and psychopomp, the new religion declared that he was the ultimate Adversary, rather than the natural complement to the powers of life.

A stag with a crucifix between its horns is an emblem of St. Hubert (possibly an attempt to Christianise a Pagan stag-cult). The stag is also an emblem of Saints Adrian, Eustace, Eustachius, Ida, Felix, and Julian the Hospitaller. In Ireland, it is associated with St Kieran of Saighir, who had a stag as a disciple; and St Cainnech, who had a stag who let him use his antlers as a book rest.

Symbolism

Deer are frequently depicted with the Tree of Life in both Pagan and Christian imagery. In the Mediterranean, the stag is identified with the Tree of Life because of its branching antlers. The Tree of Life is a symbol of perfect harmony; its fruits symbolise the rewards of spiritual growth. By association with the Tree of Life, the deer is seen as a spiritual animal.

The stag is a symbol of the Sun, of renewal, creation, fire, and the dawn. It is an enemy of the cthonic serpent. In dualistic cultures, the stag trampling the serpent underfoot represents the victory of spirit over matter. The stag is a messenger of the gods and the heavenly powers. Stags draw the chariot of Father Time; reindeer draw Father Christmas' sleigh.

Antlers are an attribute of the Horned God, and denote fertility in nature and fecundity in humans and other animals. They also represent supernatural power. The ten-tined antler is an attribute of the shaman.

In Alchemy, the stag with the unicorn represents the dual nature of Mercurius, the philosophical mercury, the nous.

To the Celts, the stag was a symbol of virility, fertility, the Sun and its therapeutic powers.

In Buddhism, deer shown on either side of the Wheel of the Law represent the Buddha preaching in the deer park at Sarnath; it was this sermon which set the Wheel of the Law in motion. The deer is a symbol of meditation, meekness, and gentleness. In Chinese Buddhism, however, it is one of the 'Three Senseless Creatures, signifying love-sickness (with the tiger as anger and the monkey as greed).

In Chinese symbolism, the deer signifies longevity, virility, high rank, official success, happiness, and wealth (deer is a homophone of lu, reward). The god of immortality, Shou-hsien, is represented by a white stag. The dragon is known as 'the celestial stag' in China. In a Chinese folk tale, a deer gives birth to a girl who is found and brought up by a man. When she dies, her body disappears. The god of salaries, Lu-Hsing, is depicted mounted on a deer.

In Japan, the deer is a symbol of solitude and melancholy, especially when associated with the maple tree. It is also an attribute of gods of longevity. The dragon is known as 'the celestial stag' in Japan. Fukurokuju, the Japanese god of wisdom and longevity, is portrayed with a deer, a crane, or a tortoise.

Poetry

"I will voyage in God's name
In likeness of deer, in likeness of horse,
In likeness of serpent, in likeness of king.

More powerful will it be with me than with all others."
(from *'Invocation for Justice'*, *Carmina Gadelica*)

The Milk White Doe

It was a mother and a maid
    That walked the woods among,
And still the maid went slow and sad,
    And still the mother sang.

"What ails you, daughter Margaret?
    Why go you pale and wan?
Is it for a cast of bitter love,
    Or for a false leman?

"It is not for a false lover
    That I go sad to see,
But it is for a weary life
    Beneath the greenwood tree.

"For ever in the good daylight
    A maiden may I go,
But always on the ninth midnight
    I change to a milk white doe.

"They hunt me through the green forest
    With hounds and hunting men;
And ever it is my fair brother
    That is so fierce and keen."

"Good morrow, mother." "Good morrow, son;
    Where are your hounds so good?"
"Oh, they are hunting a white doe
    Within the glad greenwood.

"And three times they have hunted her,
    And thrice she's won away;
The fourth time that they follow her
    That white doe they shall slay."

Then out and spake the forester,
       as he came from the wood,
"Nor never saw I a maid's gold hair
       Among the wild deer's blood.

"And I have hunted the wild deer
       In east lands and in west;
And never saw I white doe yet
       That had a maiden's breast."

Then up and spake her fair brother,
       Between the wine and bread,
"Behold, I had but one sister,
       And I have seen her dead.

"But ye must bury my sweet sister
       With a stone at her foot and her head,
And ye must cover her fair body
       With the white roses and red.

"And I must out to the greenwood,
       The roof shall never shelter me;
And I shall lie for seven long years
       On the grass below the hawthorn tree."

Dog

Latin name *Canis familiaris*   **Polarity** Masculine/Feminine

Family *Canidae*   **Element** Air/Fire

Planet Moon

Folk name Dogger (Hampshire)

Deities Diana, Hecate, Cocidius, Sucellos, Nodens, Woden, Brimo, Asklepios, Gala, Astarte, Belit-ili

Etymology from Old English *docga* (origin unknown)

Varieties

The domestic Dog (*Canis familiaris*) is related to the Wolf (*Canis lupus*), the Fox (*Vulpes vulpes*), the Coyote or Prairie Wolf (*Canis latrans*), and the Dingo (*Canis dingo*), which is believed to be descended from domestic dogs taken to Australia by people from India.

Folklore

The dog was often an embodiment of the corn-spirit in harvest ceremonies. In the Lons-le-Saulnier region in the Jura mountains, the last sheaf of the harvest was called 'the Bitch'. The corn-spirit was commonly perceived as a wolf or a dog in France, Germany, and Slavonic countries. When the wind set the corn into a wave-like motion, people would say "The mad Dog is in the corn"; children were warned not to go into the corn-field because "The big Dog sits in the corn." In some parts of Silesia, the person who cut the last sheaf was called the Wheat-dog or the Peas-pug (depending on the crop).

In North-east France, the idea of the Corn-dog was quite well-developed. If a harvester became unwell or unable to keep up, the others would say "The White Dog passed near him", "He has the White Bitch", or "The White Bitch has bitten him." In the Vosges region, the person to cut the last sheaf was said to "kill the Dog". If the crop was poor, the Dog was said to be lean. Near Verdun, the expression for finishing the reaping was that they were going to kill the Dog. At Epinal, they would say that "We will kill the Wheat-dog (or Rye-dog, or Potato-dog)." In Lorraine, they would say of the man who cut the last sheaf, "He is killing the Dog of the harvest." At Dux in the Tyrol, the man who gave the last stroke at the threshing was said to "strike down the Dog". The Romans sacrificed red-haired puppies in spring to avert the blighting influence of the Dog Star, and to make the crops grow ripe and ruddy.

The expression "It's raining cats and dogs" comes from the tradition of using cats and dogs in rain-making ceremonies. Both cats and dogs were believed to be the familiars of witches. The dog is a signal of wind, like the wolf. Both the dog and the wolf were associated with Odin, the god of wind and storm. The dog symbolises the strong gusts of wind accompanying a rainstorm.

In Welsh legend, Prince Llewellyn had a dog called Gelert. One day he returned to his castle to find the dog's jaws dripping with blood. He had left Gelert to guard his infant son, but the baby could not be found. Thinking Gelert had killed the baby, Llewellyn ran the dog through with his sword. Afterwards he found his son close to the body of a wolf, which Gelert had killed. Full of remorse, he buried Gelert. The grave lies just outside the village of Beddgelert in Gwynedd, Wales. It is not known if it is really the grave of Gelert, but tradition asserts that it is the place, and it is certainly an atmospheric site. The earliest written account of this legend dates only from around 1800, when W. R. Spencer wrote a poem about it; however, the story is illustrated in the chronicle of

John Rous (circa 1483), where a greyhound is depicted lying in a cradle in a coat of arms at the feet of the Prince of Wales.

A similar legend was related in France, where a cult developed around the dog, which was believed to heal sick children. In the diocese of Lyons, a thirteenth century inquisitor, Stephen of Bourbon, discovered the cult of Saint Guinefort (the holy greyhound). Near the enclosed nuns' village of Neuville, on the estate of the Lord of Villars was a castle. The lord and lady of this castle had a baby boy. One day, when the lord and lady had gone out of the house, and so had the nurse, leaving the baby alone in the cradle, a huge serpent entered the house and approached the baby's cradle. Seeing this, the greyhound, which had stayed behind, chased the serpent and, attacked it. The cradle was upset; the dog bit the serpent and the serpent bit the dog. Finally, the dog killed the snake and threw it well away from the cradle. The room was drenched with their blood.

When the family returned, they thought the dog had killed the child, and the lord of the castle ran the dog through with his sword. Then they found the baby to be safe and sound, and discovered the remains of the serpent. Deeply regretting the unjust killing of the dog, they threw it into a well near the house, raised a mound of stones over it, and planted trees beside it. When the people learnt of the manner of the dog's death, they came to the place to honour the dog as a martyr, and prayed to it when they were ill or in need of something. An old woman in a nearby town taught the women how to make offerings to the martyred dog, such as salt and other things; women would hang their babies' swaddling-clothes over the bushes, and drive nails into the trees. They would also pass their naked babies nine times between two trees. They would call upon the faeries of the forest of Rimite to return their children that they had stolen and take away the sickly changeling they had foisted on them. Children were also laid under the trees on a bed of straw with candles on either side of them.

According to Stephen of Bourbon, some of the babies were actually accidentally killed in this manner. In any case, he proceeded to suppress the cult by disinterring the dog, cutting down the grove, and preaching vigorously against the cult of the holy greyhound. The name of the dog was not, however, originated by the peasants; the historical Saint Guinefort was a martyr at the time of the emperors Maximilian and Diocletian. He was believed to give protection against the plague.

In later centuries, ecclesiastical authorities concerned with the diocese of Lyons enquired of the local priests whether there was any superstition, but were told that none existed. In 1823, however, it became clear that the legend of Guinefort was still extant. In 1877, an extract from Stephen of Bourbon's treatise was published, and various folklorists descended on the region to investigate. All the locals who were asked replied that Saint Guinefort was a dog, and related the story of the child and the snake with few variations from the original version, except that the knight had been replaced by a woodcutter, who killed the dog with an axe.

People were still making pilgrimages to the wood at Sandrans as a cure for illnesses in the nineteenth century. This would seem to imply that the cult had survived for six centuries, slightly modified by time and oral transmission. It is probable that the association of the name Guinefort with the legend of the dog occurred because Guinefort was a saint of the dog-days (the ascendancy of the star Sirius), owing to the manner of his martyrdom and his association with curing the plague.

Another holy dog cult (recorded in 1713) occurred in the Auvergne, where a dog called Ganelon was regarded as a saint by the locals; sadly, little is known of this cult beyond the dog's name. It was still believed in the sixteenth century in France that burying a dog under a dying tree was believed to give the tree strength and to rejuvenate it. It was also believed that the killing of a dog would bring misfortune, either to the murderer or to someone who lived in the same house. In Provence the killing of a dog was believed to bring seven years' bad luck.

Various similar narratives of a man killing a faithful dog which had protected his child from a predator occur in Europe, the Near East, and India. There are several versions of the story in the

Romans des sept sages (Novel of the seven wise men), written in the thirteenth and fourteenth centuries. Another two narratives are found in the two versions of the novel of Dolopathos. A version appeared in German around 1520, written by Johannes Pauli, in *Schimpf und Ernst*. Pausanias (who wrote a travel book about Greece) also relates a variation of the tale, and a version appears in the Panchatantra, where the protagonist is a brahman. There was also an Arabic version in the Book of Kalila and Dimma, where a pious Muslim kills the dog.

The black dog is regarded as an emissary of diabolical powers, a symbol of sorcery, the damned, and death.

Spectral dogs appear frequently in local legend and folklore, such as the Gytrash in Lancashire (mentioned in Charlotte Bronte's *Jane Eyre*), or the Moddy Dhoo in the Isle of Man. In the West of England, there is a legend of the Devil's Dandy Dogs, a pack of fire-breathing hounds led by the Devil over the moors on stormy nights. Possibly these spectral hounds are a remnant of the Wild Hunt. In Taunton, Somerset (1923), it was believed to be lucky to meet a Dalmatian - "a plum pudding dog" - and if you made a wish, it would be fulfilled. This belief was also recorded in Oxford in 1953, with the proviso that you must cross your fingers on seeing a Dalmatian to obtain success.

It was generally believed (according to the principles of sympathetic magic) that if a dog bit you, laying its hair on the wound would heal the bite. This quickly became satirically applied to the popular hangover cure of having another pint of the beverage you were drinking the night before. Various texts cite this tradition, from Heywood in 1546 to Swift in 1738, in whose book *"Polite Conversation"* the following piece of wit is recorded:

> *"Your Ale is terrible strong and heady... and will soon make one drunk and sick; what do you do then? Our way is, to take a Hair of the same Dog next morning."*

In 1872 in Lancashire, an assault case was heard before two magistrates which arose from the owner of a dog which had bitten a child refusing to give some its hairs to the mother of the child to be laid across the wound.

Hearing dogs howling is believed to portend calamity or death. This belief was recorded many times between 1507 and 1971.

Mythology

Dogs were venerated in ancient times, and there is evidence to suggest that they were domesticated in pre-dynastic Egypt (c. 7500 BCE). The dog is the oldest animal companion of humans, acting as a friend, guardian, hunter, and herder. In some societies, the dog was highly regarded; in others, it was regarded as unclean.

In many mythologies, the dog guards the boundaries between this world and the next, and is often an attribute of deities associated with the dead (Hecate, Yama, Odin). It is the guardian of the passage and of the underworld. It is also a psychopomp, guiding the souls of the dead. It is also associated with many lunar deities (Diana, Sinn); messenger deities (Hermes/Mercury, Anubis); deities of destruction (Set, Brimo); hunting deities (Diana, Cocidius); healers (Asklepios, Nodens); and Mother Goddesses (the Mother Goddess was sometimes depicted as a whelping bitch, and referred to as the Bitch). It is also a symbol of the wind, chasing away the boar of Winter or drought. The cynocephalus (a dog-headed man) imprisons or destroys the enemies of light. The dog is often a mythical ancestor or a culture hero; in many myths the dog brought fire to humanity or invented fire-making by friction. In some cultures, it is said that the dog saw the men making fire, and let the women into the secret. The dog often acquires sexual symbolism when connected with fire, as fire symbolises passion. The companionship of the dog continues beyond death, and it acts as an intermediary between the dead and the underworld deities.

In Africa, the dog is a culture hero, either the inventor or the bringer of fire. Dogs are frequently the companions of Australian Aboriginal tribes.

In indigenous American mythology, the dog is a culture hero and mythical ancestor, and intercedes with the powers of the next world. The Iroquois sacrificed a white dog at the New Year to take prayers to the next world. Dogs were regarded as guardians and protectors, representing loyalty and the tolerance of human failings.

In Aztec mythology, Xoltl, the god of death and of the setting Sun, has a dog's head and is the patron deity of dogs. The dog was regarded as a guide of the dead, and was often sacrificed at funerals to guide the soul to the afterlife.

In the Mexican Zodiac, the Dog is the last sign, representing a period of non-time or chaos, the transitional period between the old year and the new, or death and rebirth.

In Mayan culture, a dog carrying a torch denoted lightning.

In Greek myth, Hecate had a pack of war-dogs. Dogs were sacrificed to her at crossroads; they were also sacrificed to Eileithyia. Hecate was sometimes depicted as a woman with three animal heads (sometimes of a horse, a dog, and a boar; sometimes of three dogs), or as a whelping bitch. Dogs are probably associated with Hecate because they howl at the Moon, and they are good at pathfinding (one of her titles was Hecate of the Ways). The dogs of Hades represented the gloom of dawn and dusk, regarded as dangerous and demonic times of day, when malevolent powers were abroad. In later Greek folklore, Hecate and her dogs were a kind of Wild Hunt. In Greek myth, the three-headed monster dog Cerberus guarded the entrance to Hades. Hercules dragged Cerberus to earth and let him go again. The herb aconite (Monkshood or Wolfsbane) was said to have grown from the foam that dripped from Cerberus' mouths. Orpheus lulled Cerberus to sleep with the music of his lyre in order to gain entrance to Hades; the Sybil who guided Aeneas into Hades threw the dog a cake made with poppies and honey, which sent him to sleep.

The legend of Cerberus may originate from the ancient Egyptian custom of setting a dog to guard a grave. The Keres, the beings who carried out the will of the Fates (Moerae), were known as the

Dogs of Hades. They carried off the dying at the appointed hour, and hovered over battles, crying out dismally as they finished off the wounded. Geryon, a triple-bodied monster who guarded the western coast of Iberia (or, in other versions, Epirus) had two dogs, both slain by Hercules: they were the two-headed Orthos, and Gargittios. Hercules killed the dogs whilst stealing Geryon's cattle (his tenth Labour). These cattle were red oxen. When the maiden Procris fled from Cephalus in shame, Diana gave her a dog called Laelaps which never missed its prey, and a dart which never missed its target and always returned to the archer. Orion's dogs were called Ptoophagos (the glutton of Ptoon, a city in Boeotia), and Arctophonos (the bear-killer). Ulysses' dog was called Argos; he recognised his master after his return from Troy, and died of joy at seeing him again.

In Graeco-Roman mythology, the dog is sacred to Diana and Hecate, and is therefore associated with the Moon and witches. By virtue of this association, dogs appear on the Tarot card of the Moon in many decks. The dog is also a psychopomp and an attribute of Hermes and Mercury. Hermes Kriophoros is the Good Shepherd, and as such is accompanied by the dog Sirius (who also accompanies the hunter Orion). In association with Asklepios (Aesculapius), the dog heals by the process of rebirth. As in other cultures, its fidelity survives death. Dogs were also sacred to Herakles (Hercules) and Artemis (Diana). Both the Greeks and the Romans sacrificed dogs on 25 July (the setting of Sirius); the Greeks in the ceremony of Kunophontes, and the Romans in a sacrifice to the goddess Furrina, to whom all red-haired dogs were sacrificed when the waters were at their lowest.

In Mithraism, the dog was regarded as a psychopomp, and was hence associated with the bull sacrifice; in this context it is depicted with the snake and the scorpion.

In the Northern Tradition, Garmr (the Devourer), which guards the entrance to Hel (the Underworld) is often depicted as a dog, and Brimo (the Destroyer) is frequently accompanied by a dog. Odin had two dogs or wolves, Geri and Freki.

In the Slavonic tradition, the three Zoryas (goddesses of dawn, evening, and midnight) have charge of a dog chained to the constellation of Ursa Minor. According to the legend, when the chain breaks it will be the end of the world. There could be a connection here with the Teutonic myth of the Fenris-wolf, who was chained by the gods; when he breaks free, Ragnarok will begin.

The Celts used dogs for hunting (e.g. deer-hounds). In Celtic mythology, the dog is particularly associated with the healing thermal waters, especially at the temple of Nodens, the god of healing, at Lydney, and at the temple of Sequana at the source of the Seine, where many statuettes of people holding a dog were found. Many statuettes of dogs were found at the temple of Nodens at Lydney, including one of an Irish wolfhound in bronze. Various other dogs in stone and bronze have been recovered from the well at the temple, where they were clearly offerings to the god. Possibly the strange funnel-like structure above the well represented the entrance to the underworld. The dog was sacred to Nodens, possibly associated with his healing and solar aspects.

Deities of the sun and healing were also associated with water and the underworld; Nodens was also associated with hunting and fertility, and was equated with Mars and Silvanus by the Romans. At Coventina's Well at Carrawbrough in Northumberland, a small bronze terrier was found. Bones of dogs have also been found at the bottom of wells, as it was the practice to dedicate a well before its use by making offerings to the deities. The dog is a companion of hunter gods, war gods, and heroes. Epona (the horse goddess) and Sucellos (the Gallic fertility god, whose name means 'the Good Striker', possibly also a god of the dead) were also accompanied by a dog. The Germanic goddess Nehalennia, the protectress of seafaring merchants, was also depicted with dogs.

The dog is also depicted on the Gundestrup cauldron, in the scene of a bull being slain; in the scene where the god appears to be dipping a man in a cauldron, where a dog is leaping up at the cauldron; and in another scene, where a goddess appears to be nurturing both men and animals, a dog is draped across one of her breasts. In Irish legend, Garbh Ogh was a giantess who hunted the mountain deer with a pack of seventy hounds all named after birds. Many Irish heroes had names with canine elements in them: Cú Chulainn (Hound of Chulainn), Conmhael, Cu Roi, Mac Con. Cú Chulainn was said to have acquired his name by killing the dog of Culann the smith; he then had to act as a replacement for the dog for seven years until a puppy could be reared to replace it. He had his own dog, called Luath. He also had a *geas* (taboo) against eating the flesh of a dog. The breaking of this geas was to cause the hero's death. Mac Con was said to have got his name because as a child, he was inseparable from a dog called Eloir the Red, so he was called Son of the Hound. (This may, however, be a late r attempt to rationalise the name.)

The hero Finn had two dogs, Bran and Sceolang, who were his two nephews magically transformed. Ethlenn, the mother of Lugh, was killed in the form of a lap-dog. Three pups were found in the head of Conganchnes: Culann's hound, Celtchair's hound, and Mac Da Tho's hound. They were the three mythical dogs of Ireland. There was also a custom in Ireland of eating dog flesh for divinatory purposes.

In the Welsh classic, the *Mabinogion*, greyhounds are given to Pwyll by Arawn, king of Annwn (the underworld), who rides a pale horse and leads a pack of white hounds with red ears in pursuit of a stag. These white hounds frequently appear in later folklore as supernatural portents of death. Amathaon stole a dog and a roebuck from Arawn; this caused the Battle of the Trees (Cad Goddeu). The goddess Cerridwen could also assume the form of a dog; when Gwion accidentally drank from her cauldron of knowledge, one of the shapes in which she pursued him was that of a greyhound chasing a hare. Mabon, the Child of Modron, was accompanied by a wonderful hound. There was a Welsh hero called Cúnhaval (Like a Hound), and another called Cynon (Great or Divine Hound). In British tradition, the name Cunobelinus (the prototype for Shakespeare's Cymbeline) means 'Hound of Belinus'. King Arthur's favourite dog was called Cavall. Tristan had a dog called Hodain or Leon. On Culhwch's first visit to King Arthur's court (in *Culhwch and Olwen*), he is accompanied by two greyhounds. Folklore and legend from Celtic areas of Britain (Wales, Cornwall, Devon, the Isle of Man, Scotland, and Ireland) include many tales of supernatural dogs, both malevolent and helpful.

In various Near Eastern mythologies, the Good Shepherd is accompanied by a dog.

In Egypt, the dog was sacred to Anubis (Anpu), who was depicted with the head of a dog or a jackal; he led Isis to the place where Osiris' coffin had floated ashore at Byblos. Set had a pack of hunting dogs, however, with which he succeeded in finding the coffin, whereupon he cut Osiris' body into fourteen pieces and scattered them all over Egypt. The dog was also an attribute of Amenti, lady of the west and of the dead; and it was sacred to Thoth (Tehuti) as messenger god, though this may have been a Greek influence. Hapi (one of the Four Sons of Horus) was dog- or ape-headed, and guarded the lungs of the dead. He was depicted on one of the four canopic jars in which the viscera were stored. It was also the custom in ancient Egypt for graves to be guarded by dogs.

The Babylonian Moon god, Sinn, was depicted with two dogs (one coming and one going), representing the waxing and the waning Moon. The dog is also an attribute of Astarte. The physician goddess Gula (known to the Phoenicians as Gala) was also associated with the dog; she could bring either health or illness. Her symbol was an eight-rayed orb.

In Semitic mythology, the dog was associated with the scorpion, the serpent, and other reptiles, and regarded as baleful, evil, and demonic. In Hebraic belief, the dog was an unclean animal, and therefore represented impurity. The dog is also unclean in Islam, and only permitted as a guard animal. The only exception to the general dislike of dogs in Semitic culture is in the *Book of Tobit* (in the *Apocrypha*), where Tobias has a dog for a companion.

In Islam, the dog is regarded as unclean, but it does appear occasionally in legends. The Seven Sleepers (in the Eighteenth Sura of the *Koran*) had a dog called Katmir, who accompanied the seven noble youths to the cavern in which they were walled up. He remained standing the whole time, neither moving, eating, drinking or sleeping, and was subsequently admitted to heaven. The seven men slept for 309 years. Jung (in *Four Archetypes: Mother, Rebirth, Spirit, Trickster*) interprets their sleep as being a process of ritual incubation, a sojourn at the centre of all things, where there is no time, and thus they remain young for the duration. The accompanying dog is the guardian of the transitional state.

In Phoenician mythology, however, the dog is a solar animal, accompanying the Sun. It is also an attribute of Gala, the Great Physician, as an aspect of the Mother Goddess. The Akkadian goddess Belit-ili had a throne supported by dogs; or her throne had a dog sitting in it. The Assyrian version of Herakles was accompanied by a dog, according to Tacitus; so was Melkarth, the Tyrian Hercules.

In Buddhism, the Lion Dog is the guardian and defender of the Law, symbolising motionless obedience and the subjection of the passions through the Law. The dog is an attribute of Yama, god of the dead.

In China, the red celestial dog, T'ien Kou (a yang animal) helps Erh-lang chase away evil spirits. It is also associated with eclipses and comets, however, and is blamed for carrying off new-born children.

In Japan, the goddess Sarama or Devasuni is a wind goddess in the form of a brindled bitch, who conducts the souls of the dead.

In Hinduism, the hunting dog is an attribute of Indra (the Vedic storm god). Yama, god of the dead, is represented by a dog with four eyes, which also represents the gloom of dawn and dusk. He is also accompanied by two ferocious dogs who act as his messengers. The hero of the *Mahabharata* refused to enter heaven without his beloved dog.

In Oceanic mythology, the dog was either the inventor or the bringer of fire.

In Siberian shamanism, the dog was the messenger of the forest spirits.

In Inuit (Eskimo) mythology, Avilayoq was the mother of the human race by her husband, a dog. Her father threw her into the sea as a sacrifice to calm a storm. She grabbed at the gunwale of his boat, and he chopped off her fingers, which became seals, whales, and polar bears. Her legend is similar to that of Sedna; they may even be identical. Another legend tells of Keelut, a malevolent Earth spirit who looks like a hairless dog.

Symbolism

The dog symbolises faithfulness, watchfulness, and nobility (both dogs and falcons are emblems of nobility). According to Plutarch, dogs represent "the conservative, watchful, philosophical principle of life." According to Apuleius, the dog is the messenger between the higher and the lower powers. The dog also symbolises loyalty, watchfulness, courage, skill at hunting, masculinity, the Sun, Air, and Fire. The dog of the Moon was represented as three-headed (possibly to depict the three phases of the Moon).

In Alchemy, the dog and the wolf symbolise the dual nature of Mercurius, the philosophical mercury. This is interesting, as both the dog and the wolf are attributes of Woden, and both Mercury and Woden are associated with Wednesday *(Mercredi* in French, and originally *Wotanstag* in German, but now Mittwoch, midweek), since Mercury was equated with Woden.

In China, the dog is solar and yang by day, but yin and lunar by night. As guardian of the night-time, it becomes a symbol of destruction and disaster, connected with meteors and eclipses, when it is said that the dog goes mad and bites the Sun or the Moon. The Buddhist Lion Dog is often portrayed in Chinese art. By day, the dog symbolises fidelity and unswerving devotion. The coming of a dog is an omen of future prosperity.

In Japan, the dog represents protection, and is a guardian.

In Graeco-Roman antiquity, the term cynic was an insult meaning 'dog-like', implying that the person was impudent or given to flattery. According to Homer, the dog has no shame.

In Egypt and Sumeria, the dog was regarded as a solar animal. In Egypt, it was associated with the hawk-headed solar god, keeping the Sun on the right path through the sky.

Zoroastrians regard both the dog and the otter as 'clean' animals. Killing them is a sin. The *sag-dig* is a mythical white dog with yellow eyes, which may be a psychopomp. Dogs are introduced at the bedside of a dying person, and accompany the funeral procession. After the person's death, the member of the family closest to them will feed the dog for the duration of the time that the soul lingers near the body. The food is fed to the dog first, then partaken of by the mourners and priests; the ritual symbolises the feeding of the dead person. The death of a woman in childbirth necessitates two dogs for the two souls. The dog ranks next to humans in creation; it is the intermediary between the worlds, and guards the Cinvat Bridge. According to M Z Afshar (in *The Immortal Hound: The Genesis and Transformation of a Symbol in Indo-Iranian Traditions*), the dog in Vedic and Indo-Iranian thought was impure and denoted death. In Zoroastrianism, however, it signifies life and ritual purity. The dog is associated with the divine hunter and saviour, who pursues immortality. The Avestan God of Contract (Mithra) and the Roman bull-slayer (Mithras, called the Mediator) have both been representations of this divine hunter. In the early Hellenistic period, there was a cult centre of Herakles as the tamer of animals in the Caves of Karafto in Kurdistan. The motif of the divine hunter has passed into Sufism as well. In Zoroastrianism, dogs were believed to be in contact with the realm of the dead, emissaries from and to the underworld.

In Christianity, the dog is a symbol of faithfulness, watchfulness, and marital fidelity. As the guardian of flocks, the dog represents the Good Shepherd, or a bishop or a priest. The Dominican monastic order were known as the Hounds of God, a pun on their name (*Domini canes*), and are symbolised by a black-and-white dog. St Dominic (1170-1221), founder of the Dominicans, is depicted with a sparrow at his side, and a dog carrying a torch in its mouth. The Devil was said to have appeared to him in the form of a sparrow; the dog with a torch refers to his mother's dream during her pregnancy that she had given birth to a dog which lighted the world with a burning torch. When he was baptised, the lady who lifted him up to the font thought she saw a star on his forehead illuminating the earth (an implicit reference to Sirius?) There is also a poetic tradition of Christ as the Hound of Heaven (as in the well-known poem by Francis Thompson, where God pursues the errant man through all the nights and days).

The dog is an emblem of St Bernard (the legend of whose birth is similar to that of St Dominic), St Hubert (patron saint of hunters, who is invoked against rabies) St Sira, St Tobias, St Wendelin and St Roch or St Roque (to whom a dog brought bread while he was dying of plague in a forest; the knight to whom the dog belonged followed it and, on encountering the saint, was converted to Christianity). It is interesting that St Roch, who was particularly invoked to alleviate the plague, should be associated with a dog, as St Guinefort, also called upon in times of plague, is associated with a greyhound in the region of Lyons (see Folklore). In a twelfth century *Martyrology*, St Christopher is represented as cynocephalous and apparently standing guard over a fortified town. The festivals of St Christopher (9 May in the Byzantine church and 25 July in the medieval Catholic church) correspond to the rising and setting of the star Sirius (the Dog Star). According to Greek tradition, St Christopher was a giant with a dog's head who devoured men until he was converted to Christ. He came from the country of Lycopolis (wolf city) or Cynopolis (dog city). Many saints with whom dogs are associated are also invoked to ward off snakes.

The dog is associated with a number of constellations and stars. The term 'cynosure' (1. a centre of attraction; 2. a guiding star - OED) comes from the Greek *kunosoura*, a dog's tail, referring to the constellation of Ursa Minor. The dog is also associated with the constellation of Canis Major, and the star Sirius. The rising of Sirius heralded the coming of the dog days, the languid days of high summer. According to Court de Gebelin and A E Waite, the Star card in the Tarot represents Sirius. The sequel to *A Hundred and One Dalmatians*, which is called *Twilight Barking* uses the association of the Dog Star and the dog days for the basis of the story. The three Zoryas (Slavonic time goddesses) have charge of a dog chained to the constellation of Ursa Minor. In Greek myth, the dog was also associated with the star Procyon. Moera was the dog of Icarius, whom Dionysos taught the art of wine-making. Icarius was killed by some peasants who thought they had been poisoned when they got drunk on Icarius' wine. They buried him under a tree, but his daughter Erigone realised what had happened when she found his dog Moera howling by the grave. She hanged herself for grief. The gods then transformed her into the constellation of Virgo, Icarius into Boötes, and Moera became the star Procyon, which rises in July, a short time before Sirius. Moera means 'the Glistener'.

Poetry

"That instant was I turned into a hart;
And my desires, like fell and cruel hounds,
E'er since pursue me."
                    (*Twelfth Night*, I, i - William Shakespeare)

Dolphin

Latin name *Delphinus delphis*   **Element** Water

Suborder *Odontoceti*   **Planet** Sun or Moon

Order *Cetacea*

Etymology Middle English *dolphin* or *delphin*, from Latin *delphinus*, from Greek *delphis, delphinos*

Deities Apollo, Aphrodite, Poseidon, Palaemon, Leucothea, Thetis, Dionysos, Neptune, Atargatis, Ishtar, Mithras, Coventina, Borvo, Nodens

Varieties
The order *Cetacea* includes whales, dolphins, and porpoises. They are warm-blooded breathing mammals, with no external ear or trace of external hind limbs, no connection between mouth and nose, and a blowhole on the top of the head to breathe through.

Folklore
According to Pliny, the dolphin is the swiftest of all living creatures. It is regarded as kinder and more sensitive than human beings. According to Aelion, dolphins are lovers of music, and as such, they were associated with Apollo. Legend has it that the dolphin was human before it took to the sea. It is very unlucky to kill a dolphin.

Mythology
In Celtic mythology, the dolphin was associated with well-worship and the power of the waters. The god Borvo (associated with healing springs) is depicted with a dolphin and a horned serpent in a pottery fragment from Vichy. A Gaulish carving from Mavilly shows the Gaulish equivalent of Neptune with a dolphin in his left

275

hand and a trident in his right. The dolphin appears frequently in Celtic art; the Gundestrup Cauldron has a picture of a man riding a dolphin. The dolphin also appears on Gaulish coins, on a mosaic floor at the temple of Nodens at Lydney, and on the slabs of stone beside Coventina's Well at Carrawbrough in Northumbria.

In Greece, the dolphin was a psychopomp, guiding souls to the Isles of the Blessed; it had both solar and lunar associations. It was connected with Apollo Delphinos, and signified the light of the Sun. But it also has feminine symbolism because of the association between *delphis* meaning 'dolphin', and *delphys* meaning 'womb'. There are dolphins sculpted on the temple of Apollo at Delphi. Delphi was originally an omphalos and a shrine of the Mother Goddess. The dolphin is also associated with Aphrodite and Eros, and is therefore a symbol of the amatory arts. It is an attribute of Poseidon as god of the sea, and of Dionysos as the son of Leucothea. Thetis (a Nereid or sea-nymph) rides naked on a dolphin. Telemachus (son of Ulysses) and Arion were saved by dolphins. When Poseidon was pursuing Amphitrite, daughter of Oceanus, he sent a dolphin to look for her. She had fled from him when he saw her dancing with her maidens on the island of Naxos. Eventually the dolphin brought her back to Poseidon, and was placed among the stars as a reward.

The dolphin also plays an important part in the myth of Leucothea. There are two versions of the myth, one involving Melicertes (later deified as Palaemon), and the other involving Dionysos. Ino (later deified as Leucothea, the Milk-white Goddess)

276

was the wife of King Athamas of Boeotia, who had gone mad and killed her other son. To escape him, she jumped into the sea with her infant son (either Melicertes or Dionysos) in her arms. Thus far the details of the myths are the same. However, in the Melicertes version, Ino and Melicertes drown, and Ino is befriended by the Nereids and becomes Leucothea, whilst the body of Melicertes was carried to Corinth by the dolphins, where he was venerated as the god Palaemon. In the Dionysos version, Ino and Dionysos are both carried (still living) by the dolphins to the Isthmus of Corinth, where she became Leucothea, the mother-goddess of the centaurs.

In Minoan art, the dolphin represents sea power, and is associated with Apollo Delphinos.

In Roman art, cupids ride dolphins, and the dolphin also appears in funerary art as a psychopomp, depicting the soul's journey over the sea of death.

In Mithraism, the dolphin was associated with Mithras as light.

In Egyptian mythology, the dolphin was an attribute of Isis, who was also goddess of the sea.

In Sumero-Semitic art, the dolphin was used as an alternative to the fish in representations of Ea-Oannes. It was also an attribute of Ishtar. In Babylonian myth, the dolphin was sacred to Atargatis as connected with water. (Atargatis was the Babylonian name for Astarte/Ishtar.)

An Australian Aboriginal tribe has the dolphin as its totem.

To the indigenous Americans, the dolphin is a messenger to the spirit world and the essence of the Great Spirit. In South America, the river dolphin is regarded as a shape-shifter which takes human form at night.

Symbolism
The dolphin is the King of the Fishes, the Arrow of the Sea. It is

regarded as a saviour and psychopomp, and symbolises the power of the sea, safety, and swiftness. Two dolphins facing in opposite directions symbolise the duality of Nature. A dolphin with an anchor symbolises the two extremes of speed and slowness and illustrates the paradoxical saying 'Hasten slowly'.

To the Romans, the dolphin symbolised the soul's journey across the sea of death to the Blessed Isles.

In Christianity, the dolphin symbolises Christ as saviour of souls (because it was reputed to rescue the shipwrecked) and bearer of souls over the waters of death. A dolphin with a ship or an anchor depicts Christ guiding the Church; a dolphin pierced by a trident or an anchor represents Christ on the Cross.

Echidna or Spiny Anteater

Latin name *Tachyglossus aculeatus*

Family *Tachyglossidae*   **Planet** Moon

Order *Prototheria*

Etymology modern Latin from Greek, *ekhidna*, viper

Natural History
The Echidna is a monotreme (having a single vent for passing urine, faeces, and eggs or sperm) mammal belonging to the family Tachyglossidae (5 species), found in Australia, Tasmania, and New Guinea. The Australian echidna or spiny anteater has long spines among its fur, and digs for ants, picking them up with its long sticky tongue. The female lays a single egg, which is incubated in a pouch on her belly. The young echidna is suckled at a teat in the pouch. It is a nocturnal animal.

Symbolism
To the Australian Aborigines, the echidna represents initiation, death and resurrection. According to J. C. Cooper, it plays the part of the lunar hare or rabbit in Aboriginal tales; it is a trickster figure.

Elephant

Latin name (see below)

Family *Elephantidae*

Order *Proboscidea*

Folk name Oliphaunt

Element Air (as intelligence)

Planet Mercury

Deities Buddha, Akshobya, Ganesha, Ganpati, Airavata, P'u Hsien, Shoden, Mercury, Apedemak

Etymology Middle English *olifaunt*, Old English *olifant* or *elefant*, Roman *olifantus*, Latin *elephantus* or *elephans*, from Greek *elephas* (ivory) and *elephantos* (elephant)

Varieties
The African Elephant (*Loxodonta africana*) is the largest elephant, and has bigger ears than the Indian Elephant (*Elephas maximus*). They are the only two genera to survive into the present era. Most of the *Elephantidae* were extinct before the appearance of humans, except these two and the Mammoth, which may have died out because of a combination of the reduction in its habitat caused by the end of the last Ice Age and being hunted by humans.

Folklore
"The elephant never forgets."

According to Pliny, the elephant is a religious animal, worshipping the Sun and stars, purifying itself by bathing in the river at the New Moon, and invoking the heavens.

Strabo and Aelian thought that the elephant had no joint in its legs, so had to sleep standing up. Aristotle called it the most intelligent of animals, teachable and gentle.

Elephants are generally regarded as lucky. This belief was recorded in Westmorland, 1953 and Morecambe, Lancashire in 1957, where someone could remember a wedding at which the bridegroom met an elephant on his way to church and was congratulated by everyone on his good luck.

Mythology

In Buddhism, the elephant is sacred to the Buddha. Legend has it that Queen Maya (wife of King Suddhodhana), while she was pregnant with the Buddha, dreamt that a little white elephant was entering her womb. The elephant is associated with royalty in India. The white elephant is the Jewel of the Law, the *vahan* of the Bodhisattva, and a symbol of love, compassion, kindness, and the wisdom, patience, and long memory of the Buddha. Akshobya, one of the four Dyani-Buddhas (Buddhas of Meditation), ruler of the East, rides an elephant and carries a thunderbolt. Akshobya is blue in colour.

In China, the god P'u Hsien (the Vedic god Pushan) rides a white elephant.

In Graeco-Roman mythology, the elephant was an attribute of Mercury as intelligence.

In Hinduism, the elephant is the animal of the god Ganesha or Ganpati. Ganesh is patron of learning, and the Vedic god of good fortune, wisdom and literature. When his mother Parvati showed him to Shiva (his father), Shiva's glance destroyed Ganesha's head, so the gods replaced it with that of an elephant. In another version of the myth, the Devas asked Shiva to defend them from some demons who were attacking them, and from Shiva's mind there appeared the glowing image of a child with an elephant's head; Parvati then declared that no enterprise would be successful if prayers were not offered to the child. It is also related that Ganesh was formed from Parvati's sweat when she was rubbing herself with fragrant oils and powders. She then lowered him into the River Ganges, where he grew to his current magnitude; he is thus known as the child of two mothers (Dvaimatura), since he was born of both Parvati and the river goddess Ganga. The attribution of elephant characteristics may have arisen as a result of Ganesha's rank as leader of Shiva's army. On the other hand, he may be a pre-Vedic deity of the Naga tribe, responsible for writing and the harvest.

The earliest known forms of Ganesh are from the Decca region in southern India; they are often related to images of the seven mothers (the Saptamatrika), who are fertility goddesses. These early Ganesh images are often accompanied by Naga serpents coiling round stones. Ganesha's consorts are Buddhi (intuition and intellect) and Siddhi (achievement). He was the legendary scribe who wrote the Mahabharata. He has four arms, giving gifts and protection to humans. In Japan, Ganesh is called Shoden. Ganesh is one of the most popular gods in India; all actions requiring luck are commenced with an invocation to Ganesh; these include acts of business, and the laying of the first stone of a new building. The cult of Ganesh has spread throughout India, Tibet, Nepal, and South-east Asia, and even as far as Mexico. He is usually depicted with an elephant head and a large human belly. He may be shown sitting, standing or dancing; he also rides on a large rat or mouse, and sometimes has a serpent as a girdle. This may be derived from his early association with the harvest. Legend relates that Ganesh fought the demon Gajamukha, and won by breaking off his right tusk and throwing it at him, cursing him to turn into a mouse, which then became his steed.

According to European folk legend, elephants are frightened of mice - perhaps there is some connection here? The apparent incongruity of an elephant seated on a mouse may also be pertinent, bringing Ganesh's playful Divine Child aspect to the fore. The mouse also represents cunning, since it is able to slip through very narrow gaps. The snake girdle was acquired after Ganesh had been to a particularly good party, and was riding home on his mouse after eating an enormous meal of sweets and puddings. The mouse was frightened by a snake and stumbled, so Ganesh fell off, and his stomach burst open, spilling all the cakes. So he made the snake into a girdle. Then he saw that the Moon was laughing at him, so he broke off his tusk and threw it at her, saying that she would never appear in the night sky again. But then there was no twilight or night, so all the gods begged Ganesh to let the Moon reappear. He did, but now the Moon waxed and waned. For this reason, anyone who looks upon the Moon during Ganesh's festival of Ganesha Chaturthi (on the 4th of Bhadrapada, near the end of August) will soon have scandal attached to them. He has various names: Ganesha (lord of the Ganas, the hosts of Shiva); Vakratunda (of the twisted trunk); and Vinayaka (remover of obstacles), amongst others. His ears are believed to sift truth from lies, like great winnowing baskets.

The Tantric interpretation of this is that a person can learn when the inner babble has been stilled and one can pay attention to the here and now; in the Vedic worldview, it represents the idea of the all-wise guru. Ganesh's trunk represents the quality of discernment, and possibly also the sound OM. An interesting feature of Ganesh is that one of his tusks is broken, which goes against the grain of Hinduism's usual tendency towards symmetry. In one legend, the tusk was broken when Parashurama, an avatar of Vishnu, struck at him for trying to prevent him from entering Shiva's chambers. In another version, he used the broken tusk to write down the Mahabharata at the dictation of the sage Vyasa. (This is almost reminiscent of Odin sacrificing his eye to gain the wisdom of the Runes, a magical sacrifice to gain knowledge.)

In Chinchbad, near Poona in Western India, Ganapati (one of Ganesh's names, meaning elephant-headed) is believed to have been incarnated in each generation of a Brahmin family of the

Mahrattas, beginning with Moorab Gosseyn in 1640. Gosseyn strove to work out his salvation by abstinence, mortification, and prayer. Following this, the god Ganpati appeared to him in a vision and promised that a part of his spirit would abide with Gosseyn and his descendants to the seventh generation. The connection with the Gosseyn family lasted until 1810, when the seven generations were up; but afterwards the Brahmins found a successor to carry on.

Indra, guardian of the East, has the elephant Airavata (who was produced by the Churning of the Ocean of Milk) as his steed. Indra's wife Aindri or Indrani has an elephant as a footstool; she is the goddess of sensual pleasure. In ancient belief, the world was supported by four elephants.

In the Meroitic culture of Sudan, there is a lion-headed war god called Apedemak, whose emblem is the elephant.

Symbolism

In China, the elephant symbolises strength, sagacity, prudence, energy, sovereignty, and cosmic energy. The white elephant is especially lucky.

In Hinduism, the elephant symbolises prudence, kingly rank, invincible might, intelligence, and longevity. It was the preferred mode of transport for princes and maharajas, hence a symbol of status, strength, and foresight. Because of its longevity, it represents victory over death, and the dignity and wisdom of old age. It is also the strength of sacred wisdom. The elephant head of Ganesh signifies strength, good fortune, and wisdom. Ganesh is powerful and destructive, but also loyal, kind and responsive to affection. His ears sift truth from untruth; his trunk represents discernment.

To the Christians the elephant is a symbol of Christ, trampling the serpent underfoot; it also represents chastity and benevolence.

In Roman art, the elephant was a symbol of immortality, longevity, and victory over death.

The elephant is an emblem of both India and Africa in European art.

In the West, the white elephant symbolises a possession, the responsibility or expense of which is out of proportion to the value of the object. It alludes to the legendary King of Siam who used to present courtiers whom he wished to ruin with a white elephant.

In Denmark, there is an order of knighthood called The Order of the Elephant, said to have been instituted by Christian I in 1462, but possibly of earlier origin. It was reconstituted in 1693 by Christian V. It consists of the sovereign, his sons, and thirty knights. Their collar depicts gold elephants and towers.

Poetry

"Let us think of the one-toothed,
let us meditate on the crooked trunk,
may that tusk direct us.
One tusk, four arms, carrying noose and goad,
with his hands dispelling fear and granting boons,
with a mouse as his banner.
Red, with a big belly,
with ears like winnowing baskets,
wearing red, with limbs smeared in red scent,
truly worshipped with red flowers.
To the devoted a merciful Deva,
the maker of the world, the prime cause,
who at the beginning of creation
was greater than gods and men.
He who always meditates thus is a Yogin above Yogins.
Hail to the lord of vows, hail to Ganapati,
hail to the first lord, hail unto you,
to the Big-bellied, One-tusked, Obstacle-destroyer,
the Son of Shiva, to the Boon-giver, hail, hail.

(*Ganesha Upanishad*)

Elk

Latin name *Alces alces*   **Element** Air

Family *Cervidae*   **Folk name** Wapiti

Deities Garbh Ogh, Pinga

Varieties

The European Elk (*Alces alces*) is called the Moose in America; it is the largest living member of the deer family. The Wapiti or American Elk (*Cervus canadensis*) was originally distributed throughout North America.

Mythology

In Irish myth, the chariot of Garbh Ogh, an ancient but ageless giantess, is drawn by elks. She hunts the mountain deer with a pack of hounds all named after birds. The Inuit (Eskimos) have a god called Pinga who watches over the animals hunted by the Inuit for food, particularly the caribou. He is also one of the guardian deities of the dead.

Symbolism

To the indigenous Americans, the elk symbolises supernatural power and the whirlwind. In 19thC. Poland, the elk was regarded as a Romantic animal, symbolising obstinate solitude and melancholy.

Ermine or Common Stoat

Latin name *Mustela erminea*

Family *Mustelidae*

Etymology ermine: Middle English from Old French *hermine*, probably from medieval Latin *mus Arminius*, Armenian *mouse*. stoat: Middle English, origin unknown

Varieties

The stoat is related to the Marten (*Martes martes*), the Weasel (*Mustela nivalis*), the Fitch or European Polecat (*Mustela putorius*), the Ferret (*Mustela furo*). Other members of the Mustelidae include the Otter (*Lutra lutra*), the Badger (*Meles meles*), the Wolverine (*Gulo gulo*), the Grison (*Grison vitata*) found in South America, and the Skunk (*Mephitis mephitis*).

Symbolism

The ermine, being white in winter, represents purity, chastity, and innocence; it is also associated with justice, and is an emblem of the Sforza family.

Robes trimmed with ermine fur denote royalty or nobility in the ceremonial trappings of both church and state. Aristocratic Christian virgin saints are sometimes depicted wearing ermine fur, particularly St. Ursula.

Fox

Latin name *Vulpes vulpes*

Family *Canidae*

Folk names Reynard, tod, zorro, shual

Deities Inari, Uke-mochi, Aunt Piety

Etymology Old English and Old Saxon *vuhs*, Old High German *fuhs* from West Germanic *fuhs*; **vixen**, from Middle English *fixen*, Old English *fyxen* from Middle High German *vühsinne*

Varieties

The zorro is a South American fox or fox-like wild dog. The shual (a Hebrew word) is any one of a number of species of fox found in Palestine; it may also refer to the jackal. The Fox (*Vulpes vulpes*) is related to the Wolf (*Canis lupus*), the domestic Dog (*Canis familiaris*), the Coyote or Prairie Wolf (*Canis latrans*), and the Dingo (*Canis dingo*).

Folklore

In Britain and Northern Europe, the fox is often called Reynard, after the name given to the fox in the Low German beast-epic, *Reynard the Fox*, which was a satire on contemporary life and events. The name is derived from Middle Dutch Reynaerd, from Old High German Reginhart, meaning 'strong in counsel'. In the North of England, the dialect word for a fox is 'tod'.

In Scandinavia, the Aurora Borealis is called 'the light of the fox'.

In Japan, marsh-light (*ignes fatui*) is called fox-fire. According to Japanese superstition, a black fox is good luck, whilst a white fox presages disaster. Geishas and prostitutes are sometimes known colloquially as vixens.

In China, the fox is believed to be able to assume human form, and is also associated with ghosts.

Mythology

In Japan, the fox is the messenger of the rice-god Inari, the god of agriculture. Shrines of Inari usually have two statues of foxes in front of them. The personality and attributes of an earlier mother-goddess, Uke-mochi, have been absorbed by Inari. The rice-god is especially worshipped by women, and is associated with rice-growing, fire, and smithcraft.

The Chinese goddess of the magical arts, Aunt Piety, appears sometimes as a vixen and sometimes as a woman.

Among the U'wa (Tunebo) of Colombia, South America, the Fox Chant is performed in the dry-to-wet season, which spans the Spring Equinox. Since the Sun is overhead at the Equinox, it is considered particularly dangerous, as it is close to the Earth, and likely to copulate with women. When the maize fields have been sown, the men perform the Fox Chant. After the Chant, the people move to the lowlands to harvest maize, avocado, and chontadura, and the main hunting season begins.

In former times, it was performed by the women. The men no longer perform the first part of the Chant. In the second part, the skin and placenta of the fox emerge from the highland cave, endowed with sight, breath, tools, and wealth. They greet each other in the same way as siblings of the same sex, and run down the mountain into the clan territory, which is the temperate zone.

The same story is then told of the opossum (*shara*). The foxes run round the lakes and think of their cross-cousins, the male opossum. They look for honey. The opossum do the same, but they are looking for crabs. In the third part, the two creatures meet. The fox remarks that the opossum has no cutting tools, and the opossum remarks that the fox has no scraping tools. The fox climbs to get honey, and the opossum catches ground wasps. Their tools are blunt. They travel to the edge of the middle world, to the place where land and sky meet. They go below the mountain lakes, and the fox steals tools from the upper world deity of light. They return to the lowlands of the middle world, and eat honey. They then eat aphrodisiac foods and attempt to copulate, but since they are both male, this is not possible, and their genitalia are immature, or blunt. So they travel to the upper world via the stars and steal mature genitalia from another upper world deity.

In the fourth part of the Fox Chant, the fox eats too much and becomes fat. He then goes to the stone pillars that support the middle world house, at the base of the Earth. He sits and becomes like stone, and becomes pregnant by eating too much honey, which is a symbol of fertility among the U'wa. He is then banished into the middle world, and becomes an immortal and asexual deity, who is the seventh star of the Pleiades. The opossum reappears as a female in the animal purification chant (*Ruwa Reowa*). The moral of the Fox Chant is that males cannot reproduce without females, and often need aphrodisiac substances as well.

The male fox is called Thenakuba by the U'wa.

Symbolism

In Christianity, the fox symbolises the devil, deception, cunning, guile, and fraud. It is reputed to feign death in order to trap its prey, and as such symbolised the treachery and wiles of Satan. As spoiling the vines (*Song of Solomon* 2:15), it represents the depredations of heretics and enemies of the church.

In Ireland, however, Christianity took a less dim view of the fox. St Kieran of Saighir built his hermitage with the help of a fox, a wild boar, a badger, a wolf, and a stag. St Kieran of Clonmacnoise had a tame fox who used to carry his writings for him. The figure of both these saints appears to be closely associated with the mythological figure of the Lord of the Animals, and they may represent a Christianised version of the local form of Cernunnos.

In China, the fox symbolises cunning, powers of transformation, shape-shifting, and longevity.

To the indigenous Americans, the fox represents the wisdom of instinct, trickery, cunning, and craftiness.

Poetry

"Take us the foxes,
 the little foxes,
 that spoil the vines:
 for our vines have tender grapes."   (*Song of Solomon* 2:15)

Gazelle

Latin name *Gazella spp.*

Family Antelopidae   **Planet** Moon

Folk name gazal

Deities Chandra, Shiva, Astarte, Mullil, Reshpu, Set

Etymology French, possibly from Spanish *gacela*, from Arabic *gazal*

Varieties

The gazelle is a member of the Antelope family, and is related to the gemsbok (*Oryx gazella*), the White Oryx (*Oryx algazel*) the eland, the antelope, and the gnu. Gazelles are mainly found in Asia and Africa.

Mythology

In Egypt, the gazelle, the oryx, and the goat were attributes of Set in his typhonic aspect. Horus was depicted trampling on the gazelle to represent his defeat of Set.

In Hinduism the gazelle and the antelope are vehicles of Chandra, the Moon god, and a symbol of Shiva, who rides in a chariot drawn by antelopes. In the Hindu zodiac, the gazelle or antelope represents Capricorn.

In Islam, the gazelle symbolises spirituality.

292

The poet ibn Arabi wrote, "My heart, a pasture for gazelles..."

In Sumeria, the gazelle was an attribute of Astarte, the great goddess. It was associated with Mullil, god of storms, and with Reshpu, a Syrian god of lightning and thunderbolts. Reshpu was also worshipped in Egypt, where he was depicted with a gazelle projected above his forehead, probably to represent his rulership of the desert. He was also shown with the crown of Upper Egypt with a gazelle's head in front.

Symbolism
In Christianity the gazelle fleeing from predators symbolises the soul fleeing from earthly passions.

Poetry

"Listen! My lover!
Look! Here he comes,
leaping across the mountains,
bounding over the hills.
My lover is like a gazelle or a young stag.

My lover is mine and I am his;
he browses among the lilies.
Until the day breaks
    and the shadows flee,
turn, my lover,
    and be like a gazelle
or like a young stag
    on the rugged hills."

(Song of Solomon, 2)

Goat

Latin name *Capra hircus aegagrus*

Family *Caprinae*

Deities Pan, Artemis, Aphrodite, Hermes, Dionysos, Daksha, Agni, Ea-Oannes, Asshur

Etymology from Old English gat (a she-goat), Old Saxon *get*, Old High German *geiz*, Old Norse *geit*, Gothic *gaits*, from Germanic *gaitaz*, from Indo-European *ghaidos*

Polarity Masculine and Feminine

Element Earth

Planet Moon

Varieties

The goat is possibly the oldest domesticated animal apart from the dog. Its nearest relatives are sheep and goat-antelopes. The family Caprinae is a subdivision of the Bovidae.

The saiga (*Saiga tatarica*) looks like an antelope but is in fact a goat. The markhor (*Capra falconeri*) lives in the mountain forests of the Caucasus.

The Cameroon Goat (*Capra hircus*) is an African dwarf variety. The domestic goat was probably arrived at by crossing various wild species of the mountains of Asia Minor and the Mediterranean, especially the Pasang or Wild Goat (*Capra hircus aegagrus*).The ibex is a close relative of the goat. The Barbary or Aoudad Sheep appears to be an intermediate species between sheep and goats.

Folklore

The old man in fairy tales is often described as riding a goat; presumably the goat represents instinct, over which the old man has mastery, and cunning, a quality which he often displays.

In Scandinavia, a straw goat is a type of corn dolly made at Lammas; it was originally sacred to Thor. It is also part of the Winter Solstice celebrations, and symbolises the promise of plenty of food through the winter. In parts of Prussia, when the corn bent before the wind, they would say that the Goats were chasing each other, or that the wind was driving the Goats through the corn, or that the Goats were browsing there. Children were warned not to go into the cornfield because the Corn-Goat was sitting there and might kill them or carry them off. During the harvest, if a reaper became ill, they would say that the Harvest Goat or the Corn-Goat had pushed him.

In the region of Braunseberg in East Prussia, all the harvesters hurried at the task of binding the oats in case the Corn-Goat pushed him. In lower Bavaria, around Straubing, the man who cut the last corn, wheat, or oats had the Goat. Two horns were set up on the last heap of corn, and it was called "the horned Goat". At Kreutzburg, in East Prussia, the harvesters called out to the woman who bound the last sheaf that the Goat was sitting in it.

At Gablingen in Schwaben, the reapers would carve a goat out of wood while the last field was being reaped. Oat-ears were inserted in its nostrils and mouth, it was garlanded with flowers, and then it was stood in the field and called the Oats-Goat. The last sheaf was also referred to as the Goat. This was also the case in the Wiesenthal in Bavaria, and the people said that the field must bear a goat. At Spachbrücken in Hesse, the last handful of corn to be cut was called the Goat, and the man who cut it was ridiculed.

In some areas of Baden, the last sheaf was called the Goat, and was made up into a straw goat, of which it was said that the Goat was sitting in it. In addition, the person who cut or bound the last sheaf was called the Goat. In parts of Mecklenburg the harvesters called out to the woman who bound the last sheaf that she was the Harvest-Goat.

Near Uelzen in Hanover, the harvest festival began with bringing in the Harvest-Goat, which was the woman who had bound the last sheaf wrapped in straw and crowned with a harvest wreath. She was brought to the village in a wheelbarrow, and then they held a round-dance. Near Luneberg, Germany, and in St Gall and Thurgau in Switzerland, the woman who bound the corn was decked with a crown of corn-ears and called the Corn-Goat. On the Isle of Skye, the farmer who finished reaping first sent a sheaf called the *goabbir bhacagh* (the crippled goat) to a neighbour who had not yet finished, who in turn sent it on to another farmer when he had finished.

Near Bernkastel, on the Mosel, the reapers determined by lot the order in which they would reap the corn. If a reaper overtook another man, he would reap past him and leave him in a patch by himself. This patch was called the Goat, and anyone for whom "the Goat was cut" like this was teased for the rest of the day. When the tail-bearer (the man in the rear) cut the last ears of corn, they would say that he was cutting the Goat's neck. Near Grenoble in Switzerland, a live goat was adorned with flowers and ribbons and allowed to run round the field. The reapers chased it and caught it, then the farmer would cut its head off and they would eat it at the harvest supper. Some of the meat was pickled for the following year. Its skin was made into a cloak which the farmer had to wear if rain set in during the harvest. If a reaper developed back pain, the farmer would lend him the goatskin. In Baden, the last sheaf to be threshed was called the Goat. Near Marktl in Bavaria, the sheaves were threshed in the open fields, and the last sheaf, called the Goat, was garlanded with violets, other flowers and cakes, and placed in the middle of the heap, where the threshers would rush at it, tear it apart, and thresh it.

At Oberinntal in the Tyrol and Haselberg in West Bohemia, the man who gave the last stroke at the threshing was called the Goat. In Tettnang, Württemburg, the man who gave the last stroke to the last bundle of corn before it was turned was called the He-Goat, and the man who gave the last stroke of all was called the She-Goat. In the Franche-Comté region, if a neighbour had not finished threshing, the straw figure of a goat would be set up in their courtyard, and the farmer had to provide wine or money. At Indersdorf in upper Bavaria, a straw goat was thrown into the barn of a neighbour who had not finished threshing, and the man who threw it imitated a goat bleating. If he was caught, they would blacken his face and tie the goat on his back. A similar custom prevailed at Ellwangen in Württemburg, except that they did not blacken his face. At Saverne, in Alsace, a stuffed goat or fox was set up in front of the door of a neighbour who was a week or more behind with the threshing. In Traunstein, upper Bavaria, they would set up an old rake with a pot on it for a head, and tell the children to kill the Oats-Goat.

In the North of England (1858), a goat kept on a farm was believed to bring luck to the farmer and keep illness away from the other animals. In Northleach, Gloucestershire (1910), a farmer introduced a smelly billy-goat among his shorthorn cows, and they stopped losing their calves prematurely. The goat was also said to prevent foot-and-mouth disease in cattle and other diseases in sheep. Pictures of pastoral scenes from about the thirteenth century showed sheep grazing and a goat standing on its hind legs.

In Russia, the forest spirits, called the Ljesche (from *ljes*, the wood), known as Leshy in Poland, are partly human, but have the horns, ears, and legs of goats. Goats are mischievous, highly-sexed, and capricious, and these qualities are also associated with the Ljesche. Also, goats often stray into the forest, so this is probably why they are associated with it and its spirits.

Mythology

In Norse cosmology, the constellation of the Battle of the Gods includes the goats which drew Thor's chariot, and Odin's goat Heidrun, whose milk was mead for the Einherjar, the heroes of

Valhalla. (The Battle of the Gods includes the classical constellations of Auriga and Capella.) Heidrun is the nanny-goat who browses on the branches of Laerad, a tree which grows outside Valhalla.

In Scotland, there is a legend of Glaisrig or Glaistig, a beautiful and seductive water-spirit, who is a goat from the waist down. She hides this feature under a long green dress, and lures men to dance with her so that she can suck their blood. Sometimes her behaviour is benign, as when she looks after old people or children and herds cattle for farmers. A similar but always benign goat legend appears in Skye, where Gobar Bachach, the Lame Goat, was said to wander over the countryside, always lying in the richest pastures. She is always in milk, and could give enough to supply an army. The last sheaf of the harvest in Skye was known as the Gobar Bachach.

In ancient Babylon, Ea-Oannes, god of the waters, was often portrayed as a goat-fish (the origin of the astrological sign of Capricorn). This amalgam represented the joining of the fertility of the sea and the land. The goat is associated with the Babylonian god of irrigation, Ningirsu. A Chaldaean and Babylonian goddess of fortune, Gadda (and her husband Gad) may have been associated with goats, as the name Gadda may mean 'she-goat'. In Sumerian mythology, the goat is often depicted with Marduk, and with goddesses of hunting. Goats were sacrificed to Marduk and to Ningirsu. The supreme Assyrian god, Asshur, whose province was war and fertility, had a female goat as his emblem.

The goat appears in Greek myth in a number of contexts. Zeus was suckled as a baby by Amalthea the she-goat (representing protection and abundance) when Rhea was hiding him from Cronos. In this aspect, he is known as Zeus Dictynnos, which means twice-suckled, because he was also given honey by the bee-goddess Melissa. Amalthea's skin became the aegis (which Artemis had on her shield), and her horn became the Cornucopia (Horn of Plenty), though in another version it was the horn of Achelous the river god, broken off by Hercules. The wild goat is sacred to Artemis, and is an attribute or form of Dionysos, who fled from Typhon in the form of a goat. In another myth, Zeus turned the

298

young Dionysos into a kid to save him from the wrath of Hera. One of Dionysos' names was 'the Kid'. In Athens and Hermion, he was worshipped under the name of 'the One with the Black Goatskin', because of a legend that he had appeared dressed in a black goatskin.

In the district of Phlius, the husbandmen plastered an image of a goat with gold leaf to protect their vines from the blight (Dionysos was the god of wine). In the rites of Dionysos, the sacrificed kid represented the death of the god prior to his rebirth. The goat was sacrificed by the Maenads. The ritual of sacrificing a kid was one of the earliest customs of pastoralists. It was part of the ceremony of initiation into the Phrygian mysteries. The goat was regarded as a cunning and fecund animal, hence its association with both Pan and Aphrodite. Satyrs (q.v.) are half-goat, half-man, and appear in the retinue of Dionysos. Pan has the legs, horns, and beard of a goat; he was also said to have been suckled by Amalthea. As a moment of eternity, being neither morning nor afternoon, the noonday hour was sacred to Pan, and it was taboo for shepherds to pipe at noon for fear of Pan. In the Arcadian tradition Pan was the son of Hermes, who was also depicted as horned and goat-footed in Arcadia. Goat deities (Pan and the Satyrs in Greek myth, and Faunus and the Fauns in Roman myth) are depicted either in full goat form, or as half-man, half-goat, or dressed in goatskin (Silenus, Dionysos). They are usually associated with the forest. In Arcadia, Pan was called the Lord of the Wood.

In Egypt, the so-called Goat of Mendes (much feared by opponents of nineteenth-century style occultism) was in fact the Ram of Mendes. The fallacy was originated by Herodotus, who got it wrong.

The goat is the sacred animal of the Madenassana Bushmen, but to look upon a goat makes a man temporarily impure.

In Roman tradition, a kid was sacrificed to Faunus on his festival (5th December in the countryside, 13th February in the city). The rural festival was a lively occasion, described in the *Odes* of Horace. It consisted of dancing in the fields, making an offering of wine and a goat kid to the god on a smoking altar of earth. It expressed the true ancient spirit of Roman religion: "an appeal to the vague and possibly dangerous spirit that guards the flocks to be present, but not to linger too long". Faunus was essentially the spirit of the wild woodland. (The name is probably derived from *favere* and means 'the kindly one', meant in an euphemistic and propitiatory sense, in much the same way as the Faeries are referred to as 'the Good Folk'). His father was Picus (the woodpecker), one of the sons of Saturn, and his mother was Canente, who died of grief when Picus was transformed into a woodpecker. Faunus was also the father or husband of Fauna, goddess of Earth and fields, also invoked under the name Bona Dea (the Good Goddess). He protected woods, fields, and shepherds, and was worshipped in sacred groves, where he gave oracles, mostly during sleep, or by causing voices to be heard in the countryside. He was also said to have been a lawgiver and one of the first kings of Latium. His attribute is the shawm or rustic pipe, which he is said to have invented. The goat was also an attribute of Silvanus, who appears with Faunus, Bacchus, and other gods of a rustic character. The classical Mercury is sometimes accompanied by a goat (presumably in imitation of Hermes, with whom he was amalgamated). The Gaulish Mercury was accompanied by a ram.

The goat was not unknown as a sacred animal in the Romano-British tradition; a face-pot from Colchester (Camulodunum) has a pair of goat-horns springing from the centre of the head, which may suggest that there was a local cult of a deity such as Pan or Silvanus. On the other hand, the goat-horns may have been easier to fit into the design of the pot. Also, the difficulty with such finds, unless they or their like have been found in a specifically ritual context, is ascertaining whether they had any religious significance, or were purely decorative.

In Spain, the Basque witches are said to have invoked Akerbeltz ('the black he-goat') at their Sabbats, which were known as Akelarre, 'the field of the goat'.

In Hinduism, the goat and the ram are attributes of Agni, the fire god, who rides a he-goat. An early Hindu god, Daksha, who was the son of Brahma, quarrelled with Shiva, who cut off his head. Afterwards they were reconciled, and Daksha was given a goat's head. This is somewhat similar to the story of Ganesh (see elephant).

Symbolism

The goat is a symbol of masculinity, great vitality, and creative energy. The female goat represents generative power, fertility, and abundance in women.

In Hinduism, the goat symbolises superiority and the higher self, because it is a mountain animal. It also represents fire and creative heat.

In Chinese, the word for goat is a homophone of yang, so it symbolises the masculine principle, goodness, and peace.

In Christianity the goat is associated with the devil, the damned, sinners, lust, and lubricious behaviour. The scapegoat represents Christ taking on the sins of the the world.

In Hebraic tradition, the goat symbolises lewdness. It is also associated with the demon Azazael, who may have been a pre-Judaic goat god. In the *Torah*, it is forbidden to seethe a kid in its mother's milk.

Poetry

"Your hair is like a flock of goats
 Descending from Mount Gilead.
 Your teeth are like a flock of sheep just shorn,
 Coming up from the washing."

(*Song of Solomon* 4:2)

Hare

Latin name *Lepus europaeus* **Polarity** Feminine

Family *Lepidae* **Element** Fire

Order *Lagomorpha* **Planet** Moon

Folk names *Hase, liévre*

Deities Manibozho, Ostara / Eostre, Thoth

Etymology from Old English *hara*, Old High German *haso*, Old Norse *heri,* from Germanic *hason* or *hazon*

Varieties

The European Hare (*Lepus europaeus*) has twenty-one subspecies throughout Europe, Asia Minor and East Africa. The Blue Hare or Variable Hare (*Lepus timidus*) is brown in summer and white in winter. Other relatives are the Arctic Hare, rabbits, and pikas.

Folklore

Seen in certain aspects, the shadows of the mountains on the Moon resemble the outline of a hare. This is most easily seen at moonrise, and also, for some odd reason, through binoculars - the rest of the time, the surface of the Moon looks like a face to me. The features on the Moon are known as the Mark of the Hare in Tibet, China, Ceylon, Africa, and amongst the indigenous peoples of North America

(Turtle Island). The hare or the rabbit is an animal incarnation of the Moon hero. The myth of the hare in the Moon also occurs in the Far East, India, and Mexico. The hare depicts the periodic death and rebirth of the Moon. A Suffolk farmer recalled a saying that used to be repeated at the end of a month, "Let the owd hare set." In some places, it was customary to say 'Hares' three times at the end of the month, and 'Rabbits' three times at the beginning of the next month, for luck.

The hare is often associated with fire, which was regarded by many peoples as an emanation of the Moon. In England, a hare running through a town was regarded as an omen of a fire (Northamptonshire, 1851, 1884; Ely, 1866; Peterborough, 1909; Harrow, 1909).

It was bad luck to meet a hare when setting out on a journey (1584, 1587, 1603, 1614, 1631, 1691); bad luck for a bride to meet a hare (1818); and unlucky for farmers (1861). In Shropshire, it was good luck to meet a hare (1883), but unlucky if one ran across your path. In Condover, if a hare ran from right to left in front of you, it was lucky, but if it was in the opposite direction, it was very lucky. If it ran ahead of you, the outcome of your affairs was undecided.

In European folktales, the hare is generally a helpful animal, a messenger of the Moon and the Mother Goddess. In the West, the white hare is a symbol of snow. Also, because of its association with the Moon and the resurgent time of Spring, the March hare is associated with madness, hence the character of the Mad Hatter in *Alice in Wonderland*.

According to the theory of humours, the hare was a melancholy animal, and ate wild succory (*Cichorium intibus*). According to *Culpeper's Herbal*, this plant "drives forth choleric and phlegmatic humours" and is under Jupiter. The flesh of the hare was supposed to generate melancholy in anyone who ate it. Swift, in 1738, described it as "melancholy meat". In the *Torah*, the hare is one of the unclean animals listed in *Deuteronomy* 14. According to Caesar, the ancient Britons did not eat hare (probably because it was sacred). In 1507, in the *Gospel of Dystaues*, eating hare was said to cause palsy. The people of Norfolk would only eat rabbit, never hare. In Ireland, it is said to be unlucky to kill a hare (Lissduff, Co. Offaly, 1972).

The hare in the Moon acts as a messenger between lunar deities and humanity. The hare is often regarded as a companion and familiar of witches, as witchcraft is particularly associated with the Moon. Witches are also said to shape-shift into hares. The earliest mention of this belief is found in Giraldus Cambrensis' *Topographica Hibernica*. It is also mentioned in G M Trevelyan's *Folklore of Wales* (1909). In some places, the hare was believed to change sex annually, or to be sexless.

Amongst the Afro-Americans, the stories of an animal trickster hero brought from Africa met and merged with indigenous American myths to form that well-known corpus of legend, the Brer Rabbit stories.

In Chinese legend, the hare is the protector of wild animals. The white hare is regarded as divine; a red hare represents good fortune, peace, prosperity, and virtuous rulers; whilst a black hare represents good fortune and a successful reign. At the Moon festival, the Chinese make figures of hares or white rabbits.

In Judaism, the hare is regarded as an unclean animal.

In Galloway, the reaping of the last stand of corn was called "cutting the Hare". When the rest of the corn had been reaped, a handful was left standing. This was divided into three parts and plaited, and the ears were tied into a knot. The reapers then retreated to a distance and threw their sickles at the Hare to cut it down. It had to be severed below the knot; the reapers continued to throw sickles at it until it had been cut below the knot. It was then carried back to the house and placed over the kitchen door on the inside. It was sometimes kept there until the next harvest.

At Minnigaff, after the hare was cut, the unmarried reapers raced each other home. The first to arrive would be the next to be married. At Anhalt, in Germany, when only a few corn stalks were left to be reaped, they said "The Hare will soon come" or "Look how the hare comes jumping out".

These customs may have originated because hares were often trapped in the corn, and became associated with the spirit of the corn. In East Prussia, they said that the Hare sat in the last stand of corn, and the last reaper chased it out. The person to whom this task fell was greatly teased. At Aurich, cutting the last corn was called "cutting the Hare's tail".

In parts of Germany, Sweden, Norway, France, Holland and Italy, they said that the man who cut the last corn was "killing the Hare". In Norway, he had to give "hare's blood" (brandy) to the other reapers. On the island of Lesbos, if two fields were being reaped simultaneously, the reapers in each field would try to finish first, to drive the hare into the other field. It was believed that the reapers who finished first would get a better crop the following year.

Mythology
The hare is an attribute of most lunar deities. In Africa, the Hottentots associate the hare with the Moon; its mysterious qualities have led many cultures to associate it with the Moon. To the Algonquin people of North America, the Great Hare, Manibozho or Michabo is a hero, saviour, father and guardian of the people. He is a creator and transformer, enabling humans to commune with their animal natures. He created the earth, the waters, and the fish, and invented fishing nets. He is the personification of light, the Great Manitou who lives in the Moon with his grandmother. He is also said to have his house at the place where the sun rises. The souls of the just go there and are fed on luscious fruits. Michabo can change himself into a thousand different animals. He provides all waters; he is the master of the winds and the brother of the snow. As a Trickster figure, Manibozho represents an agile mind outwitting brute strength. One of his legends tells how he slew a great snake or fish which was eating people. Among the Iroquois, the Hare is a form of the Great Spirit, and is either the Moon himself, or his grandmother is the Moon. The hare finds a way through where a more belligerent approach would bring disaster, because of its docility and cunning.

In Buddhism, it is believed that the Buddha placed the hare in the Moon, because the hare sacrificed itself by leaping into the fire when the Buddha was hungry; hence it symbolises total self-lessness.

In both Buddhist and Hindu art, the hare appears with the crescent Moon. The Hindu Moon god, Chandra, carries a hare.

In Celtic mythology, the hare is an attribute of lunar deities, and is often depicted held in the hand of hunting deites. Before going into her last battle against the Romans at King's Cross in 61 CE, Queen Boudicca of the Iceni invoked the goddess Andraste and then released a divinatory hare. It may be that the hare was sacred to Andraste. The hare is also associated with shape-shifting, being one of the forms taken by Gwion whilst trying to escape the wrath of Cerridwen. When Gwion accidentally splashed himself with the magic brew in Cerridwen's cauldron and sucked his fingers, thereby becoming possessed of all knowledge, she chased him. He changed into a hare, so she changed to a greyhound; then he changed into a fish, so she changed into an otter; he changed to a bird, so she changed into a hawk. She finally caught him when he turned into a grain of corn, and she changed into a hen and ate him. Later she gave birth to a magical child. Another transformation tale involving a hare is that of *How the Leg of Cian mab Maelmuaidh mab Bran was healed.* A man slips his greyhound after a hare, which turns into a beautiful young lady, who rushes into the arms of her pursuer, leads him into a faery mound, and sleeps with him. Later in the same story she turns into a mare when she is struck. The hare occurs frequently in the iconography of the Celts; hunter gods are frequently portrayed holding a hare in their hands. A relief from Touget depicts a hunter god holding a large hare across his chest, grasping it by its front and hind legs.

In Leicestershire there is a legend of Black Annis, who lived in the Dane Hills and was said to eat children. She was associated with a May Eve hare hunt (later transferred to Easter Monday). She may be of Scandinavian origin. According to Robert Graves, because of her association with Spring, she must have had a maiden aspect as well as the character of a hag.

It is possible that Lady Godiva was associated with the hare. The story of the naked lady riding through the town may well be a description of a May Eve procession of the goddess Goda. The name Godiva is derived from Godgifu ('gift of God'). Men were frequently forbidden to see such rituals, hence the punishment inflicted on Peeping Tom. A miserere seat in old Coventry Cathedral (noticed by Robert Graves) depicted a long-haired woman wrapped in a net, riding sideways on a goat and following a hare. This lady probably represented Spring, and possibly the same goddess Goda.

In Christianity, the hare represents fecundity and lust. The Virgin Mary is sometimes depicted with a white hare at her feet, symbolising triumph over lust. It must be noted, however, that she has clearly borrowed this attribute from a Moon goddess, even though its meaning has been distorted to conform with christian mores. Several of her other attributes have been borrowed from the Great Goddess (the peacock borrowed from Hera as Queen of Heaven, the title Stella Maris from Isis, etc.) The defencelessness of the hare was used as a symbol for the submission of those who put their trust in Christ.

In Europe, the Easter hare or rabbit symbolises dawn, Spring and new life. It is an attribute of the hare-headed goddess known to the Teutons as Ostara and to the Anglo-Saxons as Eostre (probably pronounced Easter, hence the name of our festival of the Spring Equinox). In this context the hare represents rebirth and resurrection, and the waxing of the Moon. The Easter Hare lays the Easter Egg, from which new life springs forth. There is a possible connection with the name of Astarte, according to some views.

In Norse mythology, Freyja is often accompanied by hares. The Teutonic goddess Holda, Harka, or Harfa (a very ancient goddess, who, according to Jack Gale, antedates both Freyja and Hel, and gave some of her attributes to both goddesses) is followed by hares carrying lighted torches.

A later (medieval) version of this goddess was Frau Holle (or Holda or Hoide), who was the German lunar goddess of witches and the

Sabbat. In summer she bathed in the forest streams, and in winter she shook down the snowflakes from the trees. The name may have been derived from a generic term for Moon priestesses.

In Graeco-Roman myth, the hare is an attribute and messenger of Hermes and Mercury, Aphrodite and Venus, Eros and Cupid. Cupids were often portrayed with hares.

In Egypt, the hare was an emblem of Thoth, and was associated with the dawn, the Moon, openings and beginnings, rising, and periodicity.

Symbolism
The hare symbolises love, fertility, and the menstrual cycle. It is associated in many cultures with lunar magic and the Moon. It represents rebirth, rejuvenation, resurrection, intuition, and illumination. The hare also represents swiftness, cunning, and timidity.

To the Greeks and Romans, the hare represented fertility and lubricity.

In China, it is said that the hare in the Moon holds a pestle and mortar with which it grinds the elixir of immortality. The hare represents the feminine principle (yin); it also symbolised the Empress and longevity. The hare is the fourth animal of the Chinese calendar (the Twelve Terrestrial Branches).

In Japan, the white disk of the Moon is represented as a rabbit or a hare pounding rice in a mortar. It is called Mochi-zuki, meaning both 'Full Moon' and 'pounding rice for cakes'.

Poetry

The Hare Song

(adapted by Y. Aburrow from the 17th c. witch song of Isobel Goudie)

I shall gae intil a hare
Wi' sorrow and sych and mickle care
I shall gae in the Lady's name
Ay will I come home again.

Hare, hare, you creature of the Moon
I shall run with the hares in the fields
Till I return to my hearth and home.

I shall gae intil a cat
Wi' sorrow and sych and a black hat
I shall gae in the Lady's name
Ay will I come home again.

Cat, cat, you creature of the Moon
I shall hunt with the cats in the barn
Till I return to my hearth and home.

I shall gae intil a craw
Wi' sorrow and sych and a black thraw
I shall gae in the Lady's name
Ay will I come home again.

Crow, crow, you creature of the Moon
I shall sit with the corbie on the bough
Till I return to my hearth and home.

I shall dance beneath the Moon
Ploughing a furrow for Mother Earth
I shall gae in the Lady's name
Ay will I come home again.

Witch, witch, you creature of the Moon
I shall gae with the witches on the mountain
Till I return to my hearth and home.

I shall walk between the worlds
Where rivers run red in the eldritch light
I shall gae in the Lady's name
Ay will I come home again.

Blessed folk, you creatures of the Moon
I shall send my fetch to walk the night
Till I return to my hearth and home.

(For the original version of this song, see Cat)

Hares on the Mountains
[version 1]

"Young women they'll run like hares on the mountains
Young women they'll run like hares on the mountains
If I was but a young man I'd soon go a-hunting
To my right fol diddle dero, to my right fol diddle dee.

Young women they sing like birds in the bushes
Young women they sing like birds in the bushes
If I was a young man I'd go and bang the bushes
To my right fol diddle dero, to my right fol diddle dee.

Young women they'll swim like ducks in the water
Young women they'll swim like ducks in the water
If I was a young man I'd go and swim all after
To my right fol diddle dero, to my right fol diddle dee.

[version 2]

"If all those young men were as rushes a-growing
Then all those pretty maidens will get scythes go a-mowing

If all those young men were as hares on the mountains
Then all those pretty maidens will get guns go a-hunting

If all those young men were as ducks in the water
Then all those pretty maidens would soon follow after

"She turned hersell into a hare,
To run upon yon hill,
And he became a gude grey-hound
And boldly he did fill."
(from *The Twa Magicians*)

The Hare
In the black furrow of a field
I saw an old witch-hare this night;
And she cocked a lissome ear,
And she eyed the moon so bright,
And she nibbled of the green;
And I whispered 'Shsst! witch-hare,'
Away like a ghostie o'er the field
She fled, and left the moonlight there.

(Walter de la Mare)

Hedgehog

Latin name *Erinaceus europaeus Erinaceae*

Folk name hotchi-witchi, niglo (Romani); hurcheon, urcheon, urchin (English); hérisson (French)

Planet Moon

Etymology *Hurcheon* - from Scots for urchin, from Old French *herichon, heriçon*, from Latin *ericius*, a hedgehog
Hedgehog: Middle English, from *hedge* (Old English *hecg, hegg*, Middle Dutch *hegghe*, Old High German *hegga, hecka*) plus hog (Old English *hocg, hogg*, possibly from Celtic).

Deities Ishtar (Sumerian); the Great Mother

Varieties

The European Hedgehog (*Erinaceus europaeus*) has three forms in Europe. Hedgehogs are also found in Asia and Africa, and most of Europe except for Scandinavia and Iceland. It is an insectivorous mammal.

Folklore

Hedgehogs were said to collect fruit, especially grapes, by rolling on them and carrying them home. They were also said (by Aristotle, Pliny, and Aelian) to be able to foretell changes in wind direction, and accordingly change the outlook of their earth holes.

In Spain, there is a particularly colourful curse: *"Espero que te cares un elefanto con erillas en las ermillas"*.

The hedgehog is a favourite animal of Gypsies (the Romani), who bake it in clay.

Folk tale

In *Hans, my Hedgehog*, a man becomes angry when his wife cannot have any children. Finally, he becomes so frustrated that he exclaims "I want a child, even if it should be a hedgehog". It being unwise to tempt fate in this way, sure enough, his wife conceives, and gives birth to a child whose upper half is that of a hedgehog, and whose legs are those of a boy. The symbolism of this is that the parent's lack of control over the emotions produces a child who is a misfit (the hedgehog's prickles symbolise an unsocial nature). The idea of parents who desire a child too much producing half-human, half-animal offspring is an ancient and widely-distributed one. In a Turkish tale, King Solomon restores a child to full humanity. Hans the Hedgehog helps a king lost in the forest to find his way home. The King promises to give Hans the first thing he sees on his way home. This happens to be his only daughter, who marries Hans in spite of his appearance. He is restored to fully human form in the marital bed, and eventually inherits the kingdom.

Mythology

The hedgehog is an emblem of Ishtar and the Great Mother in Sumerian and Assyro-Babylonian mythology. The hedgehog was also venerated in Iran.

Symbolism

In Christianity, the hedgehog stealing the grapes from the vines symbolises the devil snaring souls; the vine symbolises Christ.

Hippopotamus

Latin name *Hippopotamus*
amphibius

Family Hippopotamidae

Order *Artiodactyla*

Folk name Hippo

Etymology
Hippo (horse) + *potamus* (river) = river horse (Greek)

Deities Amenti, Taueret, Opet

Polarity Feminine

Element Water

Star Sothis/Sopdet (Sirius)

Varieties
The only relative of the Hippopotamus is the Pigmy Hippopotamus (*Choeropsis liberiensis*).

Folklore
The hippo is sometimes equated with the Behemoth of the Old Testament.

Mythology
In Egyptian mythology, the red hippopotamus represents Set in his typhonic aspect. The hippo's thigh is the phallic 'leg of Set', representing power and virility. The hippo is also a symbol of Amenti, 'the bringer-forth of the waters', goddess of the West. Taueret, the hippopotamus-goddess, was equated with bounty and protection.

In Thebes, she was called Opet or Apet, and was the goddess of childbirth, protecting women in pregnancy and childbirth. She was also associated with rebirth. Her festival was celebrated when the star Sopdet (Sothis or Sirius) rose on 19th July.

Taueret was a pre-dynastic hippopotamus deity and mother goddess. She was sometimes known as the Eye of Ra, and regarded as his daughter. She was depicted as a pregnant female hippopotamus, standing up, with the hind legs of a lioness, pendulous human breasts, and a crocodile's tail. In her avenging aspect she was sometimes regarded as the wife of Set and depicted with the head of a lioness and brandishing a dagger.

Horse

Latin name *Equus caballus*

Family *Equidae*

Order *Perissodactyla*
(odd-toed ungulates)

Rune Eh / Ehwaz

Polarity Masculine

Element Fire

Planet Sun

Etymology Old English/Old Saxon *hors*, Old High German *hros*, Old Norse *hross*, from Germanic *horsam* or *horsaz*

Deities Epona, Rhiannon, Macha, Étain Echraide, Clidna, Medhbh of Connacht, Avalokitesvara (Kwan-yin)

Varieties

The horse is related to the ass (q.v.), the mountain zebra (*Equus zebra*), Hartmann's zebra, Grevy's zebra (*Equus grevyi*), the East African zebra (*Equus burchelii böhmi*), the rhinoceros, and the tapir. (The last two are members of the order *Perissodactyla*.) The horse developed from the Dawn Horse or eohippus, which lived in the forests of the

Eocene period. There were several varieties of Eurasian Wild Horses, only one of which survived into modern times. The Tarpan or European Wild Horse (*Equus caballus gmelini*) is now extinct; the last mare was killed by Polish peasants in 1876. There are about six separate groups of domestic horse. In Britain, horses were rather heavy and large in appearance, until the introduction of horses from the Middle East, the first one being the Godolphin Arab. There are records of the domestication of the horse from about 1750 bce, though it was probably domesticated about five thousand years ago. It was a sign of wealth to own horses, and the horse was one of the closest associates of humans.

Folklore

In the Northern Tradition, a baldrick was a girdle made of horse-hair and tied around a bell to make it magically efficacious, and an instrument of consecration. Plaited horse-hair was used as a cure for a wen in the neck in Gloucestershire (1873); and horse-hair in a bag, procured with neither thanks nor payment, was a cure for a wen in Herefordshire (1912).

In Scottish folk belief, the kelpie was a malign spirit which haunted lakes and rivers, often in the form of a horse; it is said to be the personification of the sudden gust of wind which sweeps over the lakes and pools of the Highlands. The kelpie was usually seen in the form of a young horse scampering along a river bank. When he was tired, he would strike the water three times with his tail. Each splash sounded like a crash of thunder. The kelpie would then disappear in a flash into a deep pool. The kelpie's bridle was highly magical; it could wreak enchantment by looking through the bridle's eyelets, but a magician could undo such an enchantment by looking through the eyelets in the opposite direction. Looking through the eyelets would also enable one to see spirits and faeries.

In the Highlands there is a tale of Seumas MacGregor, who encountered a kelpie by Loch Slochd. He had lost his horse, and thought he had found it again, but it turned out to be a kelpie trying to carry him off into the loch. So he called upon the Trinity and the kelpie threw him off. When he came to his senses, he was lying on the shore with the kelpie's bridle in his his hand. This became a family heirloom amongst the MacGregors, who used it for magic. In Irish folklore, the Pookah, Phooka, or Pooka was a spirit in the form of a wild shaggy colt hung with chains, which haunts wild places. In some parts of Ireland, Samhain (Hallowe'en) was known as Puca Night or Goblin Night, as such spirits walked abroad on that night. In Northern England, a spirit called the Gytrash haunted the roads, appearing in the form of a horse, a mule, or a large dog. Charlotte Brontë mentions the belief in Jane Eyre.

Until the nineteenth century, the cleaning of the local white horse on the hillside was the occasion for a local holiday. There is a nineteenth century engraving of the scouring of the White Horse at Uffington in 1889, which was known as "The Pastime". It is considered effective to make a wish whilst standing in the White Horse's eye.

The horse was also associated with seasonal festivals, in the form of the hobby horse, such as the Old Hoss of Padstow, which journeys through the town on May Day, starting from the Red Lion Inn. The Old Hoss costume is black, shaped like a boat, and equipped with a fierce horse mask with snapping jaws, like many of its counterparts in other towns. In Kent, the Hoodeners travel around with the Hooden Horse on Christmas Eve. This is possibly a survival of Woden and his horse Sleipnir - Woden was associated with the festival of Yule. However, since there is little or no evidence of the custom in early times, we must be cautious about drawing such comparisons. The custom was first recorded from 1807 to 1908, carried on by Kentish farm labourers in eastern Kent, particularly around Ramsgate. It was revived at Canterbury in 1952, and is now continued in the Whitstable area by the 'Ancient Order of Hoodeners' (pronounced 'Oodeners).

The Hooden Horse consisted of a four-foot long pole surmounted by a carved horse's head, carried by a man in a dark hood. It was decorated with horse-brasses and ribbons, and had a snapping jaw worked by a string. The bearer of the Hooden Horse was accompanied by three to seven other men, one of whom tried to mount it, another who carried a whip, and a man called Mollie (the usual appellation for a transvestite) dressed as a woman and carrying a broom. Graffiti representing a hobby-horse frame has been found in various churches, such as Girton in Cambridgeshire, Shillington in Bedfordshire, and Wallington in Hertfordshire. In Germany, hobby-horses are known as *Steckenpferde* (stick horses). The esoteric significance of the hobby-horse is that it is the steed of the shaman, for riding up and down the world tree. Odin and his magical horse Sleipnir might perhaps be the model for this. Hobby-horse dancing may have been used to induce a trance similar to that brought about by the shaman's drum - in Siberia, the shaman is said to ride the drum to the underworld.

A similar custom appears in South Wales, called the Mari Lwyd (Grey Mare), a horse's skull on a pole, decorated with ribbons and carried by a man dressed in a white sheet. The skull often had glass eyes and a clacking jaw. It was accompanied by four to seven men, who would go from house to house to get food and drink, engaging in singing contests with the occupants of the house. The Mari Lwyd was first recorded in 1800, became defunct in the early 1900s, but was revived in the 1980s. A similar custom is recorded in the Isle of Man, where it is called the Laare Vane (White Mare), and in Ireland, where it is called the Lair Bhan. The Manx Laare Vane appeared at harvest celebrations as well as at Christmas; it was brought into the communal room of a house on New Year's Eve, accompanied by a fiddler. It chased the girls; the one who was caught had to wear the white sheet of the man who carried the horse while the others performed a stick dance (rather like morris); then the fiddler was blindfolded and put through a mock beheading. After this his head was laid in the lap of the girl, and he had to make predictions for the coming year. The oracular power of a severed head is an ancient motif in Celtic literature and folklore, and this may represent a genuinely ancient custom. Another similar custom was first recorded in Derbyshire around 1840 (and also disappeared around the turn of the century), called the Old Horse. No oracular element was associated with it, however.

It is interesting that something like these ideas appears in the English pantomime tradition, with the tradition of cross-dressing and the pantomime horse. The pantomime had its origins in the

Italian harlequinade, and by the 1890s it was established that the principal boy was played by a woman and the dame by a man. The English pantomime adopted the older midwinter motifs of animal disguises and transvestism (just when they were declining in the countryside) and put them on the stage, safely toned-down as 'children's entertainment'. A similar process happened with the development of the folk-tale (which originally abounded with sex and violence, as reading the Grimm Brothers' collection will demonstrate) into the sanitised 'fairy-tale' of Charles Perrault and Hans Christian Andersen.

Harvest traditions often featured the horse. Between Kalw and Stuttgart, when the wind ruffled the corn, people would say that the Horse was running through it. At Bohlingen near Radolfzell in Baden, the last sheaf of oats was called the Oats-Stallion. In Hertfordshire, at the end of the reaping, they held a ceremony called 'Crying the Mare'. The last corn stalks left standing were tied together and called the Mare. All the reapers threw their sickles at it, and the one whose sickle cut through it won a prize. After it was cut some of the reapers all shouted three times "I have her", then the others shouted "What have you?" and they answered, "A Mare! A Mare! A Mare!" Then the others asked three times "Whose is she?" and the one whose sickle had cut through was named three times. Then they asked "Whither will you send her?", to which the answer was, to someone who had not finished reaping. A similar custom prevailed in Shropshire. The last farmer to get all his corn in was said to have to keep the Mare all winter. Near Lille, in France, when a harvester became tired, they said *"Il a la fatigue de la Jument"* (the Mare has tired him out). The first sheaf, which was called the cross of the Horse, was placed on a cross of boxwood in the farm, where they made the youngest horse on the farm step on it. The reapers danced round the last standing corn, shouting, "See the remains of the Horse". In other places, the last sheaf was given to the youngest horse in the village to eat. This may have represented passing the corn-spirit on to a real horse, which thus became the Foal for next year's harvest. The person who threshed the last sheaf was said to beat the Horse.

In an Irish legend, O'Donoghue rises from the waters of a lake on 1st May (Beltane), and visits his realm mounted on a milk-white steed. The boatmen of Killarney called the white-crested waves when the wind whips up the sea "O'Donoghue's white horses".

The Wild Huntsman or the Erl-King rides a black horse; traditionally, the black horse is an omen of death. The Wild Hunt was said to be a cavalcade of souls, led by various heroes (Odin, Charlemagne, Wild Edric, etc.) which appeared at portentous times and seasons.

In Derbyshire, according to Alison Uttley, black horses and mares were lucky, especially if they had a white star on the forehead or a white foot.

In Berkshire, it is said that if you leave a horse overnight at Wayland's Smithy (the burial mound near the Uffington White horse) with a silver coin, it will be shod when you return in the morning.

There is also a body of superstition concerning horseshoes. Ordinary people have to hang their lucky horseshoes upright (with the open end at the top), to keep luck in; whereas smiths and farriers may hang it upside-down, in order to pour luck into the smithy (or possibly to imbue the anvil with magical power). Horseshoes are also placed on doorsteps with the open end pointing into the house, to keep witches and the devil out. According to John Aubrey (1688), Elias Ashmole (founder of the Ashmolean Museum) had one on his doorstep. Apparently, Horatio Nelson had a horseshoe nailed to the mast of the Victory. Many other ships had one as well. When turned upwards, the horseshoe represents the crescent Moon and the horns of power and protection. It can also depict the female genitalia, and averts misfortune. It is generally considered lucky to find a horseshoe; the earliest evidence of this belief is from the 14th century; the belief was still extant as late as 1982, and you would not have to go far to find someone who still believed it. The horseshoe is particularly lucky if it still has nails in it. The belief is probably connected with the general belief in the protective powers of iron, which acts as a magical insulator.

In Ireland, the teeth and hooves were considered lucky. It was believed that if you found the back tooth of a horse by chance, you would never want for money (1887). In County Limerick, the hooves of a horse or a donkey were kept after its death, and hung up in the house for luck.

Once more widespread in Britain, the Horseman's Word was still in existence in North-east Scotland at the turn of the century. It was reputed to give its possessor power over horses and women, and prove that he had become a man. When a youth was old enough, he was told to present himself at eleven o'clock at a certain barn on a dark night, with a candle, a loaf, and a bottle of whisky. He was blindfolded at the barn door and led before a secret tribunal, who put him through a series of questions and made him repeat certain words. The tribunal consisted of a few older ploughmen, presided over by a master of ceremonies, who sat at an altar made by inverting a bushel measure over a sack of corn. He also had to suffer various ordeals, some of them possibly sexual. Whether this had always been the case or represented a debased form of the ceremony cannot be ascertained. At the end of his initiation he shook the Devil's hand (usually a stick covered in hairy skin). After this he was given the Horseman's Word, and all present shared the bread and whisky. The youth had now become a ploughman. It is not known what the Word was, though it may have been the phrase "Both in one", signifying complete harmony between the ploughman and his horses. Amongst the powers reputedly bestowed by the Word was to reist the horses (making them stand still so that no-one else could move them) and to call them to him from miles away. The possessor of the Word was believed to have a similar power over women - he only had to touch a girl and she would do his will. Sadly, the origins of the Ku Klux Klan are said to lie in a form of the Horseman's Word taken to America by Scottish emigrants; but it is to be hoped that the Klan is a perversion of the Horseman's Word, and not a reflection of its true nature.

Most people in Britain will not eat horseflesh; many folklore writers have speculated that this is the result of a ritual taboo which has survived from ancient times, when horsemeat could only be eaten at sacral feasts. In Denmark, a three-day feast at which horseflesh was eaten survived into Christian times among the serfs, despite official disapproval. It also had some ritual elements, such as sprinkling bowls of the horse's blood towards the South and East, which would possibly imply a solar connection. However, in order to prove that this was a similar custom to that which had allegedly died out in Britain, one would need to demonstrate that it was associated with a taboo on horsemeat for the rest of the year.

Mythology

In ancient Italy, horses were not permitted to enter the sanctuary of Virbius, the first of the Kings of the Wood in Aricia, because they were responsible for his death as Hippolytus. According to legend, the young Greek hero Hippolytus, who was chaste and fair, learned the skills of hunting from Chiron the Centaur. Hippolytus spent all his time in the forest chasing wild animals with Artemis, the virgin huntress. The divine company he kept made him immune to the charms of ordinary women. Aphrodite, goddess of love, was angered by his indifference, and inspired his stepmother Phaedra to fall in love with him. When he refused her advances, she accused him falsely to his father, Theseus, who believed her, and prayed to his father Poseidon to avenge this slight upon her honour. Hippolytus was driving a chariot on the shore of the Saronic Gulf when Poseidon sent a great and fearsome bull forth from the sea. The horses of Hippolytus' chariot bolted, and he was trampled under their hooves. Artemis was grief-stricken, and persuaded Asclepius, god of healing, to bring him back to life. Jupiter was angry with Asclepius for restoring a mortal to life, and sent the physician god to Hades. But Artemis concealed Hippolytus in a cloud and carried him to Nemi. There she entrusted him to the nymph Egeria, and he ruled there as king under the name of Virbius, and was worshipped as a god. He had a son, also named Virbius, who rode in a chariot drawn by fiery horses to fight with the Latins against Aeneas and the Trojans.

In Greek mythology, Ixion was the ancestor of the Centaurs. He wanted to make love to Hera, but Zeus tricked him by making a cloud in her shape. Ixion mated with the cloud and produced Centaurus, who mated with the mares of Pelion and produced the

Centaurs. It is possible that the myth of the Centaurs arose from the amazed response of people who had never seen men on horseback before. Centaurs are also strongly associated with the worship of Dionysos.

Horses are also sacred to the earth goddess, Demeter (along with the bee, the poppy, the snake, the pig, corn, and torches) because Demeter took the form of a mare when Poseidon made advances to her during her search for Persephone. She hid in a cave in Phigalia in Arcadia, where, robed in black, she stayed so long that the plants started to die, and humanity would have perished if Pan had not persuaded her to come out. The Phigalians set up an image of the Black Demeter in memory of this, and she was portrayed with the head and mane of a mare and the body of a woman. In another version, she hid among the herds of King Oncus, but Poseidon changed into a stallion, and found her. She bore him Arion, a horse with the gift of speech, and a daughter whose name was a secret, but who was known as Despœna (the mistress) and particularly venerated in Thessaly. The underworld goddess, Hecate, was sometimes depicted with three animal heads (horse, dog, and boar).

According to Plato, Poseidon divided the kingdom of Atlantis between the sons of Evenor and Leucippe. Evenor was one of the Earth-born primeval men of Atlantis, who fell in love with Leucippe (White Mare). She gave birth to five pairs of male twins, to whom Poseidon gave the five areas of Atlantis.

In Greek myth, Pegasus was the winged horse who was born from the blood of Medusa after Perseus killed her. Pegasus expresses the desire of humans for flight and mastery over the element of Air. He was tamed by Bellerophon, using Athene's bridle. Bellerophon then rode him in his battle with the Chimæra. It was his hoof that struck the rock on Mount Helicon, producing the Hippocrene spring (*hippos*, *horse*, *krene*, fountain). This spring is a symbol of poetic inspiration:

"Oh for a beaker full of the warm South,
Full of the true, the blushful Hippocrene."
(Keats)

Many of the gods had chariots drawn by horses, especially those associated with the sky, such as Apollo/Helios, and Eos, goddess of the dawn, (sister of Helios and Selene), who rises from the sea and rides across the sky in a horse-drawn chariot. It was believed that Poseidon was the creator of the horse. White horses draw the chariot of Phœbus, the sun god. Pegasus symbolises the transition from one plane of existence to another.

Many of the horses of Greek mythology are known to us by name. The horses of Helios, the Sun, were Actæon (effulgence), Athon (fiery red), Amethea (no loiterer), Bronte (thunder), Erythreos (producer of red), Lampos (lamplight), Phlegon (burning one), and Purocis (fiery hot). The horses of Aurora, the dawn, were Abraxa, Eos (the dawn) and Phæthon (shining one). The horses of Hades were Abaster (away from the stars), Abatos (the inaccesible), and Nonios. Hercules' horse was called Arion (warlike), and previously belonged to Poseidon. In one myth, Poseidon brought the horse forth from the earth by striking it with his trident. This may be connected with his association with earthquakes. Arion had the right feet of a man, could run at great speed, and spoke in a human voice. Another myth connects the birth of Arion with Demeter (see above). The white horses Cyllaros and Harpagus (one that carries off rapidly) were the steeds of Castor and Pollux. Ethon (fiery), Podarge (swift-foot) and Galathe (cream-coloured) were Hector's horses.

The Romans sacrificed a horse to Mars in October. After a horse-race held by the Salii (priests of Mars in his role as the ancient Italian god of crops and agriculture), the near-side horse of the winning team was sacrificed to Mars on an altar which was carved with three storks with interlaced bills. This festival of the October Horse was the last corn festival of the year. Previously a bull had been sacrificed, but as Mars gradually took on warlike associations, the horse was substituted. Apparently the sacrifice also symbolised the death of death itself. The Romans also adopted the Celtic goddess Epona, venerating her as a horse goddess and a funerary deity. The Dioscuri (Castor and Pollux) ride white horses. The horse is also an attribute of the huntress, Diana.

Caligula made his horse Incitatus (spurred-on) a senator and a consul. Incitatus had an ivory manger and drank wine from a gold pail.

The ancient Chaldaeans had a possible horse-goddess, Silili, who is mentioned in the *Epic of Gilgamesh* as the mother of a stallion who was a lover of Ishtar.

The Egyptians were famed for their horses; Solomon imported them and sold them on to the Hittite and Armenian kings. The horses were sacred to the sun god.

> *"He removed from the entrance to the temple of the Lord the horses that the kings of Judah had dedicated to the sun .... Josiah then burned the chariots dedicated to the sun."*
> (II Kings 23:11)

In Norse mythology, Odin's horse was called Sleipnir. Sleipnir had eight legs, which may symbolise the eight airts of the sky (the ancient eightfold division of the compass), or the eight legs of four men carrying a coffin (as Odin is the god of the dead, it seems apt that his steed should be associated with the final journey).

The origins of Sleipnir were unusual. Once upon a time, the Aesir agreed to give Freyja, the Sun and the Moon to a giant if he could build a wall around Asgard in a year. They thought this was a particularly safe bet, as Asgard was so large that it ought have been impossible. However the giant worked together with his horse Svadilfari, who helped him to do it so fast that he was about to meet the deadline. So the Aesir went to Loki and asked him to help them. He shape-shifted into a mare and lured Svadilfari away. While this was going on, Thor slew the giant; meanwhile Svadilfari sired a foal on Loki in mare form. This foal was Sleipnir, the grey horse with eight feet. The other gods had only slightly more prosaic steeds: Freyr's horse was called Bloodyhoof; Thor's chariot was drawn by goats; and both Freyr and Freyja possessed magical boars. The horse was particularly associated with the Vanir pantheon (Freyr, Freyja, Njord, etc.) as deities of the fields, forests, sun and rain.

The chariot drawer of the maiden Sol, the sun, was Arvak (early-waker). The chariot of the moon, the youth Mani, was drawn by Alsvid or Alswider (All-swift). The horse of Siegfried, the hero of the Nibelung cycle, was Grani (grey-coloured). The Valkyries' steeds were clouds. Night's horse was called Hrimfaxi (frost-mane), from whose bit the dew falls. Day's horse was called Skinfaxi (shining-mane). It will be noticed that Tolkien drew on these horses to name Gandalf's horse in The Lord of the Rings, Shadowfax (shadow-mane). Tolkien drew extensively on Norse mythology for his source material, which is one of the reasons why the book rings true.

Horses are frequently associated with sovereignty. Hengist and Horsa were the two leaders of the fifth century invasion of Britain; the names may be of religious significance. Contrary to popular belief, however, the two war-leaders were brothers, not husband and wife.

The Coventry legend of Lady Godiva was probably derived from a monastic description of a local procession dedicated to the Saxon goddess Goda (who is also associated with Wild Edric). The name Godiva is derived from Godgifu (gift of God). Men were often forbidden from viewing such rituals, hence the salutary fate of Peeping Tom. A miserere seat in Coventry Cathedral (the pre-war one) depicted a long-haired woman wrapped in a net, riding side-ways on a goat and following a hare. A naked lady riding a white horse represented Spring.

In early Celtic Ireland, horses were seen as a symbol of pastoral wealth. Warriors rode horses, and they were also used to pull funerary carts to the tombs of dead nobles. On Celtic farms, horses were ridden, but were also pack and draught animals. They were also eaten. They were very valuable animals: Medhbh of Connacht had a horse 'which was valued at a cumal' (a female slave). In Irish mythology, Macha, the wife of Crunnchu, had to race against the king's horses when she was pregnant. She died at the winning-post, giving birth to twins. The great mound Émain Macha (Twins of Macha) commemorates the legend. Medhbh of Connacht, the legendary queen, could outrun the fastest horse. The Irish otherworld goddess, Clidna, appears with birds (as do

Epona and Rhiannon) and presides over horse-racing in the many-coloured land (the Celtic otherworld). The horse and goose often appear together, with Epona and/or Mars. Agesilaos, a late Greek writer, tells that Epona was born of a mare:

> *"Phoulouios Stellos, who hated women, had relations with a mare. In time she gave birth to a beautiful little girl to whom she gave the name Epona."*

The Irish goddess of reincarnation, Étain Echraide, was the fabulously beautiful wife of Midir. Her name means 'horse-riding'. Horse racing was a popular sport in the otherworld, and the Celts looked forward to an afterlife in which they could race chariots and horses. The Irish god of the sea (also known in Wales in the Isle of Man) had a horse called 'Splendid Mane'. One of the Dagda's by-names was Eochaid Ollathair (Eochaid the Great Father). The name Eochaid is derived from *ech*, a horse. In the tale of The Death of Fergus, the poet Aedh is taken to the otherworld by Esirt on a magical horse which appears from the sea,

> *"of which horse the fashion was this: two fierce flashing eyes he had, an exquisite pure crimson mane, with four green legs and a long tail that floated in wavy curls. His colour was that of prime artificers' gold work, and a gold-encrusted bridle he bore withal."*

In the earliest Celtic contexts, the horse had definite solar associations. It was frequently depicted on coins with the crane (a solar bird). It also appears on the Gundestrup cauldron (found in Scandinavia). La Téne metalwork also abounds with horse motifs. One of these looks like a sea deity, holding sea-horses aloft in either hand, while across his breast is depicted a monster devouring two men. Supernatural horses are also associated with the formation of lochs and wells. In Irish mythology, Lough Neagh was formed in the following manner: the horse of Oengus urinated and formed a well, which was then given into the keeping of a woman who had to put a cover over the well; but one day she failed to replace the cover and the well overflowed and formed Lough Neagh. Lough Ri was formed in a similar fashion. Midir's horse urinated and also formed a well, which subsequently overflowed, drowning a man called Ri, and was hence named Lough Ri. Magical horses were also endowed with great strength, such as the three horses who bore the Three Horse-Burdens of Britain, one of whom was Black Moro, who carried seven and a half people on his back (the half was Gelbeinevin the cook, who swam with his two hands to the horse's crupper) across the Menai Straits. Another horse which carried a burden across the sea appears in Irish mythology in the *Colloquy of the Ancients* was the steed of Manannan, who rescues Ciabhán, one of the Fianna and two young men in a boat with a stern of copper from a storm and carries them to the Otherworld, where they serve him in exchange for their rescue.

In the Welsh epic, the *Mabinogion*, Arawn, King of Annwn (the Otherworld) rode a pale horse and led a pack of hounds with red ears in a pursuit of a stag. King Arthur's horse was called Lamri (the curvetter).

Gaulish war gods were also associated with horses; both Rudiobus and Segomo (also known in Irish mythology, as Nia Segamon). However, the strongest association of horses was with Epona (Divine Horse), who was very popular with the Roman cavalry. Indeed, she was adopted as a patroness by some units, even the Batavian imperial bodyguard, the equites singulares, who had a shrine in their stables.

Many Roman forts had a shrine to Epona. Statues and bas-reliefs of Epona have been found in Gaul, Britain, the Rhineland, the Danube basin, and at Rome. She is shown riding either a horse or an ass, usually side-saddle; standing beside a horse or between two horses; or lying half-naked along a horse's back. In Gaul, she was frequently depicted with Mars. On the cheek-piece of a Roman helmet found at South Collingham in Nottinghamshire, Epona is depicted standing beside her horse, holding the bridle in her left hand, and grasping a rope-like object, which may be a serpent, in her right hand. She is usually depicted riding side-saddle, some-times accompanied by dogs, birds, or foals. She was sometimes depicted as horse-headed. She was introduced into Britain, and may have been equated with Rhiannon and Macha (both connected with horses in their own right). She was invoked on Hadrian's

Wall at Carvoran and at Auchendavy. A cross at Kilrea in Ireland bears a depiction of her seated between horses. A fourth-century funeral tile from Roussas in France shows her riding side-saddle on the back of a goose. As well as her connection with warriors, she was also a goddess of maternity and fecundity; she appears in the company of mother goddesses in several Gaulish depictions. A small bronze from Wiltshire shows her with ears of corn in her lap, and a dish of corn in her right hand, held above a horse. Another horse is standing on her left. Both of these horses are small, wearing collars, and with protruding tongues. She appears to be holding a snake in her left hand.

Many Celtic brooches, coins, and small votive figurines of horses have been found in Britain, such as the bronze statuette of a horse found at Coventina's Well at Carrawbrough in Northumberland. The horse was connected with indigenous deities of war, and possibly with the cult of the head. Horses were also associated with the birth of heroes; at the birth of Cú Chulainn, a mare foals at the same time as Deichtine gives birth to the hero. The foals are called the Grey of Macha and the Black of Saíngliu. Cu Chulainn maintained his association with horses throughout his life; there is a description of his horses in the Tain Bo Cuálnge: "nimble, furious, small-headed, bounding, large-eared, small-snouted, sharp-beaked...". The life of his horses was bound up with his.

A similar story is associated with the birth of Pryderi, Rhiannon's son, in which a chieftain named Teyrnon was engaged to watch over a mare whose foals disappeared every time she gave birth. A foal was born, but a huge claw came through the window to seize the foal. Teyrnon cut off the monstrous arm, and opened the door of the stable. He found a small child lying there; it was Pryderi, who had been taken from his mother on the night of his birth. The foal was given to the child. Unfortunately, Rhiannon was blamed for Pryderi's disappearance, and assumed to have murdered him. As a punishment, she was made to stand at the mounting-block for seven years offering to carry every stranger who visited the court on her back. In the *Mabinogi of Math*, she was made to wear an ass's collar around her neck. A similar tale was told about the Welsh divine hero, Mabon, who was stolen from his mother when he was three nights old, but eventually rescued by King Arthur. Mabon had a swift horse and a wonderful hound.

Rhiannon had a white horse, which she could ride faster than any man, although she seemed to be travelling at a steady pace. This image may represent the Moon. The name Rhiannon means "great queen", from *rig antona*. Supernatural Celtic horses were often red; red horsemen were often an omen of disaster in Celtic myth. In the story of Dá Derga's hostel, the king's doom is presaged by three red horsemen (na trĭ Deirg). In the story of Cú Chulainn, the hero sees a chariot drawn by a one-legged red horse and driven by a red woman (the war goddess). She is accompanied by a man carrying a hazel fork and driving a cow.

A number of Celtic statuettes of a horse and rider have been found at various sites. They may have been mounted on the end of a pole for ritual purposes, or they may have been offerings to a deity. In Gaul, Mars was often represented as a rider on horseback, probably by association with indigenous deities connected with horses, who were also portrayed on horseback. An altar from Bisley in Gloucestershire depicts Mars as a warrior on horseback wielding an axe. A fragment showing Mars Corotiacus as a mounted warrior riding over a prostrate enemy was found in Martlesham (a name connected with Mars) in Suffolk. A piece of New Forest ware from Linwood shows a horseman, a radiant god, and a squatting goddess. Similarly, a relief from Kingscote in Gloucestershire depicts a mounted god and an enthroned goddess, who may be his consort.

In general, the horse was to the Celts a cult animal, a status symbol, and an icon of power. Although it had solar associations, it was not directly equated with the sun; rather the heroes who rode it were given solar attributes by the bards to endow them and their steed with splendour. The horse was also frequently associated with the otherworld; faery horsemen were frequently described as appearing from a magical mist and luring people into the otherworld. It was also associated with virility (as indeed it still is).

In Slavonic myth, there are several deities associated with horses: Triglav (a deity at Stettin) had a black horse which gave omens; and Khors, a god of health and hunting, was depicted as a stallion. The white horses of the sun were tended by Zorya Utrenyaya (Aurora of the morning), Zorya Vechernyaya (Aurora of the evening), and the stars, Zvevda Dennitsa (the morning star) and Vechernyaya Zvevda (the evening star). Horses were sacrificed to Volos, lord of the animals and protector of flocks. His functions and attributes were transferred to Saint Vlas or Blaise. Yarilo or Erilo, the god of joy and carnal love (possibly related to Eros, the Greek god of love) rides a white horse, dresses in a white cloak, and is young and handsome. He wears a crown of wild flowers in his hair, and is also the god of springtime. Corn sown in the spring is called *yarovoi*. Horses were also very important to the Slavonic heroes, known collectively as the bogatyri; they were the heroes of the epic poems known as byliny (that which has been). Ilya Muromyets, the Christianised version of Pyerun (Perkunas) rides a black horse. Another bogatyr, Mikula, rides a little horse that is faster than the finest chargers.

In pre-Islamic Iranian mythology, the chariot of Ardvisura Anahita is drawn by the four white horses of cloud, rain, sleet, and wind, and the Magi's chariot is drawn by four chargers representing the four elements and their associated divinities. In Islam, the horse signifies happiness and wealth.

In Sumero-Semitic myth, Marduk's chariot of the sun was drawn by four horses.

In Mithraism, white horses draw Mithras' chariot in his character as the sun god. Similarly, in Roman mythology, white horses draw the chariot of Apollo.

The Basque goddess Mari rides across the sky in a cart drawn by four horses.

The horse was also highly revered by the Anglo-Saxons. Hengist and Horsa were the semi-legendary leaders of the first Saxon warband to arrive in England. They were said to have arrived in Kent in 449. Vortigern offered them land in exchange for their help in fighting the Picts. Horsa is said to have been slain at the battle of Aylesford in 455, but Hengist survived to rule Kent until his death in 488. The name Hengist means stallion (modern German *Hengst*); the name Horsa means horse. The traditional badge of Kent is a white horse.

In Hindu mythology, Sanjna, the wife of the sun god Surya, bore him three children, but was eventually exhausted by his constant dazzling. She therefore persuaded her sister Shaya (the shade) to take her place. After a few years Surya (clearly an unobservant being) noticed the change, and went in search of Sanjna. She had turned herself into a mare, so he became a stallion and chased her. For a while they lived together as horses in a state of bliss, until he gave up an eighth of his brightness so that she could live with him as the sun. In some myths, Surya, the sun, is feminine.

Another appearance of the horse in Hindu mythology is the tenth and final avatar of Vishnu, called Kalki, who will appear as a white horse in the sky. The name Kalki means 'time'. Another Hindu horse deity is Varuna, the Cosmic Horse and god of the waters. In early Vedic times, the horse was one of the great sacrificial animals; the Vedic Horse Sacrifice was probably the oldest, and certainly the most famous. The horse was deeply venerated by the Indo-Europeans, and the sacrifice was attended by the King and Queen with four hundred followers. The occasion denoted an erotic spring fertility rite. The Gandhavas (half-man, half-horse) represent natural fecundity, but also music, intelligence, and abstract thought. The god Savithri (one of the Adityas or guardians of the months of the year) has a chariot drawn by luminous horses.

In Siberia, the horse is a psychopomp, guiding souls from this world to the afterlife. The horse is also a sacrificial animal in Siberia and the Altai. Its skin and head are then used in ritual; the skin represents the fat and the head contains the life-force.

In China, the Cosmic Horse is white, and is an avatar of Kwan-yin, the goddess of compassion, who is known to Buddhists as Avalokitesvara (a bodhisattva) and in Japan as Bato Kwannon. The Celestial Charger, Ma-wang, king of the horses, is the

333

ancestor of all horses. Buddha's horse (when he was Prince Gautama) was called Kantaka, and was white. In Chinese Buddhism the winged horse carried the Book of the Law on its back. In Taoism, the horse is an attribute of Ch'ang Kuo, one of the eight immortals.

In Japan, the white horse is regarded as a form of Bato Kwannon; she is often depicted either as a white horse, or horse-headed, or with a crown which includes a horse figure. The black horse is an attribute of the rain god.

There are various individual horses who are proverbial for their deeds and adventures. Some are historical, others legendary. Banks's Horse was a horse called Marocco, belonging to a man called Banks around the end of the reign of Queen Elizabeth I. Marocco was able to do many different tricks; one of his exploits was allegedly the ascent of St Paul's steeple. Bayard was a horse of great swiftness. He was given by Charlemagne to the four sons of Aymon. If all four of the brothers mounted, the horse elongated himself to four times his usual size; if only one mounted, he remained his usual size. Bayardo was Rinaldo's steed; he was associated with Bayardo's Leap, near Sleaford in Lincolnshire. Rinaldo was riding on Bayardo when the spirit of the place menaced him by leaping onto Bayardo's back behind him. Bayardo made three great leaps and unhorsed the spirit. Three standing stones, about thirty yards apart, are said to mark the leaps. Bucephalus (bull-headed) was Alexander the Great's charger; Alexander built him the city of Bucephala as a mausoleum.

Al Borak (the lightning) was the horse brought by Gabriel to carry Mohammed to the seventh heaven, and was one of the animals received into Paradise. He had the face of a man but the cheeks of a horse, and the wings of an eagle. He spoke with the voice of a man and glowed all over with radiant light; his eyes were like jacinths, but as brilliant as the stars. In Islam, the horse is regarded as a gift from Allah; it is believed to pray for its owner, to have psychic and prognostic powers, being able to foresee danger and perceive the spirits of the dead.

The mare Alfana was the steed of Gradasso in *Orlando Furioso*. Orlando's horse was called Brigliadore (golden bridle). Aquiline (like an eagle), a horse bred on the banks of the Tagus, was the steed of Raymond, the medieval French hero. Arundel (swallow) was the horse of the hero Bevois of Hampton, a dragon-slayer. Hampton is usually interpreted as Southampton, and there is an area of the town called Bevois Valley, and an administrative building called Arundel Towers. In Spanish legend, Bavieca was the horse of El Cid. The horse survived the hero by $2^{1}/_{2}$ years, during which time he would permit no-one to mount him. He was buried before the gates of the monastery of Valencia, and two elm-trees were planted on his grave. Black Bess was the mythical mare of Dick Turpin, the highwayman, created by Harrison Ainsworth in his book *Rookwood*. The mare was supposed to have carried the outlaw from London to York in one night. Warwick the Kingmaker had a famous horse called Black Saladin, whose sire was Malech. It was said that when the line of Malech died out, so would the Warwick family; apparently this actually happened. Rosinante was Don Quixote's nag, a bag of skin and bones which he believed was greater than El Cid's Babieca or Alexander's Bucephalus. The name means 'once a jade' (*rocin*, a jade, *ante*, before).

Symbolism

The white, golden, or fiery horse generally represents the Sun. It is also associated with the oceanic gods (Poseidon, Neptune, Manannan), when it is generally lunar. It is a symbol of wisdom, reason, intellect, nobility, light, swiftness (both physical and mental), instinct, the animal self, divination (the shaman's drum is a steed which can carry the drummer to the otherworld), the wind, and the waves of the sea ("white horses"). The winged horse and the white horse represent the Sun and the Cosmic Horse. The winged horse also symbolises pure intellect, unblemished innocence, life, and light. It is generally ridden by heroes (e.g. Bellerophon upon Pegasus). The lion slaying the horse or bull denotes the sun drying up mists and moisture, defeating the powers of humidity. The black horse is a symbol of death, and is traditionally used to draw hearses; it also symbolises chaos and the twelve days of misrule between the old year and the new.

In heraldry, the horse often appears prancing (invicta) and represents speed, nobility, and power. The horse's head was the emblem of Carthage, and the winged horse is depicted on Assyrian bas-reliefs and the coins of Carthage.

In Christianity, the horse symbolises courage; in the East, it is a symbol of fire and the heavens. The Four Horsemen of the Apocalypse (in the *Book of Revelations*, chapter 6) were Death (on a white horse), War (on a red horse), Famine (on a black horse) and Famine (on a pale horse). In Christian art, the horse denotes courage and generosity. It is an attribute of Saints Martin, Maurice, George, and Victor, all of whom died on horseback. Wild horses are an attribute of St Hippolytus (see Mythology) In the art of the catacombs, the horse denoted the ephemeral passage of life. By the Renaissance, it had come to represent lust.

In Buddhism, the horse represents the indestructible and the hidden nature of reality. In China, the horse symbolised the heavens, fire, yang, the South, perseverance and speed, and was a good omen. The horse's hoof is also a lucky charm. The horse is the seventh animal in the Chinese zodiac (the Twelve Terrestrial Branches).

Poetry

"The tigers of wrath are wiser than the horses of instruction."

(from *"Proverbs of Hell"* by William Blake, 1757-1827)

"Ride a cock horse to Banbury Cross
 To see a fine lady upon a white horse;
 Rings on her fingers and bells on her toes,
And she shall have music wherever she goes." (from *Mother Goose*)

Eh by₍ for eorlum   œpelinga wyn,
hors hlofum wlanc   dær him hælep₍ ymb,
welege on wicgum   wrixlap₍ spraece,
and bi₍ unstyllum   aefre frofur.
 (from Anglo-Saxon Rune Poem)

(A steed is the joy of aethlings for eorls,
A horse proud in hoofs, where men about it,
wealthy, on stallions, exchange speech,
and to the restless is ever a solace.)

I will voyage in God's name
In likeness of deer, in likeness of horse,
In likeness of serpent, in likeness of king.
More powerful will it be with me than with all others.
> (from the *Carmina Gadelica*)

Brian
(Brian was the steed of the archangel Michael.)

Michael's Brian was
As white as the snow of the peaks,
As white as the snow of the waves,
As white as the cotton of the meads,
And nearly as white as the angel victorious.

Michael's Brian was
As swift as the swift of the spring,
As swift as the wind of March,
As swift as the deadly levin,
And nearly as swift as the shaft of death.

> (from the *Carmina Gadelica*)

Human

Latin name *Homo sapiens*

Family *Primates*

Polarity Woman = yin;
Man = yang

Element all four elements

Etymology
Middle English *humain*(e), from Old French, from Latin *humanus*,
from *homo*, a human being

Planet "Men are from Mars, women are from Venus."

Woman

The great mother is the archetypal image of women; she is the
feminine principle symbolised by the Moon, the Earth, and the
waters. She represents the power of instinct. She can be either
beneficent and protective or malefic and destructive. She is both
the pure spiritual guide and the siren or seductress, the virgin
Queen of Heaven and the harpy and harlot, supreme wisdom and
utter folly, the totality of nature.

Unfortunately this either/or dichotomy has been perpetuated
throughout the history of symbolism, so that it seems impossible to
have a goddess who is both an assertive
individual and sexually active; the minute she
becomes sexually active, she either becomes
subject to a male or stigmat-
ised as a harlot.

Symbols of woman are everything lunar, receptive, passive, nourishing, hollow, concave, sinuous, cavernous, diamond-shaped (perhaps to represent the yoni; women's coats of arms in heraldry are depicted as lozenge-shaped, or oval-shaped. In particular, the cave, walled garden, well, door, gate, cup, furrow, sheath, scabbard, shield, ship, shell, fish, pearl, the waters, the crescent moon, reflected light of the moon, and the star, are all used to represent the feminine principle.

In Buddhism, the feminine principle is called the Prakriti; in Hinduism, it is called the Shakti; and in China, it is called yin. In Hinduism, Prakriti is the world womb, from which everything has its origin. Prakriti is the mother of Brahma, who is sometimes identified with the cosmic tree. In her earthly manifestation, she is called Mulaprakriti, 'primeval matter', who differentiates the elements and the myriad forms of nature from primal energy.

The Shakti (Hindu, Nepalese, Tibetan) is the feminine principle as the supreme force, the active aspect of the universe, with Shiva as the passive. Shiva cannot exist or be effective without her to provide polarity. The worshippers of Shakti are called Shaktas. The six principle aspects of Shakti are Parashakti (the great power), Jnanashakti (understanding and intellect), Ichchhashakti (will, desire), Kriyashakti (making, doing), Kundalinishakti (the serpent energy), and Mantrikashakti (charm, magic, music, and language). In Indian art a beautiful woman depicts the benevolent aspect of Maya, the great mother, whilst her terrible aspect is represented by Kali or Durga.

In Christianity, the Church is regarded as the Bride of Christ, and is depicted as a woman holding a chalice or a cross and wearing a crown. A veiled or blindfolded woman in Christian art depicted the Jewish synagogue. Figures of women were used to depict the virtues, the vices, and the seasons in medieval art.

Man

The cosmic man is the microcosm, reflecting the macrocosm and the elements. His body represents earth, his body heat is fire, his blood is the waters, and his breath is the air. The principle symbols of masculinity are the sun, sword, spear, lance, arrow, dart, spade, plough, ship's prow, pillar, pole, fircone or deal apple, obelisk, fire, flame, torch, lingam, shakta, and yang. The masculine principle is generally equated with the Sun (except in Teutonic and Oceanic mythology) and everything phallic, penetrating, piercing, upright, and associated with heat.

In Indigenous American symbolism, a white eagle feather represents the male principle. In Taoism, Man is the central and mediatory power in the great triad of Heaven, Man, and Earth. In Islam and Sufism, Man represents universal existence and the link between God and Nature. In Kabbalah, the cosmic man is called Adam Kadmon, whose body is the Tree of Life (*Ets Chaim*).

Poetry/Quotations

"When Adam delved and Eve span
Who was then a gentleman?"
 (Attributed to John Ball, 1381)

"One is not born a woman, one becomes one."
(Simone de Beauvoir)

"I expect that Woman will be the last thing civilized by Man."
(George Meredith, 1828-1909)

"Women must come off the pedestal. Men put us up there to get us out of the way."
(Viscountess Rhondda, 1883-1958)

"People call me a feminist whenever I express sentiments that differentiate me from a doormat or a prostitute."
(Rebecca West, 1892-1983)

"Every man has three characters: that which he exhibits, that which he has, and that which he thinks he has."
(Alphonse Karr, 1808-1890)

"Man is by nature a political animal."
(Aristotle, 384-322 BCE)

"Men can be analysed, women... merely adored."
(Oscar Wilde)

"Never despise what it says in the women's magazines: it may not
be subtle but neither are men."
(Zsa Zsa Gabor)

Hyena

Latin name *Hyéna hyéna*

Family *Hyéninae*

Etymology Middle English from Old French *hyene*, from Latin from Greek *huaina* (feminine of *hus*, a pig).

Varieties

The *Hyænidae* are scavengers and carrion eaters, which include the Aard Wolf (*Proteles cristata*) from South Africa. The Striped Hyena (*Hyæna hyæna*) is a member of the subfamily *Hyæninae* or True Hyenas.

Folklore

The hyena was believed to change its sex. This may be because the female of the species was long believed to be the male, because her genitalia resemble a penis. Also, the female gathers a lot of males about her, which zoologists thought were a 'harem' of females. This demonstrates how easy it is to generalise from human practices and make assumptions about animal behaviour which are not borne out by empirical evidence.

It was also said that the hyena imitated the human voice to lure men to their deaths, and that it mimicked vomiting in order to entice dogs to come to it, so that it could kill them.

In Africa, the hyena is believed to have magical powers, and is regarded with dread. It is believed that men's souls can enter hyenas in order to wreak revenge on those who have done them wrong. In East Africa, the hyena is an animal-ancestor, and the emblem of a secret society.

Mythology

The hyena was venerated by the ancient Egyptians, because it was believed that a stone called the hyænia is found in its eye. Pliny relates that when placed under the tongue, the stone would confer the gift of prophecy.

In Arabic tradition, wizards are believed to take the form of hyenas; in the east, the animal can be the incarnation of a sorcerer.

In Africa, various hyena gods are associated with elements and spirits. Generally the hyena is regarded as an unclean animal, feeding on corpses and skulking in graveyards. It also represents treachery and the desolation of the wilderness.

Symbolism

The hyena represents nameless vice, impurity, instability, inconstancy, or a two-faced person. In Christianity it was used as an image of the devil feeding on damned souls.

Ibex

Latin name *Capra ibex sibirica*   **Subfamily** *Caprinae*

Family *Bovidae*   **Order** *Perissodactyla*

Etymology from Latin

Varieties

The Siberian Ibex (*Capra ibex sibirica*) is a member of the goat family.

Folklore

According to Pliny, the ibex can hurl itself from great heights and land on its horns, which are elastic and can absorb the shock.

Mythology

The Egyptians regarded the ibex as sacred to Set and Reshep; it shares the symbolism of the gazelle. Reshep was the god of lightning; he was originally the Syrian deity Reshpu. Reshpu was depicted as a warrior with shield and spear in his left hand and a club in his right and a gazelle projected above his forehead, perhaps depicting his sovereignty over the desert. The horns of the ibex are often depicted in the art of Mesopotamia and the northern steppes of Asia.

Symbolism

The wild goat of the Bible is actually the Nubian ibex. In Arabic tradition, the ibex represents beauty.

Jackal

Latin name *Canis aureus*	**Polarity** Yin
Family *Canidae*	**Element** Earth
Order *Carnivores*	**Planet** Moon

Etymology from Turkish *Çakal*, from Persian *sagal*

Deities Anubis, Duamutef, Kali

Mythology

In Egypt, the jackal was mainly associated with Anubis, originally known as Anpu or Anup. He was depicted as a jackal-headed god, or as a black jackal. He assured the souls of the dead safe conduct to the judgment seat of Osiris. Because the jackal could see by both day and night, Anubis was given the title of the Pathfinder; because of his role as a psychopomp, he was known as the Opener of the Way. He was also associated with the cemetery, and presided over the embalming of the dead. He was a local deity of Abydos, the son of Osiris and Nephthys (a great magician-goddess who knew the words of power needed to raise the dead, and regarded as a pro-tector of the dead; originally known as Nebhet). He was exposed by his his mother (presumably so as not to be found out sleeping with Isis' consort) but Isis found him with the help of some dogs. He grew up to be her attendant and guard in her journey to seek the body of Osiris; he helped her to restore him to life. His name means 'watcher' and 'guardian of dogs'. He and his brother Upuaut (the wolf-god) presided over the abode of the dead, led them to the hall of judgment, and supervised the weighing of the heart in Maat's scales. In another story, he is the son of Set. He may have been called upon to prevent jackals eating the bodies of the dead.

Duamutef is another jackal-headed Egyptian deity. He is one of the four guardians called upon to watch over the canopic jars, and is generally depicted on the jar which contains the stomach. His name means 'he who praises his mother', and he is associated with Fire, East, and the goddess Neith.

In Hinduism, the jackal is an attribute of Kali the Destroyer, because of its scavenging.

Symbolism

In Buddhism, the jackal symbolises a person who cannot understand the Dharma, and is therefore rooted in evil.

In the Bible, the jackal is an unclean animal and a symbol of desolation.

Jaguar

Latin name *Panthera onca*

Family *Felidae*

Folk name Ounce

Deities Tezcatlipoca

Polarity dark

Planet Moon

Etymology from Tupi-Guarani *yaguara*

Varieties

The jaguar is the largest spotted cat, and the pre-eminent animal of Central American mythology. It is at the top of the food chain, and competes with humans and other felines for available prey.

Folklore

In South America, tribal magicians were believed to take the form of a jaguar, or to have a jaguar as a familiar spirit, and sometimes to become a jaguar after death. Magicians in jaguar form were believed to be able to travel through time and space. They were also believed to be able to see the future through the eyes of the jaguar. Black jaguars were believed to become demons after they had died. The Akuriyo people of Surinam believe that there are three ways to be killed by a jaguar: grabbed and killed; killed and eaten; or 'jaguar-killed', where an Akuriyo magician sends a spirit in the shape of a jaguar to kill someone.

Many peoples regarded someone who had killed a jaguar as having great kudos. The Mojo of Bolivia ate the flesh of the jaguar at a feast to celebrate the kill, in order that it might impart to them the fierceness of the jaguar. Many peoples' clothing and regalia was also imbued with jaguar symbolism. The Mocovi, Toba, Mboya, and Pilaga tribes of the Chaco wore jackets of jaguar skin for ornament and protection, and also to give the wearer the fierceness of the animal. Among the Parintintin people of central Brazil, most of the men had a jaguar tattooed on the inside of the forearm. The Suya of the Upper Xingú often wore jaguar claw necklaces, and the Caingang of Brazil readied themselves for battle by painting themselves with black spots or stripes and roaring like jaguars.

Mythology

In parts of South America, it is believed that if a soul is to be reincarnated, it passes over the rainbow into the other world; if it is not to be reincarnated, it is eaten by the cosmic jaguar. The mirrored eyes of the jaguar were the conduit to the realm of spirits.

In Mexico, the jaguar was regarded as the messenger of the forest spirits. In Central America, it was regarded as the Master of Animals (just as the lion is regarded as king of the animals in the West). It was the chief figure in Mayan ritual, and sacrifices were made to the jaguar god, who could also take on human form. The Quiche lineage (a Mayan royal house) was believed to be descended from a jaguar. In an Amazonian myth, Jaguar Woman marries Anaconda; in another story, the Jaguar married a human woman to obtain the secret of fire.

Symbolism

To the Aztecs, the jaguar symbolised the powers of darkness at war with the solar eagle. The Aztec warrior god was depicted as a jaguar; he was knocked from the sky by the Feathered Serpent (the sun), and became a jaguar when he fell into the sea.

The Toltecs regarded the jaguar as night, thunder, and rain, but his yellow skin symbolised the sun.

The jaguar remained a potent symbol in South America for a long time, representing aggressive qualities, élite status, and perceptual abilities. It was associated with magic, rulers, warfare, and sacrifice.

Kangaroo

Latin name Macropus

Family *Felidae*

Folk name boomer (male), flyer (female) joey (young)

Deities Tezcat

The kangaroo is sacred to the Moon in Aboriginal mythology.

The kangeroo owes its name to Captai James Cook, who asked the Aborigine people of the Endeavour River what they called the kangeroos, and they (not understanding him) replied 'I do not know'. Kangeroos had been seen be Westerners before, as Captain Francois Pelsært, who was wrecked on the coast of Australia while carrying Dutch colonists to the Moluccas in 1629, saw them.

The Great Kangeroo (Macropus spp) is the most well-known and largest of the kangeroo species.

Leopard

Latin name *Felis [Panthera] pardus* **Planet** Sun
Family *Felidae*

Etymology Middle English from Old French from Late Latin, from Late Greek *leopardos*

Deities Osiris, Dionysos

Varieties

The Cheetah or Hunting Leopard (*Acinonyx jubatus*) is the swiftest animal on foot; it can run at speeds of up to 75 miles per hour. The Snow Leopard or Ounce (*Felis [Uncia] uncia*) and the Ocelot (*Felis [Leopardus] pardalis*) all resemble or are closely related to the Leopard or Panther (*Felis [Panthera] pardus*).

Folklore

The leopard got its name from the belief that it was a cross between a lion and a pard (a panther without any white specks).

In some parts of Western Africa, if a man killed a leopard, he was bound and brought before the chiefs for killing one of their peers. He would offer the defence that the leopard is a chief of the forest and hence a stranger. Then he would be released and rewarded. Afterwards, the dead leopard would be given a chief's bonnet and set up in the village, where dances would be held every night in its honour.

Mythology

In Egypt, the leopard was an emblem of Osiris, and his priests wore leopard skins. In Africa, the leopard is a cult animal for many peoples, the attribute of storm gods. African priests also wore leopard skins. In Dahomey, the leopard is sacred to the royal family. It is highly revered among the Ibo, who associate it with fertility. To many peoples, it embodies the spirits of the dead, or can be the vehicle for the soul of a chief. Anyone who sees it must not mention its name; nor must its flesh be eaten, because it helped the ancestors.

In Greece, the leopard was an attribute of Dionysos in his aspect of creator and destroyer. Dionysos is frequently depicted wearing a leopard skin or riding on a leopard; his chariot is drawn by leopards, and they are his playmates.

Symbolism

The leopard symbolises cruelty, aggression, ferocity, and intrepidity. Its spots resemble eyes, so it is called the Great Watcher.

In Hebrew symbolism it represents swiftness. In the Book of Isaiah, the leopard is cited as an example of ferocity (contrasted with the kid); the coming millenium will be the time "when the leopard shall lie down with the kid" (Isaiah 11,6). The question "can the leopard change his spots? Neither can you do good who are accustomed to doing evil" (Jeremiah 13,23) represents a pessimistic view of the behaviour of the people of Israel.

In Christianity, the leopard represents the devil, sin, the duplicity of Satan, the Antichrist, and concupiscence. In Christian art, the leopard represents the Beast in Revelation 13,18 with seven heads and ten horns. Six of the heads have a nimbus, but the seventh, which is wounded to death, lost its power and is therefore depicted as bare.

"And the beast which I saw was like unto a leopard, and his feet were as the feet of a bear, and his mouth as the mouth of a lion."

In heraldry, it is a symbol of bravery, impetuous deeds, bold achievements, and activity; it is sometimes referred to as the lybbard. In China, it symbolises bravery and warlike ferocity.

Líon

Latin name *Felis [Leo] leo*

Family *Felidae*

Folk name King of the Animals

Polarity Yang

Element Fire

Planet Sun

Etymology Middle English, from Anglo-French *liun*, from Latin *leo, leonis*, from Greek *leon, leontos*

Deities Sekhmet, Bast, Pakhit, Renenet, Mekhit, Tefnut, Shezmu, Maahes, Min, Anhur, Anat, Hepatu, Shaushka, Ruti, Qedeshet, Lebiyah, Ishtar, Nergal, Marduk, Ningirsu, Yaghuth, Artemis, Phoebus, Cybele, Tyche, Apollo, Juno, Hercules, Fortuna, Bahu, Tara, Narasinha, Ratnasambhava, Vishnu, Devi, Durga, Kwan-Yin

Varieties

There were once many subspecies of Lion throughout Africa, Asia, and even in Europe. They now survive only in the grassland, forests, and hills of Central, East, and West Africa. There is a small enclave in a reserve in India.

Folklore

The lion is known as the King of the Animals, and hence is associated with kingship, the sun, fire, and solar deities. According to superstition, the lions in the Tower of London fall ill when the monarch falls ill, and die when he or she dies.

> *"Our first visit was to the Lions. My Friend [a Tory] enquired very much after their Health, and whether none of them had fallen sick upon ... the Flight of the Pretender? ... He had learned from his Cradle, that the Lions in the Tower*

were the best judges of the Title of our British Kings, and always sympathized with our Sovereigns."
(Addison, *Free-Holder*, 1 June 1716)

According to an old fable, the lion wipes out its footprints with its tail, so that it cannot be tracked. It was also believed that it slept with its eyes open, so it represented vigilance, spiritual watchfulness and fortitude. It was also said that lion cubs were born dead, but their sire breathed life into them after three days, or that their dam howled over them to bring them to life. This was associated with Christ bringing the dead to life.

The fortunes of lions' breeding was widely held to affect the breeding of other animals, even humans. Both Yorkshire and Sussex superstition held that when lions breed (every seven years), other animals are sterile, or their litters are stillborn. The old women of Wellington Workhouse in 1895 said that if a lioness died in whelping, the year would be a bad one for women to be pregnant. In Northamptonshire in 1985, a woman died in childbirth, and a neighbour was heard to remark that "a lioness must have died this year."

Mythology

The lioness was an attribute of the lunar Great Mother from the Mediterranean to Africa, the Middle East, Sumeria, India, and Tibet. The lion is the King of the Animals in many cultures, but is also associated with war gods and the Sun.

Many Egyptian deities are associated with lions. The best-known is probably Sekhmet, an early lioness-headed fire goddess. She is the consort of Ptah and the mother of Nefertum and Imhotep.

Known as the 'Lady of the West', she was one of the Memphis triad. When Ra ordered Hathor to destroy humanity, Sekhmet helped her; hence in this context the lion represents vengeance. Sekhmet was known as the Eye of Ra. Her festival is on 7 January. Later on, she was occasionally identified with Hathor. Bast, the Egyptian cat-goddess, was originally lion-headed but was later shown as cat-headed. In this guise, she represented the beneficent aspect of the Sun, whilst Sekhmet represented its destructive aspect. Maahes was an Egyptian lion-headed god, the son of Bast and Ra.

Another lioness goddess was Mekhit or Mihit, who was worshipped at Thinis. Anhur (known to the Greeks as Onuris), whose name means 'the one who leads back the distant one', was a warrior and hunter god from This, near Abydos. His name refers to the legend telling that he journeyed south to capture Mekhit, who became his consort. Pakhit was a cat or lioness headed form of the goddess Bast; she was worshipped at the Speos Artemidos, east of Beni Hasan. She was also associated with Mut. Renenet was another goddess sometimes depicted with the head of a lioness; she was the goddess of suckling, and gave the baby its name, fortune, and personality; she appeared at death with Shai (god of destiny) to weigh and judge the soul; and she acted as a general goddess of harvest and nourishment.

Tefnut was a lioness-headed rain-goddess, one of the Ennead of Heliopolis. She was the twin and wife of Shu, god of the air. Together they raised the heavens, personified by Nut.

The lion is solar and associated with Ra if depicted with the sun, and lunar and associated with Osiris if depicted with the crescent moon. It also represents protection. A lion with a head at either end of its body represents sunrise and sunset. Two lions shown back to back, with the sun between them, represent past and present, or yesterday and tomorrow. Sef, the personification of yesterday, and his brother Dua (today) were depicted as lions. Aker was an earth god, represented as the foreparts of two lions joined together, each with a human head. He guarded the point where the eastern and western edges of the Underworld met, and his back supported Ra's boat on its travels from west to east during the night. The god of the western desert and its oases was Ash, who was sometimes depicted with three heads, one of a lion, one of a snake, and the other of a vulture.

Min, the god of sexual potency, was sometimes portrayed as lion-headed, and usually as ithyphallic. Shezmu, the god of wine and unguent oil presses, was in early times depicted in human form, when he was the god who dismembered sinners. Later, he was represented as a lion, and regarded as the master of perfumes. Both roles stemmed from his original function as an attendant of the Pharaoh. According to Plutarch, the Egyptians adorned their doors with the gaping mouth of the lion because the rising of the Nile commenced when the sun was in Leo. According to Horapollo, lion figures in temples were intended to protect the temple and represented the inundation. Certainly the flood waters of the Nile were extremely important to the Egyptians, and we have already seen that the lion was associated with the rain goddess Tefnut. According to Aelian, lions were kept in temples at Heliopolis, and temples were dedicated to them.

Many Middle Eastern peoples venerated the lion. It was the cult animal of Anat (the chief Canaanite goddess of fertility, love, and war), and of Ishtar, perhaps in her aspect of goddess of battles. The Hittites had a goddess called Hepatu or Hebat (wife of their storm god Teshub). She was depicted as a matron standing on a lion, her sacred animal. Another Hittite goddess was Shaushka, an oracular goddess closely linked to Hittite ruling families. She was depicted as a winged woman standing on a lion. Ruti ('lion-like') was a Phoenician deity at Byblos, portrayed as a lion-headed man. Qedeshet or Kedesh was the Syrian goddess of life and health, also worshipped in Egypt; she was depicted standing naked on a walking lion, holding a mirror and lotus blossoms in her left hand and two snakes in her right.

Lebiyah, meaning 'lioness' is the Hebrew personification of Israel; she is called the Mother of Israel (Ezekiel 19). The winged lion represents the South and the Lion of Judah. The lion is associated with cruelty and might. It also appears in the legends of David and Goliath and Samson. The lion died out in Palestine at the time of the Crusades. The pre-Islamic Arabs north of the Yemen worshipped Yaghuth (the Helper) in the form of a lion. The Babylonians worshipped the god Ningirsu, patron of irrigation. He is sometimes depicted as lion-headed and with his claws resting on the backs of two lions. His origins lie in the region of Lagash, dating from earliest times; he may be equated with the Sumerian god Ninib, god of the summer sun, storms, and fertility. Ninib was also depicted as a lion with two heads or a lion with a bough in its paws.

In Sumeria, the lion represented solar fire, sovereignty, strength, and courage. It was an attribute of Marduk as the sun god. Inanna, Atargatis, and Ishtar, as the Great Mother, are accompanied by two lions. The Chaldaean god Nergal, associated with war and death, is shown as a lion, signifying the hostile aspect of the sun and the heat of the solstice, or as two lions' heads placed back to back, in his role of god of the sun and the underworld.

In the Meroitic culture of Sudan, Apedemak was a lion-headed war god. He was also associated with the elephant.

In Greek mythology, the lion is an attribute of Phoebus, Artemis, Cybele, the Gorgons, and sometimes Dionysos. Both Cybele's and Hera's chariots are drawn by lions. Tyche is often accompanied by lions. She is the goddess of fortune, the daughter of Oceanus and Tethys. She wears a mural crown and carries attributes representing abundance. Each city had its own Tyche.

The lion skin is an attribute of Herakles, who slew the Nemean lion, and wore its skin afterwards. The story tells that he could make no impression on it with his club, so he squeezed it to death. Herakles depicted wrestling with a lion is often used as a funerary symbol, and represents the solar hero conquering death. Hippomenes and Atalanta were turned into lions for profaning a temple of Zeus (or, in some versions, Cybele).

In the Mithraic mysteries, the fourth stage of initiation was Leo, the lion. In order to reach this stage, the initiate had to have a total and longstanding commitment to the order, being consumed in the fire of love to the extent that the intellect is subsumed. The duties of a Leo included setting up the ritual meal, during which they would drink wine, which symbolised the experience of divine love.

In Roman mythology, the lion is an attribute of Apollo, Hercules, and Fortuna, and represents solar fire, royalty, the power of death, and conversely, humanity's victory over death. Lions also draw the chariot of Juno.

In Hinduism, Bahu (the Abundant One), is the Creative Mother. She is the constellation of Leo or the star Denebola. In India and Tibet, the lion is an attribute of Tara, representing the Earth and the maternal instinct. The lion is the fourth avatar of Vishnu, called Narasinha or Agni; he is sometimes half-man, half-lion. The lioness and the lion together depict the shakti and the shakta. The lion is the supreme lord and represents rhythm, whilst the lioness is the power of the spoken word. The lion is the animal guardian of the North, and is an attribute of Durga as destroyer of demons, and of Devi.

In Buddhism, the lion is the defender of the law (Dharma). Its roar represents the Buddha's fearless teaching of the Dharma. The lion represents the wisdom of Buddha, spirituality, advancement and cognizance, enlightenment and sovereignty. Buddha is sometimes shown seated on a lion throne, or depicted as a lion with a cub under its paw, which represents his compassionate rulership of the world. He is also referred to as the Lion of the Shakya clan. A newly initiated bodhisattva is represented by a lion cub. Ratnasambhava rides a lion.

In Chinese Buddhism, Kwan-Yin, the goddess of compassion, fecundity, and healing, is sometimes depicted standing on a lion. She is also a magician and a teacher of magic, and is believed to give oracles. She is sometimes depicted as a prostitute. Chinese men usually communicate with her through a female intermediary. If they are unable to do so, they have to apologise for it. The immortal Chiu-shou was a lion who took human form and fought in the wars. He was eventually ordered to revert to lion form, and became the mount of the Buddha Wen Shu. Stone lions guarded the courts of justice; they were supposed to come alive at night and wander about. In Japanese Buddhism, Aizen Myoo has a fierce face with three eyes and a lion's head on top of a human head, but he is full of compassion for humanity.

In Taoism, the hollow lion ball or brocade ball represents the Void, emptiness, and the withdrawal of the mind.

Symbolism

The lion is regarded as both solar and lunar. In its solar aspect it is regarded as the heat, splendour, and power of the sun, fire, strength, majesty, courage (e.g. Richard the Lionheart), fortitude, justice, law, martial strength. The negative side of this is cruelty, ferocity, and the vicissitudes of war.

The lion is an attribute of war deities and a symbol of war. In its lunar aspect, it is the lioness with the Great Mother, and represents the maternal instinct. It is also associated with virgin warrior goddesses. Crete, Lycia, Mycenae, Phrygia, Sparta, Syria, and Thrace all had goddesses whose emblem was a lioness.

In heraldry, the lion represents valour, royalty, power and protection. It symbolises the wisdom and energy of the animal kingdom. The lion and the unicorn represent the contention of solar and lunar, male and female forces.

In medieval art, the lion killing the boar represents the power of the sun killing the boar of winter. The lion and dragon eating each other symbolises union without a loss of identity. The lion lying down with the lamb signifies the return of the Golden Age, the restoration of Paradise and primordial unity. It is also the end of the temporal world and conflict. The solar hero killing the lion represents the sun god controlling the heat of the noonday sun. Stone lions' heads as waterspouts or fountains represent the sun in the daytime and the gift of water poured out upon the earth. The green lion represents the young corn god before he matures into the golden corn.

In medieval legend, Sir Iwain de Galles was accompanied by a lion which he had rescued from a serpent. Sir Geoffrey de Latour took a lion into battle with him against the Saracens, but it drowned when trying to board the ship which was to carry them away from Palestine.

In *Aesop's Fables*, several animals joined the lion in a hunt, but when the prey was divided, the lion claimed a quarter for himself, one for his superior courage, one for his dam and his cubs, and 'as for the fourth, let who will dispute it with me.' The other animals quietly withdrew. Hence the expression, 'the lion's share', meaning most or all of the booty.

In alchemical symbolism, the winged lion or griffin (q.v.) depicts the union of the two natures of the androgyne. The red lion represents sulphur, the masculine principle. The unicorn represents mercury, the feminine principle. The green lion represents the beginning of the alchemical work, being the all-transmuting elixir. Two lions depict the dual nature of Mercurius, the philosophical mercury.

According to Macrobius, lions are an emblem of the Earth, the mother of the gods; pairs of lions guard doors, gates, treasures, and the Tree of Life, being 'the master of double strength', and representing vigilance and courage.

In China, the lion represents bravery, energy, and strength. The man in marriage is represented by the lion as strength and the horse as speed, whilst the woman is represented by flowers. In Japan, the lion is king of the animals, and is associated with the peony, the queen of flowers. The lion ball symbolises emptiness. The Chinese Lion Throne represents the subjugation of cosmic forces.

In Christianity, the lion represents the power of Christ and his kingship as the Lion of Judah; lions are depicted as sentinels supporting the pillars of the Church. However, the roaring lion can represent the Devil devouring sinners, who are rescued by the power of Christ. A solitary lion symbolised the hermit and solitude. As the Gospel of Mark emphasised the royalty and majesty of Christ, the lion became the symbol of Mark. It is also an emblem of various saints: Adrian, Euphemia, Gerasimus, Jerome, Mary of Egypt, Paul the Hermit, Prisca, and Thecla. The catacomb paintings used pictures of Daniel in the lions' den to represent God's redemption of his people. The story of Androcles and the lion is a well known Christian legend.

In Iran, the lion represented royalty, solar power, and light. In Islam, it represents protection against evil.

In Mithraism, the lion is solar and represents the fourth grade of initiation. The lion-headed Cronos is Aion, time and destiny devouring everything, and the sun as the fiery principle. The lion and the bull together symbolise death; with the stag, the lion represents the moment of death.

Lynx

Latin name *Felis [Lynx] lynx* **Polarity** Yin

Family *Felidae* **Element** Fire

Planet Sun

Deities Mafdet

Varieties

The European Lynx (*Felis [Lynx] lynx*) is found in Europe, the Carpathians, the Balkans, and as far east as China. The Canadian Lynx (*Felis [Lynx] canadensis*) is found in the northern forests, while the Bay Lynx (*Felis [Lynx] rufus*) is found in America.

Folklore

In early times, the lynx was believed to be a cross between a dog and a panther; it was believed to be able to see through walls.

Mythology

In Egyptian myth, the cat or lynx goddess Mafdet was renowned as a slayer of serpents, and was known as the 'Lady of the Castle of Life'. She was a first dynasty goddess, predating both Bast (the cat goddess) and Sekhmet (the lioness).

Symbolism

The lynx is associated with keenness of sight, hence the expression 'lynx-eyed'.

In Christianity, the lynx represents the vigilance of Christ.

In heraldry, it symbolises keen vision and watchfulness.

Mole

Latin name *Talpa europaea*   **Polarity** Yin

Family *Talpidae*   **Element** Earth

Planet Saturn

Folk names Moldiwarp, Moudewort, Unt, Moudie

Etymology Middle English *molle*, probably from Middle Dutch *moll(*e), Middle Low German *mol, mul*

Varieties
The American Garden Mole (*Scalopus aquaticus*) is very similar in appearance and habits to the European Mole (*Talpa europaea*).

Folklore
There are various superstitions regarding moles. In Wales in 1909, it was still believed that if a mole was found among the cabbages in the garden, then the master of the house would die before the year's end. In Bridgwater, Somerset, in 1922, it was still regarded as lucky to see a mole in the road. In 1987, in Petersfield, Hampshire, a villager observed that there were molehills along the bank at the bottom of the garden, and was told by a neighbour that it meant that someone was about to move, or if the molehills appeared in a circle around the house, it meant that someone was going to die. It appears that moles were connected with death, as diggers and delvers of the earth, but also with money, which is also associated with the element of earth - moleskin purses were believed to be lucky in Suffolk (1861), Shropshire (1883), and Forfar, Angus (1950); it was said that the owner of such a purse would never lack money to put in it.

Symbolism

As a dweller beneath the earth, the mole represents cthonic powers, darkness, and death. It also represents the misanthrope.

Literature

"The creeping tide of light gained and gained, and now they could see the colour of the flowers that gemmed the water's edge.

'Clearer and nearer still', cried the Rat joyously. 'Now you must surely hear it! Ah - at last - I see you do!'

Breathless and transfixed the Mole stopped rowing as the liquid run of that glad piping broke on him like a wave, caught him up, and possessed him utterly. He saw the tears on his comrade's cheeks, and bowed his head and understood."

from Chapter VII, *The Piper at the Gates of Dawn*, in *The Wind in the Willows* by Kenneth Graeme

The character of Mole is a down-to-earth creature who discovers the exciting world of the River one morning as he decides he has had enough of spring-cleaning, and sets out to discover the world beyond his front door.

Monkey

Latin name various   **Polarity** Masculine

Family *Cercopithecoidea*

Deities Hanuman, Sun Hou-Tzu

Varieties

There are many species of monkey. The Woolly Monkey (*Lagothrix lagotricha*) lives in South America; the Brown Capuchin Monkey (*Cebus fatuellus*) also lives in South America, and has a tuft of dark hair on its head. The Old World monkeys are generally grouped into a large family, the *Cercopithecoidea*. This includes the Rhesus Monkey (*Macaca mulata*), which is common in India and South-east Asia. The Stump-tailed Monkey (*Macaca speciosa*) lives in mountain forests from Thailand to Western China.

Mythology

The monkey is revered in Japan. In India, it is regarded as an incessant chatterbox, and represents the distracted mind which must be focused on meditation. When tamed, the monkey is very intelligent and loyal. Hanuman, the monkey god and hero of the Ramayana, symbolises cunning and strength. It was he who made the bridge over the sea to Sri Lanka so that Rama and his troops could rescue Sita from the demon-king Ravana. Hanuman's father was Vaya, the wind god, and his mother was Anjana, an Apsara or celestial nymph who could also take monkey form on occasion. When fire is used against the monkey god, he can tame it. This symbolises the Tantric ability to transform intense emotion into spiritual power.

Hanuman was also noted for his learning and his courage, speed and strength. He is the archetypal loyal friend and companion. It is possible that the original Hanuman was a king of the forest peoples, who were regarded as monkeys by the other peoples of India in the same way that the aboriginal peoples of Britain came to be seen as the faery folk. In another Indian tale, it was Vala, son of the smith god Visvakarma, who built a bridge across the ocean for Rama and Lakshmana with the help of the monkeys. At the Ram Lila festival, little boys dress as monkeys.

In China, there is a legend of a monkey god called Sun Hou-Tzu who is the king of the monkeys. He became immortal when he travelled to the Underworld, found the book where the names of all who were to die were written, and tore up the page with his name on it. He carries a magic wand, and is the hero of many tales in which he represents human nature. In Kampuchean art, the monkey is a guardian of the threshold; statues of monkeys and monsters guard shrines in Cambodia.

One of the Buddha's early incarnations was as a monkey. Monkey is also the hero of the classic Chinese tale of The Journey to the Western Paradise (shown on television as Monkey in Britain in the early eighties), in which he represents unregenerate human nature.

In Mayan mythology, the god of the North Star had the head of a monkey. Monkeys also occur in Peruvian art.

In Africa, certain monkeys can embody the spirits of the dead. Many tribes have monkey spirits that serve as guardians.

Symbolism
The mischievous monkey represents the human tendency to spread gossip and delight in the misfortunes of others. However,

the three "Mystic Monkeys" (See no evil, Hear no evil, and Speak no evil) represent the ability to transcend gossip and exercise discretion and discernment. In many cultures, the monkey represents impudence, mischief, the lower instincts, and inquisitiveness. In Buddhism, it is known as one of the Three Senseless Creatures and regarded as being always greedy and grasping. In China, it is a trickster figure, symbolising ugliness and the power of transformation. It is the ninth animal of the Chinese zodiac.

In Christianity, the monkey represents vanity, luxury, and the devil.

Folklore

According to an old Indian legend, the Hanuman monkey once stole a mango, which only grew in the garden of a giant in Sri Lanka. The giant threw the monkey into the fire. He escaped from the fire, but not before his limbs and face were scorched, which is why monkeys are black to this day.

Mouse

Latin name various

Family *Myomorpha*

Order *Rodentia*

Polarity Yin

Element Earth

Planet Jupiter

Deities Zeus, Sabazios, Apollo

Varieties

The European Harvest Mouse (*Micromys minutus*) occurs throughout Europe and Asia as far as Japan. The American Harvest Mouse (*Reithrodontomys spp.*) is larger than the European variety. The Fat Dormouse (*Glis glis*) lives in Central and Southern Europe, western Turkestan, the Caucasus, and Iran; it has a bushy tail like a squirrel. The Common Dormouse (*Muscardinus avellanarius*) is found in southern Sweden, Great Britain, Russia, central and southern Europe, and Asia Minor. It eats buds, berries, and hazelnuts. The Asiatic Dormouse (*Dryomus nitedula*) lives in south-eastern Europe, the Alps, the Carpathians, south-eastern Bavaria, southern Silesia, the Balkans, and south-western and central Asia.

Folklore

Most of the folklore of mice revolves around the fact that they are prodigious gnawers and renowned for despoiling grain stores. There were various attempts to prevent mice from eating crops. An Ancient Greek treatise on farming advises the farmer to write a request to the mice to

leave on a sheet of paper and to stick it on an unhewn stone before sunrise. In Bali, the mice in the cornfields were caught in huge numbers and burnt, but two mice let go with a little packet of white linen as a propitiatory gift, and the people bowed down before them.

In the legends of the witches of Tuscany (as related in the *Gospel of the Witches*), Diana came to earth as a mortal, but was so powerful that her greatness could not be concealed. One night there was a meeting of all the witches and faeries, where Diana declared that she would darken the heavens and turn all the stars into mice. The witches and faeries said that if she could do this, she would be their queen. So she got an ox-bladder and a piece of witch-money (which has a sharp edge) and cut the earth. She filled the bladder with earth and mice, and blew into the bladder until it burst. The earth in the bladder became the heavens, and for three days there was a torrential downpour. The mice became stars and rain. Having made the heaven and the stars and the rain, Diana became the Queen of the Witches, and was the cat who ruled the star-mice, the heavens, and the rain. She then returned to heaven and left the education of the witches to her daughter, Aradia. Diana is personified as a cat in another legend related in the Gospel of the Witches; when she desired Lucifer, he "fled from her and would not yield to her wishes; he was the light which flies into the most distant part of heaven, the mouse which flies before the cat..."

There are various folk remedies involving mice, including fried mouse as a remedy for whooping cough. In Germany, it was the custom, when one had a tooth removed, to insert it in a mouse's hole. If a child's milk-tooth was placed in a mouse hole, it was supposed to stop the child having toothache. Another formula was to go behind the stove and throw the tooth backwards over one's head, saying "Mouse, give me your iron tooth; I will give you my bone tooth." This is a form of sympathetic magic, deriving from the belief that teeth thrown away would cause the new teeth to be like the teeth of the animal that finds the old teeth, and since mice have strong teeth, it would be desirable for them to find the teeth.

370

It is alleged that Jews used to meet secretly in gardens to eat pork and mouseflesh as a religious rite, which is supposed to date back to the time of Isaiah. The pig was sacred to Adonis, who may still have been worshipped amongst some Hebrews. Presumably the mouse was also sacred.

Mythology

In Greek myth, the mouse is an attribute of Zeus, Sabazios, and Apollo. In the case of Apollo, it may represent food for the sacred snakes kept by the priestesses of Apollo.

In Pagan times in Flanders, there was a festival of moths and mice.

Symbolism

The mouse is a cthonic animal, representing movement, agitation, turbulence, and the powers of darkness. It can also represent humility, however.

In Hebrew symbolism, the mouse represents hypocrisy and duplicity. In Christianity, it represents the devil, as a devourer of food stores. In Christian art, mice are depicted gnawing at the root of the Tree of Life.

Poetry/Literature

In *The Lion, the Witch, and the Wardrobe* by C S Lewis, it is the mice who try to help Aslan when he is bound upon the Stone Table, by gnawing at the ropes that bind him. Because of this, he gives them the gift of speech, so that they become Talking Animals. In *Prince Caspian and The Voyage of the Dawn Treader*, Reepicheep, chief of the mice makes an appearance. His main values are honour and decorum, and he is very good at chess. At the end of the book he takes a small boat from the ship and sets off for Aslan's country, which lies at the end of the world.

"You have found an elephant in the moon" is an expression denoting illusory success. Sir Paul Neale, an astronomer of the 17th century, claimed that he had found an elephant on the moon, but it turned out that a mouse had crept into his telescope, and he had mistaken it for a lunar elephant.

"Wee, sleekit, cow'rin', tim'rous beastie,
O what a panic's in thy breastie!
Thou need na start awa sae hasty,
Wi' bickering brattle!"
      (from "To a Mouse", Robert Burns, 1759-1796)

"The best laid schemes o' mice an' men
Gang aft a-gley."
      (ibid.)

Mule

Family *Equidae*

Deity Mullo

Etymology Middle English from Old French *mul*(e), from Latin *mulus, mula*

Varieties

A mule is the offspring of a donkey and a horse (especially of a male donkey and a mare), and is a sterile hybrid. An ass is a small, usually grey, long-eared animal of the horse genus.

Folklore

According to legend, Mohammed had a white mule called Fadda.

Mythology

Amongst the Celts of Europe, Mullo was the patron god of muleteers; he may originally have been a mule totem divinity.

Opossum

Latin name *Didelphus virginiana*

Family *Didelphidae*

Etymology from Virginian Indigenous American *apassum*

Varieties
The opossum is a marsupial, and can carry up to sixteen young in its pouch.

Mythology
Among the U'wa (Tunebo) of Colombia, South America, the opossum appears in the Fox Chant (see Fox) and the animal purification chant (Ruwa Reowa). In the animal *purificaiton* chant, the upper world deity Rukwa sends the lower world deity Kanwara a message to say that an initiation ceremony is needed because the female animals are maturing and will eat each other. These animals include pacas, anteaters, peccaries, armadillos, coatis, porcupines, deer, sloths, and turkeys. They are about to menstruate. A female initiation ceremony and chant must be performed to prevent them turning into humans. The elders are gathered below the middle world, and Kanwara, who is immobile, gets his sister's son Sheba to chant and perform the ceremony for the elders. But Sheba chants four times, and on the fifth, returns to Kanwara crying because he has not performed the chant correctly, and must now eat and die. The ferret now puts on a hood and begins to menstruate. The opossum goes to Kanwara to tell him, and he tells the animals to put on hoods made of leaves, so that they will begin to menstruate. It is at this point that it is established that some animals will eat others.

In the second part of Ruwa Reowa, Kanwara looks for another sister's son to perform the chant correctly. He locks the elders in a house inside a mountain in the lowlands. The opossum goes to Kanwara to tell him that the elders are secreting fluid. This pleases Kanwara, because it means that he is powerful. He asks Thunder to perform the chant, but Thunder demands payment. He is promised the ferret as a wife, because she has a white blaze under her neck, which is equated with *raiya* (women's shell necklaces for initiation ceremonies, a symbol of wealth). Thunder travels through the lakes to the house of the elders (the usual procedure for a man who is courting), followed by Bibra, the monkey, playing the flute. Thunder performs the initiation ceremony but burns his penis off in the process. He blows on the elders, making them less bitter and smelly. In the menstrual initiation ceremony, women are given crab, armadillo, or paca to eat. These animals may be female clan ancestors.

Otter

Latin name *Lutra lutra*   **Polarity** Yin

Sub-family Lutrinae   **Element** Water

Family Mustelidae

Deities Dubthach

Etymology   Old English *otr, otor, ottor*, from Middle Dutch, Middle Low German *otter*, Old High German *ottar*, Old Norse *otr*, Germanic *udros*

Varieties

The subfamily *Lutrinae* includes about seven genera, all of which are semi-aquatic.   The Common Otter (*Lutra lutra*) was widespread over the whole of Europe, but in some parts has been exterminated for its fur and for the supposed damage it did to fisheries.   The otter is making a comeback in Britain, because the water supply is less polluted and less chemicals are being used which kill off insects and fish, the otter's food supply. In many areas where the otter was absent, it is now only rare, and in areas where it was rare, it is now common (*The Independent*, Monday 8 June 1998).   There is no cause for complacency, because inappropriate chemicals are still being used in some areas, but this is encouraging.   They have even been seen in urban locations.   The otter is a relative of badgers, pine martens, weasels, ferrets, etc.

Mythology

In the Algonkin (indigenous American) creation legend, their culture hero, Manibozho, took refuge on a mountain after a great lake had overflowed and submerged the world. He sent out three messengers - a raven, an otter, and a musk-rat - before he could be sure that the waters had subsided. Afterwards he married the musk-rat and became the ancestor of the Algonkin people.

The otter may be associated with the Horned One, the Lord of the Animals, in a sculpture from Meigle in Perthshire, Scotland. However, the animal depicted may be a wolf.

A Celtic deity called Dubthach had an otter on each shoulder.

In the Volsunga Saga there is the story of a man called Otur (Otter) who was a great fisherman. During the day, he appeared in the form of an otter, staying in the water and catching fish, but came ashore during the night in human form and slept in a house.

Symbolism

In Christianity, the otter is an emblem of St Cuthbert. In Zoroastrianism, it is one of the 'clean' animals (as is the dog); it is a great sin to kill it.

Panda

Latin name *Ailuropoda melanoleuca*

Family *Procyonidae*

Folk name *xiong* (Chinese)

Etymology from Nepali

Varieties

Pandas belong to the Raccoon family (*Procyonidae*). There are two varieties, the Giant Panda (*Ailuropoda melanoleuca*) and the Red Panda (*Ailurus fulgens*). The Giant Panda lives at altitudes of 11,000 to 14,000 feet above sea level in the forested mountains of Tibet and China. It  makes tunnels among the mountain bamboo. The Red Panda lives in the Himalayas, Burma, and China at altitudes of up to 12,000 feet. It generally lives in trees, but comes to the ground to hunt small vertebrates and eat bamboo shoots.

Folklore

In Chinese versions of the Little Red Riding Hood story, the wolf is replaced by a wicked bear.

Mythology

In Chinese mythology, the bear hero the Great Yu diverted the great flood which his father (also a bear) had been unable to withstand.

Symbolism

In China, the bear symbolises a man, with the snake as a woman. Dreaming of a bear portends the birth of a son. (Chinese)

Panther

Folk name *bao* (Chinese)

Etymology The name comes from the Greek πανοηρια *pan qeria (pan theria)* meaning all animals, because of its fabled ability to attract other animals

Folklore
In the Middle Ages the panther was believed to be friendly to all animals except the dragon. It was said to attract other animals with the sweet scent which it exhaled (see Poetry for Swinburne's more sinister interpretation of this myth).

Mythology
In Benin, the capital of ancient Zimbabwe, there was a panther god called Agassou, who was regarded as an ancestor of the royal house. In Haitian voodoo, Agassou is the guardian of customs and traditions, and the god of springs.

In North America, the Algonkin and Ojibwa peoples believe the panther to be a sinister creature of the underworld, but to the Cherokee people it is a sacred animal with special powers, such as being able to see in the dark.

The panther is also sacred in Polynesia, where it is depicted with flames coming from its head, back and legs.

Symbolism
In Christian legend, the panther was said to save people from the dragon or the devil. It was also believed to have sweet breath, and became thereby a symbol of the sweet influence of Christ. To the

Christian writer Physiologus, the panther was the type of Christ. Later, however, when the ferocity of the panther became known, it came to symbolise evil and hypocritical flattery.

In heraldry, the panther is always depicted as a ferocious animal, and signifies fury, anger, fierceness, impetuous behaviour and remorselessness.

In China, the panther's tail (bao-wei) was a mark of distinction, and was used as an ornament for war chariots. The panther was regarded as a savage and cruel animal, and the name *bao* signifies this. In pictures, the panther symbolises taming savagery. A beautiful, headstrong and violent young woman was called a flowery panther (*hua bao-z*).

Poetry

"As one who hidden in deep sedge and reeds
Smells the rare scent made when the panther feeds,
And tracking ever slotwise the warm smell
Is snapped upon by the warm mouth and bleeds,
His head far down the hot sweet throat of her -
So one tracks love, whose breath is deadlier."

(from *Laus Veneris*, by Algernon Swinburne)

Pig

Latin name *Sus domestica*

Family *Suidae*   **Element** Earth

Folk name Hog

Etymology Middle English *pigge*, from Old English *picga* or *pigga*

Deities Ceres, Carnea, Mars, Tellus Mater, Venus, Hercules, the Lares, Zeus, Demeter, Persephone, Rimmon, Tiamat, Phaea, Ceridwen, Manannan

Varieties

The domestic pig is related to the Wild Boar (*Sus scrofa*) and the European Wild Boar (*Sus scrofa scrofa*).

Folklore

The five dark marks on the inner side of the pig's forelegs were popularly believed to be the marks of the demons' claws as they entered the Gadarene swine (Mark 5:11-15).

The 'Hampshire Hog' is a colloquial name for an inhabitant of Hampshire; the symbol of Hampshire is a hog. Hampshire people often refer to themselves as Hampshire Hogs with great pride.

In Schwaben, Germany, the man who cut the last sheaf at harvesttime 'had the Sow'. In Baden, the last sheaf was called the Rye Sow or the Wheat Sow. Sometimes the reaper who cut the last sheaf was himself called the Sow. At Neuatz, in Courland, the farmer's wife boiled the tail and chine of a pig. The sower ate some of the chine, then buried the rest of it and the tail in the field where the seeds were sown, so that the corn would grow as long as

381

the tail. In Hesse and Meiningen, people ate pea soup with dried pig ribs at Candlemas or on Ash Wednesday. The ribs were then collected and hung in the room until sowing time, when they were buried in the sown field or put in the seed bag amongst the seed. They were believed to discourage earth-fleas and moles, and to make the flax grow tall.

In Hungary, the midsummer fire was kindled by revolving a wheel round an axle wrapped in hemp. Pigs were driven through the fire to protect them from sickness.

At the Hallowe'en bonfires in Wales, the people would wait until the last ember had gone out and then run away suddenly, shouting as loudly as possible "The cropped black sow seize the hindmost!" This saying was still current in Carmarthenshire in the 1920s, when people used the cutty black sow to frighten children.

There is a Hungarian folktale called *The Enchanted Pig*. (A similar tale appears in English under the name of *The Black Bull of Norroway*.) Once upon a time there was a king who had three daughters. The king had to leave for the wars, and told his daughters to take care of the castle, but not to go into a back room, else harm would come to them. After his departure, all went well for a while, but then the eldest daughter suggested that they looked in the room, where they found a book which told that the eldest daughter would marry a prince from the East, and the middle daughter would marry a prince from the West. The youngest daughter did not want to go against her father's wishes by looking at the book, but the other two made her, and the book revealed that she would marry a pig from the North.

After the king's return, everything happened as foretold by the book. On the way home after the wedding of the youngest daughter and the pig, he got into a marsh and covered himself with mud, then asked the princess to kiss him. After wiping his snout with a handkerchief, she did this. During their nights together, the pig changed into a man, but in the morning he was a pig again. The princess went to a witch and asked how she could stop the man turning back into a pig every morning. She was told to fasten a thread around his leg at night. She did this, but the pig awakened and told her that because she tried to hasten things along, he must leave her, and that they would not meet again until she had worn out three pairs of iron shoes and blunted a steel staff in search of him. She wandered in search of him, going as far as the Sun and the Moon and the wind to seek him. In each of these places she was given a chicken to eat, and told to save the bones. Eventually, after she had worn out three pairs of iron shoes and blunted her steel staff, she came to a mountain of glass where her husband dwelt. She could not get up the mountain, so she made a ladder from the chicken bones. The ladder was one rung too short, however, so she chopped off her little finger to use as the last rung. She was reunited with the erstwhile pig (now fully human), and they inherited her father's kingdom, where they ruled wisely and justly 'as only kings rule who have suffered many things'.

Mythology

In Greece, pigs were sacred to Demeter, goddess of fertility, and were sacrificed to her at Eleusis after being washed in the sea. Pigs and cakes of dough were sacrificed to Demeter and Persephone at the festival of Thesmophoria, which was celebrated by women only in October. They were thrown into deep ravines where there were snakes, which ate the remains of the pigs. The previous year's decayed flesh (that which remained uneaten by the snakes) was fetched from the bottom of the chasm by women, and sown with the seed corn to ensure a good crop. Later legend explained that this custom originated when Hades abducted Persephone. As Hades opened the earth to return to the underworld, a swineherd called Eubulus was herding his pigs nearby, and they fell down the chasm into the underworld. Probably Persephone's sacred animal was the pig. The sow is sacred to Dictean and Cretan Zeus, who was suckled by a sow whilst in hiding from his father Cronos. Another divine being associated with pigs is Circe (whose name means 'she-falcon'), who turned men into swine, lions, and wolves. When Odysseus landed on her island, she turned all his crew into swine.

The Romans offered pork and beans to the goddess Carnea at her festival on 1 June. They also sacrificed pigs to Mars as the god of agriculture, and to Tellus and Ceres at harvest time. The sow was sacred to Ceres because it taught men to turn up the earth. Pigs were also sacrificed to Hercules, Venus, and the Lares by people seeking a cure for illness. In Egypt, the black pig was an attribute of Set, whilst the white sow was an attribute of Isis. The pig was also sacred to Bes, the dwarf deity who helped mothers in childbirth. Both the Egyptians and Phoenicians regarded the pig as an unclean and forbidden food.

In Sumero-Semitic mythology the pig is an attribute of Rimmon, Tiamat, and the Great Mother. The boar that killed Adonis, Dumuzi, or Tammuz is believed to have been another aspect of Astarte or Ishtar, who was Adonis' lover. The Phoenicians had a god called Aleion, Aleyin, or Aleyn, who gave water to crops and vegetation, and was the god of Spring, clouds, wind and rain. With his seven companions, Aleyin led a pack of wild animals, including eight wild boars. In Haitian voodoo, Marinette is a corn-goddess to whom pigs are sacrificed.

In Hinduism, Vishnu's third incarnation was as a boar called Varaha or Varahi. His consort or feminine aspect in this incarnation was called Vajravarahi, who is a source of life and fertility. There is also a goddess called Pashadhari, who is depicted with the head of a sow. Her name means 'noose-bearer'. She is the Doorkeeper of the South with her husband Yamantaka. Her attribute, the noose, represents both the yoni and the umbilical cord; she is both nourishing and restrictive. In early Hinduism, the storm god Rudra, also a god of mountains and the dead, renowned for his skill in archery, was addressed as the 'ruddy divine boar'. The early Vedic storm and lightning goddess Rodasi was his wife in some versions of the stories; in others, his wife is Prisni, the earth and cow goddess.

In Buddhism, the pig is at the centre of the round of existence, and represents ignorance and greed. It is one of the Three Senseless Creatures, which depict the sins which bind humanity to the world of maya (illusion). In Tibetan Buddhism, the Diamond or Adamantine Sow is Vajravarahi, a Great Mother and Queen of Heaven. It is not clear whether this goddess was derived from the Hindu goddess of the same name, or vice versa.

The indigenous Americans regard the pig as a bringer of rain, giving life to the land to benefit all the children of the Great Spirit. The pig is also associated with the Moon and thunder.

The people of Banks Island (off the coast of Queensland in Australia) believe that the god Qat created both humans and pigs at the same time, and brought them to life by dancing and beating a drum. There was no difference between pigs and humans until he gave the pigs four legs instead of two.

Celtic mythology is full of pig imagery, as it was a very important animal to the Celts. Many of their great feasts involved consuming pork in huge quantities. When feasting, the hero's portion (*cauradmir*) was always a piece of pork. The flesh of a red pig was chewed for the divinatory rite of *Himbas Forosnai*. Pork was also the food of the gods at otherworld feasts. In Irish myth, the *bruidhne* (hostels belonging to otherworld gods) would hold feasts at which there were huge cauldrons of boiled pork, but the pigs were constantly reborn to be eaten again the next day. However, the Galatian Celts did not eat much pork, nor was it much eaten in the Highlands of Scotland.

According to the Welsh epic, the *Mabinogion*, the first pigs in Britain were given to Pryderi, King of Dyfed by Arawn, King of the Underworld. Afterwards there was a bloody war between Gwynedd and Dyfed for possession of these pigs. The Celtic queen, Cerridwen, is associated with the sow referred to as the Old White One. Cerridwen was often referred to as the White Sow; she could be the Crone aspect of the goddess who eats our mortal flesh after we have fed from the Cauldron of Inspiration. After this transformation, the soul follows the spiral path to Caer Arianrhod, the heart of the North Wind. There was also a goddess called

Phaea, the Shining One, a sow goddess of the Moon and fertility. Goleuddydd, a character in the Welsh epic, the *Mabinogion*, was associated with the sow; she was the daughter of Amlawdd, the wife of Kilydd, the mother of Culhwch (also associated with pigs), and the aunt of King Arthur.

The pig is an attribute of Manannan, god of the sea, who has a herd of magical pigs which are killed and eaten, but regenerate themselves. The Lord of the Otherworld is often depicted with a slain but still squealing pig slung over his shoulder. The European Celts had a deity called Moccus or Moccos, who was the god of a pig clan. The Romans identified him with Mercury. The Welsh hero, Culhwch, is also associated with pigs. His name means 'pig-run', and he may be a anthropomorphic pig. The tales relate that his mother was badly frightened by pigs when she was pregnant, and gave birth to Culhwch in her fright, abandoning him amongst the pigs. He was found and brought up by the swineherd, who gave him the name Culhwch because he found him amongst the pigs. When Culhwch grows up, he seeks the hand of Olwen, and must perform various tasks before he can marry her. One of these is to obtain the tusk of Ysgithyrwyn the Chief Boar for the giant Ysbaddaden to shave himself with. The final task is to obtain the shears, comb, and razor from between the tusks of Twrch Trwyth, another magical boar. Gwrhyr the Interpreter of Tongues (one of King Arthur's companions on the quest) speaks with one of Twrch Trwyth's seven followers, who is called Grugyn Silver-Bristle.

The Irish counterpart of Twrch Trwyth is Orc Triath, a huge and destructive boar mentioned in the *Book of Invasions*. In another Mabinogion story, that of Math and Mathonwy, one of the punishments inflicted on Gwydion and his brother for the rape of Goewin was their transformation into a boar and a sow. In this form, they produce a piglet whom Math turns into a human boy, but who retains his pig-name, Hwchdwn. In the Welsh triads, the Sow Henwen (the old white one), who was possibly a meta-morphosed prince, gave birth to a series of magical beings rather than a normal litter. She travelled around the countryside, and brought forth a grain of wheat and a bee in one place, which subsequently became famous for its wheat and bees. In another place she gave birth to a grain of barley and a bee. Among her other progeny were a wolf cub, which was given to Menwaedd of Arlechwedd; a monster kitten which grew up to be the Cat of Palug, renowned for terrorising the countryside; and a young eagle, which was given to Breat, a prince of the North.

In the Irish tale of *The Battle of Magh Mucrime*, a huge horde of pigs issue from the mouth of the Cave of Cruachan, the entrance to the underworld; they are magical pigs of death, which can be neither counted nor destroyed. In the Fionn cycle of tales, a huge and destructive boar called Formael kills fifty warriors and fifty hounds in a single day. Formael is blue-black, with stiff bristles and a spiky dorsal ridge, each spine of which can impale an apple. He also has enormous teeth, but no ears and no testicles (another sign of his supernatural status). In the story of Diarmuid and Grainne, Fionn sends Diarmuid to hunt a boar which is Diarmuid's own foster-brother in enchanted form. Fionn knows that the death of this boar will be the death of Diarmuid, but he wants him to die so that he can gain the hand of Grainne (see Boar).

In Scandinavian mythology the Black Sow represents coldness, death, and evil.

Symbolism

The pig is a symbol of fertility and prosperity. Its negative connotations are greed, gluttony, lust, anger, and the unclean (presumably in the sense of not kosher, as the pig is a very clean animal). The sow is associated with the Great Mother, and has lunar, sky, and fertility symbolism. The sow was a symbol of maternity throughout the ancient world, owing to her plentiful mammary glands and the large litters of piglets she produced.

In China, the pig is a symbol of untamed nature. It is regarded as being greedy and dirty naturally, but useful and fecund when tamed.

In Christianity the pig represents the devil, gluttony, and sensuality. It is also an emblem of St Anthony Abbot, who overcame the demon of gluttony. In Judaism and Islam, the pig is an unclean animal which must not be eaten.

Polar Bear

Latin name *Thalarctos maritimus*

Family *Ursidae*

Folk name Nanook

Polarity Masculine

Element Water

Planet Moon

Deities Sedna, Kannaaluk

Folklore
Most polar bears are allegedly left-handed.

Symbolism
Humans have a particularly tense and ambiguous relationship with the polar bear. It is associated with fear, hunger, sexual desire, prestige and power. It also symbolises male authority.

There are numerous ceremonies involving the polar bear for Inuit boys during their childhood. Polar bears are associated with the depths of the sea, as well as with land and air. They can travel by land or sea, and are therefore considered an excellent vehicle of shamanic meditation.

The Inuit regard animals that can walk on their hind legs as magical; these include polar bears, otters, lemmings, groundhogs, ermine, and weasels. The size and strength of the bear makes it pre-eminent among these; it also has a similar diet to humans, as it eats fish and sea-mammals.

The Inuit particularly admire the hunting techniques of the polar bear, especially its practice of waiting by seals' breathing holes, scratching on the ice to attract the seal's curiosity, then killing it with a blow of the paw. The Inuit have adopted this technique, using an implement to scratch on the ice, and a harpoon to kill the seal. Polar bears also kill walruses with a piece of ice or a stone while they are lying asleep on the ice floes in the sun. So the bears are tool-using animals. They also build shelters in the winter, consisting of a large pile of snow in the lee of a hill, out of the wind. The pregnant females hibernate in these shelters from the end of the autumn, give birth in the spring, and then emerge into the open.

When polar bears were plentiful, they were much in demand as a game animal. Their pelts were used as insulation for igloos, and made into trousers and boots. Its meat (which apparently tastes similar to human meat) was eaten, the fat was used for oil lamps, and the bones, claws, and teeth were made into tools, amulets, and ornaments. Polar bears were regarded as the ancestor of men.

Puma

Latin name *Felis concolor*

Family *Felidae*

Folk name Mountain Lion

Deities Tepeyollotl

Polarity Yin

Mythology

In Aztec mythology, Tepeyollotl (Heart of the Mountains) was a puma god, lord of the eighth hour of the night.

Rabbit

Latin name *Oryctolagus cuniculus*

Order *Lagomorpha*   **Planet** Moon

Folk name *rabotte* (French dialect), *robbe* (Flemish)

Etymology Middle English, perhaps from Old French.

Deities Ostara, Eostre

Varieties

All the domestic varieties of rabbit were developed from the European Rabbit (*Oryctolagus cuniculus*), which originated in Spain. They are related to hares and pikas. In North America, there are Big-eared Jack Rabbits, Snowshoe Rabbits, Arctic Hares, Swamp Rabbits, Cottontails, Pigmy Rabbits, and Pikas (*Ochotona*).

Mythology

A hare or rabbit is the attribute of Eostre or Ostara, the Teutonic goddess of Spring and dawn. However, there is now some doubt as to whether this goddess existed at all, or whether she was a figment of the Venerable Bede's imagination. In his eighth century work on the origins of the calendar, Bede claimed that the name of Easter was derived from a Germanic goddess. There is no corroborating evidence from elsewhere for the existence of this deity, except that the word seems to be cognate with a number of other Indo-European goddess names, such as the Greek Eos, the Roman Aurora, and the Indian Ushas, all goddesses of the dawn and the spring.

In the Main valley in Germany, the festival of Easter was known as Ostarstuopha throughout the eighth and ninth centuries. On the other hand, the word Easter may simply derive from

Estormonath, the month of openings. There is at any rate no doubt that both the hare and the rabbit are associated with the festival of Easter, and that this is unlikely to have originated with the Christian element of the festival.

The rabbit is a lunar animal. Both the rabbit and the hare are said to live in the Moon, and are associated in many cultures with Moon Goddesses and Earth Mothers. In Aztec mythology, the Moon is a rabbit or a hare. In China, figures of white rabbits are made for the Moon Festival. To the indigenous Americans of the eastern forests, the rabbit is a trickster animal. Wearing rabbit skins in a ritual denotes docility and humility before the Great Spirit. The Brer Rabbit stories may originate from indigenous American tales, or were perhaps brought from Africa by the slaves. There is certainly a rabbit character in the Anansi stories, which originated in Africa. The rabbit also symbolises fecundity and lust. Richard Adams uses the trickster energy of the rabbit for the character of Elahrairah in Watership Down. There are some very interesting passages in this book, such as the chapters where the smallest rabbit, Fiver, is close to death, and undergoes a shamanic experience.

Among the Hopi, rabbits are a source of food. Before the hunt, prayers are said and offerings are made to make the rabbit willing to be caught. After being caught they are covered with a white blanket or manta, then they are smudged (smoke is blown over them), an act of blessing or a prayer offering of thanks. (Other large animals are treated with the same respect.) Rabbits, deer and antelope are regarded as related species because of their tendency to speed, lope, and circle back. The rabbit is the smallest animal to be accorded the manta ceremony.

There is no rabbit *katsina* (spirit), but the rabbit appears in Hopi legend. The rabbit clan was once given the responsibility of guarding the village against outsiders.

Rat

Family *Rattus spp.*

Order *Rodentia* **Polarity** Yin

Varieties
Old English *ræt* and Old French *rat* from Roman *rattus* The Brown Rat (*Rattus norvegicus*) is larger than the Black Rat (*Rattus rattus*). Brown Rats often carry disease, and can stow away on ships and trains; they are also very fertile, so they are now very widespread.

Folklore
The rat is seen as a plague animal, signifying death, decay, and the underworld.

According to Pliny, the Romans drew omens from rats. If one saw a white rat, it was lucky. If rats gnawed clothing or equipment, it was regarded as unlucky.

According to the folklore of sailors, rats would desert a ship before she set out on a voyage that would end in her sinking. Rats are also believed to leave a falling house. In the Ardennes, France, rats were banished from farms by writing a spell on a piece of paper and leaving it in the barn. Around 1900, a farmer in America wrote a letter to the rats on his farm saying that he could not afford to keep them and asking them to move to a neighbour's farm where there would be more grain.

It was once believed in Ireland that rats could be killed by anathematising them with metrical charms or rhyming verse. In *Poetaster, Apologetical Dialogue*, Ben Jonson says, "Rhime them to death, as they do Irish rats". In Shakespeare's *As You Like It*, Rosalind says, "I was never so be-rhymed since Pythagoras' time, that I was an Irish rat." Sir Philip Sidney, in his *Defense of Poesie*, says, "I will not wish unto you ... to be rimed to death, as is said to be done in Ireland".

At Raratonga in the Pacific, they would recite a prayer when a child's tooth was extracted: "Big rat! Little rat! Here is my old tooth. Pray give me a new one." Rats' teeth were very strong, so theirs would be the best. The old tooth was thrown onto the thatch where the rats lived.

Mythology

In Hindu mythology, the rat is the steed of Ganesha, the elephant god, who is the conqueror of obstacles and the god of wisdom, successful endeavour, and prosperity. The rat is also a powerful entity in its own right, and an object of veneration.

In Japan, both the god of happiness and the god of wealth are accompanied by a white rat. The rat is depicted merging from a bale of rice, or wielding a mallet. The Ainu believe that God created the rat to punish the Devil. The rat bit off the Devil's tongue, and he was so angry that he made rats increase until they became such a nuisance that God had to create cats.

The Egyptians and the Phrygians regarded the rat as divine. In Egypt the rat was a symbol of complete destruction, but also wise judgment, because rats always eat the best bread. In Greek mythology, Apollo earned the title of 'rat-killer' when he sent a plague of rats against his priest Crinis in retribution for his neglect of his duties, but the priest saw the rats coming, and repented, so the god forgave him and killed all the rats with his arrows.

Symbolism

In China, the rat denotes meanness and timidity. It is the first animal of the Twelve Terrestrial Branches (the Chinese Zodiac).

In Christianity, the rat is a symbol of evil, but also an emblem of St Fina.

In Hinduism, the rat is a symbol of prudence and foresight.

Poetry

> *"In few, they hurried us aboard a bark,*
> *Bore us some leagues to sea; where they prepared*
> *A rotten carcase of a butt, not rigg'd,*
> *Nor tackle, sail, nor mast; the very rats*
> *Instinctively have quit it."*

(Shakespeare, *The Tempest*)

Seal

Latin name *Phoca vitulina*   **Polarity** Feminine

Family *Phocidae*   **Element** Water

Planet Moon

Etymology Old English *seolh*, Middle Low German *sel*, Old High German *selah*, Old Norse *selr*, from Germanic *selhaz*

Mythology

In Inuit mythology, seals, whales, and polar bears are descended from the fingers of Sedna (also known as Arnaknagsak), the goddess of food, who lives in the sea. Her father cut off her fingers as she was trying to get back into the boat from which he had just sacrificed her to the sea. If her prohibitions are not observed, she can call up a storm, or prevent seals, whales, and polar bears from leaving their homes. There is also a helpful iceberg spirit called Nootaikok, who procures seals for the hunters. There is also Agloolik, the spirit of seal caves, who lives under the ice and helps hunters to find game.

In Chile, in Araucania, the god Huaillepenyi, the god of fog, is depicted with the body of a ewe, the head of a calf, and the hindquarters of a seal. He is believed to be responsible for the birth of deformed children.

In early Greek mythology, Proteus was a sea god, the son of Oceanus and Tethys. He was the guardian of Poseidon's herd of seals. He had the gift of prophecy, but he had to be caught and made to speak. This was very difficult, as he could change shape.

In Old English and Norse myth, the god Heimdall assumed the form of a seal to carry the necklace Brisingamen back to Freyja. Loki had stolen it from her, and left it on a rock in the sea. Heimdall swam out to it in the form of a seal, recovered it after a fight with Loki, and took it back to Freyja in Asgard. Beowulf mentions the episode (Heimdall was called Hama in Old English):

I have heard tell of	Nænige ic under swegle
no better treasure fit	selran hyrde
for princes	hordmathm hæletha
since Hama carried back	sithan Hama ætwæg
to the Shining Citadel	to thære byrhtan byrig
Brisingamen,	Brosingamene,
ornament and gem ...	sigle and sincfæt ...

Sheep

Latin name *Ovis spp.*

Family *Ovidae*

Element Fire

Zodiac sign Aries

Polarity Masculine

Planet Sun

Etymology from Old English *scep, scaep, sceap*, Old Saxon *scap*, Old High German *scaf*, from West Germanic *skaepa*

Deities Amon-Ra, Khnemu, Osiris, Jupiter, Zeus, Sabazios, Dionysos, Pan, Hermes, Aphrodite, Agni, Thor

Folklore

A rigwelter is a sheep that has fallen over and cannot get up again because it has colic.

In Devon, there used to be a Ram Feast held on May morning at Holne on Dartmoor, where a ram was run down in the Ploy Field, and roasted in its fleece by a granite pillar. At midday, there was a scramble for a slice of the meat, which was believed to be lucky for the one who ate it. At Kingsteignton, also in Devon, a decorated sheep's carcase is paraded through the town on Whit Monday, and then roasted in the open air.

There were many superstitions associated with black sheep. In Shropshire (1878), one black sheep in the flock was regarded as lucky, and in Somerset (1923), a black ewe was believed to bring luck to the flock. In Ireland, if the first lamb of the season was black, it portended mourning garments for the family throughout the year ('Speranza' Wilde, Superstitions of Ireland, 1887). In Kent, a black lamb was good luck for the flock; in Shropshire it was bad luck.

In Orkney, if the first lamb you saw in a year was black, you would have bad luck. In Derbyshire, according to Alison Uttley, black lambs were lucky.

Mythology

In Celtic myth, the ram represents the powers of earth and the underworld. It is associated with the hearth, which is an entrance to the underworld. With the ram-headed serpent, it is an attribute of war deities. A ram-headed serpent appears on the Gundestrup cauldron with the Horned God, a deity of fecundity, wealth, and prosperity. At one time the Horned God was associated with the Roman Mercury. The ram is also one of the three sacred animals of Brighid, the Irish goddess of fire, poetry, and healing. (The other two are the ox and the boar.) Celtic art has many representations of rams, including fire-dogs found in Gaul which were in the form of a ram. Ram's heads were also carved on Gaulish tombs and monuments to underworld deities. The god of the Gauls was Belin, the ram, and his consort was Belisama, his manifestation upon earth. The Gauls also sacrificed sheep and rams. An early Irish text refers to red-eared, three-horned supernatural sheep (probably from the underworld, whose animals often have red ears). In North-west Sutherland there was a tribe called the Caereni ('People of the Sheep').

The Basque goddess Mari rides on a ram, whose horns she uses to wind wool into a ball.

In Christianity, the ram represents Christ as the leader of the flock. It is also associated with the legend of Abraham and Isaac, where a ram was substituted for Isaac as a sacrifice. This was held to prefigure the sacrifice of Christ on the cross, as the Paschal Lamb. Christ was also given the name 'the Lamb of God', after the passage in Revelation:

> *"Then I saw a Lamb, looking as if it had been slain, standing in the centre of the throne, encircled by the four living creatures and the elders. He had seven horns and seven eyes, which are the seven spirits of God sent out into all the earth. He came and took the scroll from the right hand of him who sat on the throne. And when he had taken it, the four living creatures and the twenty-four elders fell down before the Lamb. Each one had a harp and they were holding golden bowls full of incense, which are the prayers of the saints. And they sang a new song: 'You are worthy to take the scroll and to open its seals, because you were slain, and with your blood you purchased men for God from every tribe and language and people and nation. You have made them to be a kingdom and priests to serve our God, and they will reign on the earth."*

In Egyptian mythology, the ram represented solar energy, procreation, creative heat, and the renewal of the sun's powers in the year's cycle. It was the personification of Khnemu, an early ram-headed deity with long wavy horns. He was later identified with Ra, who was addressed as 'Ra... thou ram, mightiest of created things'. Amon-Ra, however, had curved horns. A ram was sacrificed to Amon at Thebes. On the feast of Opet, a boat was dedicated to Amon and decorated with rams' heads. The Ram of Mendes was sacred to Osiris, and his soul was said to be incarnate in it. It was also said to embody the souls of Ra, Kephera, and Shu. When the ram died there was great public mourning; when a replacement was found, there was great rejoicing. The name of the Ram was Ba Neb Djedet (the soul of the Lord of Djedet, the Djed being the sacred pillar of Osiris). In popular speech this was contracted to Banaded, and rendered into Greek as Mendes. (Herodotus wrongly referred to the Ram as 'the goat of Mendes', and in this form it reappeared looking sinister in the writings of 19th century occultists, whence it is regularly exhumed as an example of how sinister the occult is supposed to be) was originally the ram god of the North-east Delta, worshipped with his consort, the fish goddess Hatmehyt. There was also a ram-headed god called Kherty (the Lower One), who personified both danger and protection. In Egypt, the Pharaohs were regarded as shepherds of the people, just as Ra was the shepherd of all men.

In Greece, the ram was sacred to Zeus and Sabazios, the ram god. It represented fertility and procreation, in which capacity it was sacred to Dionysos. In Cyprus, the ram was associated with Aphrodite. (It is a little known fact that Aphrodite was a goddess of death as well as of beauty, which might explain her association with the ram here, as the ram is associated with psychopomp figures.) It was also associated with Hermes as the Good Shepherd, in his aspect of Hermes Kriophoros, the Ram-bearer. There is a statue of Hermes Kriophoros in the museum at Epidavros, in the Pelopponese. He was probably a very early Pelasgian deity, a protector of flocks and herds. He lost his pre-eminence after the 6th century BCE, and his functions were taken over by Apollo Nomios. The Ram of Mendes was regarded as an attribute of Pan by the Greeks. Pan was a herdsman too. Selene (the Greek Moon goddess) was seduced by Pan in the form of a white ram in the depths of the Arcadian woods. In another version, he clothed himself in the dazzling white fleece of a ewe. Initiates of the mysteries of Attis were bathed in ram's blood at their initiation. In the legend of the Golden Fleece, Phrixus and Helle were carried off by a magical ram. The goddess Gaia (the earth goddess, known as the deep-breasted one) was invoked in oaths, accompanied by the sacrifice of a black ewe.

In Rome, the ram was associated with domesticity and the hearth, and a ram was sacrificed to the Lar of the house in a purificatory rite. Faunus was associated with shepherds. The deity Pales, a god and/or goddess of flocks, had his/her festival on 21 April, the Palilia, traditionally the date of Rome's foundation.

In Hindu mythology, the ram is sacred to the Vedic fire-god, Agni. It is a symbol of the sacred fire, which springs from the wood. In Tibetan Buddhism, the *dorje* Lak-pa is a ram's head. A *dorje* is a thunder bolt and a divine attribute, which is often used as a kind of sceptre and an object of power. Chenrezig, the all-merciful good shepherd, is incarnated in the Dalai Lama.

In Norse mythology, Thor's chariot was drawn by rams. (In some versions, it is drawn by goats.)

In Sumero-Semitic art, a ram's head atop a column is a personification of Ea, Lord of the Ocean and of Destiny. The Phoenician Baal or Hamon, as a sky and fertility god, was often depicted with ram's horns on his head. Ammon later became associated with Jupiter, and they were worshipped as a composite deity in parts of Asia Minor. Rashap (or Reshpu as he was known in Syria, where he was a god of lightning) is depicted with ram's horns and seated on a throne supported by rams. In Israel, the *shofar* is a ritual ram's horn blown at festivals, and is associated with the ram sacrificed instead of Isaac. The tabernacle was decorated on the inside with ram's skins dyed red (Exodus, 26:14). In the Feast of the Passover, the lamb represents obedience to God's will. In Islam, the ram is seen as a sacrificial animal. There is also a saying "the divine glory is among the shepherds".

In the Orphic mysteries, Orpheus Boukolos, the Herdsman, was the Good Shepherd and carried a kid or a ram on his shoulder.

In Iranian mythology, Yima, the Good Shepherd, has the solar eye and the secret of immortality. There is an interesting parallel here with Yama, the Hindu god of the dead.

In Slavonic myth, Volos or Volusu was an early god of animals, sometimes the god of war. He became a peasants' god, the protector of sheep and cattle. He was later christianised as St Vlas or St Blaise. There was also Kurwaichin, a Polish and Slavonic deity who protected lambs.

Symbolism

The ram represents masculine energy and virility. It is associated with creative energy and procreative power, and is therefore an attribute of sky gods. The sign of Aries represents the renewal of the sun's power in Spring. It is associated with kingship and the head. The spiral of the ram's horns represents thunder, and is connected with both sun gods and moon goddesses.

Sheep in general usually stand for blindness and stupidity. Their tendency to follow without question has also made them a symbol of the disciple who closely follows the master, surrendering individual will in exchange for the teachings of the master. Such unquestioning devotion is regarded as laudable in some cultures, but usually results in an attitude of irrational bigotry and a faith easily undermined by rational enquiry. In Christianity, the sheep represents the flock of Christ, the faithful, and the Apostles, with Christ as the Good Shepherd.

In China, the sheep is the eighth animal of the Twelve Terrestrial Branches (the Chinese Zodiac). It symbolises the retired life. It is also the symbolic animal of Tui, one of the trigrams of the I Ching. The trigram Tui is one Yin line (--) above two Yang lines (=), known as the Joyous, the Youngest Daughter, the Marrying Maiden, the Lake, or the Mouth; it is two strong lines within, expressing themselves through gentleness.

Lambs represent innocence, youth, gentleness, purity, and the unblemished. Neophytes and the newly initiated were compared to lambs. A lamb with a lion represents paradise, because of the saying "the lion shall lie down with the lamb" in the book of Revelations.

In Christian symbolism, a lamb with a cross depicts the crucifixion, whilst the lamb and flag denotes the resurrection. The lamb with the seven horns and eyes represents the seven gifts of the Holy Spirit. A lamb with a hill and four streams represents Christ and the Church, with the four streams as the rivers of paradise or the four gospels. A lamb with a dove represents the human and divine natures of Christ. John the Baptist with a lamb represents him heralding the coming of Christ. The lamb is an emblem of Saints Agnes, Catherine, Clement, Genevieve, Joanna, John the Baptist, and Regina. The sacrificial lamb is a symbol of martyrdom.

The fleece represents the fat, which is regarded as the life-force of the sheep. By extension, it represents all life-giving sustenance (cattle, corn, etc.) and also offspring and long life. The Golden Fleece hung on the Tree of Life. It is solar because it is gold and because it came from the golden ram on which Zeus ascended to the heavens. Later, the voyage in search of the Golden Fleece was interpreted as a quest for spiritual illumination, with the lamb representing innocence, the gold being the treasure of immortality, individuality, and the struggle with the dragon and Medea being the overcoming of the dark side of nature.

Common to many pastoral cultures, the Good Shepherd is a symbol of care and protection of the helpless. He is the leader and protector of the flock, a saviour figure. He is also a psychopomp, associated with the god of the dead, who sometimes has a shepherd's crook and staff as his attribute. The symbol of the Good Shepherd occurs in Sumerian, Iranian, Hebrew, Orphic, Hermetic, Pythagorean, Tibetan, and Christian traditions.

In Christianity, Christ is the Good Shepherd; the role expresses his compassion and humanity, and the redemption of those who have gone astray. Hence bishops carry a crook to symbolise their role as shepherds, though curiously enough the crook also resembles the *lituus* of the Roman augurs.

Poetry

Marking the lambs

My knife will be new, keen, clean, without stain,
My plaid beneath my knee with my red robe.
I will put sunwise round my breast the first cut for luck,
The next one after that with the sun as it moves.

A male lamb without blemish, of one colour, without defect,
Allow thou out on the plain, nor his flowing blood check,
If the froth remains on the heather with red top,
My flock will be without flaw as long as I change not the name.

The Three who are above in the City of glory,
Be shepherding my flock and my kine,
Tending them duly in heat, in storm, and in cold,

With the blessing of power driving them down
From yonder height to the sheiling fold.

The name of Ariel of beauteous bloom,
The name of Gabriel herald of the Lamb,
The name of Raphael prince of power,
Surrounding them and saving them.

The name of Muriel and of Mary Virgin,   (should this be Uriel?)
The name of Peter and of Paul,
The name of James and of John,
Each angel and apostle on their track,
Keeping them alive and their progeny,
      Keeping them alive and their progeny.

              (from the *Carmina Gadelica*)

The Clipping Blessing

Go shorn and come woolly,
Bear the Beltane female lamb,
Be the lovely Bride thee endowing,
And the fair Mary thee sustaining,
      The fair Mary thee sustaining.

Michael the chief be shielding thee
From the evil dog and from the fox,
From the wolf and from the sly bear,
And from the taloned birds of destructive bills,
      From the taloned birds of hooked bills.

              (from the *Carmina Gadelica*)

Squirrel

Latin name *Sciurus vulgaris*   **Element** Air

Family *Sciuridae*   **Planet** Mercury

Folk name romen morga (Romany)

Deities Medhbh, Desana

Etymology from Middle English, from Anglo-French *esquirel*, Old French *esquireul*, from Roman *scuriolus*, diminutive of Latin from Greek *skiouros*, from *skia* (shade) + *ouros* (tail)

Varieties

The Sciuridae include the Red Squirrel (*Sciurus vulgaris*); European Alpine Marmot (*Marmota marmota*); the Prairie-dog (*Cynomys ludovicianus*); the European Ground Squirrel (*Citellus citellus*), the North American Flying Squirrel, and the Grey Squirrel.

Folklore

In southern Latin America, it is taboo for indigenous women to eat squirrels whilst planting ground nuts, as this is believed to cause the crops to dry up.

The coming of winter is heralded by catching the first good squirrel.

The Romani believe the squirrel to be a lucky animal, but will cook it and eat it also.

Mythology

In Celtic mythology, the squirrel and the bird are attributes of Medhbh of Connacht. She had a bird on one shoulder and a squirrel on the other. She also had a sacred tree, the Bile Meidbe, dedicated to her.

In Scandinavian mythology, the squirrel Ratatosk lives on the world tree, Yggdrasil, and carries insults from the eagle at the top to the serpent Nidogg, the Dread Biter, at the bottom. Ratatosk also brings rain and snow.

Among the peoples of the Amazon the squirrel is believed to be one of the forms taken by Desana, the Master of Animals. In central America, the squirrel was sacrificed to the Mayan gods.

Symbolism

In Christianity, the squirrel symbolises avarice and greed, because of hoarding its food.

In Japan, the squirrel is a symbol of fertility and is associated with the vine.

Tapír

Latin name *Tapirus terrestris*

Family *Tapiridae*

Order *Perissodactyla* (Odd-toed Ungulates)

Etymology from Tupi *tapira* (the Tupi are the people of the Amazon valley)

Varietes

There are three varieties of tapir in Malaya, and one in America.

The Guatemalan Sun god is Hun-Ahpu-Vuch (Grandfather). His wife is Hun-Ahpu-Myte (Grandmother), the Moon goddess. Both were depicted with human bodies and the face of a tapir, a sacred animal.

Tiger

Latin name *Felix tigris* or
Panthera tigris

Family *Felidae*

Order *Carnivora*

Polarity Masculine

Element Fire

Planet Sun

Etymology Middle English, from Old French *tigre*, from Latin, from Greek *tigris*

Deities Durga, Shiva, Padma-Sambhava, Dionysos, Earth Mother, Chang Tao-ling, Freyja

Varieties

The smallest Tiger is the Sumatran (*Felix tigris sumatrae*); the largest is the Siberian (*Felix tigris longipilis*). Tigers live in India, China, Mongolia, Manchuria, Korea, Eastern Siberia, and South of the Caspian Sea.

Folklore

In China, the tiger is believed to be a guardian of graves and to frighten away evil spirits. It is believed to be able to see in the dark, and as such it is a cthonic animal. In Malaysia, there is a belief in were-tigers; these are particularly dangerous because they can embody the souls of sorcerers and the dead. The tiger must not be named (speak of the devil and it will appear...), so it is referred to as 'the striped one', 'hairy face', or 'Lord'. In Sumatra and Java, they believe in benevolent were-tigers.

Mythology

The Chinese god of wealth and gambling rides on a tiger, which guards money chests. The goddess of the wind also rides a tiger. The New Moon is depicted as a child escaping from the jaws of a tiger. This child is the ancestor of humanity, whilst the tiger is the powers of darkness from which the light of the New Moon escapes. The White Tiger represents the western quarter, the region of death, the season of Autumn, and the element of earth; it must always have its head to the South and its tail to the North. The Blue Tiger represents the Eastern quarter, the season of Spring, and plant life. The Red Tiger is the South, the Summer, and the element of fire. The Black Tiger is the North, the Winter, and the element of water. In the centre is the Yellow Tiger, representing the Sun. To ride a tiger means to encounter dangerous elemental forces. In Taoist art, the Immortal Chang Tao-ling rides a tiger. He was the first leader of popular Taoism. The constellation of Orion is associated with the tiger in China.

In Egypt, the tiger was an attribute of Set as the killer of Osiris.

In Greek mythology, tigers can be substituted for the leopards drawing Dionysos' chariot.

A twelfth-century wall-painting in Schleswig Cathedral in Germany shows Freyja riding on a large striped cat which must be a Siberian Tiger. Freyja is known to be associated with cats. The painting also resembles depictions of the Hindu goddess Durga, who also rides on a tiger.

Symbolism

The symbolism of the tiger is ambivalent. It is both solar and lunar, a creator and a destroyer. If it is shown fighting a serpent, it represents celestial, solar power. Shown fighting a lion or a dragon, it is lunar, cthonic, and malefic. It also symbolises royalty, strength and cruelty, and can be a manifestation of the Earth Mother. In heraldry, the Tigre or Tyger represents ferocity and strength. Medieval heraldry depicted a mythical tiger, as a real one had never been seen in Europe; modern heraldry introduced the Royal or Bengal tiger, which is more realistic.

The Chinese revered the tiger as a symbol of ferocity and protectiveness, vitality and animal energy. Its effigy was often used as a guardian of gates and doorways. It was regarded as the king of the animals. When it represents yang, the tiger denotes authority, courage, military prowess, and fierce protectiveness. When it is yin it represents cthonic powers, and is in conflict with the celestial dragon as yang. They represent the opposing forces of spirit and matter. The tiger is the third animal of the Twelve Terrestrial Branches (the Chinese Zodiac). It was also originally one of the Four Auspicious Creatures, but was replaced by the ky-lin (Chinese unicorn). It is the emblem of gamblers and was the mark of military officers of the fourth class. In Chinese alchemy, the tiger represents lead and the strength of the body.

In Japan the tiger symbolises courage and the heroism of warriors. It is believed to live for a thousand years.

In Buddhism, the tiger is one of the Three Senseless Creatures. It represents anger, whilst the monkey is grasping greed and the deer is love-sickness.

In Hinduism, the tiger is the symbol of the Kshatriyas, the royal and warrior caste. Durga, the destroying goddess, rides a tiger; Siva wears a tiger skin in his destructive aspect. Padma-Sambhava may appear as a tiger when destroying demons.

To the Aztecs, the tiger symbolised the sun setting in the West and the powers of earth.

In Shamanism, the tiger symbolises superhuman powers. It is regarded as a messenger of the forest gods, and is ridden by gods, immortals, and exorcists.

Poetry

"The tigers of wrath are wiser than the horses of instruction."

(from *Proverbs of Hell* by William Blake, 1757-1827)

"Tiger, tiger, burning bright
In the forests of the night,
What immortal hand and eye
Dare frame thy fearful symmetry?

Burnt in distant deeps or skies
The cruel fire of thine eyes?
Could heart descend or wings aspire -
What the hand dare seize the fire?

And what shoulder, and what art
Could twist the sinews of thy heart?
And when thy heart began to beat,
What dread hand - and what dread feet?

When the stars threw down their spears
And watered Heaven with their tears,
Did he smile his work to see?
Did he who made the lamb make thee?

Tiger, tiger, burning bright
In the forests of the night,
What immortal hand and eye
Dare frame thy fearful symmetry?"

(*The Tiger* by William Blake, 1757-1827)

Weasel

Latin name *Mustela nivalis*

Family *Mustelidae*

Folk name *phurdini* (Romany)

Etymology from Old English *wesule, wesle*, Old High German *wisula*, from West Germanic *wisulon*

Varieties

The weasel is related to the ferret, the polecat, the pine marten, the stoat, and the badger.

Folklore

"My wife was usually fond of a weasel-skin purse, as being the most lucky."
> (from *The Vicar of Wakefield*, Oliver Goldsmith, 1799)

"A purse made from a weasel's skin will never want for money, but the purse must be found, not given or made."
> (from *Superstitions of Ireland,* 'Speranza' Wilde, 1887)

The flesh of the weasel, salted, powdered, and mixed with wine, was said to be a cure for snakebite.

Among the Romani, the weasel is known as a *phurdini*. When a weasel is angry or afraid, it blows or puffs. The Romani associate this with the wind, which they hate and call 'the devil's sneezing'. If you see a weasel puffing it is unlucky. If a betrothed girl sees a weasel puffing, she must wash herself in the next running water she finds, or she will have an unhappy marriage. If a pregnant woman sees a weasel on her path, the birth will be difficult and the

413

child will have a difficult life. If a Romani *vardo* (caravan) meets a weasel, it must change direction, especially if the weasel is puffing. A patteran or sign is left at the place for those who follow: a tuft of a woman's hair tied to a branch, and a sign in the road to indicate the direction taken (three parallel lines with the middle one longer than the others). If a gipsy kills a weasel, the whole tribe will have bad luck for some time. The weasel was abominated in some parts of India, but worshipped in others.

The Greeks also regard it as anathema. Similarly, in China, the weasel is one of the five animals that can bewitch people.

Mythology
The Egyptians held the weasel to be sacred. According to Aelian, the Thebans worshipped it.

Indigenous Americans regard the weasel as a creature of insight, ingenuity, and stealth. It can hear everything that is said and interpret its inner meaning. A weasel foretold the coming of the whites and the disaster they would bring. There are short- and long-tailed weasels in America, which are regarded as siblings.

According to medieval legend, the weasel and the cockerel are the only two animals capable of killing the basilisk, which is afraid of them.

Literature
When Harold Pinter was asked what his plays are about, he answered, "The weasel under the cocktail cabinet." The weasel is generally regarded as a symbol of sneaky and underhand behaviour. In Kenneth Graeme's *The Wind in the Willows*, the weasels invade Toad Hall while Toad is in prison, and conduct a life of riotous living there before being ousted by Ratty, Mole, and Badger.

Whale

Latin name various	**Polarity** Yin
Family *Cetaceae*	**Element** Water

Folk names *illhveli, hrosshveli, störfiskar*

Planet Moon

Etymology
Old English *hwæl*, Old High German *wal*, Old Norse *hvalr*

Deities Sedna, Arnaknagsak, Aumanil, Wac, Tuparan, Paikea, Tinirau

Varieties

The order Cetacea includes whales, dolphins, and porpoises. There are two suborders, the *Odontoceti* (toothed Whales) and the *Mysticeti* (whale-bone Whales). The *Odontoceti* include the Sperm Whale (*Physeter*), which is the source of ambergris; Dolphins, Porpoises, and the Narwhal (*Monodon*). The Blue Whale is the largest creature that has ever lived; its average length is 100 feet. The Orca or Killer Whale (Grampus) is black-and-white, and eats seals. There is a remarkable film of a group of orca feeding on seals, where one of the orca shepherds a baby seal back to shore, evidently having decided that it has had enough.

Folklore

In Norse legend whales have magic powers and are the mounts of witches. In Iceland, there are various mythical whales which are regarded as malevolent. These were the *illhveli* (wicked whales), which were never mentioned by name because they knew their own name and would appear if it was uttered; hence they were always referred to as *störfiskar* (big fish) instead.

There were distinct species of *illhveli*. One of these was the *stökkull* (jumper) which had flaps of skin hanging over its eyes, preventing it from seeing anything unless it leapt out of the water, which lifted the flaps. Once it could see, it attempted to destroy anything that floated. Another of these was the horse whale (hrosshveli), which was said to look like a horse and neigh like a horse; it had a huge horse's tail which made huge waves on the sea, destroying men and boats.

Mythology

According to Arabic tradition, the Earth rests on the back of a whale, and earthquakes are caused by its movements. A similar myth occurs in Russia. In Slavonic myth, four whales support the Earth.

On Mangaia Island (Polynesia), there is the god Paikea, the lord of the sea monsters; there is also a whale named Paikea. A Polynesian and Maori god, Tinirau, is sometimes a whale and sometimes a man.

There are many legends of the whale's back being mistaken for an island, where sailors land on it and light fires for cooking, whereupon the whale, feeling the heat, dives under the sea, and all the sailors drown. This story appears in the *Arabian Nights*, and was used in medieval bestiaries to illustrate the devil luring people to destruction.

Origen said that great whales represent violent passions and criminal impulses. The orc was a sea-monster fabled by Drayton,

Ariosto, Sylvester, and other poets to eat people; according to Pliny, it was a huge creature with a lot of teeth. The name was sometimes used for a whale.

The story of Jonah and the whale is reminiscent of the initiatory rites of death and rebirth. The three days inside the whale represented the dark phase of the Moon. Later the jaws of the whale came to symbolise the mouth of hell. In Judaism, the whale represented the power of the cosmic waters, the monster Leviathan. In Arabic tradition, the whale was female; the word used for it is *dagah*, a female fish. It is quite likely that the whale was a symbol of the Great Goddess.

A hero swallowed by a whale crops up in the Inuit stories of the trickster Raven. There are whale festivals among the northern peoples, and a Killer Whale clan. Whales are descended from the fingers of Sedna (also known as Arnaknagsak), the goddess of food, who lives in the sea. If her prohibitions are not observed, she can call up a storm, or prevent seals, whales, and polar bears from leaving their homes. Aumanil is another Inuit deity who lives on land and guides whales.

Amongst the Pericu people (indigenous American), Wac, or Tuparan, was a god who rebelled against Niparaya. He was defeated and expelled from heaven with followers. Confined to an underground cave, he had to look after whales and make sure they did not escape.

Symbolism

The whale is the symbol of Greenpeace, the environmental organisation. In the late twentieth century, it has been realised that the whale is a peaceful and highly intelligent creature, with a highly evolved social structure. The whale is also capable of beautiful songs.

Wolf

Latin name *Canis lupus*   **Planet** Sun

Family *Canidae*   **Element** Earth

Deity Odin, Woden

Etymology Old English *wulf*, Old Saxon *wulf*, Old High German *wolf*, Old Norse *ulfr*, Gothic *wulfs*, from Germanic *wulfaz*

Varieties

The Wolf (*Canis lupus*) is found in Europe and North America. The Coyote or Prairie Wolf (*Canis latrans*) is found in North America. The Wolf is related to the domestic dog (*Canis familiaris*) and the Dingo (*Canis dingo*), which is believed to be descended from domestic dogs taken to Australia by people from India.

Folklore

In medieval England, outlaws were known as "wolf-heads". In Norse tradition, there were warriors called Úlfhednar, who wore wolf-skins over their mail-shirts, and fought singly in battle.

There were also warriors called Úlfhamir (wolf-shirts), who probably went into battle without armour, as did the Berserkers. It is possible that the animal warriors used the cry of their animal to unnerve their opponents, perhaps even temporarily lowering their blood-pressure. According to the *Hrafnsmal* (Speech of the Raven): "The Berserks bayed ... the Úlfhednar howled." As late as the 13th century, Irish warriors were said to be able to shapeshift into wolves. A Saxon champion called Ordulph is said to have kicked in the oaken gates of Exeter with one kick.

There are also a number of kings recorded with wolf elements in their names. There were five kings of Mercia with wolf-names: Wulfhere (665-675 CE); Cenwulf (794-819 CE); Beornwulf (821-823 CE); Bertulf (838-852 CE); and Ceolwulf (874-877 CE), the last king, who lost the kingdom to invading Danes. There was also a king of East Anglia named Aldulf (664-713 CE), and five kings of Northumbria: Heodwulf (572-3 CE); Freodwulf (573-580 CE); Ceolwulf (729-737 CE); Oswulf (757-759 CE); and Erdulf (794-806 and 808-809 CE). They may or may not have been connected with some kind of warrior wolf-cult, but their names at least indicate reverence for the wolf and a desire that some of its qualities should inhere in the man so named.

According to Pliny and Plato, there was a myth that if a man sees a wolf with its mouth shut it will lose the power to open it again, but if the wolf sees the man first with his mouth shut he will lose his voice. The myth also appears in Physiologus and the medieval bestiaries.

Wolves were often associated with the corn spirit. There were various sayings to describe the wind ruffling the corn: "The Wolf is going through the corn", "The Rye-Wolf is rushing over the field", or "The Wolf is in the corn". Children who might stray into the fields were warned off with sayings like "The Wolf sits in the corn, and will tear you to pieces", "The Rye-Wolf will come and eat you up", or "The Rye-Wolf will carry you off".

In Feilenhof, in East Prussia, if a wolf ran through the cornfield, he would be watched to see if he carried his tail high or dragged it behind him. If he dragged his tail, he was blessing the corn, and would be offered titbits; if he held it high, he was witholding his blessing, and the peasants would try to kill him. This implies that the power of the wolf was believed to be in his tail. In Silesia, when the reapers gathered round the last sheaf at the harvest, they said that they were about to catch the Wolf.

In Mecklenburg, everyone feared to cut the last sheaf because the Wolf was sitting in it; whoever cut it had the Wolf, and in some places had to try and bite the other harvesters or to howl like a wolf. The woman who bound the last sheaf was also referred to as the Wolf, sometimes for the rest of the year; people said as she bound the sheaf, "The Wolf is biting her" or "She has the Wolf" or "She must fetch the Wolf".   In Germany, people in many places said that the Wolf sat in the last sheaf. In some places they called out to the reaper, "Beware of the Wolf", or they would say that he was chasing the Wolf out of the corn. At Brunshaupten, Mecklenburg, the woman who bound the last sheaf made a corn-wolf from it which was about two foot long and six inches high, with its tail and mane made from wheat ears. It was carried in procession to the farmhouse, where it was kept in the parlour. Sometimes the Wolf was made as a human-shaped effigy. In Buir, near Köln, the last sheaf was made into the image of a wolf, and kept in the barn until all the corn was threshed, when the farmer had to sprinkle it with beer or brandy. In some places the last wagon-load of corn was called the Wolf. In some places, the Wolf was believed to hide in the corn in the granary, until he was driven into the last bundle for threshing. At Wanzleben near Magdeburg, a man dressed as the corn-wolf (covered in threshed straw) was led on a chain in procession, to represent the corn-spirit having been caught trying to escape from the threshed corn.

Near Treves, the Corn-Wolf was killed at threshing, and the last sheaf was threshed till it was merely chopped straw. Near Chambéry, the reapers formed a ring around the last stand of corn and said that the Wolf was in it. At Finisterre, Brittany, the harvesters shouted, "There is the Wolf; we will catch him". Then each took a section of the field to reap, and the one who finished first shouted "I've caught the Wolf". In some places the Corn-Wolf spent the winter in the farm-house. In Poland, a man dressed in wolf-skin was led about at Yule, or a stuffed wolf was carried by people collecting money.

Until the mid-nineteenth century, at Jumièges in Normandy, the midsummer festival was celebrated by the Brotherhood of the Green Wolf choosing a new chief, who had to come from the hamlet of Conihout on St John's Eve (23rd June). After being elected the new chief acquired the title of Green Wolf and donned a long green mantle and a brimless green hat. The whole brotherhood processed to Chouquet, carrying a crucifix and a holy banner and singing a hymn of St John. A mass was held in the local church, and they ate a simple meal. In the evening a bonfire was kindled, accompanied by the sound of handbells played by a young man and woman, both garlanded with flowers. (Afterwards the handbells were given into the keeping of the new Green Wolf.) The whole brotherhood danced round the bonfire, trying to catch the man who had been the previous year's Green Wolf. He staved them off with a wand. Eventually he would be caught and they would make as if to throw him on the fire. They then returned to the house of the new Green Wolf for another simple meal and more hymn-singing. At midnight, however, the festival became more bawdy, and decorum gave way to licence. Next day, a huge loaf decked with greenery and ribbons was paraded with an accompaniment of musket fire.

Mythology

A Celtic Welsh princess of Radnor is said to have waged war against her enemies in the form of a wolf. In Malory's *Morte d'Arthur*, one of Uther Pendragon's knights was called Ulfius (wolf); he later became King Arthur's chamberlain. In Celtic cosmology, a wolf swallows the Sun, the sky father, at night. In the *Mabinogion*, one of the transformations of Gwydion and Gilvaethwy (as a punishment for their rape of Goewin) is into a wolf and a she-wolf. The wolf is generally regarded as a helpful animal in Celtic mythology, and often accompanies the Horned God. An Irish tribe claimed to be descended from a wolf, and Cormac, the King of Ireland, was suckled by a wolf.

In the cosmology of the Northern Tradition, there is a constellation called the Greater Wolf's Jaws, and another called the Lesser Wolf's Jaws. According to legend, when the Fenris Wolf was fettered, the god Tir (Tiw in England) placed his hand in the wolf's jaws as a pledge of good faith. When the wolf realised he had been tricked and the fetters closed about him, he bit off Tir's hand. Afterwards the wolf's jaws were wedged open with Tir's sword, and two streams of saliva run out of the wolf's mouth until the end of the world. The two streams are called Wan and Wil, the two branches of the Milky Way (known to the Anglo-Saxons as Ermine Street). The Pole Star, known as the Nowl or Nail, is Tir's star, and his sword-arm reaches out from the Nowl into the Wolf's Jaws. In the *Anglo-Saxon Rune Poem*, it is the Pole-Star that is referred to in the stanza on the rune Tir: "Tir is a certain sign; it keeps trust well / With aethlings; ever on course / Over the night-fogs, it never ceases."

At Ragnarok, the Fenris Wolf will eat Odin, but will be killed by Vidar, the son of Odin and Sigyn (or the son of Loki and Rinda), a strong and silent god who will inaugurate the golden age after Ragnarok. In one version of the tale, however, Vidar prises open the jaws of the wolf by stepping on his lower jaw and tearing the upper jaw away. Could this have been to release Odin from the belly of the wolf? Also at the Ragnarok, Tyr is devoured by the hound Garm, thus resuming his original role of the sky father devoured by a wolf.

The Lesser Wolf's Jaws lies on the ecliptic (the sun's apparent path through the constellations) and is opposite the group of stars known as the Battle of the Gods. Tir, as the sky god, is also associated with the Sun, so perhaps the Lesser Wolf's Jaws were seen as devouring the Sun. (It must be borne in mind, however, that the Sun is generally feminine in the Northern Tradition). The classical name for this constellation is the Hyades plus the star Aldebaran.

Odin had two wolves called Geri and Freki. Gods of the dead are often accompanied by wolves and ravens. (Odin's ravens were called Hugin and Munin, Thought and Memory.) The wolf was regarded as a bringer of victory.

Amongst the Anglo-Saxons, there was never a widespread belief in Ragnarök, but it is reasonable to suppose that they did have the legend of the two wolves devouring the sky father, as a purse-top from Sutton Hoo depicts the legend. In Norse myth, the Sun and the Moon run across the sky because they are being pursued by two wolves called Sköll and Hati. According to legend, "there lived a witch in the forest called Ironwood to the east of Midgard... the ancient witch farrowed giants by the dozen and all in the likeness of wolves: it is from them that these two wolves come. Further, it is said, a really frightful one in line of descent called Moonhound shall throw out. He shall be filled with the flesh of all men who die; he shall swallow the Moon; and he shall sprinkle with blood all the sky and heavens at which the Sun's light shall be put out and winds shall rise up and howl hither and yon."

St Kieran of Saiglir (an Irish saint) had as his disciples a wolf, a stag, a badger, a fox, and a boar. Christianity in general, however, regarded the wolf as a symbol of evil, devouring ferocity, cruelty, craftiness, heresy, and the earth. It represented the devil devouring the flock of the faithful (see Sheep), and also the stiff-necked people, as the wolf was believed to be unable to turn its head. The exception to this was the white wolf, of whom it was believed that her cubs were born dead, and the father had to lick them into life after three days. This was regarded as a symbol of the resurrection of Christ. Also, the wolf was an emblem of St Francis of Assisi, who befriended a wolf which was terrorising a town called Gubbio. Thereafter the townspeople fed the wolf and mourned him when he died two years later.

In medieval Europe, the werewolf was regarded as the violence lurking under the thin veneer of civilisation. Lycanthropy and shapeshifting were among the powers attributed to witches. In Slavonic cultures, werewolves were called Vlkodlaks, and were believed to cause eclipses of the sun and the moon. (Note the similarity here with other myths of the wolf devouring the light.) In the story of the bogatyr Volkh or Volga (derived from the Slavic word *volkhv*, a priest or sorcerer), the bogatyr is able to shapeshift into a bright falcon, a grey wolf, a white bull with golden horns, or an ant. Werewolf legends are also widespread in Armenia.

In Arcadia (in Greece), there was a cult of the wolf. Plato and Pausanias tell of the rites of Zeus Lycaeus, in which a wolf was sacrificed and eaten, so that the devotees absorbed its essence, becoming one with it, so that they were called 'Lukoi' (wolves). According to Aelian, there was a bronze image of a wolf at Delphi, associated with Apollo. Lykaon, the son of Pelasgus (the first ruler of Arcadia), was transformed into a wolf and exiled from Olympus for the crime of offering Zeus a child sacrifice. If he abstained from eating human flesh for nine years, he would be restored to human form.

In Aztec mythology, the howling wolf is the God of Dance.

Indigenous Americans have many wolf tribes and clans, some of which claim descent from a wolf-hero. The wolf is associated with the Dog Star, the home of the gods, and is regarded as a pathfinder and teacher. It is also associated with the Moon, and is believed to have psychic powers. The soul of a hunter may pass into the realm of wolves. The Inuit have a great wolf called Amarok.

There is a blues singer called Howlin' Wolf.

In Egypt, the wolf was an attribute of Khenti Amenti (the lord of the west, and hence of the dead), and of Upuaut or Wepwet, the wolf god and brother of Anubis (Anpu). Upuaut was also a cemetery god at Asyut (Lycopolis). He and Anubis rule over the Funeral Mountain. He is also known as the opener of the way, conducting souls through the gates of the West after death, and steering the boat of the sun.

In Graeco-Roman mythology, the wolf is sacred to Ares and Mars because of its fierceness. It is also sacred to Apollo and Silvanus. A she-wolf suckled the orphaned Romulus and Remus, and is frequently depicted in Roman art. Romulus and Remus were the twin sons of Mars and the Vestal Virgin, Rhea Silvia. They were cast adrift as babies by their uncle Amulius, but were rescued by the she-wolf. According to legend, they built Rome in 753 BCE, and Romulus killed Remus in an argument. Romulus became the first king of Rome, and was deified after his death as the war-god Quirinus. The wolf also denotes valour in the Graeco-Roman tradition.

The festival of Lupercalia was celebrated on 14 February in Rome (the origin of St Valentine's Day).

In Hindu mythology, the Asvins rescue the quail of day from the wolf of night. The Asvins are Dasra and Nasatya, the Divine Physicians, originally cosmic deities.

In Zoroastrianism the wolf is an ally of Ahriman, the adversary, and is called the 'flatterer, the deadly wolf', denoting the evil in human nature.

Symbolism

In alchemy, the wolf and the dog represent the dual nature of Mercurius, who is the philosophical mercury, the nous. The grey wolf was used to symbolise antimony in sixteenth century alchemical texts, because antimony was said to attack metals.

In China, the wolf symbolises rapaciousness and cupidity.

In folk tales, the wolf is the forces of darkness waiting to devour civilisation. The wolf in *Little Red Riding Hood* is an archetypally destructive animal. According to Bruno Bettelheim, it is a way of making sense of the times when Grandma is angry, without compromising the illusion of a "nice" Grandma. It also represents the departure from the straight and narrow, the asocial and wild aspects of the male. Being trapped in the wolf's belly represents an initiatory experience. In *The Three Little Pigs*, the wolf represents antisocial, destructive and devouring behaviour.

A more positive view of the wolf as the representative of wilderness has developed over the last few years, to the extent that in January 1995 the wolf was reintroduced to Yellowstone Park in Wyoming, USA. There has also been talk of reintroducing it to the Scottish Highlands, where the last wolf was shot in 1785, but the move has been opposed by sheep farmers.

Molluscs

Clam

Latin name *Mercenaria mercenaria*

Etymology 16th c., from clam, a clamp

Varieties
The North American hard or round clam (*Mercenaria mercenaria*); the soft or long clam (*Mya arenaria*).

Mythology
In the beginning there was nothing but sea, and Old Spider hovering above it. Then She made the Moon, the Sea, the Sky, the Earth, and the Sun from a clam shell that she found with two snails in it.

      (Creation legend, Nauru Island, Micronesia)

Octopus

Latin name *Octopus vulgaris*   **Polarity** *Feminine*

Family *Octopodidae*   **Element** Water

Planet Moon   **Deities** Great Mother

Etymology from Greek *oktopous, oktopodos*; *okto*, eight, *podos*, foot.

Varieties
The octopus is a cephalopod mollusc of the family *Octopodidae*. Members include the Common Octopus (*Octopus vulgaris*), and a smaller Mediterranean variety, *Philonexis catenulata*.

Folklore
There is an urban myth in which a man eats a baby octopus in a restaurant. During the following months, he experiences alarming stomach cramps, and later discovers that he has a fully-grown octopus inside him.

Mythology
In Celtic and Scandinavian art, the octopus is portrayed with straight arms (possibly symbolising the eightfold Wheel of the Year), but in Minoan and Mycenean art, it is depicted with wavy arms and takes on the symbolism of the spiral, which signifies both solar and lunar powers, the motion of the heavenly bodies, the cycle of the seasons, expansion and contraction.

Symbolism
The symbolism of the octopus is related to that of the spiral, the dragon, and the spider. It represents the unfolding of the universe from the mystic centre. In astrology, the octopus is sometimes

associated with the sign of Cancer, as it represents the Summer Solstice. It may also be a thunder symbol. It symbolises the depths of the sea and the phases of the Moon.

Oyster

Latin name *Ostrea edulis*   Polarity Feminine

Families *Ostreidae* (True Oysters);
            Margaritanidae (Freshwater Pearl Oysters)

Element Water

Planet Moon

Etymology Middle English and Old French *oistre* from Latin *ostrea*, *ostreum*, from Greek *ostreon*

Symbolism

The oyster represents the womb, the creative aspect of the feminine principle, birth and rebirth, initiation, justice and the law of life in the cosmos.

To the Chines, it symbolises cosmic life, the power of the waters, the sacredness of the moon, yin, and fertility.

Shellfish

Latin name various   **Polarity** Feminine

Families *Sphaeriidae* (Orb Cockles);
Pholadidae (Piddocks);
Mytilidae (Mussels);
Pectinidae (Scallops);
Unionidae (Freshwater Mussels)

Element Water   **Planet** Moon

Deities Venus, Vishnu, Buddha

Mythology
In Buddhism, the conch is the voice of Buddha. In Hinduism, it is
the voice of Vishnu, calling to awaken people from ignorance.

Symbolism
Shellfish have lunar and feminine associations, and denote birth,
good fortune, and resurrection. The symbol of St James of
Compostella is a shell. The shell is also associated with the birth
of Venus because of the painting by Botticelli. It is also associated
with initiation, and was used to scoop and pour the waters of
baptism.

Slug

Latin name various

Family *Arionidae*

Etymology from Middle English *slugge*, meaning sluggard

Varieties

Arionidae family: Red Slug (*Arion rufus*); Forest Slug (*Arion subfuscus*).
Limacidae (Keeled Slugs): Great Grey Slug (*Limax maximus*); Ash-black Slug (*Limax cinereoniger*).
Helicidae family: White-lipped Slug (*Cepaea hortensis*), actually a snail.

Folklore

The slug was believed to wear itself away as it left its trail of slime.

"Like a slug melting away as it moves along..." (Psalm 58:8)

Mythology

In Egypt, the slug was believed to be the semen of the sky god, the origin of life and moisture. The so-called 'horned asp' may well have been the slug.

Snail

Latin name various   **Polarity** Yin

Family *Helicidae*

Class *Gastropoda* (Gastropods)

Folk name hodmandod, hodmidod, dodman

Planet Moon

Etymology Hodmandod is perhaps related to hoddy-doddy, a dumpy person, a duped husband, a simpleton. Snail comes from Old English *snægel*, from Old High German *snegil*, and Old Norse *snigill*

Varieties

Helicidae family: *Helicodonta obvoluta; Helicigona lapicida; Helicigona rossmüssleri; Isognomostoma personatum; Zenobiella umbrosa*; Roman or Edible Snail (*Helix pomata*); *Cepaea nemoralis; Cepaea vindobonensis; and Cepaea hortensis.*
Lymnaeidae (Pond Snails): Great Pond Snail (*Lymnaea stagnalis*); Marsh Snail (*Galba palustris*).
Planorbidae family: Ram's Horn (*Planorbis planorbis*); Great Ram's Horn (*Planorbarius corneus*).
Pomatiasidae family: Round-mouthed Snail (*Pomatias elegans*)
Viviparidae (River Snails): Common River Snail (*Viviparus viviparus*); *V. fasciatus.*

Folklore

The snail's track could be used for divination if left on a slate. According to Hesiod, the time of the harvest was indicated when the snail began to climb on the stalks.

Ammonite fossils were called snake stones, from the folk belief that they were petrified coiled snakes.

Mythology

In Mayan and Aztec art, snails are portrayed on stelae. The Mexican Moon god Tecciztecatl is enclosed in a snail shell. The snail also represented rebirth, and as such was often depicted on the heads of Aztec deities.

The Zuni people (indigenous American) have a snail clan.

Symbolism

As a creature which appears and disappears, the snail is lunar and symbolises rebirth. It can also represent the dawn merging from the dark cave of night. Its spiral shell signifies the labyrinth, the spiral, and the underground cavern. As a slow creature, it represents voluptuousness. In Christianity it represents sloth and sin, because it was believed to feed on mud and slime.

Sea Snail

Latin name *buccinum*

Polarity Androgynous

Element Fire and Water

Planet Moon

Deities Tecciztecatl

Mythology
In Aztec myth, the sea snail represents the Moon god, who appears and disappears. It also signifies pregnancy and childbirth, because the child emerging from the womb is like the snail emerging from its shell.

Symbolism
The sea snail represents the androgyne and the combination of the elements of Fire and Water.

Mythical Animals

There are many different mythical animals, some utterly fantastical, and others garbled versions of travellers' tales or attempts to explain the inexplicable. The combination of characteristics is a way of looking at other possibilities, and of combining the symbolism of more than one animal (this is particularly true of heraldic beasts). Monsters symbolise primordial chaos and the frightening aspects of Nature. Fabulous and winged beasts are often associated with the Moon Tree and the Tree of Life as guardians of the gifts bestowed by the tree (either treasure or esoteric knowledge). The gates of hell are often depicted as the gaping jaws of a monster. Monsters also represent the darkness and the unconscious, and are slain or overcome by heroes of the light. Water monsters symbolise the unfathomable depths, the primordial chaos, or the manifestation of divine power.

Many mythical animals were first described in medieval bestiaries. These books were very fashionable between the eleventh and fourteenth centuries. They described the habits and peculiarities of both real and fabulous animals, as well as their legendary lore and moral symbolism. They were based on the *Physiologi* of the classical era. Bestiaries written in English were mostly translations of works produced in Europe. Some of the most popular were those of Philippe de Thaun, Guillaume le Clerc (*Le Bestiaire Divin*), and Richard de Fournival's satirical work, *Le Bestiaire d'Amour* (circa 1250).

Amemait

The amemait is a combination of a lion, a crocodile, and a hippopotamus, and symbolised retribution. It is known as the Devourer.

Amemait

Amphisbaena

The amphisbaena is like the basilisk, but with a head at each end, and therefore able to see both ways.

Basilisk

The basilisk is a combination of a bird and a reptile. It has the head and claws of a bird and the body of a serpent. In Christianity, it symbolises the devil and the antichrist. In Europe, it symbolises evil, lust, and disease, especially syphilis in 15th century Europe. Its gaze is lethal. In order to fight it, you have to look away from it and observe its movements in a mirror. The name basilisk means 'king of serpents' (from Greek *basileos*, a king). In Alchemy, the basilisk is a symbol of the philosophers' egg, the Hermetic vessel in which the Great Work was completed. There were three types of basilisk. The fiercest was hatched from a cock's egg by a serpent and was wingless; it was small, but could kill with a glance. One of these was alleged to have been killed by a weasel at Halle in Saxony. The second type was created artificially by using herbs; its venom depended on the ingredients. The third type was generated in mines, had beautiful eyes, and was coal-black with wings shining with small veins. It was harmless, and its oil and water were useful to alchemists. It sometimes had a jewel in its head.

Basilisk

Behemoth

The behemoth is usually assumed to be a mythical version of the hippopotamus. It represents the power of the land. Leviathan is the power of the sea, and Ziz (a great bird) is the power of the air.

> *"Look at the behemoth, which I made along with you and which feeds on grass like an ox. What strength he has in his loins, what power in the muscles of his belly! His tail sways like a cedar; the sinews of his thighs are close-knit. His bones are tubes of bronze, his limbs like rods of iron. He ranks first among the works of God, yet his Maker can approach him with his sword. The hills bring him their produce, and all the wild animals play nearby. Under the lotus plant he lies, hidden among the reeds in the marsh. The lotuses conceal him in their shadow; the poplars by the stream surround him. When the river rages, he is not alarmed; he is secure, though the Jordan should surge against his mouth."* (Job 40: 15-23)

Bucentaur

The bucentaur is half-man, half-
bull. Like the centaur, it symbolises the dual nature of humanity.

Capricornus

The capricornus is half-goat, half-fish. It symbolises the winter
solstice and the zodiacal sign of Capricorn. It is a form of the
Babylonian god Ea-Oannes, the lord of the abyss.

Centaur

The centaur is half-man, half-horse. Depicted as holding an arrow
and a drawn bow, it represents the zodiacal sign of Sagittarius (the
archer). The name centaur means "one who rounds up bulls".
They were originally depicted as hairy giants, only later becoming
half-man, half-horse. Their ancestor was Ixion of Thessaly, the
son of Ares. Ixion desired the goddess Hera, but Zeus duped him

by shaping a cloud to look like Hera. Ixion mated with the cloud, and the cloud gave birth to Centaurus, who mated with the mares of Pelion and produced centaurs. The myth probably arose because of the early Dorian Greeks' amazement the first time they saw someone mounted on a horse. The centaurs lived in Thessaly, and the Thessalonicans were famed for their equestrian skills. In medieval romances, the centaur was often referred to as a sagittary, and described as a creature with eyes that sparkled like fire and could strike people dead like lightning. They were believed to have fought in the Trojan armies.

"The dreadful Sagittary
Appals our numbers"
(Shakespeare, *Troilus and Cressida*, Act V Scene V).

The centaur symbolises the lower nature of humanity; the animal nature combined with the higher nature of human virtue and judgment. It represents both the savage and the benign aspects of nature, and the conflict between them. The horse is solar, and represents the strength and power of the body guided by the spirit (which is represented by the human part of the centaur). In Ovid's *Metamorphoses*, the Centaurs are depicted as a brutal species. At Heracles' wedding to Deianeira, the centaurs started a fight and Heracles killed the centaur Nessus, who had tried to rape Deianeira. Before he died Nessus gave Deianeira some of his blood as a charm to keep

439

Heracles' love. She put it on his shirt, and it burned him. After this incident, the Lapiths drove the centaurs out of the country.

In Christianity, centaurs represent sensuality, the passions, adultery, brute strength, humanity torn between good and evil, the animal and the spiritual nature. The centaur also symbolises heretics and devils, their arrows being the fiery darts of evil. The centaur is the antithesis of the knight, who controls his steed and is separate from it, whereas the centaurs are ruled by their passions. In Greek art, the centaurs are often shown ridden by Dionysos, alluding to their drunken habits. Not all the centaurs are brutish, however. The centaur Chiron typifies wisdom. He taught Aristaeus, Apollo, and Achilles the arts of war and of healing. His mother was Philyra. He is a symbol of the healing powers of nature, and his skill at archery represents the power and fertility of nature. The patron goddess of the centaurs is Leucothea (the milk-white goddess), the mother of Dionysos.

Cerberus

Cerberus is an enormous three-headed dog that guards the gate of Hades.

Charybdis

Charybdis was a roaring monster that lived at the bottom of a whirlpool in the Sicilian sea. Nearby was a monster called Scylla, and it was very difficult to steer a course between them, as Odysseus found. They symbolise a dilemma, as in the phrase "caught between Scylla and Charybdis".

Chimaera (or Grylli)

The chimaera has the head, mane and legs of a lion, the body of a goat, and the tail of a dragon. Ovid described it as having "a body all aflame". It represents winds and storms, danger (on both land and sea), and elemental chaos. Latterly it has come to be proverbial for anything non-existent. In mythology, Chimaera was the daughter of Echidne (a snake goddess of winter) and Typhon (the storm god). She was slain by Bellerophon. In modern Greek the word for utopia is χιμαιρα (*khimaira*). The name is derived from the word for a she-goat.

Cockatrice

The cockatrice was said to be hatched by a serpent from a cock's egg. It is sometimes synonymous with the basilisk. Both creatures were reputed to be able to kill anyone on whom they fixed their eyes.

> "They will kill one another by the look, like cockatrices."
> (Shakespeare, *Twelfth Night*, Act III Scene IV).

The cockatrice was used as a figure of speech to signify a treacherous and insidious person who stirs up trouble.

Cynocephalus

The cynocephalus is a dog-headed man who imprisons or destroys the enemies of light. St Christopher is sometimes depicted as a cynocephalus in his role as the guardian of the city.

Dragon

Latin name *Draco*

Polarity Masculine and feminine

Elements All four Elements

Folk name Lindworm, Orm, Worm

Planet Sun or Moon

Etymology Middle English from Old French, from Latin *draco(nis)*, from Greek *drakon*, a serpent, from a verb meaning 'to watch over'

Deities Tiamat

Dragons are often associated with mountains. In Chinese tradition, they are the lords of the sky and guardians of esoteric knowledge. In Christianity, they are deemed to be winged serpents and associated with the devil. They were the demonic opposition for saints, hermits, and anchorites. Slaying the dragon meant exorcising the mountain. In 1280, King Pedro III of Aragon climbed the Pic Canigou (9000 feet) on the border of Provence. His companions were driven back by horrible thunderclaps, but he went on alone. At the top of the mountain he saw a lake with a dragon in it. He did not kill it. The Alps were believed to be the abode of dragons. A professor of physics and mathematics at Zurich, Jacob Scheuchzer, collected accounts of dragon sightings, which included cat-faced dragons, snake-like, bat-like and bird-like dragons, fiery and non-fiery dragons, flying and slithering dragons, smelly ones and noisy ones, ones with scales and feathers, fork-tailed, fork-tongued, crested and non-crested. The dragon of Val Ferret had a diamond-encrusted tail. A crevasse in the Valais was inhabited by a dragon called an onibra, which guarded liquid gold. A peasant tried to get the gold, fell into the crevasse, and was trapped there for seven years, but the dragon did not harm him. Mons Pilatus, near Lucerne, is reputed to be the burial site of Pontius Pilate and to be inhabited by a fierce dragon. A cabinet of curiosities in Lucerne included a dragon stone said to have been dropped by the dragon when it was flying from Rigi to Mons Pilatus.

There are many myths of the hero slaying the cthonic underworld serpent, often in order to free a damsel in distress or to reach a treasure which is hard to attain.

In Norwich, there used to be a form of the hobby horse at festivals, called Snap the Dragon, which was paraded through the streets.

In the 15th and 16th centuries in Leicester, there was a pageant called the Riding of the George. The procession included St. George and the dragon (the Chamberlain's accounts for 1536 show four shillings paid for dressing the dragon). From the 14th to the early 16th centuries, there was a similar event in Norwich. The procession featured St. George; the princess was replaced by St. Margaret (who saw the devil in the form of a dragon). After the Reformation (1552), the saints disappeared, but the dragon was kept on "for pastime". It was popularly referred to as "Old Snap", and was accompanied by "whifflers", who juggled with swords, and men in motley.

Dragon myths occur in various forms, but they are usually regarded as benevolent in the East and malevolent in the West. Some mystery traditions, however, regarded them as the Logos, the vivifying spirit, or the Pleroma. The dragon is often synonymous with the serpent, especially when it represents the unmanifest, chaos, the primordial waters, the untamed power of nature, and undifferentiated potentiality (the Pleroma). It can also represent the act of creation, hurling the thunderbolt to effect the change from the unmanifest to the manifest.

There is a constellation called Draco, and in astrology the two nodes of the Moon are called Caput Draconis (Dragon's Head) and Cauda Draconis (Dragon's Tail).

The dragon was a cult animal of the Anglo-Saxon kings. Many Anglo-Saxon kingdoms had dragon banners, the most famous being the dragon of Wessex, first mentioned in Henry of Huntingdon's twelfth century account of the Battle of Burford (752 CE). The forces of Cuthred of Wessex rode into battle behind the ealdorman Edelhun carrying a golden dragon, the insignia of the king. Henry of Huntingdon also relates that Edmund Ironside went into battle in 1016 CE with a dragon banner. King Harold is depicted in the Bayeux tapestry fighting under a dragon banner. The dragon is generally regarded as a manifestation of earth energy and a guardian of treasure, especially in burial mounds. The dragon may have been the spirit of the dead man taking on a ferocious aspect to guard his grave-goods, or it may have been a manifestation of earth energy.

There are many place names with a dragon association:

Drakelow (Derbyshire) - derived from *dracan hlawan*
Drakelow (Worcestershire)
Drake's Cross (Worcestershire)
Drakenedge (Warwickshire)
Drakestone (Gloucestershire)
Dragley Beck (Lancashire)
Drake's Island (Devonshire)
Drakeholes (Nottinghamshire)
Dragon Hill (near the Uffington White Horse, Berkshire)

According to legend, Dragon Hill in Berkshire was where St George slew the dragon; a bare patch on the hill is where the dragon's blood was said to have been spilt. Nothing will grow on this spot. Another story is that Cerdic, King of the West Saxons, slew Naud the Pendragon and 5000 men on the hill.

In the year 793 CE, according to the Anglo-Saxon Chronicle, fiery dragons were seen flying through the air, and interpreted as a portent of famine. Meteors were sometimes known as flying dragons, and this may have been what the dragons in the Chronicle were.

To the Celts, the dragon symbolised sovereignty. *Y Ddraig Goch* (the Red Dragon) is the flag of Wales, and was the banner of Uther Pendragon. The dragon could also represent earth energies. The young Merlin was able to see that Vortigern's tower kept falling down because there were two dragons, one red, one white, fighting in a pool beneath the hill on which he was trying to build it, and their struggle kept undermining the foundations. He thus saved himself from being the human sacrifice that Vortigern's magicians had suggested would stop the tower from falling down. In the story of *Lludd and Llefelys*, two fighting dragons were overcome in the form of two young pigs. These fighting dragons were one of the three plagues of Britain. Hu Gadarn, another Welsh hero, dragged the monster Addanc from its lair by Llyn Llion with his team of oxen.

The dragon symbolises the Four Elements, because it dwells in Earth, breathes Fire, flies through Air, and its scales shine like

Water. It denotes the joining of opposites and primal energy, and was identified with sky gods and their earthly representatives, emperors and kings. It also represents the joining of matter (serpent) and spirit (bird), and was originally entirely benevolent, with the bird as the breath of life and the serpent as the waters of life. It later became ambivalent as both the fertilising rain that follows thunder, and the destructive forces of floods and lightning. In the East, it is a positive symbol, and in Western Paganism, it is a symbol of earth energies. In Christianity, it is a negative force, representing the devil, the serpent, chaos, destruction, base instincts, and evil. It was an attribute of Saints Cado, Clement of Metz, George, Keyne of Cornwall (daughter of Brychan, King of Brecknock in the 5th century), Margaret, Martha, Maudet, pol Samson, Sylvester, and Philip (the apostle). A dragon with a knotted tail symbolises evil defeated; it was thought that the dragon's power, like the scorpion's, was in its tail. A habitation of dragons was a place of destruction and desolation. Slaying a dragon represents the triumph of spirit over matter, or the sun god defeating darkness. This was Christianised as the Archangel Michael triumphing over Satan.

In traditions where spirit and matter are not diametrically opposed but complement each other, the dragon is seen as positive; in traditions with an emphasis on transcendent spirit, the dragon is abhorred. In dragonslaying legends, the hidden treasure represents spiritual wisdom, the virgin to be rescued represents purity and the soul, and the lance of the knight signifies masculine energy and the rays of the Sun. In the earliest version of the legend of St George and the Dragon, in The Prologue to the Passion of St George (12th c.), the dragon was subdued by the sign of the cross and led back to the city by a strand of the princess's hair. This symbolises using the power of the Anima to subdue but not destroy the Shadow. A better-known version appears in *The Golden Legend* by Jacques de Voragine, in which the Princess of Silene in Libya is chosen by lot to be fed to the dragon, and is left by a lake near its lair. St George finds her and prepares to defend her. The dragon appears, and George asks for God's help, fights the dragon, and overcomes it. Then he leads it with the Princess's girdle to the city, much to the terror of the inhabitants. Then they see that George has it under control. After converting them all to

Christianity, George cuts off the dragon's head. It would appear that the legend has been manipulated to identify the dragon with Paganism.

St. George is one of a long line of slayers of monsters and dragons. Frequently the dragon represents chaos, and must be slain to restore order. Tiamat, the Great Dragon of Sumerian myth, threatened to destroy the world she has created and kill all her children, so Marduk slew her and formed heaven and earth from her body. However, this myth can also be interpreted as a patriarchal god destroying a powerful goddess. The dragon is often associated with the sea, the great deeps, mountain-tops, clouds, and the Sun rising in the East. In Indian mythology, Indra slew the serpent Ahi to get rain for the parched world. The dragon is ambivalent in rain myths; sometimes it is an ally of the rain god, sometimes it is opposed to him. Sometimes dragons represent the power of the land, which conquerors have to overcome in order to gain possession of new territory. They are also guardians of treasure and esoteric wisdom. Killing the dragon symbolises overcoming the difficulties on the path to inner knowledge, or the light triumphing over the darkness. There are many myths of the dragon being coiled around the Tree of Life, where it acts as both a manifestation of earth energy and a threshold guardian, the Great Serpent whose coils ascend "even unto the Abyss" (the chasm between ordinary and divine perception).

These are some of the dragon-slayers whose names are recorded in legend:

Culture	Hero	Dragon / Monster
Sumerian	Marduk	Tiamat (dragon goddess)
Greek	Perseus	Sea monster
Greek	Hercules	Lernean Hydra
Greek	Theseus	Minotaur
Indian	Indra	Ahi
Persian	Mithra	Ahriman
Persian	Thraetana	Darak
Persian	Rustem	Asdeev
Egyptian	Ra	Apep

448

Culture	Hero	Dragon / Monster
Germanic	Sigurd	Fafnir (serpent)
Germanic	Siegfried	treasure-guarding monster
Germanic	Gull Thorir	winged & scaled dragon
Germanic	Grettir	Karr the Old (vampire)
Anglo Saxon	Beowulf	Grendel
English (14th c., County Durham)	Lambton heir	Laidly Worm
English (Cheshire)	Thomas Venables	man-eating dragon
English (Southampton)	Bevois	dragon
French (Rouen)	St Romanus	dragon called La Gargouille
French	St Martha	The Tarasque of the Rhöne
French	St Martial	a dragon in Bordeaux
French	St Florent	a dragon of the Loire
Christian	Archangel Michael	The Devil in the form of a dragon
Christian	St Margaret	The Devil in the form of a dragon

In some folk tales, the Laidly Worm is a boy or a girl who has been turned into a serpent by a jealous stepmother (this happens in *The Laidley Worm of Spindleston Heughs* and *The Laily Worm*), and is released from the enchantment at the end of the story. In *Assipattle and the Mester Stoorworm*, Assipattle is the youngest of seven sons, who, despite being despised by all his family except his sister, kills the dragon by sailing into its gullet in a little boat, running down into its stomach with a lump of burning peat, setting fire to the oil in its liver, and escaping just in time to watch it burn up and disintegrate. Its tongue was flung up to the moon, fell back to earth, and gouged out the sea which divides Denmark from Norway. Its teeth were scattered all over the place, and became the Orkneys, the Shetlands, and the Faroe Islands. The body coiled into a huge lump, which became Iceland, but continued to burn, which is why there are still volcanoes there. Assipattle also stole his father's magic horse, which was controlled by a blast through the windpipe of a goose. There are certain similarities with Odin (magic horse, goose), but also with the legend of Marduk, who forms heaven and earth out of the body of Tiamat, the great dragon.

In China, the dragon is regarded as a benevolent manifestation of celestial power. It symbolises spiritual and supernatural power, wisdom, esoteric knowledge, infinity, change and transformation, the rhythms of Nature, the life-giving waters, strength, wisdom, and nobility. It is also the emblem of the Emperor as the Son of Heaven. It is the Celestial Stag, and symbolises the Sun, light, life, the Heavens, sovereignty, and Yang. The principles of Yin and Yang are sometimes represented as two dragons contending, one blue for Yin, the other white for Yang. They usually have either the Sun or the Moon between them. If portrayed back-to-back, they represent the Yin-Yang duality and eternity. If they are chasing each other's tails, they symbolise the creative interaction of Yin and Yang.

The four claws of Mang, the terrestrial dragon, are the Four Elements, and the five claws of Lung, the azure imperial dragon, are the Four Elements and Spirit. Mang represents temporal power. Lung is the highest dragon and lives in the sky, its head facing North and its tail pointing South; it is the vital spirit, celestial power, and on earth, the power of the Emperor, which is delegated from heaven. The Dragon of Clouds is thunder and the fertilising rains, the waters of the deep, and Spring. The hornless dragon, Li, lives in the sea and controls the deeps; it also symbolises scholars. Chiao lives in the mountains, and symbolises statesmen.

A dragon called Kung-Kung caused the Deluge by knocking over the pillars of heaven with its head. In another version of this story, he was the leader of the tribe of Omei Shan. When they were defeated in battle, he tried to end his life by battering his head on the heavenly bamboo, and tore an enormous hole in the canopy of the sky, through which the waters of the firmament poured, flooding the earth. According to Wang Fu, the "nine resemblances" of the dragon are the horns of a stag, the head of a camel, the eyes of a demon, the neck of a snake, the belly of a clam, the scales of a carp, the claws of an eagle, the soles of a tiger, and the ears of a cow.

The dragon is often depicted with a flaming pearl or the dragon ball, which may represent the rolling of thunder or the Moon as the bringer of rain. A dragon swallowing a pearl represents the waning Moon; a pearl emerging from its mouth represents the waxing Moon. A dragon with a phoenix (*feng-huang*) represents the union of heaven and earth, the Emperor and the Empress, the macrocosm and the microcosm, the two aspects of the androgyne, and the rhythms of birth and death. A dragon with a tiger symbolises lust (dragon) and anger (tiger). The goddess Nu-kua (creatrix and sister-wife of Fu-Hsi, the legendary first emperor of China) has a woman's torso and a dragon's tail. She restored harmony in the world after it was destroyed by flood and fire. She founded the institution of marriage, taught humanity the arts of civilisation such as irrigation, is the provider of children, a tamer of wild beasts, and a mediator between men and women. A dragon-horse is said to have arisen from the Yellow River and shown Fu-Hsi a chart inscribed on its back; from the characters on this chart, Chinese writing was developed. The Dragon Kings (*Lung-wang*) are bringers of rain, and depend on the August Personage of Jade for their authority. The four main *Lung-wang* rule the four seas surrounding the earth. Their names are Ao Kuang, Ao Jun, Ao Shun, and Ao Ch'in. They live in a crystal palace with an army of crabs and crayfish.

Each area of China, each well and watercourse, has its own dragon king. If there is no rain, sacrifices are made to the dragon kings, but if the drought does not cease, the statues of the dragon kings are left in the roadside in the dust to force them to relent and ask the August Personage of Jade to send rain. People also appeal to them if there is too much rain. In Chinese Alchemy, the dragon symbolises mercury, blood, and semen. In Chinese Taoism and Buddhism, there is a goddess called Tou Mu (probably of Hindu origin) who lives at the Pole Star. She has three eyes, eighteen arms, which hold weapons, the Sun, the Moon, a dragon's head, and five chariots. The Chinese association of dragons with heavenly wisdom derives from the Taoist association of transcendence with mountaintops, where dragons are often believed to dwell.

In Japan, the three-clawed dragon (which was originally an early form of the Chinese dragon) symbolises the Mikado, and imperial and spiritual power.

In Hinduism, the dragon is the uttered word, power made manifest. It is an attribute of Soma and Varuna. Indra slew the dragon Ahi or Vritra (the encloser) to bring rain. For a thousand years it had enclosed in its coils all the waters of the world. Fields and cities lay waste and parched, and even the abode of the gods was in ruins. Then Indra flung his thunderbolt among the coils of the monster, and the waters were released to flow over the earth.

In Persian mythology, the dragon was an attribute of Haoma. The hero Rustum, son of Zal, prince of Sedjistan, killed the white dragon Asdeev.

In Hittite mythology, the dragon Illuyankas was defeated by the goddess Inara and the storm god Hooke by getting it drunk.

In Egypt, the dragon was an attribute of Osiris as the god of the dead. Apep, the dragon of darkness, attacked the boat of Ra in the underworld each night.

In Hebrew symbolism, the dragon is desolation and the wilderness. In Christianity, much of the symbolism of the dragon is derived from the passage in *Revelation* chapter 12, where the archangel Michael battles with the dragon Satan in defence of the "woman clothed with the sun, and the moon under her feet, and upon her head a crown of twelve stars", who was "travailing in birth". This has also been used as a source of imagery for the Virgin Mary. St Bernard is depicted on Mount Joux with a slain dragon at his feet. The slaying of dragons by saints and angels is a Manichaean tradition of the battle between good and evil.

In ancient Sumer, the dragon was the Adversary and the power of evil.

In Assyro-Babylonian mythology, Tiamat was the Great Dragon, the goddess of the primordial sea. Her consort (originally female and an aspect of her) was Apsu, the personification of the sweet waters. Tiamat was slain by Marduk.

In Greece and Rome, it was an attribute of Heracles/Hercules as a slayer of monsters. The chariot of Ceres was drawn by dragons. Medea escaped from Jason in a chariot drawn by winged dragons. The golden apples of the Hesperides were guarded by a dragon. Sowing dragons' teeth in the earth made warriors spring from the ground. Cadmus slew the dragon at the fountain of Dirce, then sowed its teeth in the ground. A warrior grew from each one, and they attempted to kill him. Then Athene advised him to throw a precious stone amongst them, and they killed each other trying to get it. All but five of them were killed; these five helped him to found the city of Thebes. One of Jason's ordeals was to plant the remaining teeth that Cadmus had not sown, and he slew the warriors that grew from them.

In a Balkan folktale, the dragon is a manifestation of a wicked old man who has abducted a king's sister. The king goes looking for his sister, and comes to the hut of an old woman in the forest. Near the hut is a fruit-laden tree, which the old woman warns him to avoid. The tree recedes into the forest and the king follows it. Eventually it stops and an old man climbs down from the branches. He takes the king to his castle, where the sister is living as his wife. She warns the king that the old man will kill him. Three days later, he disappears. His younger brother searches for him, encounters the wicked old man in the form of a dragon, and kills him. A young man is released from the spell that had enchanted him, and marries the sister. Here the dragon represents the guardian of treasure in the form of the princess, who is also an Anima figure.

In Alchemy, a winged fiery dragon denotes the volatile principle, and a wingless dragon denotes the fixed principle. The hermaphrodite or Rebis is often shown standing on the winged fiery dragon. The dragon guarding treasure symbolises the difficulties encountered on the way to completing the Great Work. It represents Mercurius, and undergoes many transformations during the alchemical process. A sixteenth-century alchemist, Thomas Charnock (c. 1524-81), wrote a long poetical treatise on the dragon in alchemy (the poetry is abysmal, but it is an interesting piece):

> "*The dragon speaketh:*
> *Souldiers in armour bright*
> *Should not have kylled me in fyelde of fighte,*
> *Mr Charnock neither for all his philosophie*
> *Iff by pryson and famyne he had not famysshed me.*
> *Gye of Warwick nor Bevis of Southampton*
> *Nere slew such a venomous dragon.*
> *Hercules fought with Hidra the Serpent*
> *And yet he could not have his intent.*"

The poem then relates how "Salomon the Wyse" entombed the dragon in a prison of brass, but the dragon mercury should be imprisoned in a vessel of glass. In this vessel, it would devour its own body out of hunger. It would then become black and red by a process of corruption (i.e. oxidisation, which forms mercuric oxide).

> "*But that precious stone that is in my hedd*
> *Will be worth a mille to him that hath skyll*
> *And for that stone's sake he wisely did me kyll.*"

This refers to the process of fixing the Philosophers' Mercury, which gives birth to the Philosophers' Stone. The "stone that is in my hedd" refers to the myth that reptiles have precious stones in their foreheads, but it is also the head of the alembic. Killing the dragon is fixing mercury, a metaphor that is also used in Indian alchemical texts. This is a vital element in the process of obtaining the elixir of life which is the means of transmutation. The dragon mercury gives rise to the elixir, which is then united with the feminine mercury in the mystic marriage.

> "*Dying in mine owne blood*
> *For now I doe excell all other worldely good*
> *And a new name is given me of those that be wise*
> *For now I am named Elixer of great price*
> *Which if you will make prouffe, put me to my Sister Mercury*

And I will conjoyne her into
Sylver in the twinkling of
an eye."

Echidna

The Echidna was half-woman,
half-serpent. She was the mother
of the Chimaera, the many-headed
dog Orthos, the dragon of Colchis
that guarded the golden Fleece, the
hundred-headed dragon of the
Hesperides, the Sphinx, Cerberus,
Scylla, the Gorgons, the Lernean hydra,
the Nemean lion, and the vulture that
gnawed at Prometheus' liver.

Furia

The furies are winged women with
serpent tails, who deal out vengeance
and the nemesis, particularly to oath-
breakers.

Gorgon

The three Gorgons were women with
serpent hair. They represent the
Great Mother in her terrible aspect, destruction and terror. They
are a patriarchal version of the Great Mother.

Gryphon or Griffin

The griffin has the head of an eagle and the body of a lion. It
symbolises the Sun and the wealth associated with it. It also
represents the sky and the light of dawn turning to gold. A winged
griffin is female, a wingless one is male.

Gorgon

In heraldry, the griffin is the guardian of the path to the tree of life or to salvation, and represents strength, bravery, magnanimity, vigilance and vengeance. The eagle part is the element of Air, and the lion part is the element of Fire. The griffin represents the combined powers of both, and was sometimes thought to be the offspring of a lion and an eagle. It is the guardian of hidden treasures. Herodotus relates that there were gold-guarding griffins in the north of Europe or Asia. According to Persian legend, Zal, the father of Rustum, was reared by a griffin when he was left as a child to die in the desert.

In China, the griffin symbolises wisdom and enlightenment. In Greece, it is an attribute of Apollo as a solar creature, Athene as wisdom, and Nemesis as vengeance. Nemesis' chariot is drawn by griffins. In Christianity it is a symbol of evil and represents the devil flying away with souls, and those who persecute christians. Dante, however, used it to symbolise the two natures of Christ, the divine and the human, and the dual role of the Pope as both a temporal and a spiritual power. He called it "the mystic shape that joins two natures in one form".

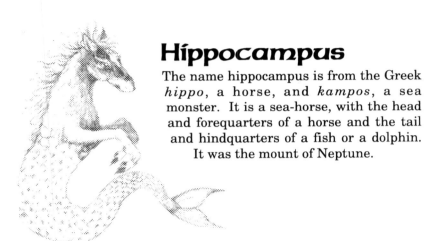

Hippocampus

The name hippocampus is from the Greek *hippo*, a horse, and *kampos*, a sea monster. It is a sea-horse, with the head and forequarters of a horse and the tail and hindquarters of a fish or a dolphin. It was the mount of Neptune.

Hippoelectryon

The hippoelectryon is half-horse, half-cockerel, and is a solar symbol.

Hippogriff

The hippogriff is half-horse, half-griffin. It is probably a solar symbol, like the winged horses of Apollo's chariot. It is the offspring of a filly and a griffin, and symbolises love. It mostly appeared in medieval legends.

Hydra

The hydra is a dragon or serpent with seven heads. It is very difficult to kill, because every time a hero chops off one of its heads, a new one would grow in its place. It symbolises blind undifferentiated life-force. Heracles killed the Lernean Hydra.

Kala-makara

The *kala-makara* was an Indian solar symbol and represented the power of the waters. It was a combination of a lion and a makara.

Kelpie

In Scottish folk belief, the kelpie was a malign spirit which haunted lakes and rivers, often in the form of a horse; it is said to be the personification of the sudden gust of wind which sweeps over the lakes and pools of the Highlands.

The kelpie was usually seen in the form of a young horse scampering along a river bank. When he was tired, he would strike the water three times with his tail. Each splash sounded like a crash of thunder. The kelpie would then disappear in a flash into a deep pool. The kelpie's bridle was highly magical; it could wreak enchantment by looking through the bridle's eyelets, but a magician could undo such an enchantment by looking through the eyelets in the opposite direction. Looking through the eyelets would also enable one to see spirits and faeries.

In the Highlands there is a tale of Seumas MacGregor, who encountered a kelpie by Loch Slochd, on the road from Inverness to Glenlivet. He had lost his horse, and thought he had found it again, but it turned out to be a kelpie trying to carry him off into the loch. So he called upon the Trinity and the kelpie threw him off. When he came to his senses, he was lying on the shore with the kelpie's bridle in his hand. This became a family heirloom amongst the MacGregors, who used it for magic.

In the mid-nineteenth century it belonged to Gregor Willox MacGregor, also known as "Warlock Willie". He lived at Gaulrig, Strathavon, Banffshire, and his clients included barren women and farmers with sick cattle, who would ask for "Taigh Maishter Willox". Kelpies have also been seen at Loch nan Dubhrachan on Skye, and Loch Treig in Lochaber. Also, in a valley between Lochearnhead and Glendochart, there is a dark loch which is reputed to be the abode of a kelpie. If you see one, you are advised not to mount it.

There were also legends of water bulls and water cows in the Highlands. One water cow had wonderful calves until the farmer offended her. Then she gave a great bellow that reverberated through the surrounding hills, and vanished with all her offspring into the lake (said to be St Mary's Loch at Yarrow).

Ky-lin or Qi-lin

The *ky-lin* is the Chinese unicorn, and represents the combination of Yin and Yang, the union of masculine and feminine, perfection, the purity of Nature, and the essence of the five elements and the five virtues, hence it is depicted as being of five colours. A white ky-lin is lunar and yin; a *ky-lin* of five colours is yin and yang combined. When not portrayed as a unicorn, it is shown as having the head of a dragon (with a single horn), the mane of a lion, the body of a stag and the tail of an ox. It represents gentleness, benevolence, good will, luck, longevity, grandeur, and fertility. It is very gentle, and its horn is soft and symbolises benevolence. The single horn represents the unity of the world under one wise emperor. The manifestation of a ky-lin portends the birth of a great emperor or sage. It appeared to the legendary Fu Hsi in 3000 bce. The birth of Confucius was heralded by the appearance of a ky-lin. "To ride a *ky-lin*" means to rise to fame. Sages and immortals are depicted riding a ky-lin to emphasise their great wisdom. "The son of a *ky-lin*" means an exceptionally clever child.

To Taoists, the ky-lin represents the essence of the five elements and virtues; it is a very important symbol in Taoism.

Lamía

The Lamiae were originally serpent goddesses (see serpent) but passed into medieval legend as a cruel queen who was turned into a serpent. The Lamia is often associated with the Sirens.

Leogryph

The leogryph is a combination of a lion and a serpent or of a lion and a griffin. It symbolises illusion and the terrible aspect of the Great Mother.

Leviathan

The leviathan is a huge fish, perhaps derived from legends of the whale. It is the primordial ocean monster, symbolising chaos, the power of the sea, and the serpent. It appears in Hebrew legend. In *Job* 41: 1-19 it appears to refer to the crocodile. In *Psalm* 104: 26, it seems to be the whale. In *Isaiah* 27: 1, it is a sea-serpent.

Lindworm

The lindworm is a wyvern or dragon with-out wings; it symbolises war and pestilence.

Loch Ness Monster

There have been several sightings of "Nessie" since the first one in April 1933, when a motorist driving along the shore of Loch Ness saw a strange object some distance away. It was afterwards described as having a snake-like head at the end of a long neck and two flippers in the middle of its body, and being about thirty feet long with two humps.

Makara

The makara is a combination of fish and crocodile, fish and antelope, or fish and elephant. It is also depicted as a shark, a dolphin, or a naga. It is the steed of Vishnu or Varuna as lord of the deeps and the western quarter of Mount Meru. It symbolises the dual nature of good and evil. In the Hindu Zodiac, it is the sign of Capricorn.

Manticore

The name manticore comes from the Persian mardkhora, a man-eater. The manticore has the body of a lion, the quills of a porcupine, the head of a man, and the tail of a scorpion. It appears in medieval bestiaries. In heraldry, it has horns, and the tail and feet of a dragon.

Mermaid or Merrow

The mermaid is half-woman, half-fish. She sometimes represents idealised feminine beauty, elusiveness, vanity, auto-eroticism and fickleness. She represents non-human instincts and desires, luring lovers to a watery grave. Archetypally, she represents the mysterious aspect of woman, the Anima and the unconscious. She is derived from early lunar fish goddesses such as Derketo and Atargatis. She may also have been inspired by the legends surrounding the dugong, manatee, or sea cow, which could be mistaken for a mermaid. The Sirens, the goddess Circe, the Selkie and Melusine are related to the mermaid.

The Irish name for a mermaid/merman was a merrow. Irish fishermen believed that seeing a merrow portended a storm. In

Ovid's *Metamorphoses*, it is related that mermaids arose from the burning ships of the Trojans. The timbers turned into flesh and blood and the green daughters of the sea. Legend has it that a mermaid was caught in Holland in 1404 and taken to Haarlem, where she was taught to spin and converted to the Catholic faith. No wonder mermaids are so elusive. In late 16th century plays, the name mermaid is used for a courtesan (Shakespeare, *The Comedy of Errors*, Act III Scene II). The Japanese mermaid, the Ningyo, is depicted as a fish with a human head. In Polynesian mythology, the creator-god Vatea is portrayed as half-human, half-porpoise.

Minotaur

The Minotaur was a man with a bull's head, conceived as a result of Pasiphae lying with a bull. He symbolises the untamed passions of Nature. The emblem of Crete is the Minotaur. The myth of Theseus slaying the Minotaur can be interpreted as the solar hero killing the bull, with the labyrinth as the path of life, and Ariadne's thread as the divine instinct in humanity.

Moddy-Dhoo

On the Isle of Man there is a legend of the Black Dog, a spaniel that haunted Peel Castle for many years. As soon as the candles were lighted in the guard room, it would enter, and it always left at daybreak. While it was there the soldiers refrained from oaths and profane talk, and always carried out their duties in pairs. One night one of their number got drunk and did the rounds alone out of bravado. He lost his speech and died within three days. The dog never appeared again. During

excavations of the castle in 1871, the bones of Simon, Bishop of Sodor and Man, were discovered. He died in 1247, and had been buried with a dog at his feet.

Naga

The Nagi are mythical Hindu serpent beings, depicted either as human-headed snakes, many-headed snakes, or monsters.

Their ancestor was Kadru, the wife of Kasyapa, and they live in the under-world and the depths of the ocean. In this realm they are kings and queens, and dwell in magnificent palaces. Female nagi can marry humans, and some Indian families claim descent from nagi. They are opposed by the solar Garuda Bird, because they represent the underworld and the element of water. They are, however, the guardians of treasure, both material and esoteric, and guardians of the threshold and the waters of life. On a microcosmic level, they correspond with the Kundalini serpent, which sleeps at the base of the spine, guarding the treasure of consciousness.

Vishnu, Lord of the Deeps, sleeps on Anata, the coiled serpent of the primordial waters, and two nagi with intertwined bodies represent the fertilised waters. The thousand-headed serpent Shesha (a king of the Nagas) cradles Vishnu between incarnations. He was born from Vishnu's mouth in his incarnation as Balarama, as he lay dying. Images of nagas are often placed under trees.

They are also guardians of cattle. They are sometimes helpful, and sometimes play tricks on people. One of the Nagas is called Ulupi. She lives in Patala, the lowest level of the underworld, a pleasant place associated with the sense of smell. Arjuna, the companion of Krishna in the Bhagavad Gita, descended to Patala and married her. The great serpent Vasuki, one of the rulers of the Nagas, was used by the gods as a rope to churn the Ocean of Milk. He had wound himself round the world mountain, and the gods and demons had a tug of war with his body, which caused the mountain to rotate and churn the Ocean. The origin of the myth of the Nagas may be a memory of a pre-Vedic tribe whose totem was the snake. In Buddhist art, the Buddha is sometimes depicted sitting on a naga. This symbolises his conquest and transformation of the knowledge hidden in the instincts.

Opinicus or Epimacus

The opinicus is a type of griffin with the legs and body of a lion, the head, neck, and wings of an eagle, and a camel's tail. It has the same symbolism as the griffin.

Ourobouros

The snake or dragon swallowing its own tail combines the symbolism of the circle and the snake. It is the equivalent of the phoenix in the realm of water. It represents rebirth, immortality, undifferentiated potentiality, and the totality of existence. It occurred in ancient Greek and Egyptian art. In Egypt, it was the circle of the universe and the path of the Sun god. In Greece, it symbolised the unity of existence. According to Epicurus, "The All was from the beginning like an egg, with the serpent as the tight band or circle around it." In Sumeria, it was the all-in-one. In Hinduism, it is equated with the wheel of samsara and the kundalini serpent. It represents the cycle of disintegration and reintegration, because it was self-generative and destroyed itself. Hence it also signifies the andro-gyne, the primordial parents, the waters of creation, and the darkness that existed before the manifestation of the light.

In funerary art it was used to symbolise immortality, eternity, and wisdom. In many mythologies, it is the serpent that encircles the world, or the ocean that surrounds the world. It is apparently still, but actually in perpetual motion. In Orphic imagery, it encircles the Cosmic Egg and symbolises Aeon, the life-span of the universe. It is also associated with the movement of the Sun, and is sometimes depicted with the Alpha and the Omega. In Alchemy, it represents the latent power of the prima materia, and the circulation of chemicals in the hermetic vessel. It is very much associated with Alchemy, and is similar to the alchemical dragon which is the symbol of Mercurius and the *prima materia*. In early depictions, it is accompanied by the motto 'εν το παν (All is One). The alchemist Thomas Vaughan (1621-65) gave an account of the ourobouros whilst explaining the mysteries of the Egyptians:

> *"First of all then, they draw a Circle, in the Circle a Serpent not folded, but Diameter-wise, and at length; her head resembles that of a Hawke, and the Tayle is tyed in a small knot, and a little below the head her wings are Volant. The circle points at Emepht, or God the Father being Infinite, without Beginning, without End. Moreover it comprehends or conteines in it self the Second Deitie Phtha, or the Second Person, who is the first Light, as we have told you in our Anthroposophia. He is said to forme all things out of the Egg, because in him, as it were in a Glasse, are certain Types or Images, namely the Distinct Concepts of the Paternall Deities, according to which by Co-operation of the Spirit, namely the Holy Ghost, the Creatures are formed."*

The ourobouros was an ideal symbol for the alchemists to represent the transmutation of matter, because it impregnates and

feeds upon itself. It also represents the unity of the cosmos.
According to Jung, it represents the process of working on the self:

> *"In the age-old image of the ourobouros lies the thought of
> devouring oneself and turning oneself into a circulatory
> process, for it was clear to the more astute alchemists that the
> prima materia of the art was man himself. The ourobouros is
> a dramatic symbol for the integration and assimilation of the
> opposite, i.e. the shadow. This feedback process is at the
> same time a symbol of immortality, since it is said of the
> ourobouros that he slays himself and brings himself to life,
> fertilizes himself and gives birth to himself."*

Pegasus

The pegasus is a winged horse, symbolising the striving of the
lower nature to unite with the higher. It is associated with the
Sun.

Ramora

The Ramora is a tiny fish,
no more than a foot long,
which is so strong that it
can anchor ships even in a
storm. It is called the
Echeneis in Greek, the
Delaya in Latin, and the
Essinus by the medieval
bestiaries. According to
both Aelian and Pliny, it
stopped Antony's ship from
going into action at the
battle of Actium, which
decided the result of the
battle. A number of
ramora saved some
children from being

massacred by Periander by anchoring his ship. It was said to live in the Indian Ocean.

Re'em

The name Re'em is used in the Torah for a unicorn, but it usually denotes a huge wild ox. There are only two of them in the world at any one time, and one lives in the East, the other in the West. They meet and mate every seventy years, and die after the female has given birth to twins, one male, one female. During the Flood, Noah tied them to the stern of the Ark because they were too big to fit inside it, and they swam along behind.

Salamander

The salamander represents the element of Fire. It is depicted as a small wingless dragon or lizard, sometimes dog-like, leaping out of flames. In the Western Tradition, it is the spirit and the guardian of the element of Fire, fabled to live in volcanoes. It lives in fire generally, but according to Pliny, it was believed that it quenched it with the chill of its body. It was thought to be sexless, so was used to denote chastity. In Christianity it represents enduring faith, a person who cannot be overcome by the fires of temptation. In heraldry, it represents bravery unquenched by the fires of affliction. The name was used by Paracelsus for the elemental beings of Fire (with Gnomes for Earth, Undines for Water, and Sylphs for Air). The same names were used by Alexander Pope in The Rape of the Lock. The badge of Francis I of France was a lizard surrounded by flames, with the motto *Nutrisco et extinguo* (I nourish and extinguish), which was derived from an Italian motto, *Nutrisco il buono e spengo il reo* (I nourish the good and extinguish the bad). Fire purifies good metal and destroys rubbish.

The name salamander is now given to a type of newt (the genus *Urodela*).

Satyr

The satyrs are nature spirits and followers of Dionysos, the Greek god of ecstasy, wine and music. They are half-man, half-goat. They originally represented the pleasure-seeking, amoral and lazy side of human nature; they were later identified with the devil in Christianity. They are associated with Silvanus, Faunus, Pan, and Bacchus, and represent untamed nature, licentiousness, and lust. They are often depicted crowned with ivy and carrying the thyrsos of Dionysos, and sometimes bunches of grapes, baskets of fruit, pitchers of wine, snakes, and cornucopiae. They are the elemental spirits of the forest and the mountains, loving pleasure and good cheer. They are sensual and lascivious, chasing the nymphs through the forest. Later they become associated with music and dancing, and join the retinue of Dionysos. They are associated with his cult.

> "Whence came ye, jolly Satyrs! whence came ye,
> So many, and so many, and such glee?
> Why have you left your forest haunts, why left
>   Your nuts in oak-tre cleft?" -
> "For wine, for wine we left our kernel tree;
> For wine we left our heath, and yellow brooms,
>   And cold mushrooms;
> For wine we follow Bacchus through the earth;
> Great god of breathless cups and chirping mirth!
> Come hither, lady fair, and joined be
>   To our mad minstrelsy!"
>   from *Endymion* by John Keats

Sea Serpent

The sea serpent is a huge beast said to live at the bottom of the ocean. It appears in many mythologies, such as Jörmungandr in Norse mythology and Leviathan in the Bible. There have also been many sightings reported by sailors. The last three were in 1857, 1875, and 1905. The serpent was described as being a long creature with a series of humps, a head rather like a horse's, with a dark back and a light belly. It appears in the summer months, and has never been known to attack anyone.

In Norse mythology, the ultimate sea being of course has to be Jörmungandr, the world serpent. In *Snorra Edda*, it is related how Thor went fishing one day and caught the world serpent on the end of his line (which was, incidentally, just such a hand line as was still being used in the nineteenth century to catch fish). The thrashings and writhings of Jörmungandr threatened to overthrow the world, so Thor had to let go. Possibly this semi-humourous episode is a foreshadowing of the events at Ragnarök, when Thor's adversary will be the world serpent, described in the *Voluspa*. It is interesting that the existence of the world serpent is necessary to maintain the equilibrium of Middle Earth, since it acts as a boundary of the seas. It is an immensely powerful being, not necessarily malevolent, but not particularly friendly if disturbed.

Silenus

The sileni are rural deities from Phrygia, the genii of springs and rivers. The name may refer to water that bubbles as it flows. The sileni are half-horse, half-human, with the tail, hooves, and ears of a horse but a human body. They are associated with the mysteries of Dionysos. The god Silenus is the son of Hermes and the Earth goddess, and is part of the retinue of Dionysos. He is very wise, but usually drunk. It was the custom to attempt to tie him up while he was sleeping off a bout of drinking, in order to compel him to reveal one's destiny. Marsyas was one of the sileni and a Phrygian river god. He held a musical contest with Apollo, and lost, although Midas (also a Phrygian) voted for him.

> "...another man remembered the tale of the satyr whom Apollo punished, after having defeated him in a competition on the reed-pipes, the instrument Minerva invented. "Help!" Marsyas clamoured. "Why are you stripping me from myself? Never again, I promise! Playing a pipe is not worth this!" But in spite of his cries the skin was torn off the whole surface of his body... Then the woodland gods, the fauns who haunt the countryside, mourned for him; his brother satyrs too, and Olympus, dear to him even then, and the nymphs, and all who pasture woolly sheep or horned cattle in these mountains. The fertile earth grew wet with tears, and when it was sodden, received the falling drops into itself, and drank them into its deepest veins. Then from these tears, it created a spring which it sent gushing forth into the open air. From its source the water goes rushing down to the sea, hemmed in by sloping banks. It is the clearest river in Phrygia, and bears the name Marsyas."
>
> (Ovid, *Metamorphoses*, Book VI)

Sphinx

The Greek sphinx is usually female, with a human head, the body of a bull, the feet of a lion, and the wings of an eagle. It symbolises the Four Elements and the riddle of existence. It is very wise. Oedipus solved the riddle of the sphinx, which was "What goes on four legs in the morning, two legs at noon, and three legs in the evening?" or "What goes on four feet, on two feet, and three, but the more feet it goes the weaker it be?" The answer being 'man'. The Greek sphinx lived in the vicinity of Thebes, and would set people riddles; if they could not answer, she would eat them. She was said to be the daughter of Typhon and Orthos, or of the Chimaera. The androsphinx (human-headed) signifies the union of the intellect with physical abilities, or the triumph of reason over the passions. The criosphinx (ram-headed) symbolises silence. The hieracosphinx (falcon-headed) is an emblem of the Sun. A sphinx with no wings and the body of a lion represents power. The Theban sphinx is a funerary symbol, denoting protection for the grave. The Minoan sphinx is crowned with lilies.

The Egyptian sphinx is a lion with the head of a Pharaoh. It symbolises royal power, vigilance, strength, wisdom and dignity, and is associated with Harmakhis (Horus of the Horizon) and Ra, the god of the rising Sun. The sphinx at Gizeh in Egypt was made of limestone around 2620 bce, and is 60' high by 180' long. It was commissioned by the pharaoh Khephren or Khafre. In the Esneh Zodiac, the goddess Ta-Repy (the Egyptian name for the constellation of Virgo, is depicted as a sphinx with the head and breasts of a woman and a lion's body.

T'ien-Kou, the Celestial Dog

T'ien-Kou is a symbol of destruction, disaster, eclipses, and meteors.

Unicorn

In heraldry, the unicorn is lunar and feminine, though its horn is masculine. It is portrayed with the head and body of a horse, the tail of a lion, the legs and hoofs of a stag, and a twisted horn in the middle of its forehead. It is often depicted with the lion as a solar and masculine animal. The Scottish coat of arms was supported by two unicorns, whilst the English was originally supported by a lion and the Welsh red dragon, until James VI of Scotland acceded to the English throne and supplanted it with one of the Scottish unicorns. The antipathy between the lion and the unicorn was often used to denote war between England and Scotland. In general, the unicorn symbolises chastity, purity, virginity, virtue, strength in mind and body, and incorruptibility.

In medieval bestiaries, the unicorn's horn was described as being white at the base, black in the middle, and red at the tip. Its body is white, with a red head and blue eyes. The earliest description of a unicorn is by the author Ctesias in 400 bce. Descriptions of its size and ferocity vary between accounts; in some it is gentle and docile, in others, fierce and warlike. Two unicorns, or a unicorn and a lion, are often depicted as guardians of the Tree of Life. The conflict between the lion and the unicorn represents the opposition of all solar and lunar powers.

In Alchemy, the unicorn is a symbol of quicksilver, with the lion as sulphur. The unicorn is fabled to be able to detect poison in any liquid and render it harmless; a design for a cup for the Emperor Rudolph II by Ottavio Strada shows a unicorn standing by as if to test the liquid. It was also believed to be the only animal that would attack an elephant. It is probable that the legend of the unicorn arose from tales of the rhinoceros. According to medieval lore, the only way to catch a unicorn was to place a virgin in its vicinity, whereupon it would lie down and place its head in her lap. This is an allegory of the birth of Christ, who entered the virgin's womb and became mortal. An old song describes Christ as "the wild wild unicorn that the virgin caught and tamed".

In Christianity, it is Christ, the "horn of salvation"; the horn as an antidote to poison represents his power to destroy sin; the single horn denotes Christ as the only Son of God, or the unity of Father and Son. As a symbol of virginity, purity, and chastity, it represents the Virgin Mary and all virtues. As a solitary creature, it symbolises the monastic life. It is an emblem of St Justina of Antioch and St Justina of Padua. A medieval Latin hymn describes Christ as the "wild wild unicorn that the Virgin caught and tamed". In ancient Egypt, it was a symbol of virtue. In Graeco-Roman mythology, it was a symbol of the lunar crescent

and an attribute of all virgin Moon goddesses, especially Diana
and Artemis, whose chariot was drawn by eight unicorns. In
Judaism, it symbolised royalty, strength, and power. It was said
to have existed in early times, but to have perished in the Flood.
In ancient Sumer, it was associated with the Tree of Life, and was
an attribute of virgin goddesses. In Persian symbolism, it denoted
perfection and virtue.

Wani

The wani is a Japanese sea-monster and messenger of the god of
the sea, Shio-Zuchi, the Old Man of the Tide, who rules all fish and
sea creatures.

Wyvern

The name wyvern comes from the Saxon *wyvere*, a serpent. The
wyvern has two legs at the front, none at the back. It is winged
and had a long curly tail. It symbolised war, pestilence, envy and
viciousness.

Appendices

When the grey owl has three times hooed,
  When the grimy cat has three times mewed,
When the tod has howled three times i' the wud
  At the reid mune cowrin' ahint the clud,
When the stars has cruppen deep i' the drift,
  Lest cantrips pyke them oot o' the lift,
  Up horses a', but mair adowe!
  Ride, ride to Lochar-brig-knowe!

(Fragment of a reputed witches' rallying song from Nithsdale
and Galloway)

Appendix One

Animals as attributes of deities

Deity	Culture	Other names*	Gender	Associated animals
Adad	Assyro-Babylonian		Male	Bull
Adonis	Mediterranean	Attis	Male	Boar
Aindri	Vedic/Hindu	Indrani	Female	Elephant
Akshobya	Buddhist		Male	Elephant
Anansi	Caribbean		Male	Spider
Anubis	Egyptian	Anpu	Male	Jackal, Dog
Aphrodite	Greek	(Venus)	Female	Bear, Deer, Dolphin, Goat
Apis	Egyptian	Hapi	Male	Bull
Apollo	Graeco-Roman	Apulu	Male	Dolphin, Griffin, Horse, Wolf, Crow
Arachne	Greek		Female	Spider
Arawn	Welsh	King of Annwn	Male	Dog, Horse
Ares	Greek	(Mars)	Male	Boar
Artemis	Greek	(Diana)	Female	Bear, Deer, Dog, Stag, Gazelle, Unicorn
Artio	Celtic		Female	Bear
Aset	Egyptian	(Isis)	Female	Heifer/Cow
Asklepios	Greek	(Aesculapius)	Male	Dog, Snake
Asshur	Assyrian		Male	Bull
Astarte	Assyrian		Female	Antelope, Dog, Gazelle
Atargatis	Sumero-Semitic		Female	Dolphin
Athene	Greek		Pallas Female	Deer, Griffin
Attis			Male	Bull

478

Deity	Culture	Other names*	Gender	Associated animals
Audhumla	Norse		Female	Cow
Bacchus	Roman	(Dionysos)	Male	Fawn, Dragon, Panther
Bast	Egyptian	Bastet	Female	Cat
Bel	Sumerian	Enlil, Rimn	Male	Aurochs
Belit-ili	Akkadian		Female	Dog
Borvo	Celtic		Male	Dolphin
Brighid	Celtic		Female	Boar
Buddha	Buddhist		Male	Elephant
Callisto	Greek		Female	Bear
Chandra	Indian (pre-Vedic)		Male	Antelope
Chinigchinich	Indigenous American		Male	Coyote
Chiron	Greek		Male	Centaur
Cocidius	North British		Male	Dog, Stag
Cronos	Greek	(Saturn)	Male	Ass
Demeter	Greek		Female	Boar, Snake
Derga	Celtic		Male	Boar
Devasuni	Japanese	Sarama	Female	Dog
Diana	Roman	(Artemis)	Female	Cat, Unicorn, Deer, Dog, Gazelle
Dionysos	Greek	(Bacchus)	Male	Ass, Bull, Dolphin, Satyr
Disa	Scandinavian		Female	Reindeer
Ea-Oannes	Sumerian		Male	Antelope, Dolphin, Goat
Enki	Sumerian		Male	Bull
Epona	Celtic		Female	Ass, Horse, Dog
Eros	Greek		Male	Dolphin
Esus	Gaulish		Male	Bull
Europa	Greek		Female	Bull
Faunus	Roman	(Pan)	Male	Satyr
Flidais	Irish		Female	Deer
Frey	Scandinavian		Male	Boar
Freyja	Scandinavian		Female	Boar, Cat
Fukurokuju	Japanese		Male	Deer

Deity	Culture	Other names*	Gender	Associated animals
Gala	Phoenician		Female	Dog
Ganesh	Hindu	Ganpati	Male	Elephant
Garbh Ogh	Irish		Female	Deer, Dog
Gula	Babylonian		Female	Dog
Gunputty	Hindu	Ganpati	Male	Elephant
Hanuman	Hindu		Male	Ape, Monkey
Hapi	Egyptian		Male	Ape, Baboon, Dog
Hathor	Egyptian		Female	Cow
Hecate	Greek		Female	Boar, Cat, Dog, Frog, Hare, Horse, Toad
Hera	Greek	(Juno)	Female	Cow, Peacock, Lamb
Herakles	Greek	(Hercules)	Male	Deer
Horus	Egyptian	Har-wer	Male	Bull
Hygieia	Greek		Female	Snake
Hu	Celtic		Male	Ox
Inari	Japanese		Male	Fox
Indra	Hindu/Vedic		Male	Dog, Elephant
Indrani	Hindu/Vedic		Female	Elephant
Io	Greek		Female	Cow
Ishtar	Sumero-Semitic		Female	Dolphin
Isis	Egyptian	Aset	Female	Cow, Deer, Dolphin
Jambavati	Hindu		Female	Bear
Jupiter	Roman	(Zeus)	Male	Bull, Eagle
Karora	Australian Aborigine		Male	Bandicoot
Kenemet	Egyptian		Female	Ape
Khons	Egyptian	Khonsu	Male	Baboon
Lahar	Sumerian		Male	Cattle
The Lares	Roman		Either	Dog
Lu-Hsing	Chinese		Male	Deer
Mafdet	Egyptian		Female	Cat, Lynx
Marduk	Sumerian		Male	Antelope
Mars	Roman	(Ares)	Male	Boar, Horse, Vulture
Matunus	Celtic	Mathonwy(?)	Male	Bear

Deity	Culture	Other names*	Gender	Associated animals
Medusa	Greek		Female	Dragon, Snake
Melusine	European		Female	Mermaid
Mehueret	Egyptian		Female	Cow
Mercurius	Alchemical	Mercury	Male	Stag, Unicorn
Mercury	Roman	(Hermes)	Male	Goat, Cock
Methyer	Egyptian		Female	Cow
Metsik	Slavonic		Male	Cattle
Minerva	Roman	(Athene)	Female	Owl
Mithras	Persian	Mithra	Male	Bull, Dolphin
Mont	Egyptian	Montu, Menthu	Male	Bull
Mullil	Sumero-Semitic		Male	Gazelle
Nandi	Indian		Male	Bull
Nandini	Indian		Female	Cow
Nehalennia	Germanic/Celtic		Female	Dog
Neith	Egyptian		Female	Cow
Nemesis	Greek		Female	Griffin
Neptune	Roman	(Poseidon)	Male	Bull, Dolphin, Horse
Ngurvilu	Chilean		Male	Wild cat
Ninhursag	Sumerian		Female	Cow
Nirriti	Indian		Female	Cow
Nodens	Celtic	Nuada, Nudd	Male	Dog
Nut	Egyptian		Female	Cow
Odin	Norse	Woden	Male	Boar, Dog, Wolf
Olle	Indigenous American		Male	Coyote
Opet	Egyptian	Taueret	Female	Hippopotamus
Orion	Greek		Male	Dog
Orore	Phoenician		Female	Fly
Osiris	Egyptian	Ousir	Male	Bull
Pakhit	Egyptian		Female	Cat
Palaemon	Greek	Melicertes	Male	Dolphin
Pales	Roman		Either/Both	Cattle, Flocks
Pan	Greek	(Faunus)	Male	Goat, Satyr
Pasiphae	Greek		Female	Bull
Pinga	Inuit		Male	Caribou

Deity	Culture	Other names*	Gender	Associated animals
Poseidon	Greek	(Neptune)	Male	Bull, Dolphin, Horse
Priapus	Graeco-Roman		Male	Ass
Prisni	Indian		Female	Cow
Prithivi	Indian		Female	Cow
Ptah	Egyptian		Male	Bull
Ra	Egyptian		Male	Bull, Sphinx
Ravana	Indian		Male	Ass
Reshep	Syrian	Reshpu	Male	Gazelle, Stag
Rohini	Indian		Female	Cow
Sadhbh	Irish	Sadv	Female	Deer
Sarama	Japanese	Devasuni	Female	Dog
Saturn	Roman	(Cronos)	Male	Ass/donkey
Sekhmet	Egyptian		Female	Lion
Serapis	Greek/ Egyptian	Sar-Hapi	Male	Bull
Set	Egyptian		Male	Ass, Boar, Gazelle
Shashti	Bangladeshi		Female	Cat
Shentayet	Egyptian		Female	Cow
Shiva	Hindu		Male	Antelope
Silenus	Roman		Male	Donkey
Silvanus	Roman		Male	Satyr
Shou-hsien	Chinese		Male	White stag
Soma	Indian		Male	Antelope
Sothis	Egyptian	Sopdet	Female	Cow
Surabhi	Indian		Female	Cow
Tammuz	Assyrian		Male	Boar
Taueret	Egyptian	Opet	Female	Hippo- potamus
Tekkeitsertok	Inuit		Male	Deer
Tethys	Greek		Female	Halcyon (Kingfisher)
Thetis	Greek		Female	Dolphin
Thor	Norse	Thunor	Male	Bear, Ram, Goat
Thoth	Egyptian	Tehuti	Male	Baboon
Tiamat	Sumerian		Female	Dragon
Typhon	Greek/ Egyptian	(Set)	Male	Ass

Deity	Culture	Other names*	Gender	Associated animals
Tyr/Tiw	Norse/Anglo-Saxon		Male	Wolf
Ukemochi	Japanese		Female	Vixen
Upuaut	Egyptian	Wepwet	Male	Wolf
Vach	Indian		Female	Cow
Varahi	Hindu	Vishnu	Male	Boar
Varahini	Hindu		Female	Boar
Venus	Roman	(Aphrodite)	Female	Bull, Dove, Swan, Sparrow
Vitiris	North British		Male	Boar
Volos	Slavonic	Volusu	Male	Cattle
Vosegus	French/Celtic		Male	Stag
Vulcan	Roman	(Hephaestos)	Male	Lion
Walgino	Polish		Male	Cattle
Xoltl	Aztec		Male	Dog
Yahweh	Hebrew		Male	Bull
Yama	Hindu/Buddhist		Male	Buffalo, Dog
Zeus	Greek	(Jupiter)	Male	Bull

* Names in brackets are Greek, Roman, or Egyptian equivalents of each other)

Egyptian deities with animal heads

Egyptian name	Greek name	Animal
Ousir-Hapi	Osorapis	Bull
Hapi	Apis	Bull
Menthu	Mont	Bull
Bast		Cat
Athyr	Hathor	Cow
Aset	Isis	Cow
Nut		Cow
Sebek	Suchos	Crocodile
Hapi	Apis	Ape

Tehuti	Thoth	Baboon
Set	Typhon	Donkey
Heket		Frog
Taueret		Hippopotamus
Anpu	Anubis	Jackal, Dog
Duamutef		Jackal
Nefertum		Lion
Sekhmet		Lion
Tefnut		Lion
Amon	Ammon	Ram with curved horns
Khnum		Ram with wavy horns
Hershef	Harsaphes	Ram with wavy horns
Khephra	Khepri	Scarab
Selkhet		Scorpion
Uadjet	Buto	Serpent
Upuaut, Wepwet		Wolf
Khenti Amenti		Wolf

Animals as attributes of saints

Ass:	Gerlach, Germanus, Philibert, Anthony of Padua
Bear:	Columba, Edmund, Gallus, Humbert, Maximinus
Bear keeping sheep:	Florentius
Bear laden with baggage:	Corbinian, Maximinus
Bear ploughing:	James
Beehive:	Ambrose, Bernard, John Chrysostom
Boar:	Emilion
Bull:	Adolphus, Regnier, Sylvester
Calves:	Walstan
Camel:	Aphrodicius, Hormisdas
Cow:	Berlinda, Bridget, Modwena, Perpetua
Crocodile:	Helenus, Theodore
Deer:	Henry
Doe:	Fructosus, Mammas, Maximus of Turin
Dog:	Benignus, Bernard, Roch, Dominic
Dolphin:	Martianus, Adrian, Calistratus
Fish:	Andrew, Eanswide, Gregory of Tours, John of Burlington, Raphael, Simon
Frog:	Huvas, Rieul, Sinorina, Ulphia
Hare:	Albert of Siena
Hind:	Catherine of Siena, Genevieve of Brabant, Lupus of Sens

Hind with two fawns:	Bassian
Horse:	Barochus, Irene, Severus of Avranches
Leopard (with ox or lions):	Marciana
Lion:	Adrian, Dorothea, Euphemia, Germanus, Ignatius, Jerome, Mark, Prisca
Ox or oxen:	Blandina, Otto, Frideswide, Fursey, Julitta, Leonard, Lucy, Luke, Medard
Pig:	Anthony the Great
Rat:	Genevieve of Nivelles
Stag:	Aidan, Eustace, Hubert, Julian the Hospitaller, Osyth, Rieul
Ploughing with stags:	Kenan, Kentigern
Wolf:	William of Montevergine
Wolf bringing child:	Simpertus
Wolf bringing goose:	Vedast
Wolf stealing pig:	Blaise
Wolf-dog:	Donatus

Animals and birds associated with the corn-spirit

(according to J G Frazer)

Ass	Bear
Boar	Cat
Cock	Cow, Bull, Calf, Ox
Dog	Fox
Gander	Goat
Hare	Horse, Mare
Kite	Mouse
Pig, Sow	Quail
Roe Deer	Sheep
Stag	Stork
Swan	Wolf

Appendix Two

Animal Pub Signs

The Bear and Ragged Staff
Arms of the Earl of Warwick

Noah's Ark
Refers to the Biblical legend of the Flood

The Cat and the Fiddle
Refers to the nursery rhyme: "Hey diddle diddle, the cat and the fiddle..."

The Bear
Alludes to bear-baiting or dancing bears

The Blue Boar
Arms of the Duke of Devonshire

The Bull and Dog
Alludes to bull-baiting

The Bull and Gate
The Bull and Mouth
A corruption of Boulogne Gate or Boulogne Mouth, a compliment to Henry VIII, who captured Boulogne in 1544.

The Cat and Wheel
A corruption of St Catherine's Wheel

The Coach and Horses
A popular sign for coaching inns

The Cock and Bull
This was a common inn sign in the 17th century. It is possibly related to the expression "cock and bull story" meaning a long and

colourful but highly improbable story, which possibly derives from animal fables where animals would converse.

The Dog and Duck
Alludes to duck-hunting

The Fox and Goose
Sometimes meant that the game of "Fox and Goose" could be played in the pub

The Golden Fleece
Refers to the story of the Golden Fleece and to the wool trade, which was the main trade of England in the Middle Ages

The Elephant and Castle
Shown as an elephant with a castle on its back, this could be a mistaken version of a howdah (a sort of tent in which ladies in purdah travelled on the backs of elephants in India); or the name could be a corruption of the Infanta de Castile, a Spanish princess.

The Golden Lion
Arms of Henry I and the Percy family of Northumberland

The Goat and Compasses
May be a corruption of "God Encompasseth Us", or the addition of a Masonic symbol to a simple animal sign. There is a pub in Dorset called the Square and Compasses, with a very Masonic-looking sign.

The Pig and Tinderbox
A facetious version of the Elephant and Castle

The Pig and Whistle
Could be a corruption of the Piggin and Wassail. A piggin was an earthenware drinking vessel. The wassail bowl was used to celebrate Christmas, New Year, and the wassailing of the apple trees.

The Red Cow
May refer to a time when red cows were regarded as more valuable than the black kind.

The Red Lion
If depicted rampant, represents Scotland; it was also the badge of John of Gaunt, Duke of Lancaster

St George and the Dragon
A sign paying tribute to the patron saint of England

The Swan and Antelope
Supporters of the arms of Henry IV

The Talbot
The talbot is a hound rather like a labrador; it was the arms of the Talbot family

The Unicorn
Appears as a supporter in the arms of Great Britain

The White Hart
The badge of Richard II

The White Lion
The badge of Edward IV as earl of March; also the device of the Dukes of Norfolk and the Earls of Surrey

The Mermaid
The Mermaid tavern in Bread Street, Cheapside, in London was the meeting place of the playwrights and writers of the early 17th century, including Jonson, Ralegh, Beaumont, and Fletcher.

Appendix Three

Terminology

Wherever possible I have given the indigenous names for peoples, places and deities. Many of the names by which they are known to the West were imposed by colonial powers, and it is important to try to restore the original names.

A glossary is given below.

Original name	Description	Imposed name	Source
Ousir	Egyptian god	Osiris	Greek
Aset	Egyptian goddess	Isis	Greek
Hoor-pa-kraat	Egyptian god	Harpocrates	Greek
Tehuti	Egyptian god	Thoth	Greek
Dineh	Indigenous people	Navaho	Spanish
Lakota	Indigenous people	Sioux	French
Inuit	Indigenous people	Esquimaux	French
Turtle Island	Place	America	Spanish

There is also the issue of cultural appropriation. Indigenous peoples are becoming increasingly distressed at "New Age" appropriation of their cultural artefacts and symbols for inappropriate purposes. They argue that their rituals are specific to their culture and heritage, and if removed from that context, have their meaning distorted. (An example of this that is closer to home is the use of the goddess image by patriarchal cultures to make women subservient, which is the exact opposite of the original meaning of the image.) Therefore they argue that Europeans should investigate our own spiritual heritage. (People of European descent who live in America will have to make their own compromise with the spirits of the land, preferably by making direct contact with the spirits of place and of animals in their own locale, and developing ways of communicating with them which arise organically out of their interaction.) Indigenous American mythology has been included in this book in the context of comparative religion. I personally object to the indiscriminate appropriation of supposedly Native American practices, which is usually done by people who cannot make a direct connection with the spirits of this land, and therefore have to go out and buy tons of shamanic paraphernalia with which they proceed to irritate everyone else by being "more shamanistic than thou", usually very loudly at four in the morning when everyone else is trying to sleep. Also, many of the people who are so keen on Indigenous peoples' spirituality have not actually done anything to help in their political struggle for autonomy. Indigenous Americans are still being oppressed today, as much of the mineral and uranium deposits in America lie under reservation land, and large corporations are trying to grab it.

An excellent organisation for all indigenous peoples is Survival International.

Recommended reading on making contact with animal spirits is *Sacred Animals* by Gordon Maclellan. For ways of making contact with the Earth, his book *Talking to the Earth* is also highly recommended.

PICTISH
ANIMAL
symbols

Bibliography and Further Reading

Yvonne Aburrow, *"The Enchanted Forest: the magical lore of trees"*, Capall Bann Publishing, 1993.

Yvonne Aburrow, *"Auguries and Omens: the magical lore of birds"*, Capall Bann Publishing, 1994.

Richard Adams, *"The Iron Wolf and other stories"*, Penguin, 1982.

M. Z. Afshar, *"The immortal hound: the genesis and transformation of a symbol in Indo-Iranian traditions"*, Garland 1990.

Freya Aswynn, *"Leaves of Yggdrasil"* (Llewellyn, 1990)

Robert Bain, *"The Clans and Tartans of Scotland"*, Collins, 1949.

R Barber & A Riches, *"A Dictionary of Fabulous Beasts"*, Boydell, 1971.

S. Baring-Gould, *"Lives of the Saints"* (quoted in the Guardian)

Brian Bates, *"The Way of Wyrd"*, Arrow Books, 1987.

Bruno Bettelheim, *"The Uses of Enchantment: The meaning and importance of fairy tales"*, Penguin, 1991.

Alvin Boyd-Kuhn, *"The Lost Light"*, Academy Press, 1940.

Brian Branston, *"The Lost Gods of England"*, Constable, 1993.

Joseph Campbell, *"The Inner Reaches of Outer Space: Metaphor as Myth and as Religion"*, Harper Perennial, 1988.

A. Carmichael, *"New Moon of the Seasons: prayers from the Highlands and Islands"*, Floris Classics, 1986.

W. A. Chaney, *"The Cult of Kingship in Anglo-Saxon England"*

Jean-Paul Clebert, *"The Gypsies"*, Pelican Books.

Juliet Clutton-Brock, *"The British Museum Book of Cats, Ancient and Modern"*, British Museum Publications, 1989.

J. C. Cooper (ed.), *"Brewer's Book of Myth and Legend"*, Helicon, 1993.

J. C. Cooper, *"An Illustrated Encyclopedia of Traditional Symbols"*, Thames and Hudson, 1993.

Donna Woolfolk Cross, *"Pope Joan"*, Quartet Books, 1997

Kevin Crossley-Holland, *"British Folk Tales (New Versions)"*, Orchard Books, 1987.

Alexander Cruden, *"Cruden's Complete Concordance to the Bible"*, Lutterworth Press, 1977.

Frank Delaney, *"The Celts"*, Guild Publishing, 1986.

Marion Davies, *"The Magical Lore of Cats"*, Capall Bann Publishing 1996

Marion Davies, *"Sacred Celtic Animals"*, Capall Bann Publishing 1998

Marion Davies, *"The Sacred Lore of the Horse"*, Capall Bann Publishing 1997

Wolfram Eberhard, "*A Dictionary of Chinese Symbolism: Hidden symbols in Chinese life and thought*", translated by G. L. Campbell, Routledge, 1986.

G. E. Evans & D. Thomson, "*The Leaping Hare*", Faber & Faber, 1972.

J. & S. Farrar, "*The Witches' Goddess: the feminine principle of divinity*", Hale, 1987.

J. & S. Farrar, "*The Witches' God: Lord of the Dance*", Hale, 1989.

Janet Farrar and Virginia Russell, "*The Magical History of the Horse*", Capall Bann Publishing 1999

Eric Fitch, "*In Search of Herne the Hunter*", Capall Bann Publishing 1995

David Fontana, "*The Secret Language of Symbols: A Visual Key to Symbols and their Meanings*", Pavilion, 1993.

J. G. Frazer, "*The Golden Bough: A Study in Magic and Religion*", abridged edn., Macmillan, 1983.

Miranda J. Green, "*Animals in Celtic life and myth*"

Mark Haeffner, "*Dictionary of Alchemy*", Aquarian Press, 1994.

M. Esther Harding, "*Woman's Mysteries, Ancient and Modern*", Shambhala, 1990.

Healey & Glanvill, "*Urban Myths... Unplugged*", Virgin, 1994.

Paul Hillyard, "*The Book of the Spider*", Pimlico (reviewed in The Big Issue, 1995).

Phil Hine, "*Sacred Elephant*", article in Talking Stick, issue XVIII, Spring 1995.

Erich Hofstetter, "*Der Herr der Tiere im alten Indien*", Otto Harrassowitz, 1980.

Christina Hole, "*English Folk Heroes*", Batsford, 1948.

Ronald Hutton, "*The Pagan Religions of the Ancient British Isles: Their Nature and Legacy*", Blackwell, 1991.

Ronald Hutton, "*The Shamans of Siberia*", Isle of Avalon Press, 1993.

Ronald Hutton, "*The Stations of the Sun: A History of the Ritual Year in Britain*", Oxford University Press, 1996.

G. & T. Jones (trans.), "*The Mabinogion*", Everyman, 1978.

C. G. Jung, "*Four Archetypes*", Arkana, 1988

Rudyard Kipling, "*Puck of Pook's Hill*", Piccolo, 1975.

Rudyard Kipling, "*Rewards and Fairies*", Penguin Classics, 1987.

A. Kitson (ed.), "*History and Astrology: Clio and Urania confer*", Mandala/Unwin, 1989.

F. Marian McNeill, "T*he Silver Bough* (Volume One: Scottish Folk lore and Folk belief)", Canongate Classics, 1989.

Payam Mohaghegh, "*Mithra the Friend*" in Sufi, Issue 32, Winter 1996-97.

Barbara Noske, "*Humans and other animals: beyond the boundaries of anthropology*", Pluto 1989.

R. M. Ogilvie, "*The Romans and their Gods*", Chatto & Windus (Ancient Culture and Society), 1969.

I. Opie & M. Tatem, "*A Dictionary of Superstitions*", OUP, 1992.

Ovid, "*Metamorphoses*", Penguin Classics, 1955. (Translated by Mary M. Innes)

Gisli Palsson, "*The idea of fish: land and sea in the Icelandic world view*", in "Signifying Animals: Human Meaning in the Natural World" (ed. Roy Willis, Unwin Hyman, 1990)

Nigel Pennick, "*Practical Magic in the Northern Tradition*", Aquarian Press, 1989.

Nigel Pennick, "*The Secret Lore of Runes and Other Ancient Alphabets*", Rider, 1991.

Nigel Pennick, "*Runic Astrology*", Capall Bann Publishing 1998

Michael John Petry, "*Herne the Hunter: A Berkshire Legend*", Wm. Smith (Booksellers) Ltd., Reading, 1972. Printed by Blackwells, Oxford.

James Riordan, "*The Sun Maiden and the Crescent Moon: Siberian Folktales*", Canongate Publishing, Edinburgh, 1989.

Anne Ross, "*Pagan Celtic Britain*", Constable, 1992.

Nicholas J Saunders "*Tezcatlipoca: jaguar metaphors and the Aztec mirror of nature*", in *Signifying Animals: Human Meaning in the Natural World*, ed R G Willis, One World Archaeology 16.N. K. Sandars (trans. & ed.), "*The Epic of Gilgamesh*", Penguin Classics, 1975.

Simon Schama, "*Landscape and Memory*", Harper Collins, 1995.

H. H. Scullard, "*Festivals and Ceremonies of the Roman Republic*", Thames and Hudson, 1981.

William Shakespeare, *The Complete Works*.

Mike Shankland, "*The Net of Ran*", Talking Stick, Issue XX, Winter 1995/6

Juliet Sharman-Burke, "*The Complete Book of Tarot*", Pan Books, 1985.

Tom Sharratt, "*Spider boxes clever in bog*", article in the Guardian, 20 January 1995.

Jerry Silverman (ed.), "*Songs of the British Isles*", Mel Bay, 1993.

Robin Skelton & Margaret Blackwood, "*Earth, Air, Fire, Water: Pre-Christian and Pagan Elements in British Songs, Rhymes, and Ballads*", Arkana, 1990.

R. J. Stewart, "*Where is Saint George? Pagan Imagery in English Folksong*", Blandford Press, 1988.

R. J. Stewart, "*Celtic Gods, Celtic Goddesses*", Blandford, 1990.

Caroline Stick, "*Anansi: Spiderman*", article in Talking Stick, Issue 18, Spring 1995

Sara Sviri, "*Where the Two Seas Meet: The Story of Khidr*" in Sufi, Issue 31, Autumn 1996.

Egerton Sykes, "*Who's Who: Non-classical Mythology*", Dent, (ed. Alan Kendall) 1993.

Jan Toman & Jiri Felix, "*A Field Guide in Colour to Plants and Animals*" (Octopus Books), 1975.

T H White, "*The Book of Beasts*", Cowell, 1959.

Brian Wicker, "*The Story-shaped World*", Athlone Press, 1975.

R G Willis (ed.), "*Signifying Animals: Human Meaning in the Natural World*", Unwin Hyman, 1990.

Chapters in the above:

"The pangolin revisited: a new approach to animal symbolism", Mary Douglas

"Sheep bone as a sign of human descent: tibial symbolism among the Mongols", Slawoj Szynkiewicz

"Cultural attitudes to birds and animals in folklore", Jawaharlal Handoo

"A semantic analysis of the symbolism of Toba mythical animals", Pablo G Wright

"Ecological community and species attributes in Yolngu religious symbolism", Ian Keen

"Pictish animal symbols", Anthony Jackson

"The idea of fish: land and sea in the Icelandic world-view", Gsli Plsson

"Animals in Hopi duality", Mark Thomas Bahti

"Eat and be eaten: animals in U'wa (Tunebo) oral traditon", Ann Osborn

"Nanook, super-male: the polar bear in the imaginary space and social time of the Inuit of the Canadian Arctic", Bernard Saladin d'Anglure

Steve Wilson, "*Robin Hood: The Spirit of the Forest*", Neptune Press, 1993.

New Larousse Encyclopedia of Mythology, Larousse, 1985.

"*Magic Animals: The Bear*" (BBC2, 1 March 1995), narrated by Miranda Richardson

Websites

http://www.amazoncity.com/soul/broomcloset   (item by Connie on the goddess Hina)

http://www.cix.co.uk/~mandrake

http://www.bioch.ox.ac.uk/~payam

http://www.geocities.com/Athens/Oracle/8173 (my home pages)

Index

Achilles, 69, 126, 440
Adad, 222, 226, 478
Adapa, 110
Adonis, 52-53, 111, 188, 193, 195,
    197, 371, 384, 478
Aeacus, 126
Aegina, 126
Aengus mac Og, 201
Agnes Sampson, 18
Alexander Hamilton, 18
Agni, 230, 294, 300, 358, 398, 401
Airavata, 280, 284
Akshobya, 280-281, 478
Alexander Hamilton, 18
Amathaon, 253, 268
Amon, 53, 56, 70, 400, 484
Amon-Ra, 398, 400
Anansi, 97, 99, 392, 478, 495
Anat, 353, 356
Anata, 465
Andarta, 184, 188
Anhur, 353, 355
Anhur, 353, 355
animal helper, 26-28, 31, 33
Anubis, 70, 264, 269, 345, 424, 478,
    484
Apedemak, 280, 284, 357
Apet, 315
Aphrodite, 53, 55, 85, 87, 111, 188,
    228, 250, 275-276, 294, 299,
    308, 323, 398, 401, 478, 483
Apis Bull, 41, 49, 53, 69, 226, 483
Apis, 41, 49, 53, 69, 128, 226-227,
    478, 483
Apollo Delphinos, 276-277
Arachne, 97, 99-100, 478
Aranyani, 46
Archangel Michael, 337, 447, 449,
    452
Ares, 57, 193, 195, 424, 438, 478,
    480
Ariadne, 229, 244, 464

Aristaeus, 132, 440
Arnaknagsak, 396, 415, 417
Artemis, 40-41, 54-55, 68, 128, 131-
    132, 184, 188-189, 195, 214,
    247, 250, 266, 294, 298, 323,
    353, 357, 476, 478-479
Artio, 184, 188, 478
Aset, 69, 96, 238, 478, 480, 483,
    489
Ashanti, 99
Ashnan, 221
Asklepios, 5, 259, 264, 266, 478
Asshur, 222, 226, 294, 298, 478
Astarte, 162, 164, 232, 259, 269,
    277, 292-293, 307, 384, 478
Atalanta, 188, 193, 195, 357
Atargatis, 41, 97, 106, 110-111,
    275, 277, 357, 463, 478
Atargatis, 41, 97, 106, 110-111,
    275, 277, 357, 463, 478
Athene, 97, 99-100, 247, 250, 324,
    453, 456, 478, 481
Athenian Bee, 132
Attis, 52-53, 61, 195, 222, 225, 401,
    478
Audhumla, 174, 235, 237, 479
Aumanil, 415, 417
Aunt Piety, 288-289
Aurora Borealis, 289
Avalokitesvara, 316, 333
Avilayoq, 271

Ba-Ronga, 17
Baal, 150, 222, 226, 402
Baal the prince, 150
Baalzebul, 150
Babi, 176-177
Bacchus, 68, 171, 242, 244, 300,
    470, 479
Badagas, 61
Bahu, 353, 358

Baiame, 150
Balarama, 465
Banebdjedet, 111
Basques, 154
Bast, 69, 208, 214, 353, 355, 363,
    479, 483
Battle of Magh Mucrime, 387
Battle of the Trees, 253, 268
Bee of Athens, 132
Beelzebub, 150
Bel, 163, 174, 226, 479
Belili, 195
Belin, 399
Belit-ili, 259, 270, 479
Bellerophon, 150, 324, 335, 441
Beowulf, 20, 185, 196, 203, 250,
    397, 449
Bhars, 61
Bhotiyas of Jahur, 61
Bishop Barnabee, 153, 155
Black Annis, 306
Blandina, 190, 244, 485
Boann, 122
boar of Formael, 201
Boar's Throng, 20, 83, 193, 197
Borvo, 275, 479
Brighid, 193, 198, 242-243, 399,
    479
Brighid, 193, 198, 242-243, 399,
    479
Brimo, 259, 264, 266
Brotherhood of the Green Wolf, 421
Buddha, 66, 77, 115, 207, 212, 241,
    256, 280-281, 306, 334, 358,
    367, 430, 466, 479
Buddhism, 15, 100, 102, 115, 148,
    183, 212, 229, 233, 241, 243,
    256, 270, 281, 306, 334, 336,
    339, 346, 358, 368, 385, 401,
    411, 430, 451
bull spectres of the Island of
    Britain, 231

Cad Goddeu, 253, 268
Caereni, 399

Cagn, 157
Cairbre Cinn-cait, 213
Calabar, 17
Callisto, 184, 188-189, 479
Canopic Jars, 69, 177, 269, 345
Carnea, 381, 384
Carp, 118, 451
Cath Paluc, 214
Celts, 3, 18, 20, 39, 59, 63, 87, 100,
    108, 122, 130, 140, 171, 188,
    198-199, 213, 220, 231, 256,
    267, 306, 328, 331, 373, 385-
    386, 446, 493
Centaurus, 323, 439
Ceres, 68, 126, 381, 384, 453
Ceres, 68, 126, 381, 384, 453
Ceridwen, 381
Cernunnos, 47, 254, 291
Chafer, 158
Chandra, 77, 162-163, 292, 306,
    479
Chang Tao-ling, 409-410
Chinigchinich, 245-246, 479
Chiron, 54, 68, 132, 323, 440, 479
Chop, 13
Christ, 27-28, 40, 62, 106, 109, 111-
    112, 135-136, 138, 140, 150,
    169-170, 172-173, 190, 234, 244,
    254, 273, 278, 284, 301, 307,
    313, 339, 354, 360, 363, 379-
    380, 399-400, 403-404, 423, 456,
    475
Clidna, 316, 327
Cocidius, 252-253, 259, 264, 479
Conch, 430
Council of Auxerre, 248
Coventina, 267, 275-276, 330
Crab, 74, 78, 97, 101-102, 375
criosphinx, 473
Cu Chulainn, 330
Cybele, 41, 61, 68, 128, 131, 225,
    353, 357
Cú Chulainn, 120-121, 221, 252,
    268, 330-331

Dagon, 106, 110
Daksha, 294, 300-301
Dasra, 425
Delaya, 468
Demeter, 3, 49, 56, 126, 128, 131,
  193, 195, 228, 324-325, 381,
  383, 479
Demne, 252
Derga, 58, 193, 198, 202, 331, 479
Derketo, 106, 110, 463
Desana, 406-407
Devi, 353, 358
Diana, 68, 71, 87, 128, 132, 215,
  242, 247, 250, 259, 264, 266,
  325, 370, 476, 478-479
Dinka, 61
Dionysos, 54, 56, 68, 128, 131, 167,
  170, 222, 228, 274-277, 294,
  298-299, 324, 350-351, 357, 398,
  401, 409-410, 440, 470, 472, 479
Divine Physicians, 425
Doctor Ellison, 153-154
Dog Star, 50, 260, 273-274, 424
Donn mac Midir, 252
Dontso, 161
Dragon Kings, 451
Druid, 251
Druids, 63, 128, 198, 220, 231
Duamutef, 69, 345, 484
Dumuzi, 196, 222, 226, 384
Durga, 339, 353, 358, 409-411
Dwyvan, 68
Dyaus, 230, 239

Ea, 102, 110, 162-164, 222, 226,
  250, 402
Ea-Oannes, 76, 106, 110, 162-164,
  277, 294, 298, 438, 479
Earth Mother, 241, 409, 411
Echeneis, 468
Eel, 119-121
Eeyore, 173
Einherjar, 197, 297
Eloir the Red, 268
Enlil, 174, 221-222, 226, 479

Enlil, 174, 221-222, 226, 479
Ennead of Heliopolis, 355
Eostre, 302, 307, 391
Epona, 167, 171, 267, 316, 325,
  328-329, 479
Erl-King, 321
Essenes, 137
Essinus, 468
external soul, 9, 16, 24

Failbhe Finnmaisech, 201
Faunus, 71, 221, 299-300, 401, 470,
  479, 481
Fenris Wolf, 83-84, 421-422
Finn, 117, 122-123, 202, 268
Fisher King, 108, 112
Five Noxious Creatures, 71, 81,
  142
Flidass, 247
Fortuna, 353, 358
Foundation rites, 60
Fox Chant, 289-290, 374
Frau Holle, 307
Frey, 196-197, 249-250, 479
Fricco, 197
Frog, 29-31, 41, 43, 45, 85-89, 93,
  136, 480, 484
Fu-Hsi, 451
Fukurokuju, 247, 251, 256, 479

Gala, 259, 269-270, 480
Gala, 259, 269-270, 480
Ganesh, 282-284, 301, 480
Ganesha, 280, 282-283, 285, 394
Ganpati, 280, 282, 284, 480
Garbh Ogh, 252, 267, 286, 480
Garelamaisama, 46
Garm, 422
Garmr, 266
Garo, 44, 61
Gilgamesh, 95, 225-226, 326, 495
Gilyaks, 16, 59
girdle of Ishtar, 77
God Almighty's Cow, 153
God of Dance, 424

Goda, 307, 327
Goldilocks, 187
Grail Chapel, 109
Great Mother, 98, 102, 109, 131,
    139-140, 162-163, 165, 229, 237,
    239-241, 250, 312-313, 338-339,
    354, 357, 359, 384-385, 387,
    427, 455, 462
Greater Wolf's Jaws, 84, 421
Greece, 59, 68, 116, 124, 135-136,
    140, 143, 151, 156-157, 170,
    188, 195, 228, 239, 243, 250,
    263, 276, 351, 383, 401, 423,
    453, 456, 466
Green Wolf, 421
Guatemala, 19, 182
Guendoloena, 47, 254
Gula, 269, 480
Gundestrup cauldron, 47, 198, 253-
    254, 267, 276, 328, 399
Gwrhyr the Interpreter of Tongues,
    65, 386

Hailer of the Dawn, 177
Hani-Yasu-No-Kami, 160
Hanuman, 67, 165, 366-368, 480
Hanuman, 67, 165, 366-368, 480
Haoma, 452
Hapi, 53, 69, 165, 176-177, 269,
    478, 480, 483
Harfa, 307
Harka, 307
Harmonia, 97, 99
Harmonia, 97, 99
Hathor, 41, 69, 111, 234-235, 237-
    238, 355, 480, 483
Hatmehyt, 106, 111, 401
Heimdall, 397
Heitsi-Eibib, 220
Hepatu, 353, 356
Hephaestus, 53, 68
Hera, 54, 74, 104, 126, 128, 131,
    188, 235, 239, 299, 307, 323,
    357, 438-439, 480
Hercules, 53, 68, 102, 265-266, 270,

298, 325, 353, 358, 381, 384,
    448, 453-454, 480
Hermes Kriophoros, 266, 401
Hermes, 5, 221, 264, 266, 294, 299-
    300, 308, 398, 401, 472, 481
hieracosphinx, 473
Hina, 113, 139-140, 496
Hodmandod, 432
Hoide, 307
Holda, 97, 99, 307
Honan, 13, 179
Honau, 13, 179
Honduras, 19
Hooke, 452
Hopi, 13, 88, 164, 179, 392, 496
Horned God, 46, 66, 188, 198, 231,
    250, 252-253, 256, 399, 421
Horseman's Word, 322
Horus, 69, 87, 96, 163, 165, 177,
    227, 238, 269, 292, 474, 480
Hounds of God, 272
Hu Gadarn, 242-243, 446
Hun-Ahpu-Myte, 408
Hun-Ahpu-Vuch, 408
Hyrax, 157

Ichthys, 106, 110
immortality, 92, 112, 132, 135-136,
    140, 143-144, 147, 159, 256,
    272, 284, 308, 402, 404, 466-468
Inara, 452
Inari, 288-289, 480
Indra, 46, 67, 126, 163, 230, 239-
    240, 270, 284, 448, 452, 480
Inuit, 43, 251, 271, 286, 389, 396,
    417, 424, 481-482, 489, 496
Io, 235, 239, 480
Ishtar, 77, 95-97, 102, 110, 196,
    225, 275, 277, 312-313, 326,
    353, 356-357, 384, 480
Isis, 41, 69-70, 85, 87, 96, 102, 104,
    106, 110-111, 171-172, 214, 227,
    235, 237-240, 247, 250, 269,
    277, 307, 345, 384, 478, 480,
    483, 489

500

Islam, 28, 71, 137, 269, 292, 332, 334, 340, 361, 387, 402
Ixion, 323, 438-439

Jain, 163
Jambavan, King of the Bears, 189
Judas Iscariot, 96
Julietta, 244
Juno, 68, 102, 104, 244, 353, 358, 480
Jupiter-Ammon, 53
Jupiter, 68, 76-77, 222, 228, 244, 303, 323, 369, 398, 402, 480, 483
Jörmungandr, 471

Kadru, 465
Kaggen, 157
Kali, 58, 339, 345-346
Kalmuck, 58
Kama, 128, 132
Kannaaluk, 388
Karora, 180, 480
katsina, 13, 88, 179, 392
Keelut, 271
Kelpie, 6-7, 108, 317-318, 459-460
Kenemet, 165, 480
Keres, 265
Khenti Amenti, 70, 424, 484
Khepera, 158
Khephra, 158, 484
Khidr, 28, 106, 114, 495
Khons, 176-177, 480
King Gollowa, 153, 155
King Math, 198, 200, 253
Kingu, 39
Kisa, 13
kobong, 12
Krishna, 66-67, 132, 189, 222, 466
Kshatriyas, 411
Kurmis, 61
Kuruvikkarans, 58
Kwahu, 13
Kwan-Yin, 116, 316, 333, 353, 358

Lady Godiva, 307, 327
Lady Horse-Head, 160
Lady Lanners, 153-154
Lady of the Animals, 46
Lady of the Flowers, 47, 254
Lady of the Fountain, 48
Lady of the Wood, 46
Lahar, 218, 221, 480
Lares, 68, 381, 384, 480
Latis, 122-123
Lebiyah, 353, 356
Leviathan, 110, 417, 437, 462, 471
light of the fox, 289
Lindworm, 443, 462
Little Miss Muffet, 97
Lobster, 103
Lord of the Elephants, 46
Lord of the Flies, 150
Lucan, 132
Lupercalia, 425
Lykaon, 424

Maahes, 214, 353, 355
Macha, 316, 327, 329-330
Mafdet, 214, 362-363, 480
Mallans, 61
Manannan, 201, 237, 329, 335, 381, 386
Manibozho, 302, 305, 377
Mao, 208
Marduk, 39, 162-163, 174, 222, 226, 250, 298, 332, 353, 357, 448, 450, 453, 480
Mari, 153-154, 239, 319, 332, 399
Mari Gorri, 153-154
Mari Lwyd, 319
Marmoo, 149-150
Mars, 55, 68, 73, 77, 95, 174, 193, 195, 228, 267, 325, 328-329, 331, 338, 381, 384, 424, 478, 480
Marsyas, 472
Matrilineal descent, 15
Medard, 244, 485
Medhbh of Connacht, 220, 316,

327, 406-407
Mehueret,, 239, 481
Mekhit, 353, 355
Melissa, 128, 131, 298
Mellonia, 128, 130
Menthu, 69, 227, 481, 483
Mercury, 5, 60, 68, 74-75, 77, 94,
    135, 199, 231, 253, 256, 264,
    266, 271, 280-281, 300, 308,
    360, 386, 399, 406, 425, 451,
    454, 481
Merlin, 47, 60, 127, 254, 446
Merovingian, 14, 136, 197
Metzik, 218
Michaelmas, 51
Midsummer, 61-62, 171, 219, 237,
    382, 421
Min, 353, 356
MInerva, 37, 68, 188, 472, 481
Minoan Great Mother, 140
Mithra, 77, 135, 225, 272, 448, 481,
    494
Mithraism, 96, 135, 230, 233, 250,
    266, 277, 332, 361
Mithras, 135, 222, 230, 272, 275,
    277, 332, 481
Moccus, 199, 386
Moddy Dhoo, 263
Moerae, 97, 99, 265
Mohammed, 71, 98, 137, 172, 206,
    334, 373
Monswa, 13
Mont, 69, 227, 481, 483
Moon Tree, 41, 435
Mullil, 292-293, 481
Mullo, 171, 373
Murigen, 122-123
Myrmidons, 126

Nanshe, 106, 110
Nantosuelta, 128, 130
Narasinha, 66, 353, 358
Nasatya, 425
Nefertum, 69, 214, 354, 484
Nehalennia, 267, 481

Neith, 69, 97, 99, 239, 346, 481
Neptune, 68, 275, 335, 457, 481-
482, 496
Nergal, 353, 357
Nia Segamon, 329
Nina, 95, 101-102, 110
Ningirsu, 298, 353, 357
Ninhursag, 237, 481
Nirriti, 235, 240, 481
Noah, 67-68, 71, 469, 486
Nodens, 113, 122, 259, 264, 267,
    275-276, 481
Norns, 97, 99, 131
Nu-kua, 451
Nu-Wang, 242, 244
Nuah, 68
Nungeena, 150
Nut, 69, 227, 238, 355, 481, 483

O'Donoghue, 321
Oceanus, 276, 357, 397
Odin, 51, 54, 83, 190, 196, 213, 251,
    254, 260, 264, 266, 283, 297,
    319, 321, 326, 418, 422, 450,
    481
Oisin, 251-252
Old Spider, 97, 99-100, 426
Olle, 245, 481
Onuris, 355
Opet, 314-315, 400, 481-482
Opochtli, 114
Order of the Elephant, 285
Orm, 443
Orore, 150, 481
Osgar, 252
Osiris, 41, 49, 53, 69, 96, 102, 109,
    111, 163, 172, 226-227, 232,
    237-239, 269, 345, 350-351, 355,
    398, 400, 410, 452, 481, 489
Ostara, 302, 307, 391

P'u Hsien, 280-281
Pa-Cha, 156
Padma-Sambhava, 409, 411
Paikea, 415-416

Pakhit, 214, 353, 355, 481
Pakwabi, 13, 88
Pakwabi, 13, 88
Palakapya, 46
Pales, 218, 221, 401, 481
Palilia, 221, 401
Palug's Cat, 199-200, 213-214
Pan, 4, 76, 128, 131, 155, 165, 171,
    294, 299-300, 324, 379, 398,
    401, 467, 470, 479, 481, 495
Paschal Lamb, 400
Pasiphae, 41, 229, 464, 481
Passion of St George, 447
Pavana, 162-163
Perkunas, 44, 332
Persephone, 56, 97, 99, 181-182,
    228, 324, 381, 383
Phaea, 381, 386
philosophers' egg, 436
Phoebus, 353, 357
Picts, 22, 333
Pindar, 132
Pinga, 286, 481
Plato, 77, 87, 132, 324, 419, 423
Pole Star, 83-84, 422, 451
Pooh, 173, 186
Poseidon, 50, 55, 68, 111, 228-229,
    275-276, 323-325, 335, 397, 481-
    482
Priapus, 111, 128, 131, 167, 170,
    482
Prisni, 240, 384, 482
Prithivi, 230, 235, 239, 482
Proteus, 397
Psyche, 1, 4, 34-35, 109, 139-140,
    156

Qedeshet, 353, 356
Quetzalcoatl, 245-246
Ra, 53, 96, 128, 131, 158, 214, 227,
    238-239, 315, 355, 400-401, 448,
    452, 474, 482
Ragnarok, 83, 267, 422
Ramman, 222, 226
Rashin Coatie, 27

Ratnasambhava, 353, 358
Renenet, 353, 355
Reshpu, 250, 292-293, 344, 402,
    482
Rhea Silvia, 424
Rhiannon, 316, 328-331
Rig Veda, 47, 239
rigwelter, 398
Rimmon, 174, 381, 384
Romani, 163, 312, 407, 413-414
Romany, 406, 413
Rudiobus, 329
Rudra, 46-47, 195, 230, 240, 251,
    384
Rustum, 452, 456
Ruti, 353, 356

Sabazios, 91, 93, 95-96, 369, 371,
    398, 401
sacrificing bulls, 39
St. Benyo, 62
St. Eligius, 37, 156
St. John's Day, 61, 168
St. Maelrubha, 62
St. Ursula, 287
St Anthony Abbot, 387
St Bernard, 136, 273, 452
St Blandina, 190
St Christopher, 273, 442
St Cuthbert, 39, 377
St Fina, 395
St Florentinus, 190
St Francis of Assisi, 423
St Gall, 190, 296
St George, 38, 445-448, 488
St Hubert, 255, 273
St Kieran of Saiglir, 423
St Leonard, 244, 485
St Maol Ruadh, 39
St Martin, 39
St Maximus, 190
St Roch, 273
St Roque, 273
St Sira, 273
St Sylvester, 244, 417, 447, 484

St Tobias, 273
St Valentine's Day, 425
St Wendelin, 273
Salmon, 22, 36, 39, 42, 66, 109,
    112, 122-123, 185, 201
Sanjna, 333
Sappho, 132
Saturn, 76-77, 167, 170, 300, 364,
    479, 482
scapegoats, 49, 60
Sea urchin, 105
Sebek, 69, 483
Sedna, 271, 388, 396, 415, 417
Segomo, 329
Sekhmet, 69, 214, 353-355, 363,
    482, 484
Selene, 325, 401
Selkhet, 69-70, 95-96, 484
Sequana, 267
serpent, 5, 14, 17, 22-23, 39, 42, 48,
    57, 66, 68, 75, 77, 93, 105, 147,
    154, 160, 198, 214, 228, 254-
    256, 261, 269, 275, 282, 284,
    329, 337, 339, 348, 359, 399,
    407, 411, 436, 441, 444-445,
    447-449, 454-455, 457, 461-462,
    465-467, 471, 476, 484
Set, 15, 30-31, 57, 65, 70, 73, 89,
    95-96, 102, 111, 123, 125, 155,
    163, 167, 171-172, 188, 203,
    214, 220, 223-224, 227, 237-238,
    245, 256, 259, 264, 269, 292,
    295-297, 303, 314-315, 324, 344-
    345, 351, 384, 393, 410, 473,
    482, 484
Seumas MacGregor, 7, 317, 459
Shashti, 215, 482
Shaushka, 353, 356
Shesha, 465
Shezmu, 353, 356
Shiva, 128, 132, 163, 222, 229-230,
    239, 251, 282-283, 285, 292,
    301, 339, 409, 482
Shiva Nataraja, 229
Shiva, 128, 132, 163, 222, 229-230,

239, 251, 282-283, 285, 292,
    301, 339, 409, 482
Shoden, 280, 282
Shosti, 215
shual, 288
Siberia, 9, 16, 32, 51, 59, 125, 203,
    208, 228, 319, 333, 409, 494
Sien-Tsan, 160
Silenus, 170, 299, 472, 482
Silvanus, 252, 267, 300, 424, 470,
    482
Sinn, 264, 269
Siva, 162, 411
Snap the Dragon, 38, 444
So-wing, 13, 195, 243, 382, 453
solar animals, 23
Soma, 128, 132, 162-163, 230, 452,
    482
Sophocles, 132
Sow Henwen, 199-200, 214, 386
Stag of Rhedynfre, 65-66
Stella Maris, 104, 307
Sucellos, 259, 267
Sucellos, 259, 267
Suchos, 69, 483
Sumer, 95, 110, 135, 452, 476
Sun Hou-Tzu, 366-367
Surabhi, 229, 235, 239-240, 482
Surya, 333
Sutton Hoo, 196, 250, 423
Svinfylking, 20, 83, 193, 197

T'ien-Kou, 474
Ta-Repy, 474
taboos, 12, 15, 36, 42, 52
Tacoma, 99
Tammuz, 110, 195-197, 384, 482
Tara, 201, 353, 358
Taueret, 70, 314-315, 481-482, 484
Te Tuna, 106, 113
Tecciztecatl, 433-434
Tefnut, 69, 353, 355-356, 484
Tellus Mater, 381
Tepeyollotl, 390
Teshub, 222, 226, 356

Tethys, 68, 357, 397, 482
Tezcat, 349
Tezcatlipoca, 347, 495
Thesmophoria, 56, 383
Thor, 51, 83, 174, 189, 232, 295, 297, 326, 398, 402, 471, 482
Three Senseless Creatures, 256, 368, 385, 411
Tiamat, 39, 114, 163, 381, 384, 444, 448, 450, 453, 482
Tinirau, 415-416
Tir, 83-84, 421-422
Toad, 19, 33, 41, 45, 71, 86, 91-94, 149, 414, 480
Todas, 57
Tou Mu, 451
Tuparan, 415, 417
Twelve Terrestrial Branches, 78, 230, 243, 308, 336, 394, 403, 411
twins, 73, 78, 123, 185, 324, 327, 469
Twrch Trwyth, 65, 199-200, 386
Tyche, 353, 357
Typhon, 54, 76, 167, 170, 172, 298, 441, 473, 482, 484

Uke-mochi, 288-289, 483
Úlfhamir, 418
Úlfhednar, 418-419
Ulfius, 20, 421
Ulfius, 20, 421
Upuaut, 53, 70, 345, 424, 483-484

Vajravarahi, 195, 384-385
Valkyries, 130, 327
Varaha, 66-67, 384
Varahi, 195, 384, 483
Vasishtha, 239
Vasuki, 67, 466
Vaya, 247, 251, 366
Vedas, 230
Venus, 68, 73, 75, 77, 85, 87, 104, 106, 110-111, 164, 228, 244, 308, 338, 381, 384, 430, 478, 483
Vesta, 171, 221
Vestal virgins, 55
Virgil, 132, 136
Vishnu, 66-67, 113, 126, 128, 132, 195, 283, 333, 353, 358, 384, 430, 463, 465, 483
Volga, 423
Volkh, 423
Volus, 218
Volusu, 218, 222, 402, 483

Wac, 415, 417
Walgino, 218, 222, 483
Wepwet, 424, 483-484
whooping cough, 5, 86, 109, 169, 370
Wild Edric, 113, 321, 327
Wild Hunt, 113, 249, 254-255, 263, 265, 321
Woden, 196, 251, 259, 271, 318, 418, 481

Xenophon, 132
Xoltl, 265, 483

Yaghuth, 353, 357
Yaghuth, 353, 357
Yama, 204-205, 229, 264, 270, 402, 483
yom, 13
Yonyosona, 13
Young Spider, 97, 100

Zeus, 53-55, 57, 68-69, 73-74, 76, 96, 100, 126, 128, 131, 150, 188-189, 222, 228-229, 239, 298, 323, 357, 369, 371, 381, 384, 398, 401, 404, 423-424, 438, 480, 483
Zoroastrianism, 65, 93, 272, 377, 425
zorro, 288
Zoryas, 267, 274

FREE DETAILED CATALOGUE

Capall Bann is owned and run by people actively involved in many of the areas in which we publish. A detailed illustrated catalogue is available on request, SAE or International Postal Coupon appreciated. **Titles can be ordered direct from Capall Bann, post free in the UK** (cheque or PO with order) or from good bookshops and specialist outlets.

Do contact us for details on the latest releases at: **Capall Bann Publishing, Freshfields, Chieveley, Berks, RG20 8TF.** Titles include:

A Breath Behind Time, Terri Hector
Angels and Goddesses - Celtic Christianity & Paganism, M. Howard
Arthur - The Legend Unveiled, C Johnson & E Lung
Astrology The Inner Eye - A Guide in Everyday Language, E Smith
Auguries and Omens - The Magical Lore of Birds, Yvonne Aburrow
Asyniur - Womens Mysteries in the Northern Tradition, S McGrath
Begonnings - Geomancy, Builder's Rites & Electional Astrology in the
 European Tradition, Nigel Pennick
Between Earth and Sky, Julia Day
Book of the Veil , Peter Paddon
Caer Sidhe - Celtic Astrology and Astronomy, Vol 1, Michael Bayley
Caer Sidhe - Celtic Astrology and Astronomy, Vol 2 M Bayley
Call of the Horned Piper, Nigel Jackson
Cat's Company, Ann Walker
Celtic Faery Shamanism, Catrin James
Celtic Faery Shamanism - The Wisdom of the Otherworld, Catrin James
Celtic Lore & Druidic Ritual, Rhiannon Ryall
Celtic Sacifice - Pre Christian Ritual & Religion, Marion Pearce
Celtic Saints and the Glastonbury Zodiac, Mary Caine
Circle and the Square, Jack Gale
Compleat Vampyre - The Vampyre Shaman, Nigel Jackson
Creating Form From the Mist - The Wisdom of Women in Celtic Myth and
 Culture, Lynne Sinclair-Wood
Crystal Clear - A Guide to Quartz Crystal, Jennifer Dent
Crystal Doorways, Simon & Sue Lilly
Crossing the Borderlines - Guising, Masking & Ritual Animal Disguise in the
 European Tradition, Nigel Pennick
Dragons of the West, Nigel Pennick
Earth Dance - A Year of Pagan Rituals, Jan Brodie
Earth Harmony - Places of Power, Holiness & Healing, Nigel Pennick
Earth Magic, Margaret McArthur
Eildon Tree (The) Romany Language & Lore, Michael Hoadley

Enchanted Forest - The Magical Lore of Trees, Yvonne Aburrow
Eternal Priestess, Sage Weston
Eternally Yours Faithfully, Roy Radford & Evelyn Gregory
Everything You Always Wanted To Know About Your Body, But So Far
    Nobody's Been Able To Tell You, Chris Thomas & D Baker
Face of the Deep - Healing Body & Soul, Penny Allen
Fairies in the Irish Tradition, Molly Gowen
Familiars - Animal Powers of Britain, Anna Franklin
Fool's First Steps, (The) Chris Thomas
Forest Paths - Tree Divination, Brian Harrison, Ill. S. Rouse
From Past to Future Life, Dr Roger Webber
Gardening For Wildlife Ron Wilson
God Year, The, Nigel Pennick & Helen Field
Goddess on the Cross, Dr George Young
Goddess Year, The, Nigel Pennick & Helen Field
Goddesses, Guardians & Groves, Jack Gale
Handbook For Pagan Healers, Liz Joan
Handbook of Fairies, Ronan Coghlan
Healing Book, The, Chris Thomas and Diane Baker
Healing Homes, Jennifer Dent
Healing Journeys, Paul Williamson
Healing Stones, Sue Philips
Herb Craft - Shamanic & Ritual Use of Herbs, Lavender & Franklin
Hidden Heritage - Exploring Ancient Essex, Terry Johnson
Hub of the Wheel, Skytoucher
In Search of Herne the Hunter, Eric Fitch
Inner Celtia, Alan Richardson & David Annwn
Inner Mysteries of the Goths, Nigel Pennick
Inner Space Workbook - Develop Thru Tarot, C Summers & J Vayne
Intuitive Journey, Ann Walker Isis - African Queen, Akkadia Ford
Journey Home, The, Chris Thomas
Kecks, Keddles & Kesh - Celtic Lang & The Cog Almanac, Bayley
Language of the Psycards, Berenice
Legend of Robin Hood, The, Richard Rutherford-Moore
Lid Off the Cauldron, Patricia Crowther
Light From the Shadows - Modern Traditional Witchcraft, Gwyn
Living Tarot, Ann Walker
Lore of the Sacred Horse, Marion Davies
Lost Lands & Sunken Cities (2nd ed.), Nigel Pennick
Magic of Herbs - A Complete Home Herbal, Rhiannon Ryall
Magical Guardians - Exploring the Spirit and Nature of Trees, Philip Heselton
Magical History of the Horse, Janet Farrar & Virginia Russell
Magical Lore of Animals, Yvonne Aburrow
Magical Lore of Cats, Marion Davies
Magical Lore of Herbs, Marion Davies
Magick Without Peers, Ariadne Rainbird & David Rankine
Masks of Misrule - Horned God & His Cult in Europe, Nigel Jackson

Medicine For The Coming Age, Lisa Sand MD
Medium Rare - Reminiscences of a Clairvoyant, Muriel Renard
Menopausal Woman on the Run, Jaki da Costa
Menopause and the Emotions, Kathleen I Macpherson
Mind Massage - 60 Creative Visualisations, Marlene Maundrill
Mirrors of Magic - Evoking the Spirit of the Dewponds, P Heselton
Moon Mysteries, Jan Brodie
Mysteries of the Runes, Michael Howard
Mystic Life of Animals, Ann Walker
New Celtic Oracle The, Nigel Pennick & Nigel Jackson
Oracle of Geomancy, Nigel Pennick
Pagan Feasts - Seasonal Food for the 8 Festivals, Franklin & Phillips
Patchwork of Magic - Living in a Pagan World, Julia Day
Pathworking - A Practical Book of Guided Meditations, Pete Jennings
Personal Power, Anna Franklin
Pickingill Papers - The Origins of Gardnerian Wicca, Bill Liddell
Pillars of Tubal Cain, Nigel Jackson
Places of Pilgrimage and Healing, Adrian Cooper
Practical Divining, Richard Foord
Practical Meditation, Steve Hounsome
Practical Spirituality, Steve Hounsome
Psychic Self Defence - Real Solutions, Jan Brodie
Real Fairies, David Tame
Reality - How It Works & Why It Mostly Doesn't, Rik Dent
Romany Tapestry, Michael Houghton
Runic Astrology, Nigel Pennick
Sacred Animals, Gordon MacLellan
Sacred Celtic Animals, Marion Davies, Ill. Simon Rouse
Sacred Dorset - On the Path of the Dragon, Peter Knight
Sacred Grove - The Mysteries of the Forest, Yvonne Aburrow
Sacred Geometry, Nigel Pennick
Sacred Nature, Ancient Wisdom & Modern Meanings, A Cooper
Sacred Ring - Pagan Origins of British Folk Festivals, M. Howard
Season of Sorcery - On Becoming a Wisewoman, Poppy Palin
Seasonal Magic - Diary of a Village Witch, Paddy Slade
Secret Places of the Goddess, Philip Heselton
Secret Signs & Sigils, Nigel Pennick
Self Enlightenment, Mayan O'Brien
Spirits of the Air, Jaq D Hawkins
Spirits of the Earth, Jaq D Hawkins
Spirits of the Earth, Jaq D Hawkins
Stony Gaze, Investigating Celtic Heads John Billingsley
Stumbling Through the Undergrowth , Mark Kirwan-Heyhoe
Subterranean Kingdom, The, revised 2nd ed, Nigel Pennick
Symbols of Ancient Gods, Rhiannon Ryall
Talking to the Earth, Gordon MacLellan
Taming the Wolf - Full Moon Meditations, Steve Hounsome

508

Teachings of the Wisewomen, Rhiannon Ryall
The Other Kingdoms Speak, Helena Hawley
Tree: Essence of Healing, Simon & Sue Lilly
Tree: Essence, Spirit & Teacher, Simon & Sue Lilly
Through the Veil, Peter Paddon
Torch and the Spear, Patrick Regan
Understanding Chaos Magic, Jaq D Hawkins
Vortex - The End of History, Mary Russell
Warp and Weft - In Search of the I-Ching, William de Fancourt
Warriors at the Edge of Time, Jan Fry
Water Witches, Tony Steele
Way of the Magus, Michael Howard
Weaving a Web of Magic, Rhiannon Ryall
West Country Wicca, Rhiannon Ryall
Wildwitch - The Craft of the Natural Psychic, Poppy Palin
Wildwood King , Philip Kane
Witches of Oz, Matthew & Julia Philips
Wondrous Land - The Faery Faith of Ireland by Dr Kay Mullin
Working With the Merlin, Geoff Hughes
Your Talking Pet, Ann Walker

FREE detailed catalogue

and

FREE 'Inspiration' magazine

Contact: Capall Bann Publishing, Freshfields, Chieveley, Berks, RG20 8TF